THE SHAPING OF THE REFORMED BAPTISMAL RITE IN THE SIXTEENTH CENTURY

The Shaping of the Reformed Baptismal Rite in the Sixteenth Century

Hughes Oliphant Old

William B. Eerdmans Publishing Company
Grand Rapids, Michigan

To Mary,

Domus et divitae dantur a parentibus;
A Domino autem proprie uxor prudens.

Proverbs 19:14

255 Jefferson Ave. S.E., Grand Rapids, Mich. 49503

Printed in the United States of America

Library of Congress Cataloging-in-Publication Data

Old, Hughes Oliphant.
The shaping of the Reformed baptismal rite
in the sixteenth century / Hughes Oliphant Old.
p. cm.
Includes bibliographical references and index.
ISBN 0-8028-3699-2
1. Baptism (Liturgy)—History—16th century.
2. Reformed Church—Liturgy—History—16th century.
I. Title.
BX9427.5.B36043 1992
264′.042081—dc20 92-3652
CIP

Contents

Preface and Acknowledgments

This is my second book on the origins of Reformed worship. To be sure, it treats a different facet of the subject than the first. That book, *The Patristic Roots of Reformed Worship,* studies the service for the Lord's day; this one takes up baptism. But more than that, this second volume looks at Reformed worship from some very different perspectives. Without this second book the first is hardly complete. The work before us comes more than ten years after the first and finds me that much further into the subject. I have gained a firmer grasp on the subject in several very specific areas. Most important is the matter of a greater appreciation of what the Reformers meant by a reform of worship which is according to Scripture. That their worship should be according to Scripture was indeed of the greatest possible importance to the Reformers. It was in regard to their practice of baptism that the Reformers were forced to think out more exactly what they meant by ordering worship according to Scripture. The phrase "according to Scripture" had a very specific meaning to them. They did not have in mind a biblicistic literalism, as many have so often imagined. They neither accepted the principle that what is not forbidden is allowed, nor the position that what is not commanded is forbidden.

A second matter which this work treats is the importance of the controversy with the Anabaptists. From this controversy much of the Reformers' understanding of worship developed. In the research for my first book the importance of this controversy did not become apparent. It was there; I just had not seen it. In studying the reform of the rite of baptism in the early sixteenth century, it became more and more clear that to get the full picture, great attention had to be given to the source literature of the Anabaptist movement. So, learning all I could from George Huntston Williams and John Howard Yoder, I started out on a fascinating study. I had a hard time resisting the temptation to add studies of Melchior Hofmann, Peter Riedemann, Pilgram Marpeck, Jacob Hutter, and Sebastian Franck to those which I had already written. In my first church, at Atglen, Pennsylvania, right on the edge of the Dutch country, I had come to have friendly feelings toward the Mennonites; I rather like their emphasis on farm and family. On the question of pacifism I sometimes come very close to being convinced. How fascinated I was to find out what the Mennonites' historical roots were. I cannot help wondering, however, if they would not do themselves greater justice by emphasizing Menno Simons rather than Thomas Müntzer, Konrad Grebel, and Balthasar Hübmaier. More and more it has occurred to me that the big issues between the Anabaptists and the Reformers of classical Protestantism are still among the biggest unresolved agonies of modern American Protestantism. But if I was ever to finish my book I had to get beyond my fascination with one aspect of it.

The third important matter in which I have gained considerable insight in the last few years is the relation of the South German Reformation to Luther. Paul Rorem and Mark Edwards have convinced me that I should not believe everything I have heard about Luther and have encouraged me to try reading him for myself rather than accepting the cultic Romanticism of so many of his liturgical interpreters. In the next ten years I will probably look at Luther much more closely. After all, the High Rhenish Reformers always protested their loyalty to Luther; perhaps we do them an injustice by not believing them. Maybe Calvin was at least as faithful an interpreter of Luther as Westphal, and perhaps we would be much more fair to Calvin if we looked at him as a disciple and interpreter of Luther. As Calvin scholars have shown again and again, to look at Calvin as the founder of a denomination is to get a distorted image. He is best understood as a staunch member of the Church universal.

A fourth important matter which I have come to appreciate more and more in the last years is that the liturgical reforms of classical Protestantism are to be seen in the context of what the Reformers taught about grace. The primary thrust of classical Protestantism is a revival of the Augustinian theology of grace. The Reformers reacted strongly against the Pelagianism of the late medieval Nominalists. In studying how the earliest Reformed theologians worked out their practice of baptism this concern for the sovereignty of grace is patent. And if our day finds Luther and Calvin hard to understand on some subjects, it is because we look at them through our own brand of Pelagianism.

In our ecumenical age there are those who question whether there is any sense in trying to discover just what the Reformed tradition has to say about worship. Some even regard a concern for what is Reformed as a perverse resistance to the ecumenical thrust of our day. These same questions are raised again and again. Would it not be better simply to let the Reformed tradition drop since we obviously have not convinced everyone? Would it not be better to jump in the ecumenical swim and start all over again with a new investigation of the question of the sacrament of baptism? Would it not be better to construct a patchwork ecumenical quilt of liturgical forms ranging from Abyssinian Orthodox to Southern Baptist? Well, that is obviously not the way I look at it. There is more than one way to approach ecumenism. This study has been undertaken with the conviction that the ecumenical movement is greatly enriched by a wide variety of confessional, ethnic, denominational, national, and conventicular traditions. Most of us have spent time worshiping with some other liturgical tradition and found inspiration from the experience.

This research was greatly aided by my becoming involved in a wide variety of other liturgical traditions. My association with these other traditions helped me gain a perspective on my own tradition which I would have never gotten otherwise. The same was true for my first book, which was written in Europe, where I was constantly worshiping with other churches quite different from my own. This book was written for the most part in Indiana. How could one be more immersed in mid-America? Yet, it must be said, Indiana is not a bad place to study liturgics. South Bend is only a few hours' drive to the north and St. Meinrad's only a few hours to the south, and I have spent hours in each place and gotten piles of books from each library. But of course, the greatest delight, particularly at Notre Dame, has been the shoptalk with William Storey, John Barry Ryan, John Melloh, Leon Mitchel, Edward Kilmartin, and James White. How much I have treasured those drives up to South Bend!

The benefits of doing my studies in Indiana are by no means limited to Notre Dame and St. Meinrad's. The people at Goshen College are the nicest people in the world, and their library has some real gems. On Sunday morning I can count on a covey of Goshen graduates in my congregation. I wouldn't trade them off for anything. They are people of such refreshing integrity. And then, too, John Howard Yoder lives in Indiana. His son Dan was a student here at Purdue, and his daughter-in-law Thea performed a significant ministry to my wife Mary at the time of the birth of our first child. Balthasar Hübmaier notwithstanding, I want to be counted as a friend of the Mennonites.

Not many places boast a religion department the equal of Indiana's Wabash College. Its chairman, Professor Eric Dean, has served as the dean of Indiana theologians for many years now, and we rookie Hoosier theologians hold him in the highest esteem.

If most of this book was written in Indiana, there are a few exceptions. The first is that at one point my congregation gave me a Sabbatical leave, and Princeton Theological Seminary gave me a grant to work in the Speer Library for several months. To President James I. McCord, I therefore wish to express my appreciation. Then at other times, when I needed to escape from the worst of the northern winter, I have taken refuge in the Yucatán. I got my work done while I was sitting in a beautiful, flower-filled patio in Mérida. I wish to express my appreciation to the pastors and elders of the Mexican Presbyterian Church who have made my repeated visits to the Yucatán so enjoyable, particularly to Pastor and Señora David Pat and Dr. and Señora Rubén Madera y Reyes. Viewing the Reformed liturgical tradition from a patio in the Yucatán gave me an exciting new perspective.

In the early days when he was still Assistant Professor in the History Department at Purdue, Leslie Fairfield, now of the Episcopal Seminary in Pittsburgh, gave me lots of valuable leads in bibliography. Reverend Stuart Robertson of the Federated Church in Brookston typed some of the more difficult chapters over and over again for me and went around and around with me as I was trying to straighten out my thoughts on the subject. Since the Federated Church of Brookston is a Federation of Baptist and Presbyterian congregations, the discussion was often carried out against a counterpoint of the most diverse practical problems in regard to baptism. What a marvelous thinking partner he was! The same must be said about Reverend John Niederhaus, pastor of St. John's United Church of Christ in Vera Cruz, Indiana, and St. Luke's United Church of Christ in Honduras, Indiana, whom I never convinced on the subject of infant baptism but who otherwise is a perfectly good Reformed theologian. Reverend Charles Hackett, pastor of the First Assembly of God, Reverend Joe Wick, pastor of the First Christian Church, and Reverend Joe Bell, pastor of Grace Chapel, must also be numbered among my theological thinking comrades. I can assure you, Indiana is a good place to write theology.

In writing this book I have had some very good assistants among the young people of my own congregation. Phyllis Post, a computer-literate librarian, worked her own special wizardry on the bibliography. Arthur Suggs did a lot of typing for me one summer. As the manuscript finally approached completion, Chris Borgert once again served as one of my thinking partners, letting me know if my writing had achieved clarity, running down innumerable problems with the footnotes and bibliography, and keeping me company when I just could not work any longer. Without such devoted friends this work would never have been completed.

HUGHES OLIPHANT OLD
West Lafayette, Indiana
July 30, 1985

CHAPTER I

The Latin Baptismal Rites on the Eve of the Reformation

There was a unique genius to the Latin baptismal rites at the end of the fifteenth century. This genius needs to be appreciated before we can get a feeling for what the Reformers were really trying to do. The baptismal rites which the early sixteenth century inherited had already undergone many developments, many reforms, and many revisions. They preserved much that was of great antiquity side by side with much that was more recent. Being filled with vestiges of the past as well as attempts to be relevant to their age and reflecting many different and conflicting theological insights all tempering and balancing each other, these rites are both confusing and fascinating in their complexity. Their many-sidedness is both their greatest problem and their greatest charm. Several characteristics of these rites are particularly deserving of our attention.

The Abbreviation of an Earlier Rite

The first of these characteristics is that the baptismal rite as it was celebrated in the Upper Rhineland about the year 1500 was a telescoped rite. It was a rite made up of many rites which in earlier centuries had extended over a period of several weeks and then in the Middle Ages had been compressed into a single rite which could be performed in about a half an hour. In New Testament times baptism had been celebrated in a very simple and straightforward way.[1] Then in the next three or four centuries of Christian history, the

1. A bibliography on baptism in the New Testament should include the following:

rite of baptism developed from a very simple performing of the baptismal washing into an elaborate mystery drama.[2] This process reached its culmination in the elaborate paschal baptisms of the fourth and fifth centuries. The Christian literature of this period has preserved many records of these dramatic ceremonies.[3] One cannot help but be impressed by the dramatic splendor of these

---

Beasley-Murray, G. R., *Baptism in the New Testament* (London: Macmillan and Company, 1962).

Betz, O., "Die Proselytentaufe der Qumransekte und die Taufe im Neuen Testament," *Revue de Qumran* 1 (1958-59): 213-34.

Bieder, Werner, *Die Verheissung der Taufe im Neuen Testament* (Zurich: EVZ-Verlag, 1966).

Böcher, Otto, *Christus Exorcista, Dämonismus und Taufe im Neuen Testament* (Stuttgart, Berlin, Cologne, and Mainz: W. Kohlhammer, 1972).

Coppens, J., and D'Ales, A., "Baptême," *Dictionnaire de la Bible, Supplément,* pp. 852-924.

Delling, Gerhard, *Die Taufe im Neuen Testament* (Stuttgart: W. Kohlhammer, 1952).

Flemington, W. F., *The New Testament Doctrine of Baptism* (London: S.P.C.K., 1948).

Gnilka, J., "Die essenischen Tauchbäder und die Johannestaufe," *Revue de Qumran* 3 (1961-62).

Leenhardt, F. J., *Le baptême chrétien, son origine, sa signification* (Neuchâtel-Paris: Delachaux et Niestlé, 1946).

Marsh, H. G., *The Origin and Significance of the New Testament Baptism* (Manchester: University of Manchester Press, 1941).

Oepke, Albrecht, "βάπτω," *Theologisches Wörterbuch zum Neuen Testament* 1: 527-44.

Reitzenstein, Richard, *Die Vorgeschichte der christlichen Taufe* (Leipzig and Berlin: B. G. Teubner, 1929).

Schnackenburg, Rudolf, *Baptism in the Thought of St. Paul,* trans. G. R. Beasley-Murray (Oxford: Basil Blackwell, 1964).

Schneider, Johannes, *Die Taufe im Neuen Testament* (Stuttgart: W. Kohlhammer, 1952).

Thomas, Joseph, *Le mouvement baptiste en Palestine et Syrie* (Gembloux: J. Duculot, 1935).

Wagner, Günter, *Das religionsgeschichtliche Problem von Römer 6,1-11* (Zurich: Zwingli Verlag, 1962).

2. For a guide to the history of the rite of baptism from the earliest times to the eve of the Reformation the following works are among the most helpful: Jules Corblet, *Histoire dogmatique, liturgique et archéologique du sacrement du baptême,* 2 vols. (Paris: Société Générale de Librairie Catholique, 1881-82); J. D. C. Fisher, *Christian Initiation: Baptism in the Medieval West, a study in the disintegration of the primitive rite of initiation* (London: S.P.C.K., 1965), abbreviated as Fisher, *Christian Initiation: Medieval;* George Kretschmar, "Die Geschichte des Taufgottesdienstes in der alten Kirche," *Leiturgia: Handbuch des Evangelischen Gottesdienstes,* eds. Karl Ferdinand Muller and Walter Blankenberg, 5 vols. (Kassel: Johannes Stauda-Verlag, 1970), pp. 1-349, abbreviated as Kretschmar, "Taufgottesdienst"; Burkhard Neunhauser, *Baptism and Confirmation,* trans. John H. Hughes (New York: Herder, 1964); Pierre de Puniet, "Baptême," in *Dictionnaire d'archéologie chrétienne et de liturgie* 2/1, cols. 251-346; and Alois Stenzel, *Die Taufe, eine genetische Erklärung der Taufliturgie* (Innsbruck: Verlag Felizian Rauch, 1958). This study will be abbreviated as Stenzel, *Die Taufe.*

3. Recently the *Sources Chrétiennes,* published by Henri de Lubac and Jean Daniélou, has given us a series of studies on patristic catechetical sermons. These ancient documents were originally the sermons preached during the course of the paschal baptisms. Tertullian, *Traité du Baptême,* eds. R. F. Rafoulé and M. Drouzy (Paris: Les Editions du Cerf, 1952); Ambroise de Milan, *Des Sacrements, de Mystères,* ed. Dom Bernard Botte (Paris: Les Editions du Cerf, 1959); Jean Chrysostome, *Huit Catéchèses Baptismales,* trans. Antoine

liturgical dramas. They were designed to initiate into the Christian Church the pagan population of antiquity. This population was accustomed to the dramatic rites of the Hellenistic mystery religions. The Church sought to win over these pagans with Christian mysteries more splendid than the old pagan mysteries.

These Christian initiation rites typically began several weeks before Easter with a solemn enrolling of the candidates for baptism. This initial enrolling was followed by several weeks of catechetical instruction; this was a period of intensive teaching, in which the basic doctrines of the Church were explained. Each of these meetings for catechetical instruction was accompanied by special prayers, exorcisms, and other rites. Often the bishop himself preached at these services. On the morning before Easter, the candidates for baptism came to the church to recite the Creed; then that night the paschal vigil began. Toward dawn those who were to be baptized were taken into the baptistry, a building especially designed for baptism. The bishop consecrated the waters of the font with a long prayer which recounted the types of baptisms. The candidates disrobed, they were anointed with oil, and then, after renouncing the devil and all his works and confessing their faith in God the Father, Son, and Holy Spirit, they were immersed in the baptismal font. After the baptismal washing each one was anointed with chrism by the bishop and received the laying on of hands. The newly baptized were then clothed in white and led into the church to join with the congregation to celebrate the Easter Eucharist.

In the sixth, seventh, and eighth centuries when the Roman sacramentaries were produced, the celebration of baptism had begun to lose some of its dramatic splendor. The Roman sacramentaries were produced for a church which was much more confident of its position in the world. While there were still converts from paganism, Italy, Provence, Greece, Asia Minor, Syria, Egypt, Spain, and many other areas were predominantly Christian. Conversion from paganism was no longer in the spotlight. Less and less attention was given to the celebration of baptism. The Roman sacramentaries indicate that more and more the great majority of candidates for baptism were children and that both church authorities and parents wanted to expedite the process of Christianizing the next generation. The many services celebrated over a series of weeks were compacted into a single service taking but a short time. By the High Middle Ages the paschal baptismal rites survived only in vestigial form. Most children were baptized shortly after birth and it was important that these

---

Wenger (Paris: Les Editions du Cerf, 1958); Augustin D'Hippone, *Sermons pour la Paque,* ed. Suzanne Poque (Paris: Les Editions du Cerf, 1966); and Cyrille de Jerusalem, *Catéchèses Mystagogiques,* ed. Auguste Piédangel (Paris: Les Editions du Cerf, 1966). The introductions and notes to these volumes are of particular value.

services be celebrated with dispatch. The parish priest was a busy man in those days, and if each child had to be baptized shortly after birth, it meant that, practically speaking, each child had to be baptized separately. That took time, and it probably became something of a routine to the busy priest. By the beginning of the sixteenth century baptism was greatly affected by the desire to get it over quickly.

The Variety of Local Rites

The second characteristic of these rites is their variety. The High Rhenish baptismal rites were flamboyantly Gothic, just like the churches in which they were celebrated. On the eve of the Reformation nothing characterized the liturgical books of the different German dioceses quite so much as the infinite variety of detail. To be sure, it was basically the same baptismal rite which was celebrated, whether in Mainz or in Strasbourg or in Constance, but in each of these dioceses the books of ritual prescribed a variety of local rites and customs. Prayers in the rite of Mainz, for example, were formulated in a slightly different way from those which appeared in the rite of Constance. The rubrics vary widely from one diocesan book to another. To be sure, we do meet much that was always or nearly always the same. The same prayers had been inherited from the ancient Roman sacramentaries. One basic shape of the whole rite is easily detected. The combination of continuity and variety was much the same as the architecture of the churches of the period. How often one sees in a late fifteenth-century Rhineland church a row of Gothic windows. The windows are all the same size and shape, and yet the tracery in each one is different. Again, it is not at all surprising to find that part of a German church is Romanesque, part High Gothic, and part very late Gothic. The baptismal rites reflect the same spirit, the same delight in infinite variety.

With the growing popularity of printing, the larger dioceses of Germany began to have their ritual books printed. Before the year 1500 we find the following diocesan rituals in print: Mainz, 1480; Würzburg, 1480; Bamberg, 1481; Constance, 1482; Cologne, 1485; Augsburg, 1487; Regensburg, 1491; Salzburg, 1496; Magdeburg, 1497; and Breslau, 1499. By the eve of the Reformation the number of diocesan rituals in print had risen to several dozen.[4]

For the study of the origins of the Reformed baptismal rite two of these

4. For a complete description of these rites, see Herman Josef Spital, *Der Taufritus in den deutschen Ritualien von den ersten Drucken bis zur Einführung des Rituale Romanum* (Münster: Aschendorffsche Verlagsbuchhandlung, 1968), pp. 212-84. This study will be abbreviated as Spital, *Der Taufritus*.

diocesan rituals will be of particular interest. The ritual of Constance was, of course, the ritual used by the church of Zurich.[5] It was given a German translation by the Reformers of Zurich as early as 1523. The ritual of Strasbourg is equally important for this study.[6] It was translated into German by the local Reformers as early as 1524, and became the point of departure for the Reformed baptismal rites of Strasbourg. To help put these two rites into perspective, we will study them alongside the ritual of Mainz.[7] As our study progresses, we will become aware of the many variations among these rites.

How one viewed this variety in the rite of baptism at the beginning of the sixteenth century depended on the age to which one belonged. Those who were still of the Middle Ages cherished the unique features of their particular diocese and regarded such uniqueness as the particular prerogative of the Church. In the ritual of Constance we have a clear statement of the respect which was given to local customs. A rubric directs that the Renunciation is to begin the rite, using the same text which is found later in the service. The rubric admits that this double renunciation is a custom not followed by all churches, but goes on to say that in such matters the local custom is to be observed.[8]

As we will see, the earliest Protestant Reformers were careful to maintain many of these local customs. On the other hand, there were certainly those who would have preferred a greater consistency, believing such variety to be a sign of decadence from a supposed original uniformity. Particularly the Christian Humanists tended to look on these variations as unfortunate. They had experienced the problem of establishing the pure text of ancient authors. They regarded these variations much as they regarded the variant readings of a text, namely as unfortunate deformations caused by centuries of inaccurate manuscript copying.

While the spirit of the late Middle Ages cherished the local variety, the

5. *Obsequiale sive benedictionale secundum ecclesiam Constantiensem* (Augsburg, 1510). It is reprinted in Alban Dold, *Die Konstanzer Ritualientexte in ihrer Entwicklung von 1482-1721* (Münster: Aschendorff, 1923), pp. 1-48. This text will be abbreviated as *Obsequiale Constantiensis.*

6. *Agenda sive Exequiale sacramentorum, et eorum que in ecclesiis aguntur* (Strasbourg: Renatus Beck, 1513). It is reprinted in Gustav Kawerau, "Liturgische Studien zu Luthers Taufbüchlein von 1523," *Zeitschrift für kirchliche Wissenschaft und kirchliches Leben* 10 (1889): 411-15. This text will be abbreviated as *Agenda Argentinensis.*

7. *Agenda Maguntinensis cum utilissimis scitugue dignissimis (prioribus tamen non insertis) notabilibus: iam nouiter ac diligenter impresse* (Mainz, 1513). It is reprinted in Hermann Adalbert Daniel, *Codex liturgicus ecclesiae universae* (Leipzig: T. O. Weigel, 1847), pp. 183-89. This text will be abbreviated as *Agenda Maguntinensis.*

8. *Obsequiale Constantiensis,* p. 6.

spirit of the Renaissance and the new Christian Humanism preferred a more universal approach. In regard to the rite of baptism, the new desire for liturgical uniformity first emerged in the work of the Venetian Dominican Alberto Castellani, who in 1523 published an order for the administration of baptism which aimed at establishing a more universal rite.[9] One notices that the work of Castellani first appears in 1523, the same year in which both Martin Luther and Leo Jud published their first German baptismal rite. The work of Castellani was destined for every bit as much success as the work of the Reformers. On his work would be based the final formulation of the Roman baptismal rite which was established by Pope Paul V in 1614, and was used by Roman Catholic Churches until very recently.

Adapted to Infant Baptism

Another important feature of the High Rhenish baptismal rites is that they are rites for infant baptism, yet when one looks more closely at the most ancient core of the rites, one discovers something quite different: the center of the ritual seems intended for adults. One might say that the rites contain an ambiguity in this respect. Although almost everyone baptized in the upper Rhineland at the beginning of the sixteenth century was baptized in infancy, many of the texts assume adult baptism. Let us consider, for example, one of the most ancient prayers in the rites, *omnipotens sempiterne deus,*

> Almighty everlasting God, Father of our Lord Jesus Christ, graciously regard these your servants, whom you have called to the beginning of faith. Drive out from them all blindness of heart, destroy all the the snares of Satan which bind them. Open to them, O Lord, the gateway of piety. Instruct them with the sign of your wisdom that they might be released from all evil desires, and that rejoicing in the sweet odor of thy teaching they might serve thee in thy Church and might advance from day to day, in order that they approach the grace of baptism by means of the medicine of thy teaching through Christ our Lord. Amen.[10]

9. *Sacerdotale juxta s. Romane ecclesie et aliarum, ecclesiarum apostolice bibliothece . . . ad optatum commodum quorumcumque sacerdotum collectus . . . ac summorum Pontificum authoritate multoties approbatum,* ed. Alberto Castellani, 1523 (Venice, 1554). This text will be abbreviated as *Sacerdotale.*

10. "Omnipotens sempiterne deus, pater domini nostri ihesu cristi respicere dignare super hos fideles tuos, quos ad rudimenta fidei uocare dignatus es; omnem cecitatem cordis ab eis expelle, disrumpe omnes laqueos sathane, quibus fuerant colligati. Aperi eis domine ianuam pietatis tue: ut signo sapiencie tue imbuti omnium cupiditatum fetoribus careant et

The prayer goes back through the Gregorian Sacramentary to the Gelasian Sacramentary.[11] This means that it goes back at least to the sixth century. It must be still older because it assumes a long and earnest period of catechetical instruction. We notice that this prayer speaks of the convert as having the beginnings of faith.[12] Because both of these sacramentaries originated in the city of Rome, this prayer must go back to a time when a good portion of those baptized in the city of Rome were adult converts from paganism.[13] The prayer may have originated as early as the fourth century. By the time the Gelasian Sacramentary was put together, the rite of baptism was normally performed for children; however, the basic order remained essentially the same. A few new forms were added and adjustments were made, but the same things were done and the same prayers were said. To us this seems rather insensitive to the pastoral needs of children, but evidently that was not the way it was regarded in those days. The ambiguities and anachronisms of this approach still marked the High Rhenish baptismal rites almost a thousand years later.

We can show how these late medieval German rites for infant baptism adapted the forms of adult baptism as it was practiced in ancient Rome with another example. From numerous patristic sources we learn of the rite of the *redditio symboli*, the recitation of the Creed. Back in the fourth century the recitation took place on the morning of Holy Saturday; it showed that one had successfully completed the catechetical instruction. It served as a statement of the personal faith of the candidate and admitted the candidate to baptism. When we look at the rite of Constance more than a thousand years later, we find that the Creed is still there to be recited, but by the priest rather than the one to be baptized.[14] This was a significant adaptation, to be sure, but other adaptations

---

ad suauem odorem preceptorum tuorum leti in ecclesia tua tibi deseruiant et proficiant de die in diem: ut ydonei efficantur accedere ad graciam baptismi tui precepta medicina. Per cristum dominum nostrum. Amen." *Obsequiale Constantiensis,* p. 21. See also the *Agenda Maguntinensis,* p. 183, and the *Agenda Argentinensis,* pp. 411-12. For variations in the text, see Spital, *Der Taufritus,* pp. 59-60.

11. *Das Sacramentarium Gregorianum nach dem Aachener Urexemplar,* ed. Hans Lietzmann, Liturgiegeschichtliche Quellen (Münster: Aschendorff, 1921), pp. 49. This text will be abbreviated as *Sacramentarium Gregorianum.* See also the *Liber Sacramentum,* ed. Leo Cunibert Mohlberg (Rome, 1968), pp. 42ff. This text will be abbreviated as *Sacramentarium Gelasianum.*

12. On the origins of this prayer, see Stenzel, *Die Taufe,* pp. 207ff.

13. For the sources of the baptismal rites used in Upper Germany, see the following: Stenzel, *Die Taufe;* Fisher, *Christian Initiation: Medieval;* Neunheuser, *Baptism and Confirmation;* and Kretschmar, "Taufgottesdienst," pp. 145-273 and 297-335.

14. "Deinde teneat presbiter manum super capita singulorum infancium et dicat. . . ." *Obsequiale Constantiensis,* p. 9. This text is followed by the Lord's Prayer, Ave Maria, and Apostles' Creed. The same pattern is found in the *Agenda Maguntinensis,* p. 185.

of the recitation of the Creed were made which entirely changed the liturgical function of the rite. The rite of the *redditio symboli* has been changed not only by having the priest say the Creed instead of the child, but also by prefacing the Creed with a reading of the story of Jesus blessing the children.[15] Still another adaptation is made. Just as Jesus lays his hands on the children in the Gospel story, so now the priest lays his hands on the head of the child. With this gesture, he then recites the Creed. With these two additions the liturgical function of the *redditio symboli* has completely changed. For the baptismal rite of Constance, the Creed functions not as a confession of faith, but as a formula for the blessing of the children.

In the rite of Constance the saying of the Creed is adapted in yet another way. After the reading of the story of Jesus blessing the children, there is a very brief word of interpretation, "through these sacred words our Lord remits all of our sins and trespasses."[16] The story is interpreted to be a statement of the basic Christian gospel: in Christ there is the forgiveness of sins. This is followed by a rubric directing the priest to admonish the godparents to teach the child the Creed.[17] Then the Creed is recited. What the priest is clearly doing is delivering the faith to the godparents in order that they in turn might deliver it to the child when he or she grows older. In the rite of Constance we find two distinct ways of adapting the recitation of the Creed to the baptism of infants. Each adaptation must come from a different hand. Each implies a different understanding of what is being done. Each is an attempt to make an ancient rite relevant to a new age.

In the case of Constance, the priest confesses faith for the child. In the original Roman rite, the candidate confessed his or her own faith. A way was found of adapting a previously existing liturgical form, originally intended for adults, for use in a service at which the sacrament was administered to children. The basic liturgical text was preserved, but its meaning was changed by the addition of supplementary customs and rubrics.

One should not imagine that the case was always that rites intended for adults were adapted for the baptism of children. The process of adaptation sometimes went in the opposite direction. Certain parts of the High Rhenish baptismal rites were attempts to adapt a traditional rite intended for infants to the

15. *Obsequiale Constantiensis,* p. 9.

16. Several editions (1502, 1510, 1560, and 1570) follow the text of Matthew with "per istos sacros sermones indulgeat dominus noster uniuersa peccata nostra et delicta." *Obsequiale Constantiensis,* p. 9, footnote to line 30.

17. "Hic doceat presbiter Patrinos, ut paruulos informent in oracione dominica et in salutacione angelica et in simbolo. Deinde teneat presbiter manum super capita singulorum infancium et dicat. . . ." *Obsequiale Constantiensis,* p. 9.

baptism of adults. A good example is the Exsufflation. In Mainz, the priest meets the child at the door of the church and, after seeking his name, blows in his face and says, "Go out from him, unclean spirit, and give place to the coming of the Holy Spirit and give honor to the living and true God."[18] The practice goes back to the classical Roman baptismal orders of the sixth century. It is described in the Gelasian Sacramentary as a rite for admitting a pagan to the catechumenate.[19] The form as we find it there was developed when the ordinary Roman rite of baptism was so naturally associated with the baptism of infants that when converts from paganism appeared, it was felt that something must be added to the usual rites. A rite for infants was adapted for use with adults. When the Roman liturgical books were taken into the mission fields of Germany in the ninth century, a normal baptism used both the regular Roman rite and this supplementary rite, the Exsufflation, when baptizing converts from paganism. Within a few generations, however, the same process took place in Germany which had taken place in Rome. More and more the people who were baptized were children, but the Exsufflation was by this time part of the traditional baptismal service whether it was adults or children who were baptized.

Over the centuries the baptismal rite had been adapted to fit the age of the candidate in very slow, almost imperceptible ways. A few rites or formulas were added here and there, but in the eyes of those who made the changes, the rite had never changed and needed never to change. As we find so clearly stated in the rubrics of the ritual of Constance, "the rite should not be . . . one way for adults and another way for children, but rather one way of performing it should be maintained."[20] Although the author of the rubric was surely sincere in this observation, in fact over the centuries the rites had been changed profoundly by the need to adapt them to children, then to adults, and then to children once again. The many ambiguities which this caused remain one of the most fascinating features of the rite.

18. "Exi ab eo immunde spiritus et da locum advenienti Spiritui Sancto et da honorem Deo vivo et vero." *Agenda Maguntinensis,* p. 183. Cf. Andrieu, *Pontifical Romano-Germanique.* For variations on the text, see Spital, *Der Taufritus,* pp. 52-54.

19. *Sacramentarium Gelasianum,* p. 93. Blowing in the face of the person to be baptized was not an uncommon rite in Christian antiquity. It is found at various points in the baptismal orders, sometimes after the exorcisms and sometimes in connection with the renunciation of the devil. See Bernard Botte, *La Tradition apostolique de saint Hippolyte* (Münster in Westfalen: Aschendorff, 1963), p. 43; and F. Dölger, *Die Sonne der Gerechtigkeit und der Schwarze* (Münster in Westfalen: Aschendorff, 1918), p. 13. The regular Roman baptismal rites of the Gelasian and Gregorian Sacramentaries do not contain it. It is found only in a supplementary section of the *Gelasianum Vetus,* which contains a number of rites and prayers for special baptisms. See Chavasse, *Sacramentaire Gélasien* (Tournai: Desclée, 1958), pp. 172ff.

20. *Obsequiale Constantiensis,* p. 13.

Preponderance of Exorcism

The rites of baptism on the eve of the Reformation were dominated by exorcisms. All kinds of exorcisms were used, and they were sometimes repeated several times. In fact, the whole service gave the impression of being a long series of exorcisms concluded by a baptism. Let us take a brief look at this long series of exorcisms.

The service as it was celebrated about the year 1500 commenced at the door of the church with a number of ancient rites which had at one time accompanied the solemn enrolling of candidates for baptism.[21] Although in the fourth and fifth centuries this enrolling had taken place at a special service several weeks before Easter, the Rhenish baptismal orders of the early sixteenth century had telescoped it together with all the rest of the prebaptismal rites into one service.[22] In the baptismal order of the Diocese of Constance, these rites of enrollment began with the Exsufflation mentioned above.[23] This blowing in the face of the child was a common gesture of exorcism.[24] Then came the signation by which the candidates for baptism were solemnly signed with the cross on both forehead and breast.[25] This usage had, at least, strong overtones of exorcism, as is shown by the prayer which followed, which among other things asked God to "take away from him all blindness of heart, shatter all the troops of Satan by which he has been held."[26] This is followed by

21. B. Capelle, "L'introduction du catéchuménat à Rome," *Recherches de théologie ancienne et médiévale* 1 (1933): 129-54.

22. Michel Andrieu, *Le pontifical Romain au moyen âge,* 4 vols., Studi e Testi 86-89 (Città del Vaticano: Vaticano Biblioteca apostolica vaticana, 1938-41).

23. The following discussion of exorcisms is based on the *Agenda Constantiensis,* although some of the variations in the other rituals will be mentioned. For an extensive study of these variations, see Spital, *Der Taufritus,* pp. 54-59.

24. On the Exsufflation, see K. Traede, "Exorcismus," *Reallexikon für Antike und Christentum,* cols. 44-117, particularly col. 89. See also F. J. Dölger, *Der Exorzismus im altchristlichen Taufritual, Studien zur Geschichte und Kultur des Altertums,* vol. 3, parts 1 and 2 (Paderborn: Ferdinand Schöningh, 1909), pp. 118-29.

25. The signation, or putting the sign of the cross on the candidate for baptism, appears in all the German baptismal rites of this period, although the formula which accompanies it differs widely from place to place. The formula found in the Strasbourg rite is completely different from that found in the *Obsequiale Constantiensis.* On the variety of formulas, see Spital, *Der Taufritus,* pp. 54-59. On the meaning of the signation in the celebration of baptism, see E. Delaye, "Baptême," *Dictionnaire de la Spiritualité,* and F. J. Dölger, "Beiträge zur Geschichte des Kreuzzeichens," *Jahrbuch für Antike und Christentum* 10 (1962). See further, J. H. Rondt, "La croix sur le front," *Revue des Sciences Religieuses* 42 (1954): 388-94.

26. ". . . omnem cecitatem cordis ab eo expelle, disrumpe omnes laqueos sathane, quibus fuerat alligatus. . . ." *Obsequiale Constantiensis,* p. 6.

putting exorcised salt into the mouth of the child.[27] The text for the exorcism of salt is very old.[28]

> I exorcise you, creature salt, in the name of God the Father Almighty, and in the love of our Lord Jesus Christ, and in the power of the Holy Spirit. I exorcise you through the living God, through the true God, through the holy God, through God, who created you to protect the human race.[29]

The next group of exorcisms in these German liturgical books consists of exorcisms which in earlier centuries had belonged to the catechetical services. In the fourth and fifth centuries these catechetical services were held daily for a period of several weeks, although their frequency and total number could differ from place to place.[30] At each of these services the same rites and the same exorcisms were repeated. In the days when all these separate services were being telescoped into a single service, some dioceses did a more radical work of telescoping than others. This explains the fact that in some of the Latin rites of the early sixteenth century the exorcisms are used only once and in others they are repeated three times. The following two texts suffice to give the general impression.

> Hear, accursed Satan, adjured through the name of the eternal God and of our Savior the Son of God, depart with your envious ways, trembling and moaning; let nothing be common with you and this servant of God who already is thinking of heavenly things, of renouncing you and your age and of winning a blessed immortality. Therefore give honor to the coming Holy Spirit, who descending from the highest realms of heaven comes to upset your frauds and to cleanse this breast by a divine fountain, that it be sanctified to God as a temple and habitation for God and that, freed from all penalties of past sin, this servant of God, N., always give thanks to God and bless his holy name forever.
>
> Therefore, accursed devil, recognize your sentence and give honor to the living and true God; give honor to Jesus Christ his Son and to the Holy Spirit and recede from this servant of God, N., because our Lord Jesus Christ

27. On the use of exorcised salt in the celebration of baptism, see Dölger, *Der Exorzismus,* pp. 92-99.

28. *Sacramentarium Gelasianum* 1.31.43.

29. "Exorziso te creatura salis in nomine dei patris omni potentis et in caritate domini nostri ihesu cristi et in uirtute spiritus sancti. Exorziso te per deum uiuum, per deum uerum, per deum sanctum, per deum, qui te ad tutelam humani generis procreauit. . . ." *Obsequiale Constantiensis,* p. 3.

30. On the relation of exorcism to the catechumenal rites, see Dölger, *Der Exorzismus,* pp. 45-62.

> has deigned to call this one to his holy grace and benediction and to the font of baptism for the gift of the Holy Spirit. O accursed devil, do not dare to violate this holy sign of the cross (makes the sign of the cross with the thumb on the forehead of the child) which we have put on his forehead, through Christ our Lord. Amen.[31]

Most striking is the way these formulas of exorcism see Satan as an all-present and all-pervading power determined to delude, deceive, and dissuade every single human soul he can possibly entangle in his traps and snares. As the candidate approaches baptism, one can expect the devil to use all his wiles to prevent this event; and so the exorcisms are especially necessary, that the path to the baptismal font be cleared of Satanic interference. For Christians of the Middle Ages, this was evidently much more real and much more important than the catechetical teaching which in an earlier day had formed the core of the catechetical services. Originally the exorcisms had supported the catechetical instruction, but as the instructions were gradually given up, the exorcisms survived alone. It is interesting to ponder the implications of this, that an infant could be exorcised but not instructed. Why was it that the exorcism survived when the catechetical instruction disappeared?

Another significant group of exorcisms in the Rhenish rituals is that group of exorcisms which in the fourth century had belonged to the service of the recitation of the Creed, usually held on the morning of Holy Saturday. This was the service which concluded the catechumenate. The first of this group of exorcisms addressed the Prince of Darkness directly:

> Let it not be hidden from thee, O Satan, the pains which await thee, the torments which await thee, the day of judgment which awaits thee, the day of everlasting humility, the day which is to come as a burning furnace in which everlasting destruction will come upon you and all your angels. Therefore, O damned and damning one, give honor to the living and true God, give honor to Jesus Christ his Son and to the Holy Spirit, by whose name and virtue I warn thee, unclean

31. "Audi maledicte sathana adiuratus per nomen eterni dei et saluatoris nostri filij dei cum tua uictus inuidia tremens gemensque discede; nichil tibi commune sit cum seruo dei iam celestia cogitanti renunciaturo tibi ac seculo tuo et beate immortalitati uicturo; da igitur honorem aduenienti spirituisancto, qui ex summa celi arce descendens perturbatis fraudibus tuis diuino fonte purgatum pectus, id est deo santificatum, deo templum et habitaculum perficiat et ab omnibus penitus noxijs preteritorum criminum liberatus hic seruus dei N. gracias perhenni deo semper referat et benedicat nomen eius sanctum in secula seculorum. Amen.

"Ergo maledicte diabole, recognosce sentenciam tuam et da honorem deo uiuo et uero; da honorem ihesu cristo filio eius et spirituisancto et recede ab hoc famulo dei N., quia istum sibi deus et dominus noster ihesus cristus ad suam sanctam graciam et benedictionem fontemque baptismatis dono spiritussancti uocare dignatus est: et hoc signum sancte crucis *Cum pollice fac crucem in fronte pueri,* quod fronti eius damus tu maledicte diabole nunquam audeas uiolare. Per cristum dominum nostrum. Amen." *Obsequiale Constantiensis,* p. 8.

> spirit, whoever you may be; go out and depart from this servant of God, N., whom today our Lord Jesus Christ has deigned to call so graciously to the holy blessing of baptism, that he might become a temple to him through the water of regeneration in the remission of all sins in the name of our same Lord Jesus Christ who shall come to judge the living and the dead and this age through fire. Amen.[32]

The text of this exorcism speaks for itself. Here we catch sight of the Church struggling with the Satanic powers which infest the world. She is confident that, armed with the power of the risen Christ, she will lead her people safely through the waters of baptism. We notice with particular interest the rubrics with which this prayer is introduced. "Again the presbyter admonishes all those standing about to pray, and he catechizes the children individually with these words, saying. . . ."[33] Here we have it! The repetition of this long exorcism is understood as "catechizing." The catechumenal rites had by this time been so reduced to exorcism that to catechize simply meant to exorcise.

One would think that there had been enough exorcism by this time, but one more comes directly on the heels of this last one. This is the "Effeta" exorcism, which is a dramatization of the story of Jesus healing the deaf-mute (Mark 7:31-37).[34] The priest is to touch the candidate's ears and nostrils with the spittle of his own mouth. While doing this the priest is to use the formula, "Effeta, that is, be opened."[35] Finally the child is taken into the church, thus ending the catechetical rites.

Not even this ends the series of exorcisms. Another group of exorcisms

32. "Nec te lateat sathana imminere tibi penas, imminere tibi tormenta, imminere tibi diem iudicij, diem supplicij sempiterni, diem qui uenturus est uelut clibanus ardens, in quo tibi atque uniuersis angelis tuis eternus superueniet interitus. Proinde damnate atque damnande: da honorem deo uero et uiuo, da honorem ihesu cristo filio eius et spirituisancto, in cuius nomine atque uirtute precipio tibi, quicumque es spiritus immunde, ut exeas atque recedas ab hoc famulo dei N., quem hodie dominus noster ihesus cristus ad suam sanctam graciam et benedictionem fontemque baptismatis dono suo uocare dignatus est, ut fiat ei templum per aquam regeneracionis in remissionem omnium peccatorum in nomine eiusdem domini nostri ihesu cristi. Qui uenturus est iudicare uiuas et mortuos et seculum per ignem. Amen." *Obsequiale Constantiensis,* p. 10.

33. "Item moneat presbiter omnes astantes orare et cathezizet eos singulariter hijs uerbis dicens." *Obsequiale Constantiensis,* p. 10. Compare: "Moneat abstantes, ut orent et catechiset: Nec te lateat Satana. . . ." *Agenda Maguntinensis,* p. 185; "Quibus completis publice catecizet eum his verbis." *Agenda Argentinensis,* p. 413. For the beginnings of this attitude, see Stenzel, *Die Taufe,* pp. 201-3.

34. On the "Effeta" exorcism, see Dölger, *Der Exorzismus,* pp. 130-37.

35. "Deinde cum digito tangat ei aures et nares cum sputo oris sui, ita dicens: 'Effeta.' Ad aures 'quod est adaperire in odorem suauitatis.' Ad nares et uideat caute ne tangat sputo labia infantis: Quomodo, ne id fiat, de consecracione distinctione quarta capite 'propter gloriam' prohibetur. 'Tu autem effugare diabole, appropinquabit enim iudicium dei.' " *Obsequiale Constantiensis,* pp. 10-11.

is found among those rites which had many centuries before been celebrated in the baptistry during the Paschal Vigil. In the Rhenish baptismal rites used just before the Reformation, these rites were performed around the baptismal font, which by this time had been moved from the baptistry into the church. Once the baptismal party has arrived at the font, the water must be exorcised.[36] Even at the beginning of the sixteenth century the baptismal fonts of cathedral churches were still consecrated by the bishop. The prayer for the blessing of the baptismal waters which the bishop used is one of the oldest and most venerable prayers in the history of the liturgy. By the end of the Middle Ages, most baptisms were performed in parish churches rather than in cathedral churches, and they were most often celebrated at some time other than Easter. For this reason we can assume that for the great majority of baptisms the water had not been consecrated by the bishop at the Paschal Vigil. In place of the long and solemn ancient prayer filled with its typological allusions, the ritual of Constance provided a short prayer for the blessing of the font in case it had not already been blessed. It is clearly an exorcism.

> I exorcise thee, O creature of water, in the name of God the Father Almighty, and in the love of Jesus Christ the Son, and in the power of the Holy Spirit. If there be any fantasy, any unfriendly power, any incursion of the devil, to erase, flee from this creature of water, that it be a fountain of water springing up unto eternal life. And when you baptize this servant of the Lord, that he become a temple of the living God in remission of all sins. In the name of our Lord Jesus Christ, who shall come to judge the living and the dead and this age through fire. . . .
>
> Hear us, O Omnipotent God, and mix into the substance of this water thy power, that being washed through this he might gain both health and eternal life. . . . This font is sanctified and made fertile in the name of the Father and of the Son and of the Holy Spirit.[37]

Not only had catechetical instruction degenerated into exorcism, but the blessing of the font had gone the same way. The old prayer with its magnificent

36. On the consecration of the font and its relation to exorcism, see Dölger, *Der Exorzismus,* pp. 160-67.

37. "Exorzizo te creatura aque in nomine dei patris omnipotentis et in caritate ihesu cristi filij eius et in uirtute spiritussancti: Si qua fantasia: Si qua uirtus inimici: si qua incursio dyaboli eradicare et effugare ab hac creatura aque, ut fiat fons aque salientis in uitam eternam. Et cum baptisatus fuerit hic famulus domini fiat templum dei uiui in remissionem omnium peccatorum. In nomine domini nostri ihesu cristi, qui uenturus est iudicare uiuos et mortuos et seculum per ignem. Deinde dicat: 'Exaudi nos omnipotens deus et in huius aque substanciam tuam immisce uirtutem, ut abluendus per eam et sanitatem simul et uitam mereatur eternam. . . .' Sanctificetur et fecundetur fons iste in nomine patris et filij et spiritus sancti." *Obsequiale Constantiensis,* p. 11.

eucharistic cast was put aside. The rite did not so much bless the font as it exorcised it.

One wonders why exorcisms had become so important in the baptismal rites of the late Middle Ages. In the New Testament Church, exorcism does not seem to have accompanied baptism. There is at least no solid evidence that exorcisms were performed as part of the baptismal services we read about in the New Testament.[38] The *Didache* mentions no baptismal exorcisms in its description of the administration of baptism. Justin Martyr does not indicate any baptismal exorcisms in his description of the service in the middle of the second century. They first appear at the beginning of the third century.[39] The reason usually given to explain their appearance seems quite solid. At the beginning of the third century most of those baptized were converts from paganism. The Christians of the period tended to think of the pagan gods as demons and of their worshipers as demon possessed. Those coming over from paganism needed, therefore, to be exorcised. One would expect, then, that with the disappearance of paganism the exorcisms would disappear too. The Gallican Sacramentaries show that by the eighth century the exorcisms were beginning to disappear, but with the liturgical reforms of the Carolingian Age in the following century the exorcisms begin to become increasingly important once more.[40] That Alcuin found the exorcisms important is without doubt to be explained by his great interest in the mission to the Saxons and the Avars.[41] By the High Middle Ages, the baptism of converts from paganism was almost unknown in Germany; nevertheless, the liturgical importance of the baptismal exorcisms wanes not at all.

There is another side to this coin. What was happening in theology was quite different from what was happening in the liturgy. Scholastic theology in its treatment of the sacrament of baptism essentially ignores the baptismal exorcisms. According to the Scholastic theologians, a perfectly valid baptism could be performed without exorcism.[42] Thomas Aquinas expressed a widely held opinion that the exorcisms belonged to the solemn celebration of baptism but were not a necessary part of it.[43] If the late medieval baptismal service

38. Rudolf Schnackenburg, *Baptism in the Thought of St. Paul,* trans. G. R. Beasley-Murray (Oxford: Basil Blackwell, 1964), p. 9. Jean Daniélou, "Exorcism," *Dictionnaire de Spiritualité* 4, cols. 1995-2004, argues the other point of view.

39. Dölger argues for the last third of the second century, *Der Exorzismus,* pp. 9-17. For a more nuanced position, see André Benoît, *Le baptême chrétien au second siècle* (Paris: Presses Universitaires de France, 1953), pp. 11, 38ff., and 52.

40. Mortimort, *L'église à priére* (Tournai: Desclée et Companie, 1961).

41. Neunheuser, *Baptism and Confirmation.*

42. Alfons Müller, *Die Lehre von der Taufe bei Albert dem Grossen* (Munich: Verlag Ferdinand Schöningh, 1967), pp. 68-70.

43. Thomas Aquinas, *Summa Theologica* 3.67.2-4.

was dominated by a concern to drive out the devil, it was not because of the teaching of the Scholastic theologians.

While other things disappeared from the baptismal rites during the Middle Ages, the exorcisms only seemed to flourish and even to multiply. Why was this? It seems, more than anything else, to be a natural reflection of the age. As the barbarian invasions began to darken the light of classical civilization and the lamps of learning went out one by one, the Church found herself struggling against powers of darkness. These powers of darkness took the form of demonic monsters and little gremlins. The exorcisms were relevant to the common people, to the Hans and Hilda who brought their little Gretchen to be baptized. Evil spirits were all about. Gargoyles infested every church tower. From every illuminated choir book dozens of griffins winked at even the most pious. Who could blame the parish priest for catering to the needs of the simple people he served? Why should the good parson not explain baptism as the chasing out of the devil? When he did that everybody understood him. He was being relevant. He was meeting the needs of his people. It was easy to explain baptism in terms of exorcism. Why should he burden his people with good Scholastic theology?

Disappearance of Catechetical Instruction

At the beginning of the sixteenth century, the Rhenish baptismal rites did not include any genuine catechetical instruction. Both the rite of Constance and the rite of Strasbourg made a strong point of admonishing the godparents of their responsibility to teach their godchildren the Apostles' Creed, the Lord's Prayer, and the Hail Mary. In the rite of Strasbourg, for instance, we find the following rubric, "Then the priest enjoins the godparents, that they teach him, when he shall come to the use of reason, the Our Father, the Hail Mary, and the Creed."[44] The rite of Constance provides a similar rubric, "Here the presbyter teaches the godparents that they should inform the little ones of the Lord's Prayer, the Angelic Salutation, and the Symbol."[45] This usage was recommended by the various pastoral manuals of that time.[46] There is, to be sure,

44. "Tunc sacerdos iniungat patrinis, ut eum doceant, cum habuerit usum rationis, Pater noster, Ave Maria et Credo, dicendo: Ir sollent es lernen so es zu syner vernunfft kumpt das Pater noster und Ave Maria und den heiligen cristenlichen glouben." *Agenda Argentinensis,* p. 414.

45. "Hic doceat presbiter Patrinos, ut paruulos informent in oracione dominica et in salutacione angelica et in simbolo." *Obsequiale Constantiensis,* p. 9.

46. For example, John Beleth required godparents to know the catechetical pieces. "Et notandum est, quod, ut supra dictum est, nullus debet suscipi in patrinum, nisi sciat

an awareness that with baptism there should be teaching. Yet the rite contains no more than this consciousness that there ought to be instruction. No longer do we find the "frequent instructions" about which Leo the Great speaks.[47] No longer do we find the series of catechetical sermons given by the bishop during Lent, as in the days of Ambrose of Milan, Cyril of Jerusalem, John Chrysostom, and Augustine.

Catechetical instructions began to disappear when more and more of those baptized were infant children of Christians rather than adult converts from paganism. This is often said and it is certainly true. After all, it would take a strong-lunged cleric to preach a series of catechetical sermons to a whole year's crop of babies every Lent. In the city of Rome, for example, it was about the beginning of the sixth century when adult converts from paganism became a rarity at the Easter baptisms. By that time the bishop of Rome found himself preaching to a whole roomful of infants carried in the arms of their parents. No wonder the traditional catechetical instruction ceased.

This was not the only reason. With the barbarian invasions, which we remember took place during the lifetimes of Augustine and Leo the Great, the whole level of education began to plummet. Schools disappeared; fewer and fewer bishops were able to preach. Who had the leisure in those days to cultivate the fine art of oratory? Augustine had been a great preacher, but as a young man he had had the leisure to spend years studying the art of rhetoric. One need only compare Augustine to Isidore of Seville two centuries later to see what had happened to education. With the disappearance of the learning of classical antiquity, Western society had become almost inarticulate. The cultivation of literary skills was neglected. Appreciation for clear and intelligent public speaking declined. The Church no longer had leaders who could preach catechetical sermons. Christian congregations no longer demanded preaching which was clear and instructive. Catechetical preaching did not have

---

dominicam orationem et *Credo in Deum,* que duo omnes patrini docere tenentur filiolos suos, quia sunt fideiussores fidei illorum et eos custodire debent pro posse suo, ne a fide et iustitia deuient, utpote responsuri de omni excessu eorum in die iuditi. Sacerdos quoque pater est et patrinus omnium illorum, quos baptizat, et eos tenetur docere. Sed quia non posset tot uacare, idcirco cure patrinorum illos conmendat." Johannes Beleth, *Summa de ecclesiasticis officiis,* ed. Heriberto Douteil (Turnholt: Brepols, 1976), p. 206.

47. "His itaque, fratres charissimi, tot ac tantis existentibus documentis, quibus omni ambiguitate submota, evidenter agnoscitis, in baptizandis electis, qui secundum apostolicam regulam et exorcismis scrutandi, et jejuniis sanctificandi, et frequentibus sunt praedicationibus imbuendi, in duo tantum tempora, id est Pascha, et Pentecosten, esse servanda; hoc vestrae indicimus charitati, ut ab apostolicis institutis nullo ulterius recedatis excessu." Leo the Great, "Epistle XVI," 6, in Migne, *Patrologiae cursus completus,* series Latina 54: 702. Cf. Stenzel, *Die Taufe,* p. 203, note b.

to disappear when infant baptism became generalized. The Church could have done this teaching after baptism. There were already the beginnings of such a tradition. Augustine had preached series of sermons to those who had just been baptized. Today we call this the photizimate and carefully distinguish it from the catechumenate, which was instruction given before baptism. The idea was that one could not understand the mysteries of initiation until one had been illuminated by baptism. Why did the Church not build on this tradition? Why was prebaptismal catechetical instruction not replaced by postbaptismal catechetical instruction? Why was it that instead of moving catechetical instruction, the Church had simply allowed it to disappear? Was it because it had lost sight of the relation of teaching and baptism? Had it forgotten the command of Jesus to teach them "all things whatsoever I have commanded you"? In the sixth century learning had come on hard days.

To understand more exactly what happened to the catechetical instruction of the fourth century, we can look at a rite in the sixth-century Gelasian Sacramentary.[48] At a single session during Lent the child is to be taught the "Gospel."[49] The four Gospel books are carried out in splendid ceremony, each in turn. The first few verses of each Gospel are read and the symbolic beasts are explained. With this ceremony, the Gospel is somehow understood to have been communicated to the infant.[50] Today we read through this rite and wonder how those liturgists perceived what they were doing. Did they think they were performing a ritual illumination in the way the dramatized cult mysteries of ancient Greece had claimed to illumine those who participated in their rites? This approach to catechizing is probably beyond our understanding, but no doubt it went hand in hand with the growing importance of exorcism as a means of catechizing.

Yet even at the time of the Gelasian Sacramentary there were converts from paganism for whom that sacramentary included a rite of catechism. As far as one can tell from the catechetical rites of the Gelasian Sacramentary, adults were given no more genuine catechetical instruction than infants were given. From this it should be quite clear that the generalizing of infant baptism was not the only reason catechetical instruction fell out of the baptismal rites. Far more important was the general drop in the level of education and a magical understanding of what instruction actually is.

The Carolingian reform did see an attempt to re-establish catechetical

48. *Sacramentarium Gelasianum* 1.23.46-48.

49. Cf. Stenzel, *Die Taufe,* p. 190, for a commentary on this rite.

50. Stenzel points out that John of Rome, about the year 500, was of the opinion that the "catechetical instructions" were to be understood under the sign of the struggle between Satan and Christ. The instructions were purely ritual. Stenzel, *Die Taufe,* pp. 190ff.

instruction. This reform was led by Alcuin, a native of York and a man of great learning for his day. Alcuin rightly deserves to be numbered among the great reformers of the Church. Under his leadership the tide began to turn. Learning began to increase. Schools were once more established. The Carolingian reform was both educational and liturgical.[51] The education of the clergy was an essential element, but there was another aspect of this reform. Alcuin was a strong advocate of the re-establishment of catechetical instruction.[52] He insisted that in the missionary work among the Saxons and Avars there should be teaching before there was baptism.[53] He appealed to the text of the last chapter of Matthew, "Make disciples of all nations, baptizing them . . . and teaching them."[54] One wonders why the Church in the time of Alcuin did not restore catechetical instruction to the actual rite of baptism. Why did Alcuin not find some way of integrating baptismal teaching into the baptismal liturgy? Liturgical reform was also a central concern of the Carolingian Age. What a perfect time this would have been to restore the old catechetical rites. Once more, adult converts from paganism were being baptized. The answer is to be found in another concern of the Carolingian reform, the concern for *romanitas*.

Let us look for a moment at this concern for *romanitas,* particularly as it was related to the liturgy. The object of *romanitas* as it affected the liturgy was to make the rites of the Frankish Church north of the Alps conform to the rites of the city of Rome. All the ancient prayers found in the Gregorian Sacramentary were to be said. The Roman formulas and rubrics of the Gregorian Sacramentary given by Pope Hadrian to Charlemagne were to be carefully maintained despite the difference in time and situation. Even though that rite was suited for a church which had been Christian for centuries, Char-

51. On the Carolingian liturgical reforms cf. Erna Patzelt, *Die Karolingische Renaissance,* and Cyrille Vogel, *La reforme culturelle sous Pepin le Bref et sous Charlemagne,* both works published together (Graz, Austria: Akademische Druck, 1965); Kretschmar, *Die Geschichte des Taufgottesdienstes,* pp. 314-27; Edmond Bishop, "The Liturgical Reforms of Charlemagne: Their Meaning and Value," *Downside Review* 38 (1919): 1-16; Fernand Cabrol, "Alcuin," *Dictionnaire d'archéologie chrétienne et de liturgie* (hereafter *DACL*) 1/I: 1072-92; and Eleanor S. Duckett, *Alcuin, Friend of Charlemagne* (New York: The Macmillan Company, 1951).

52. On the liturgical works of Alcuin cf. Kretschmar, "Taufgottesdienste," pp. 301, 309. Particularly helpful in the works which he quotes is G. Ellard, *Master Alcuin, Liturgist* (Chicago: Loyola University Press, 1956).

53. On the role of catechetical instruction in the mission of the Avars, cf. Stenzel, *Die Taufe,* p. 216. For a period a bit before the Carolingian time see Stenzel on the practice of Pirmin the founder of Reichenau (c. 680-755) and Boniface the founder of Fulda (c. 675-743). In both cases there was a clear interest in real instruction. Cf. Kretschmar, "Taufgottesdienste," p. 309.

54. Cf. Kretschmar, "Taufgottesdienste," pp. 310ff.

lemagne wanted it to be used to baptize the tribes of northern Europe. As Charlemagne understood it, such a rite would both Christianize and Romanize. The prebaptismal instruction so important to Alcuin was seen as one issue and the Gregorian baptismal rites were perceived as something entirely different. The catechetical instruction of the missionary monks was done before the baptism. It was considered desirable to have forty days of preparation before the pagan converts were baptized.[55] All during these forty days, the missionary monks instructed, exorcised, sprinkled holy water, and blessed the new converts with solemn signations. Yet at the end of the forty days, the whole Roman rite had to be performed just as it appeared in the Gregorian Sacramentary. That these very rites had once stretched out over forty days worried no one. Apparently no one considered this repetitious. No one thought it burdensome to go through all these rites in one session. It was not burdensome repetition, but rather the holy and glorious endowment of *romanitas*.

Thus even when the Church was again faced with the need to give catechetical instruction to converts from paganism, there was no recasting of the baptismal service so that the old catechetical rites were restored.

The older rites were simply compressed to make room for missionary preaching which never became ritualized or institutionalized. When the need for instructing converts from paganism arose, such preaching was supplied, but it was supplied outside the rite.

Having attempted to explain why catechetical teaching disappeared from the rite of baptism and having tried to explain why it did not reappear with the Carolingian reform, let us look once again at those early sixteenth-century baptismal rites.

What about the catechetical instruction of the children baptized in infancy? Was there instruction for them once they reached the age of reason? The rites of Strasbourg and Constance indicate that the godparents promised to see that the children would learn the catechetical pieces, but evidently the Church did not provide any regular means for giving catechetical instruction. Perhaps no one up to that point felt the need for more than memorizing the Creed, the Lord's Prayer, and the Hail Mary. Whatever the reason, the fact is that there was no widespread catechetical teaching for Christian children. Things were going to change. The growing awareness of the need for Christian education was one of the chief forces behind the desire in the sixteenth century to reform the rite of baptism.

55. Stenzel, *Die Taufe,* p. 246.

The Beginning of a Movement to Translate Certain Parts of the Rite

Another noteworthy characteristic of these texts is the movement to translate the baptismal rite, or at least portions of it, into German. The first place we find this is at the very beginning of the service. Both the rite of Constance and the rite of Mainz begin with the question posed in German, "Wie sol das kyndt heissen." "What is the child to be called?"[56] The Strasbourg rite does not give the question but rather provides a rubric directing the priest to inquire whether the child is masculine or feminine, whether the child has been baptized out of necessity, and what the child's name is. Presumably the questions would be asked in German. Furthermore, at the crucial moment when the baptismal vows renouncing the devil are made, the Latin question is translated into the German and a German answer is expected. "Abrenuncias Satanae? Widersagest Du dem Teufel? Responsio: Abrenuncio. Ich widersag."[57] The second place where these rites frequently used the German language is in the question which the priest asks regarding the intention to be baptized. "Do you will to be baptized?" "I so will." "Vis baptizari? Willst Du getauft werden? Responsio: Volo. Ich will."[58] We find that in the rite of Constance this exchange is also given in both Latin and German.[59] In the Strasbourg rite the question is put to the godparents, "Do you will that the child be baptized?" They respond, "We so will."[60] This question and answer appear first in Latin and then in German.

Why is it that German has been introduced into certain parts of the baptismal rite? Is it part of a general concern to translate liturgical forms into the common language? One could understand it in this way, but there is something else at work here. In the late Middle Ages voluntarism was beginning to have an effect on the way the sacrament of baptism was understood.[61] We will have more

56. *Agenda Maguntinensis,* p. 183; *Obsequiale Constantiensis,* p. 6.

57. *Agenda Maguntinensis,* p. 185.

58. *Agenda Maguntinensis,* p. 187; *Agenda Argentinensis,* p. 414.

59. *Obsequiale Constantiensis,* p. 6.

60. *Agenda Argentinensis,* p. 415.

61. Stenzel understands the question "vis baptizari" as arising from the concern of Scholastic theology that the intention to be baptized needed to be established. *Die Taufe,* p. 256. Surely he is correct. The question may go back to the days of Alcuin. At that time it may have served to establish that the candidate was being baptized of his own free will. Cf. Ordo 28, where the question is not present, and Ordo 50, where the question is present. Michel Andrieu, *Les Ordines Romani du haut moyen âge,* 5 vols. (Louvain: Spicilegium Sacrum Lovaniense, 1931-61); for Ordo 50, vol. 5, pp. 284 and 285; for Ordo 28, vol. 3, p. 407. Several of the early baptismal rites collected by Martène, e.g., Limoges, Moissac, and Jumieges, contain the questions of intention. Edmund Martène, *De antiquis ecclesiae ritibus,* 3 vols. (Rouen: G. Behourt, 1700), 1: 192, 195, and 207.

to say about voluntarism later. Here we simply want to notice that voluntarism had already made its mark on the baptismal rites. For the voluntarist it was very important that there be the intention of being baptized. Evidently those who directed that the questions regarding the intention to be baptized be asked in the common tongue felt that these questions had to be understood even if the rest of the rite did not have to be understood. Nicholas de Plove, in his *Tractatus sacerdotalis* printed in Strasbourg in 1512, directed that this question and answer be repeated three times so that it could be ascertained that the person was being baptized by his own voluntary intention.[62]

With this emphasis on the intention of those to whom the rite is administered, the strong objectivity indicated in the expression *opus operandi* is beginning to give way to a more subjective understanding of the sacrament. This subjectivism is fostered primarily by the voluntarism of the late medieval Nominalists. Clearly a voluntarist understanding of salvation led to the translation of what the voluntarists considered the core of the rite, the expression of the intention. A more Augustinian theology might have chosen the words of Christ, namely the baptismal formula, for translation into German. The tendency toward subjectivism which puts at the heart of the rite the intention of the baptized and which leaves the word of Christ or the action of God untranslated gives the impression of Pelagianism.

Whatever the reasons, there clearly was a growing tendency to celebrate certain parts of the rite of baptism in German. In the time of Charlemagne, the passion for *romanitas* kept the whole rite in Latin. By the beginning of the sixteenth century, other concerns were able to introduce German translations of at least portions of the service.

Disappearance of Paschal Baptisms

Neither the Strasbourg nor the Constance baptismal rite gives any hint that baptism should normally be administered on any particular day or any particular season of the year. At the end of the Middle Ages baptism could be held *quolibet tempore,* at any time one wished. In those days, most children were baptized within a few days after birth. By the beginning of the Reformation the great baptismal celebrations of the Easter season were a thing of the past.[63]

62. The section of the *Tractatus sacerdotalis* regarding baptism has been printed in Gustav Kawerau, "Liturgische Studien zu Luthers Taufbüchlein von 1523," *Zeitschrift für kirchliche Wissenschaft und kirchliches Leben* 10 (1898), pp. 415-17. This work will be abbreviated as Kawerau, "Taufbüchlein." Cf. p. 417.

63. They had not been completely forgotten, as we learn from Henry Bullinger. See

The mounting expectation during the forty days of catechetical preparation, the magnificent Paschal Vigil with its reading of the Old Testament types of baptism, the solemn consecration of the font, the baptisms themselves near the dawn of Easter morning, and the celebration of communion in the full light of the resurrection, which back in the fourth century had made such an exciting liturgical drama, had all disappeared. There were few traces of all that Easter glory in the baptisms celebrated on the eve of the Reformation. The rites we find in Strasbourg and Constance can be celebrated with dispatch, in less than half an hour and at the time most convenient for either priest or parent.

The great paschal baptismal services of the fourth century were not inherited from the time of Christ and the apostles. It is doubtful that the New Testament Church limited baptism to Easter or Pentecost. While precedent for baptism at Pentecost could be found in the second chapter of Acts, it was a different matter with the Ethiopian eunuch, the Philippian jailer, and Cornelius. They were probably baptized on some other day of the year. Possibly the custom of baptizing on the Lord's Day goes back to New Testament times. It seems well established in the second century, but the evidence is too scanty to be sure. We gather from Cyprian that in the middle of the third century North African infants were baptized soon after birth.[64] Just when the tradition of baptizing on Easter and Pentecost originated is not clear, and it would take us far afield to search it out. Certainly the practice was in full flower in the fourth century, the time when we first encounter detailed accounts of the rite of baptism.

Our interest at this point is a brief account of how and why the custom of Easter baptisms disappeared.[65] Already in the sixth century there was some movement to allow baptisms on the feast of Epiphany since that feast celebrated the baptism of Christ. Christmas, since it celebrated the birth of Christ, was also thought of as an appropriate time for the sacrament of new birth. Clovis, we remember, was baptized on Christmas Day in the year 496. In some circles the *dies natales* of certain martyrs were thought of as appropriate. This tendency to proliferate the occasions for baptism was opposed quite early. Leo I, the bishop of Rome in the middle of the fifth century, opposed the celebration of baptism

---

the author's article on Bullinger's knowledge of the history of the rite of baptism, "Henry Bullinger and the Scholastic Works on Baptism," *Henry Bullinger, 1504-1575* (Zurich: Theologischer Verlag, 1975).

64. "Quantum uero ad causam infantium pertinet, quos dixisti intra secundum uel tertium diem quam nati sint constitutos baptizari non oportere et considerandam esse legem circumcisionis antiquae, ut intra octauum diem eum qui natus est baptizandum et sanctificandum non putares, longe aliud in concilio nostro uisum est." Louis Bayard, *Saint Cyprien Correspondance, texte établi et traduit,* vol. 2 (Paris: Société d'édition "Les Belles Lettres," 1925), p. 214.

65. For a much more detailed account see the work of Fisher, *Christian Initiation: Medieval,* pp. 109-19.

on Christmas and Epiphany. As he saw it, baptism should be reserved, except, to be sure, in cases of necessity, to the traditional celebration of Easter and Pentecost.[66] At the end of the fifth century, Pope Gelasius insisted on retaining Easter and Pentecost as the normal seasons of baptism. With such authority, the maintaining of paschal baptisms should have been assured; nevertheless, we hear these appeals to reserve the celebration of baptism to the traditional seasons repeated again and again. From these constantly repeated pleas for the maintenance of paschal baptisms one gets the impression the custom was having a hard time maintaining itself. Charlemagne understood the preservation of the paschal celebration of baptism as a Roman tradition, and he was therefore eager to continue this tradition; nevertheless, there is evidence that in the Carolingian period the custom was less than universal. While the Council of Mainz in 813 and the Council of Paris in 829 were eager to maintain paschal baptism, the prominent Carolingian theologian Rabanus Maurus favored more frequent baptisms.[67] For several centuries the custom was maintained in some areas more successfully than in others. What seemed to change this insistence on the two classical occasions for baptism was the growing conviction of the absolute necessity of baptism. The necessity of baptism was considered so absolute to such theologians as Bernard, Peter Lombard, and Hugh of St. Victor that by the end of the twelfth century no one dared wait for Easter, particularly if that meant waiting the better part of a year.[68] Such insistence, coupled with the cold reality that a quarter to a half of these infants would not live a year, effectively undermined the tradition of paschal baptisms. At the beginning of the twelfth century, Rupert of Deutz lamented that in his day only a few children were kept waiting until the feasts of Easter and Pentecost.[69]

By the thirteenth century we begin to find assurances that children could be baptized at any time. Regarding the delay of baptism until Easter or Pentecost, Thomas Aquinas taught that a distinction should be made between the baptism of infants and that of adults. He tells us that while the baptism of infants should not be delayed, adult baptism should be reserved for the tradi-

66. Leo the Great, "Epistle XVI," para. 6 in Migne, *Patrologia latina* (hereafter *MPL*) 54: 700-702.

67. Fisher, *Christian Initiation: Medieval,* p. 76.

68. Fisher, *Christian Initiation: Medieval,* p. 112.

69. "At, postquam Christianitas crevit, et sagena illa verbi dei piscibus impleta est, quia periculosum erat tantam multitudinem differe propter occasiones mortis, quae in multitudine hominum multae sunt, maxime propter turbam infantum, ex Christianis parentibus succrescentium, quorum tenera vita persaepe levei occasione succiditur, visum est sanctae Ecclesiae, passim indulgentia baptizandi concessa, imo oblata, cuncta antevenire pericula, baptismi tamen solemnitatem vel in paucis cum Dominica resurrectione, cui similis est, celebrare." *De divinis officiis, MPL* 170; 112.

tional seasons. Citing the well-known decree of Leo I, he argues that the tradition of delaying baptism until Easter or Pentecost should be understood to include the exception of the danger of death, which is always a fear when children are involved.[70]

Concerned Christian parents would have their children baptized *in necessitate* rather than run the risk of having their children die without baptism. This practice became so common that the canon lawyers and theologians were prompted to take another look at the subject. There was evidently the danger that if they continued to insist on both the absolute necessity of baptism and on the traditional dates of Easter and Pentecost, they would be confronted with the *fait accompli* that most children would receive their baptism at the hands of midwives.[71] It is not surprising, therefore, that by the fourteenth century we find that baptism is required by the eighth day after birth.[72]

With this information in mind, we look again at the opening pages of the ritual of Constance. Almost as a preface, a short treatise on the seven sacraments opens the text. In this little treatise we find this thumbnail sketch of the Church's teaching on baptism.

> Baptism is the doorway to and the foundation of all the other sacraments. Without baptism it is impossible to enter the kingdom of heaven. It is simply necessary. Its material, therefore, is the most common of all materials, pure water. In necessity it can be conferred by a layman of either sex, even from a heretic, or a schismatic, or a Jew, if only there is the intention and if the formula is used. The formula comes from the words used by the Lord when he said, "Go baptize in the name of the Father and of the Son and of the Holy Spirit." The formula, therefore, used equally by all, is: "I baptize you in the name of the Father, and of the Son and of the Holy Spirit." Nor ought "Amen" to be added. The effect, therefore, is the remission of all sins and punishments.[73]

With such accents on necessity and simplicity, one marvels that anyone was baptized in church at all. It is easy to understand why midwife baptism was

70. Thomas Aquinas, *Summa Theologica* 3.68.3.

71. Midwives were properly instructed in the baptism of infants *in necessitate.* In regard to this practice in the fourteenth century see Jules Corblet, *Histoire du sacrament de baptême,* vol. 1, pp. 321ff.

72. Stenzel, *Die Taufe,* pp. 264-66.

73. "Baptismus est Ianua omnium et fundamentum, sine quo impossibile est intrare regnum celorum. Ideo simpliciter est necessarium. Eius ergo materia communis omnibus, quia pura aqua elementaris; Et in necessit a layco utriusque sexus conferri potest, ab heritico, Scismatico uel iudeo, si intensio uera adest et forma uerborum seruatur, quam dominus expressit dicens: Ite baptizate in nomine patris et filij et spiritussancti. Forma igitur est ab omnibus equaliter tenenda: Ego te baptiza in nomine patris et filij et spiritus sancti. Nec addi debet: Amen. Effectus ergo est remissio omnium peccatorum et penarum." *Obsequiale Constantiensis,* pp. 1-2.

so popular. Indeed, it was very popular. Many of these late medieval baptismal rites began by asking whether the child had previously been baptized. This gives us a very good clue as to what was going on. Baptism was in danger of becoming a household religious rite. There is no longer any tension between paschal baptisms and *quolibet tempore* baptisms. There was another, quite different tension, and that was the tension between *quolibet tempore* baptisms at church and *in necessitate* baptisms at home. Put more plainly, it was a tension between church baptism and midwife baptism.

The Presbyterializing of Baptism

Still another characteristic of these baptismal rites is that the celebrant is the parish priest rather than the bishop. This is evident first from the fact that the rites are found not in a pontifical, the book of rites celebrated by the bishop, but rather in the ritual, the book of rites to be celebrated by the local priest.[74] The *Obsequiale* of Constance, the *Agenda* of Mainz, and the *Agenda* of Strasbourg were all early forms of what today is technically called the ritual. They were published by the bishops of these cities for the guidance of their priests. The ritual contained the occasional services which were normally conducted by the parish priest. In the ritual we find not only the baptismal service, but also the marriage service and the burial service. Throughout these rituals themselves it is equally clear that the usual celebrant is the priest. It had not always been this way. In earlier centuries baptisms were celebrated by the bishop.

This presbyterializing, that is, this turning over of the rite to the presbyter, brought about a corresponding change in the way the baptismal rites were celebrated and in the way these rites were understood. It was really the presbyterializing of baptism which was responsible for separating baptism and confirmation and for making them two separate sacraments. When this change took place, what the priest did was considered one sacrament, the sacrament

74. On the distinction between pontifical and ritual see the appropriate entries in the *New Catholic Encyclopedia.* The *Rituale Romanum* was not published until 1614. "The *Rituale Romanum* had a long prehistory, however. It evolved slowly from the need of the local priest to have a service book for the ordinary services other than the mass and the daily office, such as baptisms, burials, and marriages. The *Agenda* of Strasbourg, the *Obsequiale* of Constance, and the *Liber Sacerdotalis* of Alberto Castellani were all rituals, i.e., liturgical books intended for priests and containing the rites for baptism, marriage, anointing of the sick, care of the dying, burial of the dead, and a number of other ceremonial blessings. On the evolution of the ritual see Spital, *Der Taufritus,* p. 141.

of baptism; and what the bishop did was considered another sacrament, the sacrament of confirmation.[75]

However clear the rubrics may have been, the actual rites themselves were at best ambiguous on this question. In the rite of Constance we read:

> *Next the godfather receives the child, holding him above the baptismal font, while the presbyter finds the chrism. He brings it out while saying the following:* "God omnipotent, Father of our Lord Jesus Christ, who has regenerated you from water and the Holy Spirit and who has given to you remission of all sins" *(here he makes a cross with the chrism on the crown of the child's head, saying),* "himself anoint you with the chrism of salvation in Christ Jesus our Lord unto life eternal. Amen."[76]

After this a white cap is put on the head of the child with an appropriate word of interpretation. Then the service is concluded by a benediction, "Go in peace; may thy faith bring thee salvation."[77] Even though the priest performs these rites rather than the bishop, the baptismal service is ended with an act which had in earlier times been regarded as an "episcopal" act, namely the anointing of the head with oil and the giving of a benediction. As this anointing appears in these rites, it would be hard to distinguish it from the historic rites, which in the course of time had come to be understood as the sacrament of confirmation. If indeed baptism was not a sign of the giving of the Holy Spirit, one wonders why the child was anointed with oil at this point. Is oil not a sign of the Holy Spirit? Is it not a sign of the penetrating and abiding presence of the Holy Spirit who by his sanctifying presence in the Christian brings to pass the inner purification promised in the sign of washing? One wonders why the accompanying prayer blesses God for regenerating the child "from water and the Holy Spirit." Are we to imagine that the Holy Spirit is present at the spiritual

75. Among the more recent books on the relation of baptism and confirmation the following may be listed: G. W. H. Lampe, *The Seal of the Spirit* (London: S.P.C.K., 1951); Burkhard Neunheuser, *Baptism and Confirmation;* N. M. Haring, "One Baptism," *Medieval Studies* 10 (1948): 217-19; Fisher, *Christian Initiation: Medieval;* B. Leeming, *Principles of Sacramental Theology* (London: Longmans, Green and Company, 1956); and J. Crehan, "Ten Years' Work on Baptism and Confirmation 1945-1955," in *Theological Studies* 17 (1956): 494-515.

76. *Deinde compater puerum recipiat tenens eundem supra fontem baptismatis; donec presbiter crisma requirat preferat interim quoque ita dicens:* Deus omnipotens pater domini nostri ihesu cristi, qui te regenerauit ex qua et spiritusancto quique dedit tibi remissionem omnium peccatorum *(Hic faciat crucem cum crismate in uertice pueri dicens):* Ipse te liniat crismatesalutis in cristo ihesu domino nostro in uitam eternam. Amen." *Obsequiale Constantiensis,* p. 13.

77. "Uade in pace. Fides tua et saluum fecit." *Obsequiale Constantiensis,* p. 13.

birth of the Christian and then leaves him to come back another time to take up a more permanent residence? Anointing with oil is performed, but the natural meaning of this symbolism is avoided.[78]

One would naturally like to know how this change came about. Others have gone into this question in far greater detail than we can discuss here, but very briefly we will look at two aspects of the question. There is the aspect of polity. How was it that the presbyter became the celebrant of baptism rather than the bishop? Then there is the more properly liturgical aspect of the problem. How was it that the emphasis on the work of the Holy Spirit fell out of the baptismal service? These two aspects intertwine as one would expect, but we can begin with a look at the polity.

As the Church spread out, the bishoprics became larger and larger. North of the Alps the number of bishops did not increase nearly as fast as the number of Christians. In the smaller bishoprics of fourth- or fifth-century Italy or North Africa, it was not at all unrealistic to expect the bishop to baptize all the Christians in his diocese. Even the small cities around the Mediterranean had their own bishops, but in Gaul and Germany the situation was quite different. Only the big cities had bishops.[79] It was quite unrealistic for the bishops of Constance, Augsburg, Basel, Strasbourg, or Mainz to baptize all the Christians in their bishoprics. Furthermore, how many parents wanted to carry their children all the way from Zurich to Constance to be baptized? One practical solution would have been to appoint enough bishops so that each could remain shepherd of his flock, but if bishops were appointed for Zurich, St. Gallen, Schaffhausen, and Winterthur, it would have unfortunately cut down on the revenue in Constance. There was, of course, a much more important reason. The bishops in northern Europe, precisely because they presided over such large territories, were able to exercise important leadership in medieval society. They were often the only leaders of society who could stand up against the politicians and feudal warlords of the day. Cutting the wings of the bishops would only have sharpened the claws of the princes.

78. For examples of prayer which draw out the meaning of the anointing and the laying on of hands cf. *Sacramentarium Gelasianum* 1.44. "Deus omnipotens, pater domini nostri Iesu Christi, qui regenerasti famulos tuos ex aqua et spiritu sancto quique dedisti eis remissionem omnium peccatorum: tu domine, inmitte in eos spiritum sanctum tuum paraclytum et da eis spiritum sapeintiae et intellectus, spiritum consilii et fortitudinis, spiritum scientiae et pietatis; adimple eos spiritum timoris dei: in nomine domini nostri Iesu Christi, cum co uiuis et regnas deus semper cum spiritu sancto per omnia saecula saeculorum. Amen."

79. The Diocese of Constance at the time of the Reformation included a number of fairly large cities which were located quite a distance from their bishop: Zurich, Winterthur, St. Gallen, Schaffhausen, Rottenburg am Neckar, Reutlingen, Tübingen, and Freiburg im Breisgau, just to name a few.

When we turn to the more specifically liturgical aspect of the problem, we must go back to that point at which the Church began to lose sight of the essential relation between the sign of the washing with water and the pouring out of the Holy Spirit. We must go back to that point where to the sign of water the sign of oil was added. This must have taken place about the end of the second century. From that point on it was all too easy to explain the water as the washing away of sins and the oil as the giving of the Holy Spirit. When the washing away of sins became one moment in baptism and the giving of the Holy Spirit became another moment, the splitting of the sacrament became almost inevitable.

Even when back in the fourth century the bishop presided during the solemn celebrations of baptism, most of the service was actually conducted by those who assisted him. The immersing of the candidates was carried out by the deacons and deaconesses. This was no doubt done for very practical reasons. They were probably younger than the bishop and the immersion of any significant number of people would have been an exhausting task. In view of this it was quite understandable that someone else should do the actual immersion, but that something should be left whereby the bishop would put on the final touches, as it were. That is just what happened. Two parts of the service were traditionally reserved for the bishop: the consecration of the font before the baptism and the anointing with oil after the baptism.[80] Both parts of the service were understood to confer, each in a different way, the gift of the Holy Spirit.

Let us consider the consecration of the font. The consecration of the baptismal font found a most ambiguous place in the rituals of the later Middle Ages.[81] These liturgical books almost always include a prayer for the blessing of the font, "if it has not been blessed."[82] There is no suggestion that in such

80. In the Gelasian Sacramentary, presumably it is the presbyter who blesses the font. *Sacramentarium Gelasianum* 1.10/4. In the Gregorian Sacramentary it is presumably the bishop who blesses the font. *Sacramentarium Gregorianum,* no. 85, pp. 52ff.

81. The history of the consecration of the font has recently attracted much attention. Among the most important works are the following: Pierre de Puniet, "Bénédictions de l'eau," *DACL* 2, cols. 685-713; Burkhard Neunheuser, "De benedictione acquae baptismalis," *Ephemerides Liturgicae* 44 (1930): 194-207, 258-81, 369-412, 455-92; Hubert Scheidt, *Die Taufwasserweihegebete im Sinne vergleichender Liturgieforschung untersucht* (Münster: Aschendorff, 1935); Eduard Stommel, *Studien zur Epiklese der romischen Taufwasserweihe, Theophaneia,* vol. 5 (Bonn, 1950); Per Lundberg, *La typologie baptismale dans l'ancienne église* (Uppsala: Lundequista bokhandeln, 1942). This work will be abbreviated Lundberg, *La typologie baptismale;* J. Magne, "La bénédictione romaine de l'eau baptismale: Prehistoire du texte," *Revue de l'histoire des religions* 68; and S. Renz, "Zur Vorgeschichte des Textes der römischen Taufwasserweihe," *Revue Bénédictine* 65 (1966): 218-55.

82. The usual rubric is: "Post hoc benedicetur fons, si non fuerit benedictus," *Obsequiale Constantiensis,* p. 4.

a case the font really needed to be consecrated by the bishop. The rubric in the *Obsequiale* of Constance tacitly recognizes that the water was supposed to be consecrated by the bishop on Easter or Pentecost, but that in all probability it had not. While a large diocese might have a number of suffragan bishops, there must have been a good number of baptismal fonts in a large diocese on which the passing shadow of the bishop never fell. Even when the bishop did consecrate a font, one wonders how long after Easter or Pentecost the water was still considered blessed and efficacious for baptism.

Conclusion

The baptismal rite the Reformers inherited was ripe for reform. At the end of the fifteenth century, it is best understood as the revision of the rite as it had been celebrated in the fourth century. For a thousand years it had been abbreviated, revised, and adjusted. It contained formulas which were no longer understood and prayers which did not address the pastoral needs of the day. For almost a thousand years most of those baptized were infants, yet the prayers were largely insensitive to this fact. Most of the prayer texts had been inherited from the Roman sacramentaries and were suited to pastoral needs of adults. These baptismal rites had dropped catechetical instruction, but had not found a satisfactory way of providing the introductory teaching which belonged to the sacrament. The whole relation of baptism to the giving of the Holy Spirit had disappeared. Evil spirits were chased out of the child, but the Holy Spirit was not invoked to take their place. In the High Middle Ages, when the attempt to maintain the paschal baptisms was entirely given up, a privatizing of the rite set in. Baptisms administered *quolibet tempore* were for the most part still administered at the church, but without the presence of the congregation.

Yet with all these problems baptism was still essentially faithful to much that was clearly Christ's institution. It was still the sacrament of the washing away of sins and entrance into the kingdom of God. Baptism was celebrated within a few days of birth, and consequently it did stand at the beginning of the Christian life. Baptism usually coincided with the first time the child came to church. Baptism clearly marked the beginning of the Christian life. In spite of the influence of Nominalism it still preserved an amazing objectivity. Maintaining the Latin language had helped in preserving the objectivity of what was done. In spite of the heavy overlay of supplementary rites, the words of Christ were still in place. In spite of the Pelagian tendencies of much late medieval Scholasticism, there was much in the rite which did speak of God's free grace. The sacrament was available to every child in Christendom. No one was denied baptism regardless of social class, education, the legitimacy of one's birth, or the moral standing of one's parents. Baptism was free to all. What could speak more clearly of the grace of God? The rites spoke very well of both the unity and the variety of the Church. There was local variety, but it was nevertheless clearly the same rite whether in Sicily or Norway, Ireland or Finland. That, too, one must regard positively. Christ had sent his apostles out to baptize in all the world, and on the eve of the Reformation their successors were baptizing in such distant places as Poland and Peru, Mexico and Malta. It was essentially the same rite which was being used. It would be a mistake to imagine that in all regards the changes which had occurred between the fifth century and the fifteenth century had been unfortunate. The fact that Constantine was not baptized until the end of his life was certainly a deformation of the New Testament practice. The Philippian jailer, who was also a Roman soldier, had been baptized immediately upon his conversion. In the fourth century one had to prove one's faith before being baptized. One had to undergo a long and often rigorous scrutiny. Few people were baptized at the beginning of their Christian life. That was very different from the practice of the New Testament Church. The fact that in the fifteenth century baptism was open to all and actually stood at the beginning of the Christian life may be regarded positively.

One might well say the same thing about the resemblance of fourth- and fifth-century Christian baptism to the pagan mysteries. Baptism as practiced by the New Testament Church bore little resemblance to the pagan mysteries. While many contemporary liturgists greatly admire the highly dramatized baptismal celebrations of late antiquity, they bore little resemblance to the sacrament as we find it celebrated in the book of Acts. One might well regard favorably the fact that many of the mystery drama elements had disappeared from the rite. In this respect the simpler baptisms of the fifteenth century were much more like the sacrament celebrated by the apostles. The pagan mystery religions were long gone, and no longer did the Church feel the need to offer Christian mysteries to take their place.

While there was much which needed to be reformed, there was also much which needed to be preserved.

CHAPTER II

The First Translations of the Latin Rites

Luther's German Baptismal Book of 1523

Early in the year 1523, Martin Luther presented to the German church a baptismal rite in the common tongue.[1]

It was the first major attempt of the Reformation to translate a liturgical form. Although there would be attempts by various Reformers in the following year to celebrate a German Mass, Luther himself would not begin to celebrate a German Mass until late in 1525. To be sure, Luther had written some suggestions for a German Mass as early as 1524, but these suggestions were not intended for immediate implementation. The case with his *Taufbüchlein* is quite different. It aimed at providing a liturgical text which would make possible the celebration of the sacrament of baptism in the common language.

Luther's work is basically a translation of the Latin rite. Protestant historians of the liturgy have been slow to recognize this fact. This reticence is due in part to a certain delight in individuality and creativity which pervaded the work of historians of a few generations ago. They wanted to justify Luther by showing his initiative. The Reformer would have been embarrassed by such pride in his "innovations." There is another reason behind this misperception.

1. *Das Taufbüchlein verdeutscht* (1523). *D. Martin Luthers Werke: Kritische Gesamtausgabe,* vol. 12 (Weimar: Hermann Bohlau, 1891), pp. 42-46. To be abbreviated as *WA* 12. For an English translation, see "The Order of Baptism, 1523," *Luther's Works,* vol. 53, *Liturgy and Hymns,* ed. Ulrich S. Leupold (Philadelphia: Fortress Press, 1965), pp. 96-101. To be abbreviated as *LW* 53. On Luther's understanding of baptism see Paul Althaus, *The Theology of Martin Luther,* Eng. trans. by Robert C. Shultz (Philadelphia: Fortress Press, 1966), pp. 353-74; Lorenz Gronvik, *Die Taufe in der Theologie Martin Luthers* (Göttingen and Zurich: Vandenhoeck & Ruprecht, 1968); Werner Jetter, *Die Taufe beim jungen Luther* (Tübingen: J. C. B. Mohr [Paul Siebeck], 1954).

Too few Protestant scholars were aware of the great variety of Latin baptismal rites found in Germany at the beginning of the sixteenth century. Luther's *Taufbüchlein* was often compared naively with the liturgical books of Mainz, Strasbourg, or even to the *Rituale Romanum* in attempts to evaluate Luther's reforms. With the work of Gustav Kawerau the true picture began to emerge.[2] With great care, Kawerau attempted to reconstruct the Latin baptismal rite as it would have been celebrated in Wittenberg at the time of Luther. He achieved this by a comparison of some thirteen liturgical books, especially the *Agenda Magdaburgensis* of 1497. It was to this archdiocese that Wittenberg belonged. Kawerau demonstrated that many features of Luther's baptismal liturgy previously thought to be innovations were in fact taken over from the liturgical practice of Magdeburg.

As much as the work of Kawerau advanced the subject, the matter was further clarified by the work of Fr. K. Nümann, who proposed that even more features of Luther's work can be explained by a comparison to the 1512 edition of the *Agenda communis.*[3] When compared to this text, still more of Luther's supposed innovations do indeed disappear. The question of just which Latin text Luther used to make his translation has not been completely solved; nevertheless, it would seem to be increasingly clear that Luther stayed fairly close to the Latin rite as it was traditionally celebrated in Wittenberg.[4] If Luther's *German Mass* (1524) is a full revision of the Latin liturgy, we cannot say the same for his baptismal rite of 1523.

While Luther's first *Taufbüchlein* was basically a translation rather than a revision, there were some significant revisions. Three of these revisions should be noted. After investigating these differences we can better appreciate

2. Gustav Kawerau, "Liturgische Studien zu Luthers Taufbüchlein von 1523," *Zeitschrift für kirchliche Wissenschaft und kirchliches Leben* 10 (1898): 407-31, 466-77, 519-47, 578-99, and 625-43. To be abbreviated as Kawerau, "Taufbüchlein."

3. Fr. K. Nümann, "Zur Entstehung des lutherschen Taufbüchleins von Jahre 1523," *Monatsschrift für Gottesdienst und kirchliche Kunst* 33 (1928): 214-19. Four editions of the *Agenda communis* are known to exist: *Agenda communis: Agenda sive Benedictionale commune agendorum cuilibet pastori ecclesie necessarium* (Leipzig: Melchior Lotter, 1501 and 1512; Basel: Thomas Wolff, 1518 and 1520). A. Kohlberg has published a modern edition: *Agenda communis. Die älteste Agende in der Diozese Ermland und im Deutschordensstaate Preussen nach den ersten Druckausgaben von 1512 und 1520* (Braunsberg: R. Rudlowski, 1903). To be abbreviated as *Agenda communis.*

4. In the following pages the *Agenda communis* will be quoted in the edition of A. Kohlberg as the Latin text most probably underlying Luther's translation. This is done with a certain hesitancy. One cannot follow the work of Schmidt-Clausing with complete confidence. The quotations which he claims to make from the *Agenda communis* do not agree with the text of the *Agenda communis* edited by A. Kohlberg. Cf. Fritz Schmidt-Clausing, *Zwingli als Liturgiker* (Göttingen: Vandenhoeck und Ruprecht, 1952), pp. 146ff.

exactly what Luther has done. The first of these variations regards the exorcisms. In our day these exorcisms seem foreign; students of Luther often take pains to justify his use of them. The fact is that for Luther the presence of Satan was a constant reality in the spiritual life. For him, exorcism had a legitimate place in the baptismal rite. Nevertheless, Luther omitted some of the exorcisms used in the Latin baptismal rite.

The most important exorcism omitted was the *Nec te latet sathana.*[5] Luther's reason for dropping this particular exorcism is not clear. The reason often given is that he simply took the opportunity to shorten the rite. This exorcism was by far the longest and most elaborate exorcism in the baptismal service, and its omission certainly lightens the diabolical load. There is also a slight and puzzling abbreviation of the *effeta* exorcism. As it appears in all the Latin liturgical books which Luther might have used, it is a threefold exorcism, anointing with spittle first the right ear, then the nostrils, and finally the left ear. With each action there is a different formula: for the right ear, the biblical *effeta;* for the nostrils, *in odorem suavitatis;* and for the left ear, *Tu autem efulgare diabole, appropinquauit enim iudicium dei.* Luther simply dropped the formula for the nostrils. Scholars have made numerous attempts to explain Luther's omission, none of which is completely convincing.[6] With Luther's omission of the exorcism of salt, we have a different situation. There were several liturgical books of the period which did not contain the exorcism of salt. These were not the sources apparently used by Luther.[7] Taking these three omissions as a whole, one must admit that Luther does appear to be interested

5. *Agenda communis,* pp. 21ff. Kawerau wanted to show that Luther significantly decreased the place of the exorcisms, which would be true enough if Luther had been dependent only on the rite of Magdeburg. Kawerau, "Taufbüchlein," pp. 588-89.

6. *Agenda communis,* p. 22. *Taufbüchlein: WA* 12, p. 45; *LW* 53, p. 99. Kawerau remarks, "Offenbar muss er an dem in odorem suavitatis Anstoss genommen haben." Kawerau, "Taufbüchlein," p. 590. Kawerau rules out quite rightly the possibility that it had offended the aesthetic sensitivities of Luther. He suggests that what might have displeased Luther was a confusion of biblical images. The phrase in Scripture usually stands for God's acceptance of the sacrifices made by men. It does not, argues Kawerau, concern the human appreciation of God's gifts. Although this is quite persuasive, Kawerau himself raises an important objection: Luther has left unchanged the phrase *ad suavem odorem praeceptorum tuorum* in the prayer *omnipotens sempiterne Deus.*

Bruno Jordahn draws back from the conclusion that Luther has tried to remove a theologically clumsy phrase: "Der Taufgottesdienst im Mittelalter bis zum Gegenwart," *Leiturgia: Handbuch des evangelischen Gottesdienstes,* vol. 5, eds. Karl Ferdinand Müller and Walter Blankenburg (Kassel: Johannes Stauda-Verlag, 1970), pp. 369-70. This extensive study, pp. 349-640, will be abbreviated as Jordahn, "Der Taufgottesdienst."

7. The rite of Bamberg 1491 had no exorcism of salt, and the rituals of Constance and of Mainz used salt that was exorcised before the service. Kawerau, "Taufbüchlein," pp. 428-29. See also Spital, *Der Taufritus,* pp. 64-67.

in trimming them down even if he did understand exorcism to have a legitimate place in the rite of baptism.

The medieval exorcisms took the place of the prayers of confession and repentance in the earliest Christian baptismal rites. This constituted the *metanoia,* the turning away from the world and toward God. Thus Luther should have substituted a prayer of repentance or confession of sin for some of these exorcisms. One might regret that Luther did not perceive the matter this way, but then to expect such a clear insight into the history of worship from a sixteenth-century theologian is a bit much to ask. If Luther's baptismal rite still looks like a rather long series of ingeniously varying exorcisms to which a short baptismal rite has been appended, it was not because he himself set it up that way. Luther did take some steps to lighten a preponderance of exorcisms in his first baptismal rite of 1523, but he would take bigger steps in this direction in his baptismal rite of 1526.

The second important variation in Luther's first German baptismal rite concerns the catechetical instruction. We notice that Luther's service did not provide for the reciting of the catechetical pieces other than the Lord's Prayer, nor does it contain an admonition to the godparents. Regarding the first omission, most late medieval baptismal rites included at least the Creed and the Lord's Prayer. Sometimes the Ave Maria or the Ten Commandments were also included. It had been the teaching and explaining of the Creed, the Lord's Prayer, and the sacraments which formed the core of the rites of catechetical instruction in the ancient church. That Luther should leave out these last vestiges of the old catechetical instruction is indeed strange when one remembers how much he did to revive the actual practice of such instruction.

The best explanation of this omission is that Luther was unaware of the original function of the Creed and Lord's Prayer in the baptismal liturgy. Kawerau suggests that Luther had a completely different perspective on this part of the liturgy. Rather than understanding the rite historically, Luther had followed the line of the medieval commentators.[8] According to this tradition, the Lord's Prayer and the Creed were an acting out of the Gospel lesson which had just been read. The lesson tells of parents bringing their children to Jesus that he might pray for them. They tell how Jesus laid his hands upon the children and blessed them. Luther's rubric makes it explicit that the minister is to put his hand on the head of the child while reciting the Lord's Prayer. The relation of this recitation of the Lord's Prayer to catechetical instruction

8. Bruno Jordahn has shown the roots of Luther's thinking in the works of Leidradus of Lyon, Honorius of Autun, Sicard of Cremona, and Theodulf of Orleans. "Der Taufgottesdienst," pp. 406-11.

has been completely forgotten. The reciting of the Lord's Prayer has become a prayer for the blessing of the child. If the Creed was left out, it was probably because Luther had a hard time seeing it as a prayer for the blessing of children.

But why has the admonition to the godparents been omitted? Luther undoubtedly recognized that it was not really part of the rite. It was spoken in the vernacular, which made it clear that it was not really part of the rite but rather a sort of explanation of the rite which the celebrant was supposed to extemporize either before or after the celebration. In the previous year, 1522, Luther had begun his program of catechetical instruction, and one can be sure that he found some way of letting people know that their children were supposed to attend it. There was probably another reason. Understanding the Lord's Prayer as a blessing rather than as catechetical instruction, Luther viewed the admonition to the sponsors as inappropriately placed.[9] Most of the German liturgical books were confused about what was supposed to be happening at this point in the rite; Luther probably thought this admonition cluttered the service.[10]

The third innovation in Luther's *Taufbüchlein* of 1523 is his famous *Sindtflutgebet,* or Great Flood Prayer. This prayer enjoyed considerable popularity, being adopted by a variety of Protestant and Catholic liturgies. Naturally found in many of the German and Scandinavian Lutheran rites, it was also revised by Leo Jud and then by Zwingli for use in German-speaking Switzerland. From there it found its way into the Reformed liturgy of the Netherlands, and even into the Church of England's *Book of Common Prayer.* Here we have an actual example of Luther creating a liturgical formula. Viewed in terms of biblical imagery, liturgical history, and pastoral sensitivity, Luther's prayer is a masterpiece. The controversy over his sources for the prayer has been long and does not seem to be settled yet.[11] While there is good reason for regarding the prayer as Luther's own composition, it must also be emphasized that Luther put the prayer together from traditional material. Three prayers in the Latin rite should be named.

First, Luther's Great Flood Prayer took the place of the Latin prayer

9. A very similar reason has been given for eliminating the *nec te latet* formula of exorcism, about which we have already spoken. If Luther intended the reciting of the Lord's Prayer to represent Christ laying his hands on the children, then it was too far into the baptismal rite for an exorcism to be appropriate. Kawerau, "Taufbüchlein," pp. 589-90.

10. On the confusion of the German rituals of the time, see Spital, *Der Taufritus,* pp. 91-95.

11. On the history of the discussion see Jordahn, "Der Taufgottesdienst," p. 380, n. 150. See also Fritz Schmidt-Clausing, "Die liturgietheologische Arbeit Zwingli's am Sindtflutgebet des Taufformulars. Ein weiterer Blick in Zwingli's liturgische Wekstatt," *Zwingliana* 13 (1972): 516-43, 591-615.

Deus patrum nostrorum, and in fact it incorporates much of that prayer into itself. The two parts of the prayer which Luther does not take over are the invocation, "God of our fathers, O God, founder of the created universe," and the petition, "as he has received this first taste of the food of salt, so do not permit him to hunger but fill him with heavenly food."[12] Luther replaced the invocation with his threefold typology of the great Flood, the crossing of the Red Sea, and the baptism of Jesus in the Jordan River.

The second possible source of Luther's material is the petition *Deus Abraham.* Although Luther removed this prayer in order to make room for his *Sindtflutgebet,* its allusion to the Exodus may have reminded Luther of the Red Sea typology. It makes considerable use of Old Testament imagery, but it does not really strike at the heart of the major Old Testament types of baptism:

> God of Abraham, God of Isaac, God of Jacob, God who appeared to thy servant Moses on Mount Sinai, and led the children of Israel from the land of Egypt sending an angel of thy pity who led them day and night, we beseech thee, Lord, that thou shouldst deign to send thy Holy Angel that he might likewise lead this thy servant and bring him to the grace of thy baptism.[13]

While the imagery of this prayer would not be completely foreign to the day of baptism, it is much more appropriate to the receiving of the catechumen into a period of forty days of prebaptismal instruction. The prayer was written for the reception of the catechumen, not for the baptismal rite proper. It was never intended to be said on the day of baptism, but rather forty days before. In the year 1523, Luther was also concerned with the questions of allegorical exegesis, typological exegesis, and the Christian interpretation of the Old Testament. In recasting this prayer, his new insights into the proper use of typology may have prodded him to select biblical types more appropriate to baptism. From the standpoint of the Christian interpretation of the Old Testament, both the story of Noah and the Flood, which 1 Peter 3:20-21 explains as a type of baptism, and also the story of the passage through the Red Sea, which 1 Corinthians 10:1-4 presents as a type of baptism, were unimpeachable

12. "Deus patrum nostrorum, deus uniuerse conditor creature, . . . et hoc primum pablum salis gustantem non diutius esurire permittas, quominus impleatur cibo celesti. . . ." *Agenda communis,* p. 18.

13. "Deus abraham, deus ysaac, deus iacob, deus qui moysi famulo tuo in monte synai apparuisti et filios israel de terra egypti eduxisti, deputans eis angelum pietatis tue, qui custodiret illas die ac nocte: te quesumus domine, ut mittere digneris sanctum angelum tuum, ut similiter custodiat hunc famulum tuum N. et perducat eum ad gratiam baptismi tui. Per christum dominum nostrum." *Agenda communis,* p. 18.

images for baptism. Christ's baptism in the Jordan as a consecration of all baptismal water is not an idea so clearly attested in Scripture, but it was certainly popular enough in the ancient Church.[14]

What conclusions can we draw about Luther's first baptismal rite? The Reformer ended his text with a short commentary on his translation, and from that we can be led in our evaluation. In the first place Luther has intended merely to make a translation which would serve as a provisional form. He is not interested in reforming the rite. As he sees it, there is much still in the rite which is merely decorative. The rite could be improved by leaving out these human inventions. He specifically mentions the exsufflation, the signation, the exorcised salt, the *effeta* exorcism, the anointing with oil before the baptism and with chrism after baptism, and the clothing of the child in white and placing a burning candle in his or her hand.[15] These are external things, outward forms not affecting the substance. Baptism can quite properly be celebrated without all these human additions. For the time being, Luther tells us, he was not interested in removing these things, but only in translating the rite.

Luther obviously intends this rite to be a cautious move toward reform. He gives us reasons for his caution. In the first place he tells us that he did not want to burden weak consciences. The Reformer has in mind the words of the apostle Paul cautioning the progressive-minded Corinthians not to offend the consciences of their brethren in regard to meat sacrificed to idols. Besides that he did not want people to complain, nor did he want to imply that those baptized with traditional rites had been improperly baptized.[16] He admits that a more thoroughgoing reform is indeed to be desired, but for the time being a simple translation would have to be enough.

Luther gives several reasons for wanting to translate the rite. He believes that people will take baptism more seriously if they understand what is being said. The rite should inspire the faith of those who participate. It should lead them to pray for the child who is being baptized. The Reformer of Wittenberg puts it this way, "Remember, too, that it is very necessary to aid the poor child with all your heart and strong faith, earnestly to intercede for him. . . . And I suspect that people turn out so badly after baptism because our concern for them has been so cold and careless; we, at their baptism, intercede for them without zeal."[17]

One notices how important the prayers of the parents and godparents are

14. On Luther's understanding of Christ's baptism by John the Baptist in the Jordan see Gronvik, *Die Taufe in der Theologie Martin Luthers,* pp. 68-72.

15. *WA* 12, pp. 47-48; and *LW* 53, pp. 102-3.

16. *WA* 12, p. 48; and *LW* 53, p. 103.

17. *WA* 12, p. 47; and *LW* 53, p. 102.

to Luther's understanding of the baptism of infants. This is one of the most significant things the Church does at baptism. She intercedes for those whom she baptizes. If the prayers are in German, then those attending the baptism can join in those prayers. Luther even makes a point of how important it is for the minister to speak the prayers slowly and distinctly so that the parents and godparents can say the prayers with him. Seen in this light, then, the addition of the Great Flood Prayer is particularly significant. It is a long and comprehensive prayer, and in the addition of this prayer the Reformer has significantly added to the prayer content of the whole service. The addition of this prayer has the effect of giving some balance to the exorcisms. With Luther's final revision of the rite in 1526, the prayers of the rite so overweigh the exorcisms that the overall impression is greatly changed. In 1526, one no longer gets the impression that the rite of baptism is a series of exorcisms culminated by the baptismal washing, but rather one has a much stronger impression that baptism is accompanied by Christian prayer. Already in the rite of 1523, Luther has made a strong move in that direction. The Great Flood Prayer has clearly brought to light the epicletic nature of baptism.[18]

Leo Jud's German Baptismal Book of 1523

It was probably not more than a month or two later that Leo Jud, pastor of St. Peter's Church in Zurich, published a German translation of the Latin baptismal rite.[19] Leo Jud was a colleague of the Swiss Reformer Ulrich Zwingli. Educated in the Latin school of Sélestat along with Martin Bucer, he continued his studies at the University of Basel, where he became a fast friend of Zwingli. On leaving the University, Jud took a church in his native Alsace while Zwingli hid himself away in the mountains of Glarus. Both young men spent the next dozen years maturing in their pastoral work and reading great quantities of theological literature. In the cellars of their minds they stored away good books as wine connoisseurs age their best bottles. In 1518, Leo Jud followed Zwingli as preacher at the Benedictine monastery of Einsiedeln. Then in 1523, he once

18. Gronvik is undoubtedly right; the key to understanding Luther's baptismal theology is to recognize that for Luther baptism is first of all a work of God. What Luther says here is quite consistent with this. It is precisely because it is a work of God that the baptismal invocation is so important. *Die Taufe in der Theologie Martin Luthers,* pp. 46-54 et passim.

19. *Ein kurtze und gemeine forme für die schwachgleubigen, kinder zu touffen* (Zurich: Christof Froschouer, 1523). There was a second edition in 1523, and another in 1524. It has been reprinted in *Corpus Reformatorum,* vol. 91, pp. 710-13. For further bibliography on this text, see Kawerau, "Taufbüchlein," p. 470.

again followed his old friend, this time to Zurich. The translation of the baptismal service was only the first of many literary commissions which Leo Jud executed for Zwingli. It was Leo Jud who edited Zwingli's expository sermons into commentaries. It was also Leo Jud who was the leading spirit behind the Zurich Bible. Jud was particularly gifted as a translator, having translated a number of works from Latin into German. The most important of these translations was Augustine's *The Letter and the Spirit.* Jud was the most faithful supporter Zwingli could possibly have had; nevertheless, Leo Jud was a theologian in his own right and we should not simply regard him as Zwingli's understudy.[20]

Luther's German would not have been easily understood in Switzerland and some adjustment of vocabulary, syntax, and spelling was necessary; but this was only a minor consideration. Essentially, Jud adapted Luther's translation to the local version of the Latin baptismal rite as found in the ritual of the Diocese of Constance, the diocese in which Zurich was located.[21] This pattern of adapting Luther's translation to the local rite of a German diocese became a frequent practice. It is worth taking a brief look at some of these early adaptations because, although Jud's version was probably the first, these other versions help put his work in perspective. Leo Jud's translation of the baptismal rite was largely dependent on Luther's *Taufbüchlein.*

Sometime in 1524, Kaspar Loener, a reform-minded priest in Franconia, published a version of Luther's *Taufbüchlein* which he had adapted to the rite of Bamberg. Shortly afterward, Loener published a version adapted to the liturgical traditions of Würzburg.[22] There is no particular point in describing all the differences between the Würzburg ritual and that used in Wittenburg except to notice the following. Although Loener availed himself of Luther's translations of the Latin prayers, he did not use Luther's Great Flood Prayer, but rather translated the Latin prayers which Luther had discarded. It is also of interest that Loener omitted the Credo and the Ave Maria from the catechetical rites, but did include an admonition to the godparents to teach the child the Ten Commandments, the Apostles' Creed, and the Lord's Prayer. Loener did not omit the exorcism *nec te latet,* nor the formula *in odorem suavitatis* in the *effeta* exorcism. In other words, while accepting Luther's lead in translating

20. On Leo Jud see the article of Emil Egli in *The New Schaff-Herzog Encyclopedia of Religious Knowledge,* vol. 6, pp. 242ff.

21. This text, the *Obsequiale sive benedictionale secundum ecclesiam Constantiensem,* is discussed in Chap. I above, beginning with n. 2.

22. Cf. Kawerau, "Taufbüchlein," pp. 468-69 and 519-25. Kawerau gives the text only of the Würzburg ritual.

the Latin baptismal service, Loerner did not accept Luther's revisions of the service. But of even greater interest for our understanding of Jud's work is the note which Loener appended to the end of his version of the Würzburg baptism rite:

> In the case that this baptismal order should be used in other bishoprics where other collects or prayers are appointed for use . . . it would be proper for the parson . . . to perform the rubrics and order of that bishopric, so that this German baptismal rite bring about no change or innovations to the diocesan customs.[23]

The strong feelings of territorial autonomy within Germany are perhaps difficult for foreigners to understand, but not even the authority of Luther's appeal to German nationalism would overcome the Teutonic respect for territorial and even metropolitan autonomy.[24]

The Reformer of Nuremberg, Andreas Osiander, also published a local variation of Luther's German baptismal rite.[25] Osiander did use Luther's Great Flood Prayer, although he revised it with considerable freedom. He preserved those formulas of exorcism which Luther dropped. He did follow Luther in dropping the reciting of the Creed,[26] but then he reintroduced an admonition that the child should receive catechetical instruction. Osiander obviously felt that Luther had been too free in his omissions. Osiander, like Luther, saw considerable virtue in moving with caution, and, like Loener, he too was eager to preserve the local traditions of his city.

23. "So dise Tauff in andern Bistumben gebraucht werden wolt, und dann in denselben Bistumben (ausserhalb der wesentlichen stuck) andere Collecten oder gebette verordent, Mag ein ygklicher Pfarherr oder Caplon, so zutauffen angesucht würdet, dieselbigen Collecten oder gebete, vermöge der Bistumben Rubricken oder ordnung, darzu thun und sprechen, Damit durch dise teutsche Tauff keinem Bistumb Enderung oder eintrag geschehe." Kawerau, "Taufbüchlein," p. 525.

24. It was only in the wake of the violent reactions of the Counter Reformation that a contrary insight, that of universalism, a viewpoint which had always been furthered by the Roman Empire, would gain complete ascendancy in Roman Catholic liturgical matters. With the liturgical reforms of Pius V, local custom would have less and less authority in those areas accepting the authority of the Roman See.

25. *Ordnung wie man Tauffet, bissher im Latein Gehalten, verteütscht, hierin ist, auss etlichen ursachen, was die andern, als uberflussig, veracht haben, nicht aussgelassen* (Nuremberg: Jobst Gutknecht, 1524) in Kawerau, "Taufbüchlein," pp. 471ff. and 524-46. See also the modern editions in Osiander's *Gesamtausgabe,* vol. 1, ed. Martin Stupperich (Gütersloh: Gerd Mohn, 1957), pp. 104-21; and in Emil Sehling, ed., *Die evangelische Kirchenordnungen des XVI Jahrhundert,* vol. 11:1 (Tübingen: J. C. B. Mohr [Paul Siebeck], 1905-). This work will be abbreviated *Kirchenordnungen.*

26. This is contrary to the rite of Bamberg, the diocese in which Nuremberg is found. See the note in Kawerau, "Taufbüchlein," p. 539.

Now let us return to the work of Leo Jud. We will look at several of his revisions of both Luther's German rite and the Latin rite of Constance.

1. Luther's formula for the exsufflation has been slightly augmented by Jud so that the Holy Spirit is given the epithet, "the comforter." This is to bring the rite into conformity with the liturgical usage of Constance.[27] Even in such a minor detail Jud finds it important to follow the local liturgical customs.

2. The liturgical books used by Luther contained two collects for the reception of the catechumen, the second of which, *Deus immortale praesidium,* is omitted by Jud. It is missing from a great number of pre-Reformation liturgical books used in South Germany, including the rite of Constance.[28] Here again Jud is adjusting Luther's service to the rite of Constance.

3. An important modification of Luther's work is Jud's very free revision of Luther's Great Flood Prayer. Jud obviously appreciated Luther's prayer. Yet he also felt free to revise it quite considerably. These revisions we will look at in detail in Chapter IX.

4. The three catechetical exorcisms found in Luther are reduced to a single exorcism by Jud. Here Jud is departing both from Luther and the rite of Constance. Here most obviously we see Leo Jud at work pruning the traditional rite.[29]

5. Another prayer, *Eternam ac justissimam,* asking God's guidance of the catechumen into the fullness of the Christian life, Luther translated from the Latin rite. This prayer is found in the rite of Constance, but Jud did not include it in his version.[30] The omission may be simply explained by a concern for brevity.

6. Jud follows Luther in omitting two of the catechetical pieces, that is, the Creed and the Ave Maria, but he goes even further and also leaves out the Lord's Prayer. No doubt Jud, along with Luther and most everyone of that age, was confused about what the catechetical pieces were doing there.

7. Once again in the omission of the *nec te latet* exorcism, Jud follows Luther in omitting a common formula of the Latin baptismal rite.

8. Jud follows Luther in directing that the child is to be immersed in the

27. The *Agenda communis* of 1512: "Exi, immunde spiritus, et da locum spiritui Sancto." Luther: "Far aus, du unreyner geyst, und gib raum dem heyligen geyst," *WA* 12, p. 42; *LW* 53, p. 96. Constance: "Exi abeo immunde spiritus et de locum aduenienti spiritui sancto parachito," *Obsequiale Constantiensis,* p. 6. Jud: "Far uss, du unreiner geist und gib statt dem troster, dem heyligen geist," *Corpus Reformatorum* 91, p. 710. *Corpus Reformatorum* is abbreviated *CR.*

28. According to Spital, *Der Taufritus,* p. 59, at least five different collects appear at this point in the various German rituals.

29. *CR* 91, p. 711; and *WA* 12, p. 44.

30. *Obsequiale Constantiensis,* p. 9.

water. Luther's rite reads, "Here he takes the child and dips him into the baptism"; Jud's reads, "Then the priest takes the child and dunks him into the water."[31] Here we have an example of Jud following Luther rather than the ritual of Constance. This revision will be taken up at greater length in Chapter X.

9. The clothing of the child in a white baptismal gown is accompanied by a formula which has been abbreviated by Jud. Luther followed the Latin rather closely with, "Receive the white, holy, and spotless robe, which you are to bring without spot before the judgment seat of Christ, in order that you might have eternal life." Jud omits the last phrase, "in order that you might have eternal life."[32] In this omission, Jud is departing from both Constance and Luther. Perhaps Jud found this formula misleading. It sounds as though living a sin-free life is the way to achieve eternal life. This appears to be another example of Jud exercising a theological critique on the text.

10. Finally we notice that Jud, in agreement with Constance and a good number of the rites of South Germany, has no presentation of a burning candle to the child. Luther, in agreement with most North German rites, included this presentation.[33] Here again Jud is simply adapting Luther's rite to the liturgical traditions of the diocese of Constance.

Perhaps the best way to characterize Leo Jud's baptismal rite is to call it an adaptation of Luther's translation to the local rubrics and traditions of the Diocese of Constance. The claim of Schmidt-Clausing that the *Agenda communis* used by Luther is the parent rite of the Reformed baptismal rites of Zurich is misleading.[34] However much he may have used Luther's translation of the *Agenda communis,* Leo Jud was concerned to alter those features of Luther's version which were peculiar to the *Agenda communis* and to reflect instead the forms and formulas of the ritual of Constance. Yet Jud also exercised a certain amount of theological pruning on both the rites of Luther and the rites of Constance. One might well ask why Jud bothered to use the *Taufbüchlein* of Luther as a basis for his work. Why did Jud not simply make a

31. Luther: "Da neme er das kind und tauche es ynn die tauffe," *WA* 12, p. 45; *LW* 53, p. 100. Jud: "Denn so nem der priester das kind und duncke es in das wasser," *CR* 91, p. 713.

32. The *Agenda communis* of 1512 reads, "Accipe vestem candidam, sanctam et immaculatam quam preferas sine macula ante tribunal christi, ut habeas vitam eternam," which Luther translates as "Nym das weysse, hejlige und unbefleckts kleid, das du on flecken bringen sollt für den richtstul Christi, das du das ewige leben habst." *WA* 12, p. 46; *LW* 53, p. 101. Jud's abbreviated version: "Nimm hin das wyss unnd unbefleckt kleid, das du on flecken bringen solt für den richterstul Christi." *CR* 91, p. 713. Constance reads: "tribunal sancte trinitatis, ut habeas uitam eternam," *Obsequiale Constantiensis,* p. 13.

33. Spital, *Der Taufritus,* pp. 123-25.

34. Schmidt-Clausing, *Zwingli als Liturgiker,* p. 145.

fresh translation, based on the rite of Constance? It was probably because Luther had made a breach in the wall of liturgical form through which Jud and his colleagues in Zurich also wanted to pass. They wanted to follow Luther and wanted to appear to follow Luther. They hoped that Luther would go further. Luther himself in his own commentary on his work implied that others might do well to go further. Leo Jud only did what Luther had encouraged him to do. Indeed, Luther himself would go further with another baptismal rite which he would publish in 1526. There is in Osiander's title, *Order for Baptism, formerly held in Latin now translated into German, in which is to be found all that which . . . others have omitted as superfluous,* a reproach suggesting that Luther had gone too far. The title of Leo Jud's baptismal rite, *A Short and Common Form for those weak in faith, to be used in the baptism of children,* makes it clear that the reform of the baptismal rite has only just begun. For the Reformers of Zurich, a mere translation of the inherited rites was only a step along the way. It would be another year and a half before they would take the next stride along that road. In the meantime, their colleagues in Strasbourg were to make a different attempt at translating the Latin baptismal rite.

The Strasbourg German Baptismal Service of 1524

When the Strasbourg pastors published their German Mass on June 24, 1524, they included with it a German baptismal rite.[35] The reform-minded priests in that cathedral city of Christian Humanism had been using this translation of the Latin baptismal rite for a few months before its publication. In January of 1524, Matthis Zell, who held the position of endowed preacher at the cathedral, began to baptize using the German language. This step made quite an impression on the city.[36] The people of Strasbourg reacted in a variety of ways. Some parents wanted their children baptized in German, and some in Latin; in some churches

35. *Teütsche Mess und Tauff wie sye yetzund zu Strassburg gehalten werden. Register buchlin über die geschrift von disputierlichen puncten. Georgij Spalatini Christliche gebett. Betbuchlin auss den Evangelien und Episteln samt den glauben, vater unser und den siben Busspsalmen* (Strasbourg: Wolff Kopphel, 1524). On the final page is given the date of publication: "am xxiii, tag Brachmonds, im jar M.D. xxiiii." This baptismal service appeared by itself in the same year, *Das Tauffbuchlin, nach rechter Form uff Teütsch zu Tauffen.* The service will be cited as the *Strasbourg German Baptismal Service of 1524,* and will be quoted from Friedrich Hubert, *Die Strassburger liturgischen Ordnungen in Zeitalter der Reformation* (Göttingen: Vandenhoeck und Ruprecht, 1900), pp. 25-36. To be abbreviated as Hubert, *Ordnungen.*

36. *Quellen zur Geschichte der Taufer,* vol. 7, *Elsass I. Teil, Stadt Strassburg 1522-1532,* eds. Manfred Krebs and Hans Georg Rott (Gütersloh: Verlaghaus Gerd Mohn, 1959), #5, p. 7 and #9, p. 19. To be abbreviated as *QGT* 7.

the priests wanted to baptize only in Latin, in others only in German. On the thirty-first of August, the city council allowed that priests might baptize as each priest wished, either in German or in Latin. It was Diebold Schwartz, Matthis Zell's young assistant at the cathedral, who translated both the baptismal rite and the German Mass, which were published in June 1524. He had evidently prepared the baptismal rite for Zell's use in January and then a few weeks later prepared a translation of the Mass for his own use. It was Schwartz who first celebrated the Mass in German in February 1524.[37]

While the Strasbourg German Mass was what might be called an expurgated mass translated into German, the baptismal service was a considerably more conservative project. Given that Luther and the reform-minded pastors of Zurich had already published baptismal rites which not only translated but also revised the Latin texts, one wonders why the Strasbourg service is so very close to that city's Latin baptismal service.

The *Strasbourg German Baptismal Service of 1524* is a translation of the Latin service found in the *Agenda Argentinensis.* It follows the Latin rite of Strasbourg closely. Whenever possible it uses Luther's translations. This means that about half of the text depends on Luther. The following items come from his translation: the prayer "O Almighty eternal God," the two exorcisms "Therefore, thou miserable devil" and "So harken now, thou miserable devil," the prayer "Lord, holy Father, Almighty eternal God," the benediction which accompanies the anointing with chrism, "The Almighty God and Father," and the formula which goes with dressing the child in the white christening gown, "Receive the white, holy, and spotless robe."[38] Schwartz has revised the translations of Luther, but these revisions are only a matter of making the text of Luther conform to the orthography and perhaps the dialect of Strasbourg. For example, in Luther's German text of the exorcism, "Therefore, thou miserable devil," we read, "Darumb, du leydiger teuffel, erkenne deyn urteyl und las die

37. According the Hubert, *Ordnungen,* p. 56, the manuscript of the Strasbourg *German Baptismal Service of 1524,* found in the Thomas Archive, is written in the very clear and polished professional hand of Diebold Schwartz. The manuscript does not appear to have been prepared for the printer, but was rather a text for the use of those priests who wanted to celebrate baptism in German. At some time it was revised, perhaps in consultation with the other reform-minded priests of the city. This hand- written liturgical text may well have been in use for several months before it was printed.

For further discussions of this service, see Johann Martin Usteri, "Die Stellung der Strassburger Reformatoren Bucer und Capito zur Tauffrage," *Theologische Studien und Kritiken* 57 (1884): 456-525; J. D. C. Fisher, *Christian Initiation: The Reformation Period* (London: S.P.C.K., 1970), pp. 30-33. This work will be abbreviated as Fisher, *Initiation: Reformation;* H. O. Old, *Patristic Roots of Reformed Worship* (Zurich: Theologische Verlag, 1975), pp. 18-22. To be abbreviated as Old, *Patristic Roots.*

38. *Luther's Works* 53, pp. 96-100; *WA* 12, pp. 44-46.

ehre dem rechten und lebendigen got. . . ." Whereas the Strasbourg text reads: "Darumb du verfluchter teuffel erkenn dein vorteyl vnd lass die ere dem rechten lebendigen gott."[39] We must leave to German philologists an exact analysis of this, but this does not appear to be at all significant.[40]

The translation of Schwartz departs very little from the *Agenda Argentinensis.* Where Luther has revised the Latin rite, the Strasbourg service has not followed his lead. Formularies omitted by Luther or Leo Jud are still found in the Strasbourg service.

There is a full set of exorcisms; all the catechetical pieces are in place, as well as the admonition to the godparents.[41] Luther's masterpiece, the Great Flood Prayer, is not used. The preference for immersion expressed by both Luther and Leo Jud has made no impact.[42]

How are we to understand this baptismal rite published by the Strasbourg Reformers? Why does it lag behind the work of Luther and Leo Jud? Three reasons may be suggested. In the first place it may be a matter of prudence. The Strasbourg Reformers may have felt that they had to proceed with greater caution. Although the baptismal rite was not published until June of 1524, it had probably been put together as early as January, when Zell began to use the German language in performing baptisms. Bucer had been in Strasbourg only a few months and had not yet begun to provide the strong leadership he later provided. Capito likewise had only recently come to Strasbourg. The reforming party did not yet have the strength it would have by the end of 1524. The success of Zell's German baptisms encouraged the reform-minded priests

39. *WA* 12, p. 44; Hubert, *Ordnungen,* p. 28.

40. Hubert, who takes such care in orthography, does not consider these variations of sufficient significance to comment on them.

41. In regard to the catechetical pieces, the Strasbourg Reformers were evidently as puzzled as Luther as to how these pieces functioned in the Latin rite. The manuscript inserts the gloss, "O Lord, through the honor of your name, hear us and be gracious to us." Hubert, *Ordnungen,* p. 32. This is not, contrary to J. D. C. Fisher (p. 31), found in the 1513 *Agenda Argentinensis.* What we find here is an attempt to make sense out of the medieval tradition that the catechetical pieces are to be "prayed" at this point. Later on, in the Admonition to the godparents, there appears a gloss on the manuscript that the godparents are to teach the child not only the Creed, the Lord's Prayer, and the Ave Maria, but the Ten Commandments as well. Hubert, *Ordnungen,* p. 34.

42. The rubric on how the baptism itself is to be done is rather curious since it departs from the 1513 *Agenda* as well as Luther and Zwingli. The *Agenda Argentinensis* directs that the priest either wash with water or immerse, "Tunc sacerdos vel abluat cum aqua vel immergat infantem. . . ," while the Strasbourg *German Baptismal Service* tells the priest to pour water on the child in the form of the cross three times, "Da nem der priester das kind und gyess dreymal creutzweiss wasser über das kind. . . ." Hubert, *Ordnungen,* pp. 35-36. On the variety of the way baptismal washing was done in the German rituals of the late Middle Ages, see Spital, *Der Taufritus,* pp. 112ff.

of Strasbourg to try a German Mass a few weeks later. The German Mass was more than a translation. It was a revision which removed much from the Mass which was objectionable to the Reformers. Particularly it removed those texts and ceremonies which made the celebration of the Lord's Supper a sacrifice. The German Mass which was published together with the German baptismal service was a more daring attempt at reform simply because it was actually produced after the German baptismal service. The German baptismal service had been a success, so when they set themselves to a German Mass, they were encouraged to go further.

A second reason should be taken into account. It is by no means clear that in January of 1524 Zell and Schwartz had in mind going much further in the reform of the baptismal service than the rite which was later published. One does not get the impression that early in 1524 the Reformers of Strasbourg were as negative about the traditional baptismal rites as they were about the Mass. In the fall of 1524, as we shall see in the following chapter, Capito was still able to say that the two essential things in the baptismal service were the use of water and the reciting of the words of Jesus. The Scholastic theologians before him had insisted on the same point, and whatever additional ceremonies may have cluttered up the baptismal service, the basic core of the rite was still there. The baptismal rite the Reformers had inherited they still regarded as being the Christian sacrament of baptism. It was a different matter with the Mass. As the Reformers saw it, by making the Mass into a eucharistic sacrifice, it was no longer the Lord's Supper. Even at the beginning of 1524, there was a different attitude toward the reform of the baptismal rite than toward the reform of the Mass. The Reformers of Strasbourg could tolerate a simple translation of the baptismal rite in a way they could not tolerate a simple translation of the Mass. The revision of the Mass was much more pressing than the revision of the baptismal rite.

A third reason needs to be considered. In January of 1524, Zell and Schwartz had in all probability not yet developed the principles of liturgical reform expressed by the Strasbourg Reformers in their letter to Luther in November of 1524, and then more fully in the *Grund und Ursach* published at the end of December.[43] Ideas about liturgical reform were developing rapidly in 1524, and what the Reformers of Strasbourg thought about the matter in December of 1524 may have been quite different from what they thought in January of 1524. What they found hard to live with by the end of the year may not have bothered them so much at the beginning of the year. In January of 1524, Zell and Schwartz were still trying to do the best they could with the

43. In Chap. III this subject will be treated at greater length.

traditional baptismal service. They were evidently not terribly critical of the rites at first. This we can gather from the report of Clement Ziegler about the middle of the year.[44] It took several months of celebrating the rites in German for the Reformers to become dissatisfied with them. As long as some of those exorcisms were said in Latin, they were not nearly as problematic as they became once everybody understood what was really being said. In Latin it all sounded very reverent and solemn, but once it was translated it lost its magic and far more was needed. It was at this point that the ideas of the Strasbourg Reformers began to develop. The presence of Bucer and Capito certainly helped them as they began to shape the principles of liturgical reform.

44. *QGT* 7, p. 14.

CHAPTER III

The First Reformed Baptismal Rites

The German translations of the Latin baptismal rites produced in 1523 and 1524 were not what should be called "Reformed baptismal rites." For Zurich and Strasbourg, churches which would take the lead in establishing the Reformed liturgical tradition, those German translations were merely stages in a transition. In Zurich this was recognized very early and was said quite explicitly on the title page of Leo Jud's *Taufbüchlein* of 1523. Leo Jud and his colleagues saw the purpose of their translation as transitional. It was a concession to the slow and weak of faith. The purpose was to help them make the adjustment, but the Reformers of Zurich hoped that it would soon be surpassed with the adoption of an order of baptism true to the institution of Christ. In Strasbourg there was a certain hesitation in the matter. There were those who at first thought a simple translation would be sufficient, but once that translation was made and was put into use, the need for a more radical reform of the rite became evident to them.[1] Nicholas Gerbel was perhaps one of those who held out the longest for a simple translation.

The Reform of the Rite in Strasbourg

Our knowledge of the first attempt to restore the baptismal liturgy of the primitive Christian Church is based on several documents.[2] The first of these

1. Early in 1524 the city council of Strasbourg supported the idea of holding worship services in German. Perhaps this was as far as the council was prepared to let the Strasbourg pastors go. The citizens of Strasbourg were most supportive of the pastors; church attendance increased dramatically. *Martin Bucers Deutsche Schriften,* vol. 1, *Frühschriften 1520-1524,* ed. Robert Stupperich (Gütersloh: Gerd Mohn, 1960), p. 187. To be abbreviated as *BDS* 1.

2. On the more general principles of liturgical reform in the High Rhenish Reformation, see Old, *Patristic Roots,* pp. 23-28.

is Wolfgang Capito's *Was man halten unnd antworten soll, von der Spaltung zwischen Martin Luther und Andres Carolstadtt,* which appeared in October 1524.[3] The irenic tone of this work is typical of Capito. Capito advised that one not get involved in a controversy over infant baptism. The important thing as Capito saw it is the Christian experience signified in baptism. Christians should experience in their own lives a dying to the life of sin and a rising to a new and holy life. This dying is something which should take place through the whole of life.

> We have taught that those baptized in the Lord Jesus are made one body with him in his death, and through baptism they die with him and are buried with him and in his Resurrection they rise to new life. Therefore, the true use or observance of baptism is that we regularly die to the old Adam and this kind of dying we must do as long as life shall last.[4]

Capito makes a point here which is essential to understanding the further development of the Reformed rite of baptism. Baptism is not a ritual which saves one as if by magic at a particular time or occasion. It is not as though before one is baptized one is lost and after baptism one is saved. Baptism is far more a sign under which the Christian lives out the whole of life. It is a sign of a continual washing from sins and a continual renewal in new life. It is not so much the ritual of a once-and-for-all crisis experience as it is a prophetic promise of what is and always will be the character of Christian life.

In regard to the more specifically liturgical aspects of the celebration of baptism, Capito tells us,

> To baptism belongs only water and this word, I baptize thee in the name of the Father and of the Son . . . etc. All the rest is supplementary which from ancient times was used for decoration. We leave out the chrism and the oil,

3. *Wass man halten unnd antworten soll von der spaltung zwischen Martin Luther und Andres Carolstadtt* (Strasbourg: Wolff Köpphel, 1524). For a commentary, see Johann Martin Usteri, "Die Stellung der Strassburger Reformatoren Bucer und Capito zur Tauffrage," *Theologische Studien und Kritiken* 57 (1884): 464-65. To be abbreviated as Usteri, "Die Stellung."

4. "Wir haben gelert, das die in den herren Jesum getaüfft sein, die sein eingeleibt seim tod, und durch den tauff mit im gestorben und begraben, und in seiner uffersteung zum newen ufferstanden. Desshalb ist gebrauch des tauffs in dem, das wir dem alten Adam stetiglich absterben, welches sterben weren soll, so lang disses leben weret." *Wass man halten unnd antworten soll,* fol. B iiij r; Usteri, "Die Stellung," p. 464. (In this document, as well as a number of other sixteenth-century documents on which this study has been based, there has been no attempt to reproduce some of the orthography unique to that age. For example, the dash above a vowel indicating that it is followed by an *n* or *m* and the superscribed *o* or *e* above some vowels have not been reproduced. To such problems a very relaxed approach has been taken.

> when people come who will allow us to leave it out, because those things have been considered far too highly and for us they darken the grace of baptism. One gives more respect to the chrism and the oil which the suffragan bishop has bewitched with his consecration formulas than to simple water which God has blessed with his Word. It is from this that has arisen that other misuse, that so many ignorant people have their sickly children baptized once again in the Church, who without chrism and oil had been baptized at home by midwives. When occasion and time present themselves, which we hope will be soon, we want to bring this into greater conformity with the Word and to improve the entire procedure in a Christian manner.[5]

One notices with particular interest how Capito attached himself clearly to the Scholastic tradition that only the water and the repeating of the baptismal formula were necessary. On this matter the Reformers were never at odds with the Scholastic theologians.[6] On the matter of the consecrated water used for baptisms, Capito, true to the Scholastic tradition, finds the consecration of the water to have been accomplished in Christ's institution of water for use in the sacrament.[7] Nothing is said about the exorcisms. Were they still used in the German baptismal services of Strasbourg at the time? The fact that they are not mentioned may indicate a certain hesitation as to their appropriateness. The remark about midwife baptism reflects the struggle we have already noticed between baptism at home and baptism at church. Here we have another characteristically Reformed point of view emerging in this work of Capito's. The struggle against midwife baptism and private baptisms became a primary concern of the Reformers. Even today American Protestant ministers have to

5. "Und zum tauff, gehort nurt wasser, und disse wort. Ich tauff dich im namen des vatters und des suns etc. Das ander alles ein zusatz, von alten, zu zierug des tauffs inbrocht. Wir underlassen den Chrisem und das ol, wo leut komen die es leide moge. Da solich ding, zu vil gross ansehe habe und bey uns, die gnad des tauffs verdunckeln. Man achtet hoher den Chrisam und das ol, so der weybischoff mit seinen weispruchen bezaubert hatt, weder des schlechten wassers, das gott durch sein wort gesegnet hatt. Dar auss auch gefolget das der unuerstedig hauff die schwachen kinder noch ein mol in der kirchen taufft, die on Chrisam und ol, in hauss von den weibern zu vor getaufft sein. Wan es gelegenheit und die zeit erfordern wurt, also wir in kurzem verhoffen, wollen wir naher uff das wort tringen, und den ganzen vorhack, uff christlich weiss bessern." *Wass man halten unnd antworten soll,* fol. B iiij r f.; Usteri, "Die Stellung," pp. 464-65.

6. H. O. Old, "Bullinger and the Scholastic Works on Baptism: A Study in the History of Christian Worship," *Heinrich Bullinger, 1504- 1575. Gesammelte Aufsätze zum 400 Todestag:* vol. 1, *Leben und Werk,* eds. Ulrich Gäbler und Erland Herkenrath (Zurich: Theologischer Verlag, 1975), pp. 191-207. As we shall see, the Reformers would go on to consider it necessary to accompany baptism with appropriate prayers, catechetical instruction, and a profession of faith, but these were not insisted on in such a way that they could not agree to there being an essential core of the rite.

7. Old, "Bullinger and the Scholastic Works. . . ," p. 198.

struggle against the desire of parents to have baptisms performed privately at home rather than before the congregation. Finally, one notices that in Strasbourg, at the time Capito wrote, the new baptismal service was optional. It was provided for those who were attracted by the growing reform movement. For others there were plenty of priests in the city who would be willing to baptize in the old way and in the old language.[8]

Now let us turn to Martin Bucer's *Grund und Ursach,* which appeared the day after Christmas, 1524.[9] This rather long work gives the reasons behind the liturgical revisions which had recently taken place in Strasbourg. While the book was actually written by Bucer, it was published under the names of nine of Strasbourg's reform-minded priests, including Capito, Kaspar Hedio, Matthis Zell, and Diebold Schwartz.[10]

The *Grund und Ursach* is a systematic explanation of the liturgical reforms which were being carried out in the different congregations of the Church of Strasbourg. The largest part of the work is devoted to the reform of the eucharistic liturgy and to the reforms of the daily office, but there is also a chapter on baptism.[11] This chapter on baptism speaks about three reforms which have been under discussion. First there should be a doctrinal reform. Much of what Bucer has to say is worked out in terms of the Augustinian distinction between the outward sign and the inward grace.[12] Bucer complains that many people attach too little attention to the inner baptism performed by Christ who baptizes us with the Holy Spirit.[13] What is important about baptism is, according to Bucer, the inner cleansing from sin, the new birth, and the renewal of spirit. Much of what Bucer says grows out of his interpretation of the saying of John the Baptist, "I baptize you with water for repentance, but he who comes after me . . . will baptize you with the Holy Spirit and with fire" (Matt. 3:11).[14] For Bucer as for many Reformed theologians who will follow him, the water baptism of both John and

8. For this earlier period see also the letter of the Strasbourg Reformers to Martin Luther, November 1524. *D. Martin Luthers Werke: Kritische Gesamptausgabe, Briefwechsel,* vol. 3 (Weimar: Hermann Bohlau, 1891), pp. 381-87.

9. *Grund und ursach auss gotlicher schrifft der neüwerungen an dem nachtmal des herren, so man die Mess nennet, Tauff, Feyrtagen, bildern und gesang in der gemein Christi, wann die zusamenkompt, durch und auff das wort gottes zu Strassburg fürgenomen. BDS* 1, pp. 194-278.

10. *BDS* 1, pp. 277-78.

11. *BDS* 1, pp. 254-62.

12. "Also ist am tauff unser fürnemste reformation, das wir durch das wort leren den eüsserlichen tauff für ein zeichen des rechten tauffs Christi, das ist der innerlichen reinigung, widergepurt und ernewung halten. . . ." *BDS* 1, p. 258.

13. *BDS* 1, p. 255.

14. *BDS* 1, pp. 254-55.

the apostles was a sign of that baptism performed by the ascended Christ, who pours out his Holy Spirit upon the elect (Acts 1:5).[15] "The outward water of baptism is nothing other than a sign of that inner, spiritual baptism which is the cleansing from all sins, which we must accept by faith and which the Spirit of God works within us as long as we live."[16] Particularly revealing is Bucer's comment on the story of the apostle Paul's baptism as it is found in the book of Acts. Ananias tells Paul, "Rise and be baptized, and wash away your sins, calling on his name" (Acts 22:16).[17] The fact that Paul was directed to call on the name of the Lord indicated that Paul was to pray that Christ wash away his sins through the pouring out of the Holy Spirit. Not only does the story of Paul's conversion and subsequent baptism show us the importance of the epicletic nature of baptism, but Bucer's commentary shows us that the Strasbourg pastors understood its liturgical significance as well. For the taste of contemporary Reformed theologians, Bucer has doubtlessly drawn too great a distinction between the outward sign and the inward grace, but in coming years Bucer himself would do much to rectify this. However this may be, Bucer has gotten Reformed theology off to a good start by putting a strong emphasis on the work of the Holy Spirit.

The second reform suggested by the *Grund und Ursach* is the restoration of the form of baptism practiced in the primitive Church. To this end all those human traditions which have cluttered the baptismal liturgy should be discontinued.[18] By this is meant the frequently repeated exorcisms, the prebaptismal and postbaptismal anointings, the use of consecrated water, exorcised bread and salt, and the handing over of the baptismal candle. According to the Strasbourg pastors, all these things are the inventions of humans and serve only to increase superstition.[19] They obscured what was the essential sign that Christ himself had given the Church.

Here it should be observed that Bucer and his colleagues had in mind the restoration of baptism as it was observed by the New Testament Church. They were not concerned to re-establish the baptismal rites of the fourth century. They knew about the dramatic baptismal rites of the Paschal Vigil from Ambrose of Milan, Cyril of Jerusalem, Augustine, and many others, but those rites were not their pattern. As the Strasbourg pastors saw it, there was

15. *BDS* 1, p. 255.

16. ". . . der eusserlich wassertauff nichts dann ein zeichen ist, des innerlichen, geystlichen tauffs, das ist der reinigung von allen sünden, die wir glauben mussen, welche der geist gotes in uns würckt, so lang diss leben weret. . . ." *BDS* 1, pp. 256-57.

17. *BDS* 1, p. 257. See also Acts 22:16.

18. *BDS* 1, pp. 254 and 258.

19. *BDS* 1, p. 258. (Also in Luther: *WA* 12, p. 47.)

much in those fourth-century rites which faithfully witnessed to the institution of Christ. For example, they found in the patristic sources a record of catechetical instruction which they regarded as a faithful witness to the teaching of Scripture. This aspect of the patristic practice they were eager to revive. On the other hand, they were well aware that even in the fourth-century rites the exorcisms and anointings, which the Reformers so much opposed, had a firm place.

In accordance with this plan to restore the worship of the primitive Church, the *Grund und Ursach* gives a short plan for the celebration of baptism:

> Therefore after a short exhortation on what baptism is and what it means, we offer prayer together that Christ would baptize the child through his Spirit and purify him from all sin. Quite simply then, the children are baptized. The sponsors, together with the other brethren, are admonished to love these children as fellow members of the body of Christ and, as soon as possible, they should be brought to Christ through sound teaching. For such a service we have a basis in Scripture, but for these other things we do not.[20]

The *Grund und Ursach* mentions a third reform which has been suggested by certain people,[21] namely discontinuing the baptism of children. Although the Anabaptist controversy had already begun in Zurich, it had not yet broken in full force upon the Church of Strasbourg. Undoubtedly Carlstadt's visit in September of 1524 had provoked a certain amount of discussion on the matter. Capito, who managed to maintain a gentlemanly piety and a scholarly calm in all matters, did not think the question was such as should provoke a controversy. Bucer was not quite as ambivalent as Capito. At this point he was still open to the possibility of discontinuing infant baptism; he nevertheless gives a number of reasons for which the Church of Strasbourg might be justified in continuing the practice.[22] One thing is clear from both these early documents. At the end of 1524, the Strasbourg pastors were still unsure as to how they should treat the question of infant baptism.

In the following spring the Anabaptist controversy became exceedingly heated, and in the following decade many of the Anabaptist leaders tried to

20. ". . . nach kurtzer verkelerung, was der tauff sey und bedeut, auch gemein gepett, das Christus wolle das kind durch sein geist taüffen und sye den pfettern sampt andern brudern befelhen, das sye solche wollen als ire glider in Christo lieben und, so bald moglich, durch die heilsam lere zu Christo furen. Des haben wir grund in der schrifft und nit weiters." *BDS* 1, p. 258.

21. *BDS* 1, p. 258. The footnote 161 provided by Robert Stupperich is misleading.

22. *BDS* 1, pp. 258-62.

make Strasbourg the center of the movement. Nevertheless the reforms of the baptismal liturgy discussed in the *Grund und Ursach* are not significantly motivated by the Anabaptist controversy.

Four features of the baptismal rite in the *Grund und Ursach* stand out. First we notice how important catechetical instruction is to the proper celebration of baptism. The older generation of Protestant liturgists would no doubt decry this as terribly didactic, but it is true to the oldest traditions of Christian baptism. To the Christian Humanists it was the most urgent reform of the baptismal liturgy.[23] They were very favorably impressed with the great attention given to catechetical instruction in the patristic age. Second, it is quite clear that the sacrament of baptism has to do not only with the washing away of sin, but with the gift of the Holy Spirit as well. There is no place for splitting baptism into two sacraments, water baptism for the forgiving of sins, and baptism of the Holy Spirit by which one receives the gift of the Holy Spirit. Neither the High Church Anglican nor the modern Pentecostal would be happy with the rite Bucer proposed. Third, the Baptismal Invocation or baptismal epiclesis is at the very heart of the rite. It asks that Christ accomplish inwardly, through Christ's baptism by the Holy Spirit, both the regeneration and sanctification of which the washing with water is a sign. Fourth, we find the vows replaced by an admonition to the sponsors, as well as to the rest of the congregation, that the child should be led to Christ by love and sound teaching. As we shall see, the catechetical instruction and the making of the vows of faith are not neglected by the Strasbourg Reformers. This will occur later in the life of the baptized child. The baptismal service itself, however, as it is outlined in the *Grund und Ursach,* has but two essential elements, the Baptismal Invocation and the baptismal washing accompanied by the words of Christ.

Now let us turn to the actual liturgical texts. Two documents have come down to us which provide the liturgical texts for the rite of baptism outlined in the *Grund und Ursach.* The *Strasbourg Church Order of 1525* (D) is the first of these documents.[24] It is not altogether clear for how long the liturgy described in this book had been in use, but it would seem to be the first genuine Reformed baptismal liturgy. This document was not published by the Re-

23. John Barton Payne, *Erasmus, His Theology of the Sacraments* (Richmond, Va.: John Knox Press, 1970), pp. 160 and 171-73.

24. *Ordnung des Herren Nachtmal: so man die Messz nennet sampt der Tauff und Insegung der Ee, Wie yetzt die diener des Wort gots zuo Strassburg Erneüwert und nach götlicher gschrifft gebessert haben uss ursach in nachgender Epistel gemeldet* (Strasbourg: Johannes Schwan, 1525). See Hubert, *Ordnungen.* (Scholars have assigned to the various evangelical liturgical orders of Strasbourg capital letters. This order is known as D.)

formers of Strasbourg themselves, but rather by Johannes Schwan, an enthusiastic supporter. The Reformers themselves were hesitant to put their first attempts into print. Somehow Schwan had gotten a copy of the baptismal service as it was being celebrated. About the same time Wolff Köpphel published the *Strasbourg Church Service* (E).[25] Köpphel was a cousin of Wolfgang Capito. (The name Capito is but a latinized form of Köpphel.) This text has unfortunately been lost. In 1526, Köpphel published the *Strasbourg Psalter* (F).[26] In a preface Köpphel tells his readers that the Reformers were not completely satisfied with their product. Nevertheless, the publisher was confident that a printed form of the services as they were being celebrated would be of use.[27] Let us look at these two documents.

In a short paragraph of explanation at the beginning of the baptismal service we are told that oil, chrism, and consecrated water are no longer used in the baptismal service.[28] Furthermore, we are assured that just as it was proper to give circumcision to infants under the law, so it is proper to baptize infants under the gospel. These infants must, of course, be the infants of Christian parents. When Christian parents bring their children to baptism, then they offer them up to God and promise before the Church to bring up the children in the Christian faith.[29] It is the parents, rather than the godparents, who now begin to function in the rite. Midwife baptism is discouraged as a lack of faith in God's saving power. It makes of the sign of baptism a magical act. The child is a member of the congregation because he or she is the child of Christian parents, and so the baptism should be before the congregation. Baptism should be administered amid the prayers of the congregation.

The actual service starts with the traditional questions as to the intention of the parents or godparents. "Do you wish this child to be baptized," to which they answer, "Yes." Then the minister asks the name of the child. It is not at all clear why these questions stand at the beginning of the service. No theological importance is given to them. These questions are not mentioned as being important to the proper celebration of baptism in Bucer's *Grund und Ursach*. Perhaps they were regarded as a solemn way to begin the service. The

25. *Straszburger kirchen ampt, nemlich von Insegung d'Eeleüt, vom Tauf und von des herrn nachtmal, mit etlichen Psalmen; die am end des büchlins, ordenlich verseychnet sein* (Strasbourg: Wolff Köpphel, 1525). Hubert, *Ordnungen,* p. 16. (This order is known as E.)

26. *Psalmen gebett und Kirchen ubung wie sie zum Straszburg gehalten werden* (Strasbourg: Wolff Köpphel, 1526). Hubert, *Ordnungen,* pp. 16-17. (This order is known as F.)

27. This comes out very clearly in the preface to the Strasbourg Psalter written by Köpphel. Hubert, *Ordnungen,* pp. 140-41.

28. Hubert, *Ordnungen,* p. 37. This explanation is found only in F and G.

29. Hubert, *Ordnungen,* p. 37.

voluntarist implications of asking whether the parents or godparents willed to have the child baptized, at first may not have occurred to the Reformers. As we will see, the Anabaptists would point out the voluntarist implications. In the *Strasbourg Psalter of 1530* (G) they disappear from the Strasbourg baptismal rite.[30]

Next we find the Baptismal Exhortation. This Baptismal Exhortation is a short sermon on the meaning of baptism. The minister assures the congregation that when we ask anything of God it will be done for us, and then asks the members of the congregation to pray for the child. First, they are to pray that the child be given faith, which is the gift of God's grace. Second, the congregation is to pray that our Lord himself baptize the child in water and in the Holy Spirit to the end that the outward washing, which God does through the minister, might be accomplished inwardly through the Holy Spirit. The Baptismal Exhortation became extremely important in following years because of the growing popularity of the Anabaptist movement. What was being done and why it was being done had to be explained. As the Reformers deepened their appreciation of baptism, so the exhortations became more elaborate. Great variety is found in these exhortations, and the minister was supposed to use his good judgment in deciding what aspects of the baptismal teaching he should emphasize on any particular occasion.[31]

After the Baptismal Exhortation the minister leads the congregation in reciting the Lord's Prayer and the Apostles' Creed. Here the catechetical pieces of the late medieval baptismal rite are used in the way they had been used on the eve of the Reformation.[32] One gets the impression that the Strasbourg Reformers are still uncertain as to how the catechetical pieces should be handled. They obviously consider it appropriate to say the Lord's Prayer and the Creed at baptism, but they have not discovered their original function. How the Creed and the Lord's Prayer actually function in this baptismal service is quite clear, in spite of whatever doubts the Reformers might have had about how they should function in a truly Reformed baptismal service. Both pieces clearly function as prayers. The Lord's Prayer is a prayer for the forgiveness of sins; the Creed is a prayer for the gift of faith. That the two catechetical pieces function as prayers is evident from the fact that the Baptismal Exhortation leads to prayer. The congregation is told to pray for the giving of faith to the child, "Bitten um den glauben." When the minister directs the saying

30. Hubert, *Ordnungen,* p. 38.

31. At the end of the baptismal service we find the following rubric concerning the Baptismal Exhortation: "aber etwan nach gelegenheit der personen würt mer oder minder geredt, etwan gar kein fürwort. . . ." Hubert, *Ordnungen,* p. 43.

32. See above, Chap. I.

of the Creed, he tells them to continue with "den Glauben."[33] What is implicit in the praying of the Lord's Prayer and the Creed is now made explicit in another prayer which follows. This method of interpreting a liturgical text by following it with a collect is an old method well known in the history of worship.

The Baptismal Invocation which follows the reciting of the Creed and the Lord's Prayer is one of the most important of the early liturgical formulations of Strasbourg. Here is the earliest version:

> Almighty, eternal God, most merciful Father, because the righteous shall live by faith alone and because without faith it is impossible to please thee, so we ask you to grant this child whom you have created the gift of faith. According to the promise of your Son, seal and establish his heart with the Holy Spirit. Truly accomplish in him that inward renewal and rebirth of spirit signified by our baptism. Grant that this child be buried as in the death of Christ Jesus and through him be awakened from the dead to walk in the newness of life to the praise of God's glory and the building up of his neighbors. Amen.[34]

The prayer is a petition that the child receive the benefits of the sacrament. This is done in terms of a wealth of biblical images. The image of sealing from Ephesians 1:13-14 is used, as are the image of new birth from John 3:5 and Titus 3:5 and the image of being buried and raised with Christ found in Romans 6:3-5. The prayer, as it is translated above, is from the edition of 1525, but each succeeding edition found the prayer slightly altered. This prayer was obviously extremely important to Bucer. For him, as for Luther, the epicletic nature of baptism was essential. Baptism was not only a matter of the sign of washing, but also that the washing be while calling on the name of the Lord. This point had been carefully made in the *Grund und Ursach,* where Bucer

33. While in English we do not call the Creed "the faith," such is the common usage in German. The pun is not so far afield as might appear to English-speaking people. What, after all, does Creed really mean? Fisher has evidently missed this point. J. D. C. Fisher, *Christian Initiation in the Reformation Period: Some Early Reformed Rites of Baptism and Confirmation and Other Contemporary Documents* (London: S.P.C.K., 1970), p. 36. To be abbreviated as Fisher, *Christian Initiation: Reformation.*

34. "Almechtiger, ewiger got, barmehertziger vatter, dieweyl der gerecht lebt allein ym glauben und unmüglich ist, das dir etwas on glauben gefall, so bitten wir dich, das du disem kindt, das da ist dein creatur, die gab des glaubens, verluhen wellest, in welchem du sein hertz mit dem heylgen geist noch deins suns verheissung versiglen und versicheren wollest, uff das dein innerliche ernewerung warhafftiglich bedeutet werde, und das es als in den todt Christi Jesu getaufft mit ym begraben und durch yn von den todten vfferweckt sy, zu wandeln in eim newen leben zu lob der herrlicheit gots und zu vffbauwung seiner nechsten, Amen." Hubert, *Ordnungen,* pp. 40-41.

calls attention to the two passages of Acts which speak of the baptism of the apostle Paul, namely Acts 9:17-19 and 22:16. In these passages Ananias tells Paul to be baptized while calling on the name of the Lord.[35]

The traditional baptismal Gospel of Jesus blessing the children is then read from either Matthew 19, Mark 10, or Luke 18 and is followed by a short exhortation to believe the words that have been read and to pray that these children may be such as receive the kingdom; that they may receive the gift of faith by which they will become true children of God, heirs and fellow heirs with Christ. The congregation is to pray that these children may partake of the covenant promises found in Christ, that they may become members of his body, and that in years to come they might be true Christians living a true Christian life.[36] In the Scripture passage Jesus had prayed for the children; from this the congregation should learn that the Church should continue the ministry of prayer begun by Christ.

The godparents and other brothers and sisters, that is, the rest of the congregation, are told that it is their responsibility to bring up the child in Christian order, discipline, and the fear of God.[37] They promise to do this, whereupon the minister takes the child and again asks the name of the child.

The baptism itself is performed "with the pouring of water" and the repeating of the traditional formula. Nothing is said about immersion or threefold pouring. This completed, the minister returns the child to the godparents and gives the benediction.

> God grant to all of you his grace and increase in his knowledge. Amen. The peace of God be with you all. Amen.[38]

As it stands in this first attempt at producing a baptismal service which is truly reformed according to the Word of God, this benediction is not terribly important; but as the Reformers develop a more and more profound understanding of the biblical benedictions, the benediction at the end of the baptismal service will become increasingly important.

In evaluating this service several things should be noted. Although it is

35. *BDS* 1, p. 257.

36. In succeeding editions the idea of becoming participators in the covenant and receiving the gift of the Holy Spirit is strengthened. Hubert, *Ordnungen,* p. 42.

37. Presumably the reference to other brothers and sisters is a reference to the whole congregation. In this we begin to see the appearance of the idea that it is the congregation which is the true baptismal sponsor. In later editions this admonition to the sponsors and congregation is moved to a position after the actual baptism. Hubert, *Ordnungen,* p. 43.

38. "Gott verleyhe vch allen sein gnad vnd fürgang in seiner erkantnüss, amen. Der fryd gottes sey mitt vch allen, amen." Hubert, *Ordnungen,* p. 43.

not simply an adaptation of the Latin baptismal rite, a number of things survive from the old Latin rite. To be sure, the essential core of the rite is still there. The baptism is done with water in the name of the Father and the Son and the Holy Spirit. We still find the catechetical pieces as well as the Gospel story of Jesus blessing the children, but the order of these is considerably rearranged. While the Baptismal Invocation, so essential to the service, is not a reworking of the old Latin prayers for the catechetical rites, it does, however, serve something of the same function. It prays, as did the old Latin catechetical prayers, for the benefits of the sacrament. The primary virtue of this service is that it puts the emphasis on the actual sign of the sacrament, the washing in the name of Jesus. This concern to emphasize the baptismal sign itself had been expressed by the Reformers again and again. This rite makes the basic sign very clear.

Reform of the Rite in Zurich

Meanwhile in Zurich the Anabaptist movement was growing. In an attempt to meet the challenge, Zwingli produced a work *Of Baptism.* To this he appended a new baptismal rite.[39] Although this work is not a full presentation of the doctrine of baptism but rather a polemical tract against the Anabaptists, we nevertheless find in it the beginnings of lines of thought which in the course of time have become characteristic of the Reformed theology of baptism. For example, we find baptism explained as a sign of the covenant. We find a strong emphasis on the work of the Holy Spirit, and we also find that Zwingli emphasizes the ecclesiological aspect of baptism. Baptism is initiation or entrance into the Church. In all this Zwingli considers himself to be making a radical departure from the commonly accepted viewpoints of the theologians usually quoted on the subject. Zwingli feels no need to construct his argument within the confines of Scholastic theology or to be limited by the quotations of the Fathers gathered by either Lombard or Gratian.

39. *Von dem Touff. Vom widertouff unnd vom kindertouff durch Huldrych Zwingli* (Zurich: Johannsen Hager, 1525). Reprinted in *Huldreich Zwinglis Sämtliche Werke,* vol. 4, eds. Emil Egli, Georg Finsler, Walther Köhler, and Oskar Farmer, *Corpus Reformatorum,* vol. 91 (Leipzig: M. Heinsius Nachfolger, 1927), pp. 206-337. Eng. trans.: *Zwingli and Bullinger: Of Baptism,* ed. G. W. Bromiley, The Library of Christian Classics, vol. 24 (Philadelphia: The Westminster Press, 1952), pp. 129-75. The work will be abbreviated as *Of Baptism.* Quotations from this work will be from the English translations except as noted. Reference to the appended baptismal rite will be in the German text in the *Corpus Reformatorum* and will be abbreviated *CR* 91. The English translation does not cover the appended baptismal rite.

> For all the doctors have ascribed to the water a power which it does not have and the holy apostles did not teach. They have also misunderstood the saying of Christ about water and the Holy Ghost in John 3. Our present task is to see what baptism really is. At many points we shall have to tread a different path from that taken either by ancient or more modern writers or by our own contemporaries. We shall be guided not by our caprice, but by the Word of God.[40]

He emphasizes this especially in relation to the interpretation of certain texts on baptism. For example, he insists on the unity of John's baptism and the apostles' baptism. He gives us a fresh interpretation of John 3:5 on the relation of water baptism and baptism by the Spirit. He spends some time developing his interpretation of Matthew 28 in a way quite independent from the Scholastic interpretation, which put the emphasis on the saying of the formula. He investigates Romans 6 and draws from it that baptism is initiation into the Church and, therefore, should stand at the beginning of our Christian experience. Some of these interpretations have been followed by Reformed theologians, others not.

For our purpose, however, Zwingli's baptismal rite is more important.[41] It is a very brief service. It begins with an invocation, "In God's name, Amen. Our help is in the power of the Lord, who created heaven and earth."[42] This is an adaptation of Psalm 124:8, so often used as an invocation in Reformed churches. The traditional questions on the intention of the sponsors and the name of the child are asked. The words have been slightly expanded, "Do you

40. *Of Baptism,* p. 130.

41. This new baptismal service as it was then being celebrated in Zurich comes as an appendix to Zwingli's tract *Von dem Touff.* "Ietz volgt die form des touffs, wie man die yetz ze Zürich brucht, und sind alle zusätz, die in gottes wort nit grund haben, underlassen." *CR* 91, pp. 334-37.

Secondary literature on Zwingli's first Reformed baptismal service: F. Schmidt-Clausing, ed., *Zwinglis liturgische Formulare* (Frankfort am Main: Otto Lembeck, 1970), pp. 39-41; *Zwingli als Liturgiker,* pp. 143-45; "Die liturgietheologische Arbeit Zwinglis am Sintflutgebet des Taufformulars. Ein weiterer Blick in Zwinglis liturgische Werkstatt," *Zwingliana* 13 (1972): 516-43 and 591-615. Joh. Martin Usteri, "Darstellung der Tauflehre Zwinglis," *Theologische Studien und Kritiken* 55 (1882): 205-84.

Corpus Reformatorum, vol. 91, pp. 671-77, contains a Zurich Church Order which is not dated but which the editors say must come after Easter of 1525. According to Schmidt-Clausing, *Zwinglis liturgische Formulare,* pp. 7-9, this service, which contains some noteworthy additions, could not have come until 1529. In Chap. VI we will see compelling reasons for rejecting the theory of Schmidt-Clausing.

42. *CR* 91, p. 334. On Zwingli's paraphrase of "name" with "power," see *Of Baptism,* p. 145: "but what we understand by the words, 'I baptize thee in the name' is this, I dedicate thee to the name, that is, the power, the majesty, the grace of the Father, the Son, and the Holy Ghost."

want this child to be baptized into the baptism of our Lord Jesus Christ?" They are to answer, "Yes."[43] This is followed by the Baptismal Invocation. Zwingli's prayer is a further reworking of Luther's Great Flood Prayer.[44] The Scripture lesson on Christ's blessing the children is still in use. After once more asking the intention of the sponsors and asking them once again to name the child, the words of Jesus from Matthew 28 are repeated, but with the literal translation of the Greek, "I baptize thee *into* the name of the Father and of the Son and of the Holy Ghost."[45] There is no rubric indicating that the baptism is by either immersion, pouring, or sprinkling. Zwingli here has departed from Leo Jud, who directed immersion as had Luther. On this subject Zwingli is now silent. After the baptismal washing, the child is clothed in the traditional white baptismal gown and given an accompanying benediction. The whole congregation is likewise given a benediction and dismissed in peace.

Five things stand out. In the first place, the service itself contains no catechetical instruction. One notices that there is neither a vow that the child will receive catechetical instruction when he or she reaches the proper age, nor an admonition to that effect. Nevertheless, while this is not mentioned in the text, it is clearly brought out in the foregoing tract that baptism should be followed by instruction.[46]

In the second place, there are no vows in the service confessing the faith of the godparents, the faith of the parents, the faith of the child, or even the faith of the congregation. The Creed and the Lord's Prayer are not recited.[47] The service contains no confession of faith or vows of any kind.

In the third place, all exorcisms and anointings have been discontinued. This Zwingli explains as a positive contribution of the Anabaptist controversy.[48] Zwingli does not mean by this that he would not have thought of

43. "Wellend ir, das kind getoufft werd in den touff unsers herrn Jesu Christi? Ihr antwurt: Ja." *CR* 91, p. 334.

44. The revisions of the Great Flood Prayer will be taken up at greater length in Chap. IX.

45. "N. Ich touff dich in den namen des vatters und des suns und des heiligen geistes." *CR* 91, p. 336. One should note that J. D. C. Fisher, *Christian Initiation: The Reformation Period* (London: S.P.C.K., 1970), p. 131, has completely overlooked this important modification of the baptismal formula. This is a serious mistake on Fisher's part and should bring into question the reliability of his collection of translations.

46. We shall see that the admonition to the baptismal sponsors will reappear in the Zurich Baptismal rite when the controversy with the Anabaptists begins to make it necessary.

47. The saying of the Creed and the Lord's Prayer quickly reappears in Zurich's baptismal rites. In Zwingli's reply to Johann Faber in 1526, he wrote "wir touffend in den namen des vatters und suns unnd heyligen geysts, mit dem vatterunser, glouben und andren christenlichen gebätten." *CR* 92, p. 50.

48. *Of Baptism,* p. 153.

removing them from the baptismal service if it had not been for the Anabaptist objection to them. Such things had been kept in the 1523 rite only as a temporary concession to the slower brethren. The Anabaptist objection to these usages was for Zwingli just one more reason for discontinuing them. The Reformer of Zurich had much more basic objections to these rites. Although Zwingli recognizes that these forms came down from early times, he finds that many people have built false hopes and beliefs on them and used them as a form of magic. For these forms Zwingli found no basis in Scripture, as is clearly said in the works introducing this baptismal service: "all additions, which have no basis in God's word, have been left out."[49]

In the fourth place, we are surprised that suddenly the mention of immersion disappears. Zwingli's tract *Of Baptism* indicates that Zwingli is still of the opinion that baptism was originally by immersion. Why does he suddenly withdraw this rubric? It would appear that it was for very practical reasons. While the progressive citizens of the city of Zurich liked to have their children baptized in German, they did not like to go through all the fuss and bother of undressing their children, immersing them in a cold stone church, and then having to dry off and reclothe a screaming child. It made for an unseemly operation the unpleasantness of which outweighed their pleasure in having the baptism done in their native language. This is only a guess, but it seems to explain the withdrawal of the rubric on immersion. The good citizens of Zurich, given their choice of immersion in German or sprinkling in Latin, chose sprinkling in Latin. Zwingli, who never was at loss to recognize the ways of humankind, quickly made sure his preference for immersion did not endanger what was to him of infinitely greater importance, worship in the common tongue.

In the fifth place, we are surprised to find that the clothing of the child in a baptismal gown has been retained. This is indeed a most puzzling feature of the rite. Why has the giving of the white baptismal gown been retained when one would expect that it would be dispensed with just as the anointing and all those other things which have no basis in God's Word? Possibly it is best explained as an inconsistency. On the other hand, one might attempt to explain it in several ways. Possibly it was because the Zurich Reformers intended to reintroduce immersion. Immersion may still have been practiced on an optional basis even though there was no longer a rubric directing it. If immersion was to be used, the Reformers realized that it would be necessary to undress the child and consequently to reclothe him. This, of course, would not necessarily require the accompanying benediction; however, it would not be the first time that practical

49. *CR* 91, p. 334. See n. 45 above.

necessity had been the mother of liturgical invention. Another possible explanation is that Zwingli and his colleagues felt the need to conclude the service with some sort of benediction or final prayer. The revised version of this benediction has indeed taken on the character of a final benediction of the child. "May God grant to you that, being now clothed bodily with a white robe, you may at the last day appear before Christ the judge with a pure conscience. Amen."[50] Leo Jud's text reads, "Receive now a white and spotless robe which you are to bring undefiled before the judgment seat of Christ. Amen." Zwingli's version makes this much more clearly a benediction. It reinforces the biblical image of the baptismal washing, making it clear that it is the pure conscience which is the ultimate goal of the sacrament (1 Pet. 3:21 and Gal. 3:27). Furthermore, it puts the whole rite in an eschatological perspective.

Basel Service Book of 1526[51]

Basel was in many respects the seedbed of the South German Reformation. Less than a century before this, the city of Basel had played host to an ecumenical council, where in conversation with the theologians of Byzantium the conciliarist movement had flowered. Concern for church reform was still very much alive. Basel was a university city. For generations the Church of Basel had known excellent pastoral leadership. At the beginning of the sixteenth century theologians and learned preachers prospered. Johann Heynlin von Stein, Johann Ulrich Surgant, and Thomas Wyttenbach led the Christian community of the city. Christoph von Utenheim sat on the episcopal throne for some twenty-five years as a model of enlightened pastoral leadership. The leaders of the Reformation in Zurich, Constance, and Strasbourg had all spent their years in Basel. In 1514 Erasmus made his home in Basel. This made Basel a major center of Christian Humanism. In Basel, Erasmus found plenty of earnest young scholars ready to assist him. They had all been well trained in the literary methods of Christian Humanism.[52] Here the first printed edition of the Greek New Testament appeared in 1517, just a few months before Luther

50. "Gott verlich dir, das, wie du yetz mit dem wyssen kleid liplich angezogen wirst, also am jüngsten tag mit reiner unvermassgoter conscientz vor imm erschinist. Amen." *CR* 91, p. 336.

51. *Form und gstalt wie der kinder tauff, Des herren Nachtmal, und der krancken heymsuchung jetz zu Basel von etlichen Predicanten gehalten werden* (Basel: Thomas Wolff, 1526). To be abbreviated as *Form und gstalt.* This is the second of two editions in 1526. On the two editions, see Old, *Patristic Roots,* p. 44.

52. On Erasmus's reasons for settling in Basel, see Johan Huizinga, *Erasmus* (New York: Charles Scribner's Sons, 1924), pp. 190-93.

nailed his ninety-five theses on the church door of Wittenberg. The great publishing houses of Froben and Cratander were in the midst of editing the first printed editions of the writings of the Church Fathers.

When the Reformation began, some of the citizens of Basel greeted it with enthusiasm but others were quite resistant.[53] Among the strongest opponents of the reform was the learned Erasmus, the prince of scholars. At first he was sympathetic, but before too long he recognized that Protestantism was proposing a reform quite different from the reform he had envisioned. Unlike Erasmus, the High Rhenish Reformers had been trained in the Christian Humanism of Jakob Wimpeling, which was far too Augustinian for Erasmus.[54] The Christian Humanism of Erasmus was much more influenced by Italian Humanism. The Protestant Reformers of Basel were a long way from making their reform into the religion of the Renaissance. They accepted the Christian Humanism of their teachers as a literary method that put great emphasis on returning to the source documents of Christian antiquity. It was above all the recovery of biblical Greek and Hebrew. It was the exercising of grammatical-historical exegesis in an attempt to better understand the text of Holy Scripture.[55] To put it very simply, the coming of the Reformation to Basel drove a wedge through the school of Christian Humanism, dividing it into those who were going more in the direction of the humanism of the Italian Renaissance and those who were going in the direction of a more biblical and more Augustinian renewal of Christianity.

John Oecolampadius, one of those capable young scholars who had assisted Erasmus, effectively took the leadership of the Protestant party in Basel from the time of his lectures on Isaiah in 1523, but it was not until 1529 that he and the other reform-minded priests of Basel had clearly won the city for the Reformation. From 1523 to 1526 the Protestant party in Basel had to work under a very different situation than their colleagues in Strasbourg or Zurich, where the city council gave strong backing to the Reformers. In Basel

53. On the history of the Reformation in Basel see Ernst Staehelen, *Das Theologische Lebenswerk Johannes Oecolampads,* Quellen und Forschungen zur Reformationsgeschichte, vol. 21 (Leipzig: M. Heinsius Nachfolger, 1939). To be abbreviated as E. Staehelin, *Lebenswerk Oecolampads;* and *Das Buch der Basler Reformation* (Basel: Helbing & Lichtenhahn, 1929).

54. On the meaning of Christian Humanism, see Lewis W. Spitz, *The Religious Renaissance of the German Humanists* (Cambridge, Mass.: Harvard University Press, 1963), pp. 1-19.

55. On the Alsatian Christian Humanists, see Bernd Moeller, "Die deutschen Humanisten und die Anfänge der Reformation," *Zeitschrift für Kirchengeschichte* 70 (1959): 46-61; and Rudolf Wackernagel, *Humanismus und Reformation in Basel* (Basel: Helbing & Lichtenhahn, 1924).

the city council tried to keep peace between the two parties. The first *Basel Service Book of 1526* could not be published in Basel itself because the council had denied Oecolampadius the right of the printing press.[56] The Reformers of the city were allowed to conduct services as they wished, but the traditional services were also maintained. The reform party was allowed the pulpit, but it was not supposed to arouse any commotion. It is in such a way that we must understand the first Reformed baptismal rite of Basel. The old Latin rite was still in use often in the same church and at the same baptismal font. Those who wanted their children baptized according to the old rite went to the priests who preferred to use the old rite, and those who wanted their children baptized according to the new rite went to the priests who supported the reform.[57]

The baptismal rite drawn up by Oecolampadius for the Protestants of Basel profited from the attempts of the Reformers of both Zurich and Strasbourg which had appeared in the preceding year. The service begins much in the way the Zurich service began. The priest asks, "Do you seek baptism for the child?"[58] On receiving an affirmative answer, the priest asks the name of the child and then begins the service with the same Biblical Invocation as the Zurich rite, "Our help is in the power of the Lord, who made heaven and earth" (Ps. 124:8).[59]

A Baptismal Exhortation follows which briefly outlines the plan of salvation. First the need of mankind for a savior is treated. Then, in the terms of the Epistle to the Ephesians, the mystery of God's eternal plan of salvation is unfolded. The people are urged to pray that the child before them may grow to recognize the coming of the Savior and so be born again through the work of the Holy Spirit, and be fully endowed with the gifts of the Spirit. The people are to pray that the child may be delivered from the power of darkness, be enlightened by faith and grow in the knowledge of Christ, bear fruit to God, and be added to the fellowship of the Christian community. The Exhortation ends with these words, "Let us pray that as we sacramentally through baptism

56. Old, *Patristic Roots,* pp. 44-46, 98.

57. Staehelin, *Lebenswerk Oecolampads,* pp. 429-47.

58. "Ir begert das man das Kind Tauff," *Form und gstalt,* fol. A iiij r. One notices that Oecolampadius has used the word "begert" or "seek" rather than the "wellend" or "do you will." This reflects a different Latin version of the same question: "Quid petis." Cf. Spital, *Der Taufritus,* 110ff.

59. The service designates the minister of baptism as "der Priester." The Reformed ministers of Basel, were, of course, all ordained priests serving in the diocese of Basel. Practically speaking, in the imperial free cites of the Upper Rhineland, it was the city council which appointed priests to the various parishes. Basel, having for centuries been a prince bishopric, had experienced a power struggle between bishop and city council which left the city council holding many powers which today we would regard as ecclesiastical rather than civil.

add this child to the number of the faithful, he might also be received by our heavenly Father and be enrolled in the book of life."[60]

The service follows the Exhortation with a prayer. The prayer remembers at length the rich covenant promises of God and then asks, "according to thy promise grant your good Spirit to this child, that he not be counted among the children of wrath, but rather among the children of light. . . ."[61] This prayer is not the actual Baptismal Invocation, but rather a prayer designed to take the place of the baptismal exorcisms of the old Latin rite. This is apparently the point of referring to the Holy Spirit as the good Spirit. As the foregoing admonition to prayer had made clear, here the congregation is to pray that the child be delivered from the power of darkness and enter the realm of light. The prayer goes on to ask that the child be established as a member of the Church that is without spot or wrinkle and trust Christ in faith and love. Here again it is clear that Oecolampadius is reworking the theme of the ancient catechetical rites.

The traditional Gospel from Mark 10 is read and then followed by an admonition encouraging the parents and godparents to teach the child the Christian faith.[62] The admonition, however, does not lead to the taking of vows but rather to a second prayer, "Now in particular I ask you to pray with me that as I baptize this child with water and receive him into the number of Christians, that God himself inwardly baptize him with his Spirit and hold him in the number of his elect."[63] With this the congregation prays together the Lord's Prayer, after which the minister offers the Baptismal Invocation. The rite of Basel has adopted the Baptismal Invocation of Strasbourg for this purpose.[64] Then the minister invites the parents and godparents to the font, repeats the traditional questions, and asks the godparents to answer in the name of the child the traditional questions for the renunciation of Satan and the trinitarian confession of faith.

60. ". . . und wie wir es Sacramentlich durch den tauff zuzelen den glaubigen, das es also von unserem himlischen vatter angenommen werd und in das buch des lebens eingescriben sey." *Form und gstalt,* fol. A iiij r.

61. ". . . nach deiner verheyssung verleyhen dein guten geist disem kind, das es nit under den kindern des zorns sonder des liechts. . . ." *Form und gstalt,* fol. A iiij v.

62. *Form und gstalt,* fol. A v v.

63. "Jetz in sonderheit bitt ich eüch, das jr mit mir bittet trewlich, das, so ich das kind mit dem wasser tauff, und nem es in die zal der Christen, das es gott mit dem geist innerlich tauff, und halt es in der zal seyner ausserwelten. . . ." *Form und gstalt,* fol. A v v.

64. *Form und gstalt,* fol. A vi r-v. The original text of this invocation is found in the *Strasbourg Church Order of 1525* (D) and is given above in n. 34. One notices a few slight revisions. Oecolampadius has dropped the phrase "zu wandeln in eim newen leben." He has added another phrase. The Strasbourg prayer asks for "the inner renewal signified by the sacrament." Oecolampadius adds to this by asking for "the inner renewal and regeneration of spirit signified by the outward baptism."

N. Do you renounce the devil?
Answer: Yes

All his works?
Answer: Yes

His worldly pride?
Answer: Yes

Do you believe in God, the Almighty Creator of heaven and earth?
Answer: Yes

Do you believe in Jesus Christ his only begotten Son, our Lord, born and suffered?
Answer: Yes

Do you believe in the Holy Spirit, one Christian Church, the communion of the saints, the forgiveness of sins, the resurrection of the flesh, and after this life eternal?
Answer: Yes[65]

The child is then baptized. "N. I baptize you in the name of the Father, and of the Son, and of the Holy Spirit."[66] We notice that Oecolampadius does not follow the suggestion of Zwingli that the Greek be rendered "into the

65. "N. Widersagstu den tüfel, Antwurt, ja. Allen seinen wercken, Antwurt, Ja, Der weltlichen yppigkeit, Antwurt, ja.

"Glaubstu in Gott den almechtigen vatter, schöpfer himels und erden, Ja.

"Glaubstu in Jesum Christum seyn eingebornen sun unsern herren, geboren und gelitten, Antwurt, Ja.

"Glaubst inn den heyligen geyst, eyn Chrystlich Kirch, gemeynschafft der heiligen, vergebung der sünd, aufferstentnüss des fleisch, nach dem leben das ewig, Antwurt, Ja." *Form und gstalt,* fol. A vi v to vii r.

There is nothing defective here in the second article of the confession of faith. This is by long tradition not the same as the Apostles' Creed. No doubt it goes back to an early form of the Creed. The Reformers of Strasbourg as elsewhere felt the need to fill in with the whole text of the Creed. See Hubert, *Ordnungen,* p. 35; and Spital, *Der Taufritus,* p. 108.

In the third article of the confession, which is identical with the Creed, it should be observed that even before the Reformation the traditional reading in German was "I believe in . . . the Christian Church" rather than the "Catholic Church." This is clear from the German translation of the Creed found in Johann Ulrich Surgant, *Manuale curatorum* (Basel: Michael Furter, 1503) consideratio V. fol. I xxx r. For a discussion of the inference of this work on the pastoral practice of the upper Rhineland cf. Old, *Patristic Roots,* pp. 7-10.

66. On the renunciation, see Hans Kirsten, *Die Taufabsage, Eine Untersuchung zu Gestalt und Geschichte der Taufe nach den altkirchlichen Taufliturgien* (Berlin: Evangelische Verlagsanstalt, 1960).

"N. Ich Tauff dich in dem namen des vatters, und des suns, und des heiligen geysts." *Form und gstalt,* fol. A vii r.

name" but uses the traditional "in the name." There is no rubric on the method of baptizing. After the baptism, the child is clothed in white. This is accompanied by the same benediction as in Zurich.

At this point Oecolampadius inserts a prayer of thanksgiving from the psalter.

> I kept my faith, even when I said,
> "I am greatly afflicted";
> I said in my consternation,
> "Men are all a vain hope."
> What shall I render to the LORD
> for all his bounty to me?
> I will lift up the cup of salvation
> and call on the name of the LORD,
> I will pay my vows to the LORD
> in the presence of all his people.
> Precious in the sight of the LORD
> is the death of his saints.
> O LORD, I am thy servant;
> I am thy servant, the son of thy handmaid.
> Thou hast loosed my bonds.
> I will offer to thee the sacrifice of thanksgiving
> and call on the name of the LORD.
> I will pay my vows to the LORD
> in the presence of all his people,
> in the courts of the house of the LORD,
> in your midst, O Jerusalem.
> Praise the LORD! (Ps. 116:10-19)[67]

The psalm is concluded with the *gloria patri.* At the time the psalm was read rather than sung, because the city council had not allowed congregational singing. The psalm is set up in stanza form. Perhaps Oecolampadius intended to have it read responsively until such a time as it could be sung in a metrical version.

The selection of this psalm is most appropriate. It is a psalm of covenant thanksgiving which pledges faith in God because of the divine acts of salvation. It was from passages of Scripture such as these that the Reformers developed their appreciation of the theology of covenant and from which they were able to develop a rich sacramental theology. The psalm itself is a prayer of thanksgiving for having received the grace of God, and yet it recognizes the obligation which receiving that grace places on the believer who promises to give witness

67. *Form und gstalt,* fol. A vii r and v (RSV translation).

to God's grace before the whole congregation. The psalm affirms the servant relation into which one has entered because of God's mercy and promises to God a life of service and worship. Those who participated in this baptismal rite could hardly miss the point. The child had received the covenant sign and so was obligated to serve God. The congregation had prayed that the child would be given faith and be freed from the bonds of Satan, and when these prayers would be answered, as surely they would be, then the child would be obligated as a child of the covenant, "the son of thy handmaid," to pledge to God his own faith and lifelong service. These vows would be made in church before the Lord's people.

This psalm perfectly expresses the Reformed understanding of baptism as the sign of God's prevenient grace. The giving of this sign initiates the covenant relationship. It lays upon us the obligation that, when the promises of this sign are fulfilled by the work of God's Spirit in our hearts, we pay God our vows in witnessing before the people of God his faithfulness to us. This we do in our worship and in our life of service. Here we see, as is often the case in the early Reformed liturgies, how the psalmody often carries the deepest insights of the worship.

The minister concludes the service by charging the godparents to bring the child up in the fear of the Lord, and gives them a benediction, "You godparents, bring up the child in the fear of the Lord. The peace of God be with you."[68]

Of the three earliest Reformed baptismal rites, the rite of Basel gives the impression of being the most finished attempt. It is more mature theologically and liturgically better balanced. It is not a dramatizing or ritualizing of Reformed theology, but an attempt to be faithful to the principle that Christian worship should be according to God's Word. It is not an imitation of the worship of the first Christians, but rather an attempt to worship God faithfully in the situation in which the Church found itself at the beginning of the sixteenth century. The theological insights of the earliest Reformed theologians, nevertheless, come through quite clearly.

The baptismal rite of Basel makes one thing clear above all; baptism is in the end a work of God. The minister, as the apostles before him, administers the sign of washing, but it is God who through his Holy Spirit cleanses the heart. One might say that the service underlines the epicletic nature of baptism. Having begun the service with the affirmation that our salvation is in the power of God alone, "Our help is in the power of the Lord," the minister calls the

68. "Ir gevätter ziecht das Kind zu der forcht gottes. Der fryd sey bey eüch." *Form und gstalt,* fol. A vii v.

church to prayer. We are reminded that our part is to pray for the salvation of the child. It is God's part to give the child faith and by the inner baptism of the Holy Spirit to regenerate him. The power to save remains with God, who works when and where and how he pleases. The power is not in our hands. It resides not in the proper performing of liturgical rites. This was one of the essential insights of Reformed theologians. Our part is to administer obediently the sign God has given, to proclaim the rich promises of grace, to call on God to fulfill these promises, and to trust that he will fulfill them. Zwingli and Oecolampadius were quite close in their theology of the sacraments, but somehow when one hears Oecolampadius, one hears more forcefully the affirmation that the sacramental signs are not empty signs. They are signs of divine promises to which God will surely be faithful. If it is true that God's Spirit works when and where and how he pleases, it is equally true that God works where he has promised to work. That was the heart of the theology of the covenant.

Conclusion

Within the year 1525, three churches which stood in the tradition of High Rhenish Christian Humanism produced baptismal rites which they understood to be reformed according to God's Word. Strasbourg led the way, Zurich followed, then Basel. For the Reformers of these cities a simple translation of the Latin baptismal rite was not a sufficient reform. They pressed on to a more thoroughgoing reform of the whole baptismal rite which would order baptism according to Scripture. By this they meant first of all that they wanted to order baptism according to the specific directions of Jesus and the apostles. In this respect the great commission of Jesus, "Make disciples of all nations, baptizing them in the name of the Father and of the Son and of the Holy Spirit, teaching them to observe all things whatsoever I have commanded you," was basic to the ordering of baptism. Not only were the specific directions of Scripture to be used, but the example of the baptisms recorded in Scripture was to be followed. The baptism of Jesus in the Jordan and the baptisms by the apostles recorded in the book of Acts were to be followed as examples of how baptism was to be celebrated.

What these High Rhenish Reformers meant by "according to Scripture" did not stop there. This was true from the outset, and it became increasingly clear to them as they went along. As their controversies with the Anabaptists became more intense, they became increasingly aware that according to Scripture also meant according to biblical principles. Right from the beginning this

South German school of reformers was concerned that their worship be consistent with Christian teaching, with the general principles of God's Word. They were concerned that the worship of the Church witness to the biblical concept of prevenient grace, to the New Testament doctrine of justification by faith, as well as to the principle of Christian love. They were concerned that worship be celebrated with a simplicity consistent with Christian charity, that it be free from all aspects of superstition and magic, that it be understandable and ethically edifying, and that the signs and symbols used be those which God had given to the Church in his Word.

Let us try to formulate how this approach to liturgical reform was worked out in regard to the shaping of these three baptismal rites. The Reformers saw four things as essential to the rite of baptism: the washing, the baptismal invocation, catechetical instruction, and the baptismal vows. All three of the baptismal services put the baptismal washing in high relief. This was the basic biblical sign. The many supplementary rites are removed in order to make the baptismal washing itself clearly the central action of the rite. This washing was done "in the name of the Father and the Son and the Holy Spirit." While they did not understand this in terms of the form and the material of baptism as the Scholastic theologians had, they did understand this to be the central core of the rite, and they continued to celebrate this central core in much the same way it had been done during the Middle Ages.

All three of these early Reformed services give great importance to the baptismal prayers. Each of these services has a Baptismal Invocation. Recalling the text of 1 Peter 3:21, they found an epicletic aspect of baptism, an "appeal to God for a clear conscience." Bucer finds the scriptural ground for this in the story of the apostle Paul's baptism by Ananias, from which he understood that not only was there the washing but also prayer which called upon the name of the Lord. For Zwingli this aspect was more a theological necessity. This theological necessity arose from the nature of the relationship between the outward sign of water and the inward grace of purifying the heart. Here the Reformers made the distinction between a magical understanding of baptism and a sacramental understanding. It is not a matter of washing sins out of the soul in the same way dirt is washed off the body, but rather the appeal to God for a clear conscience (1 Pet. 3:21). Ever since these earliest baptismal rites, Protestantism has put the emphasis of worship not on the proper performance of rites or on the reciting of correct formulas, but rather on the inward working of God's Holy Spirit. This is a basic principle of Reformed worship, and it is clearly illustrated in the Baptismal Invocation of the earliest Reformed baptismal rites.

The third thing which belonged to baptism was catechetical instruction.

This the Reformers drew from the words of Jesus, "teaching them to observe all things whatsoever I have commanded you." In addition to this biblical root of their worship we need once again to call attention to the patristic roots of Reformed worship. The Reformers greatly admired the catechumenate of the patristic era, and they clearly intended to revive it. For the Reformers the vestigial remains of the old catechetical instruction found in the late medieval baptismal rites hardly fulfilled the commission which Jesus gave to the apostles before his Ascension. In the first place they did not realize that the reciting of the Lord's Prayer and the Creed, and the reading of the Gospel story of Jesus blessing the children were remnants of the ancient catechetical instruction which the Reformers so greatly emulated. Even if they had realized it, these ritualized catechetical rites were hardly sufficient for what they had in mind. For them the old tradition of passing on to the godparents this responsibility was likewise quite insufficient. The Reformers had in mind the establishing of genuine catechetical instruction which would follow baptism when the children were of sufficient age to receive such instruction. In other words, the catechetical instruction was postponed.

It was the same way with the baptismal vows. The Reformers understood this to be the fourth essential part of the service of baptism. Those who received baptism must make a profession of faith in Christ. Here again the old settlement of having the confession of faith made for the child by the sponsors was not satisfactory for the Reformers. The godparents have not yet been dispensed with, or at least not entirely. In Basel the godparents still make a confession of faith for the child; nevertheless that does not take the place of the confession of faith which the child will need to make when he reaches sufficient age. The Reformers considered an intelligent confession of faith on the part of those baptized essential. This, too, they postponed until after the child had received catechetical instruction.

What we have in these first attempts to achieve a Reformed baptismal rite is a complete recasting of the rite of baptism which takes into account that it is children who are being baptized and yet also takes very seriously the part played by prayer, teaching, and profession of faith in a true celebration of baptism. The sign of washing was administered to the child in the name of the Father, the Son, and the Holy Spirit. This was accompanied by appropriate prayers. The catechetical instruction and the profession of faith were postponed until later in life. They did not understand this as though the child were only half baptized until such a time as the catechetical instruction was completed and the vows of faith performed. The washing itself was the covenant sign, but that covenant sign entailed the instruction and the profession of faith. The covenant sign entailed far more, of course; it entailed a new life. This new life would be characterized by hearing God's Word, serving God in prayer, turning away from sin, and bearing witness to one's faith before the world. Baptism becomes a sign at the beginning of the Christian life which will be actualized throughout the whole of the Christian life. The sign of washing is only the beginning of a lifelong experience of being washed from our sins and renewed by the Holy Spirit. The Christian is baptized into repentance, unto a new life, and unto the ways of God. The Christian is baptized into the covenant people in order that he may experience the fulfillment of that covenant. Baptism is a prophetic sign standing at the beginning of the Christian life.

There is no doubt that the Reformers of Strasbourg, Zurich, and Basel were becoming aware of the stirring of the earliest proto-Anabaptists toward the end of 1524. By the middle of 1525, they were fully aware that Anabaptist churches were being founded. The influence of these groups, however, was not of primary importance in the shaping of the Reformers' baptismal rite. As we have seen in both Capito's *Was man halten soll* and Bucer's *Grund und Ursach,* the Reformers were aware of the concerns of these people, but they already had their minds on their own program of reform, which they considered more pressing. The Reformers of Zurich became involved in the Anabaptist controversy at an earlier date than those of Strasbourg and Basel. As we have already noticed, the first text which we have for the Reformed baptismal rite of Zurich comes as an appendix to a work which Zwingli wrote as an answer to the Anabaptists. Zwingli tells us that the conversations with the Anabaptists have helped make clear the need for the reform of the baptismal rites, but the actual text of the service which he gives shows no trace of being shaped by the Anabaptist controversy. The Reformers of Zurich had one approach to reform and the Anabaptists another. The appearance of the Anabaptists made it necessary for Zwingli to be quite explicit about his approach to the reform of baptism. For this reason it was indispensable for him to publish a baptismal rite which exemplified his approach as an appendix to his first tract against the Anabaptists. For Zurich, at least, the general direction for the reform of the rite of baptism had been fairly well set as early as the publication of Leo Jud's *Taufbüchlein* in 1523. Shortly after these first services were published in 1525, the Reformers began to give increasing attention to the Anabaptist concern. The controversy forced them to think through the meaning of baptism in relation to two very different fronts. On the one side were the supporters of the traditional Latin rites, and on the other the ideas of the Anabaptists. From this point on the Anabaptist influence and the reaction of the Reformers against the movement will be increasingly reflected in the baptismal rites. Let us turn now to look at the concerns of the growing Anabaptist movement.

CHAPTER IV

The Anabaptist Bid for the Reform of the Baptismal Rite

At the time the Reformers were actually in the position of being able to carry out some of their liturgical reforms, they discovered that there was a growing circle of people who were urging a completely different reform of the rite of baptism. The main thrust of this circle was opposition to the baptism of infants. They believed in baptizing only those who had undergone a profound conversion experience. This circle, which the Reformers would later call the Anabaptists, held that the key to the whole reformation of the Church was their program of baptismal reform. What was at issue was far more than simply a concern to worship God according to Scripture. At issue in this question of believers' baptism was an attempt to found a new church for the spiritually elite. Let us look at a number of the more significant statements of this position. We will want to study a variety of most diverse and fascinating personalities in order to get a well-balanced picture.

The Source of Anabaptism in Saxony and Thuringia

In all probability it is indeed to Andreas Carlstadt, the appearance of the Zwickau Prophets in Wittenberg, and the revolutionary ministry of Thomas Müntzer that we must trace the opposition to infant baptism as it appeared in the sixteenth century.[1] Andreas Carlstadt, who was in charge of the Reforma-

1. At least this is one of the starting points. Karl Holl and Ernst Troeltsch debated whether Anabaptism began with Müntzer or with the Swiss Brethren. Harold Bender and John Yoder

tion of Wittenberg while Luther was being kept in seclusion on the Wartburg, began in Luther's absence to introduce a number of liturgical reforms.[2] In December of 1521, he celebrated communion in German and without vestments. He published shortly thereafter a work against the liturgical use of art, *Von Anbietung der Bilder.*[3] This was followed by an iconoclastic riot. In the meantime, Carlstadt's theology was becoming increasingly subjectivist and spiritualist.

It was at the height of Carlstadt's influence in Wittenberg that the Zwickau Prophets arrived in town and laid before the university theologians their own particular brand of millenarianism and spiritual exegesis. Among the ideas which they laid before the Wittenbergers was their opposition to infant baptism. The ideas of the Zwickau Prophets won the support of some of the theologians of Wittenberg, notably Carlstadt, Martin Cellarius, and Dr. Gerhardt Westerburg. With Luther's return to Wittenberg in March of 1522, the growing revolutionary element was quickly called to a halt. The Zwickau Prophets were repudiated as *Schwärmer* and Carlstadt left Wittenberg for the parish church of Orlamunde, where he continued to develop his ideas, publishing in 1523 his *Vom Priestertum und Opfer Christi.*[4]

Another very original and creative reformer influenced by the Zwickau Prophets was Thomas Müntzer.[5] Müntzer had read extensively in the German

---

took up the position of Troeltsch, insisting on the Swiss origin of Anabaptism, while Hans Hillerbrand supported Holl. Recent research has shown quite convincingly that there were several sources to Anabaptism. For an analysis of this discussion see James M. Stayer, Werner O. Packull, and Klaus Deppermann, "From Monogenesis to Polygenesis: The Historical Discussion of Anabaptist Origins," *The Mennonite Quarterly Review* 49 (1975): 83-121.

2. Ronald J. Sider, "Karlstadt's Orlamünde Theology: A Theology of Regeneration," *The Mennonite Quarterly Review* 45 (1971): 191-218, 352-76. Sider's ideas are further developed in *Andreas Bodenstein von Karlstadt: The Development of His Thought, 1517-1525,* Studies in Medieval and Reformation Thought, vol. 11 (Leiden: E. J. Brill, 1974). The standard biography of Carlstadt has been Hermann Barge's two-volume work *Andreas Bodenstein von Carlstadt* (Leipzig: F. Brandstetter, 1950).

3. *Von abtuhung der Bylder, Und das keyn Betdler unther den Christen seyn soll* (Wittenberg: Nicholas Schirlentz, 1522). A modern edition of this work was edited by Hans Lietzmann (Bonn: Marcus and Weber, 1911). A small collection of the works of Carlstadt was edited by Erich Hertzsch, *Karlstadts Schriften aus den Jahren 1523-25* (Halle: Niemeyer Verlag, 1956-57).

4. Andreas Bodenstein von Carlstadt, *Von dem Priesterthum, und opffer Christi* (Jena: Michael Buchfüher, 1524). Neither a sixteenth-century edition nor a modern edition of this work could be obtained for this study.

5. On Müntzer, see Harold S. Bender, "The Zwickau Prophets, Thomas Müntzer, and the Anabaptists," *The Mennonite Quarterly Review* 27 (1953): 3-16; Otto H. Brandt, *Thomas Müntzer, sein Leben und seine Schriften* (Jena: W. Diederichs, 1933); Norman Cohn, *The Pursuit of the Millennium,* rev. and exp. edn. (New York: Oxford University Press, 1970),

mystics, and in Joachite millenarianism.[6] As pastor of a proletarian parish in Zwickau, he developed a concern for social reform. Müntzer's social reforms have commended him to many advanced thinkers of our own day, and in certain circles this has led to a careful and sympathetic study of Müntzer. Moving to Allstedt in 1522, Müntzer began to institute a number of ingenious liturgical reforms. His *Das deutsche Kirchenamt* (1523) and his *Deutsche evangelische Messe* (1524) were attempts at a celebration of the Mass in the vernacular with a strong emphasis on the doctrine of the priesthood of all believers.[7] These two documents show Müntzer's tremendous originality, foreshadowing much which today is thought of as being very modern. It appears that during his pastorate he discouraged the baptism of infants; however, there is no indication that he proposed the rebaptism of adults. Müntzer was in fact far more occupied in millenarian speculations than in liturgical reform. He became increasingly involved in what finally developed into the Peasants' War. His "Sermon before the Princes" gives us a good look into his theology of revolution. Müntzer's eschatology was closely related to his theology of baptism. What happened in the social revolution was for Müntzer an exact parallel to the crisis of the conversion experience. It is the same dramatic reversal, whether on the objective plane of history or in the subjective experience of the soul. Premillenarianism and Anabaptism are logical twins.

For our concerns, the most important of Müntzer's works is his *Protestation oder Entbietung Thomas Müntzer's . . . seine lehre betreffend und zum Anfang von dem rechten Christenglauben und der Taufe.*[8] The work is an attack on fictitious faith and misunderstood baptism. Toward the end of the work he tells us that his purpose was to give a summary statement of the ruin that has befallen the Church through misunderstood baptism and fictitious faith.

Let us begin with a look at what Müntzer means by fictitious faith. The

---

pp. 233-51; Eric W. Gritsch, *Reformer without a Church: The Life and Thought of Thomas Muentzer, 1488?-1525* (Philadelphia: Fortress Press, 1967); Karl Holl, "Luther und die Schwärmer," *Gesammelte Aufsätze zu Kirchengeschichte* 1, fourth and fifth edn. (Tübingen: J. C. B. Mohr, 1927), pp. 420-67; Reinhard Schwarz, *Die apokalyptische Theologie Thomas Müntzers und der Taboriten* (Tübingen: J. C. B. Mohr, 1977); Wilhelm Wisswedel, "The Inner and Outer Word: A Study in the Anabaptist Doctrine of Scripture," *The Mennonite Quarterly Review* 26 (1952): 171-91.

6. M. M. Smirin, *Die Volksreformation des Thomas Münzer und der grosse Baurenkreig* (Berlin: Dietz, 1952), pp. 87-184.

7. Karl Schulz, "Thomas Müntzers liturgische Bestrebungen," *Zeitschrift für Kirchengeschichte* 47 (1928): 369-401.

8. Brandt, ed., *Thomas Müntzer, sein Leben und seine Schriften,* pp. 133-44. To be referred to as Brandt, *Thomas Müntzer.* Also in Müntzer's *Schriften und Briefe. Kritische Gesamtausgabe,* eds. Paul Kirn and Gunter Fraz (Gütersloh: Gerd Mohn, 1968), pp. 225-40.

German, *gedichtiten glauben*, might also be translated "artificial faith." Müntzer tells us that it is the sort of faith preached by scholars who have nothing but book learning. It is the sort of inherited faith that children of Christian parents are born into and so easily grow up taking for granted and never doubting. This kind of faith, Müntzer claims, does not have its source in the heart. The scholars claim that man is justified by this kind of faith, but to say that we are justified by faith rather than works is much too easy. One must follow the footsteps of Christ and bear His cross through a life of trials and sufferings. Only by experiencing the suffering of Christ, according to Müntzer, can one be saved. The hypocrites, he tells us, follow the sweet Christ, but the true Christian must follow the bitter Christ. It is not enough that Christ should suffer for us; we must suffer with him. As we read these words of Thomas Müntzer, we cannot help but come to the conclusion that Müntzer's attack on fictitious faith is an attack on the Reformation as it was preached at Wittenberg.

In chapters 5, 6, and 7, Müntzer focuses on the question of baptism. The problems of the Church begin with the appearance of infant baptism and the disappearance of the discipline of the catechumenate. In the early days of the Church, Müntzer tells us, only grown people, after a long period of instruction, were baptized; but now baptism is totally misunderstood. One regards more the holy sign than the inner essence. All the doctors of the Church have completely missed the point of baptism. Nowhere in the Bible do we read that a single child was baptized by Christ or the apostles. Nor for that matter do we find any evidence that Mary, the Mother of God, or the disciples of Christ were ever baptized with water. Presumably, Müntzer has in mind that it was an inner experience or baptism of suffering and martyrdom which the Virgin and the apostles received. If artificial faith was the malady of Wittenberg, according to Müntzer, then misunderstood baptism was the fatal illness of Catholic orthodoxy.

In chapter 6 Müntzer gives us an exposition of the true meaning of baptism. Because no one has truly understood baptism, this entrance or initiation into Christianity has become a clumsy monkey business. The scholars have always quoted John 3:5, "Whoever is not baptized in water and the Holy Spirit will not enter the kingdom of God." This is true, although the scholars have not explained it properly. Müntzer sees in the text an expression of his unique understanding of inner and outer baptism, outer baptism being baptism by water and inner baptism by the Spirit. In a boldly imaginative fashion he draws on the various references to water in the first seven chapters of the Gospel of John in order to develop his thoughts on baptism. The references are not always precise, and so it is only with hesitation that one reports his ideas. Inner baptism is explained by the text of John 7:37, "If any man thirsts, let him come to me and drink. He who believes in me, as it is said in the Scriptures, streams of water shall flow from his body, which is living water. This he said of the Holy Spirit, which the believers would receive in the future."[9] It is clear to Müntzer that water means moving of our spirits in the Spirit of God. Inner baptism is when the Holy Spirit performs within us the ministry of John the Baptist, "Prepare the way of the Lord."[10] It starts one moving in the way of the Cross, the *imitatio Christi.*[11] In the second chapter of John we read the story of turning water into wine, which Müntzer tells us means the movements of our spirits toward a desire to suffer. In the third chapter we read that John baptized where there was much water, that is, where there is so much movement that one hears the voice of the bridegroom and is able to lay hold of it. Presumably what Müntzer means is that there is so much spiritual turmoil that one comes to a crisis experience and there finds Christ. It is important to see here that this crisis experience within the soul is the natural counterpart of the premillenarian revolution which accompanies the return of Christ. The crisis experience is the soul's Armageddon.

In the fourth chapter of John, Müntzer learns that the true water springs up from the source of life. In the fifth chapter of John, Müntzer finds another reference to the movement of the water in the story of the healing of the man at the Pool of Bethesda.[12] Presumably, what is meant here is that the movement of the waters stands for the spiritual *anfechtung* or the trials of life. The suffering of these trials is the source of spiritual healing. Just as the angel was sent from God to move the waters which would heal the lame man, so God

9. "So jemand dürtet, der komme zu mir und trinke. Wer da glaubt an mich, wie die Schrift sagt, die Wasserstrome werden fliessen von seinem Leibe, die lebendigen Wasser. Das sagete er vom heiligen Geiste, den die Gläubigen zukünftig werden empfangen." Brandt, *Thomas Müntzer,* p. 135.

10. If I am correct here, Brandt and G. H. Williams have misunderstood the text.

11. Hans-Jürgen Goertz has very carefully shown the relation of the initiation of the salvation process through the Holy Spirit and the relation of this to Müntzer's understanding of baptism. *Innere und äussere Ordnung in der Theologie Thomas Müntzers* (Leiden: E. J. Brill, 1967), pp. 107-14. To be referred to as Goertz, *Innere und äussere Ordnung.* Compare this to Gabriel Biel in Heiko A. Oberman's *The Harvest of Medieval Theology. Gabriel Biel and Late Medieval Nominalism* (Cambridge, Mass.: Harvard University Press, 1963), pp. 175-78 and 224-35.

12. "Siehst du, lieber Geselle, dass sich der Evangelist selbst auslegt und redet von den Wassern, wie die Propheten tun, denn die Wasser sind Bewegung unsers Geistes in dem Gottes, wie Johannes sich durch Jesajam erklaret im ersten Kapitel. Aber im andern Kapitel werden solche unsere Wasser zu wein. Unsere Bewegungen werden lustig zu leiden. Im dritten tauft Johannes, wo viel wasser sind, viel Bewegung. . . ." Brandt, *Thomas Müntzer,* p. 135.

sends to his people spiritual trials that they might be saved. In the sixth chapter of John, Müntzer points to the story of Christ walking on the stormy waters. Here, says Müntzer, is the Christ we follow, going through the misery and suffering of life. Nicodemus was moved through the sign of water to come to Christ. That is why Christ referred him to the water. The sign of Jonah is the same thing. For the contemporary New Testament scholar, Müntzer's interpretation of the Gospel of John is fanciful and individualistic. It is a good example of illuministic exegesis. It is much more closely related to a highly subjective sort of mystical poetry than an attempt to understand what the author of the Gospel of John is really saying; nevertheless, by means of this illuministic exegesis of the Gospel of John, Müntzer makes abundantly clear to us what he means by real baptism. Real baptism is the imitation of Christ. It is through such a baptism that the Christian arrives at salvation. It is only by this lifelong union with the suffering Christ that anyone is initiated into the Kingdom of God. One immediately recognizes the influence not only of Thomas à Kempis, but also of Meister Eckhart and John Tauler.

In chapter 7 of his work, Müntzer returns to the theme of the degradation of baptism. Of all the heathen ceremonies and gestures which have sprung up in the Church, it is the baptism of infants which has been the most harmful. It is because children have been baptized before reaching the age of accountability, and because the catechumenate has been discontinued, that all Christians have become children. With the institution of godparents, true baptism faded.[13] It was then that the Roman Church became disunited with the other churches, insisting that her gestures and ceremonies were better than those of any other church. These ceremonies she gathered from paganism. All of this mockery has as its basic source the baptism of those who have no understanding.

For both the Wittenberg and the Rhenish Reformers it was primarily the disappearance of biblical preaching and the turning of the Lord's Supper into a sacrifice which needed liturgical reform. For the classical Reformers, whether in Wittenberg, Zurich, or Strasbourg, the reformation of the rite of baptism was not a cardinal concern. With Müntzer we find a full-scale demand for the reform of the baptismal rite. It is not just a matter of translating the rite into the common language, recasting the prayers, or eliminating extraneous ceremonies. This radical recasting of baptism calls for several distinct reforms. First,

13. "Hier ist der Ursprung wider alle Auserwählten also ganz verführerish entsprossen mit allen andern heidnischen Zeremonien oder Gebarden des ganzen Greuels in der heiligen Stätt. Da man unmündige Kinder zu Christen machte und liess die Catechumenos abgehen, wurden die Christen auch Kinder. . . ." Brandt, *Thomas Müntzer,* p. 136.

there is the restoration of the catechumenate, a reform in which almost anyone influenced by Christian Humanism was interested. Second, there was the demand to discontinue the institution of baptismal sponsors which was under attack from several quarters, even among the Reformers of classical Protestantism.[14] Third, and most significantly, Müntzer attacks the baptism of children. As yet there is no suggestion that those baptized as children must be rebaptized as adults. In this work of Müntzer's we have one of the first published demands for a radical reform of the rite of baptism.

Above all we should notice this fact: this call for the radical reform of the rite of baptism is found in a work which looks for the reform of the Church not in the direction of justification by faith, nor in a rediscovery of the authority of Scripture, nor in a renewed appreciation of the sovereignty of grace, but rather in a book which sees the reform of the Church in terms of medieval German mysticism.[15] For Müntzer, salvation is not through faith but through the imitation of Christ.[16] Müntzer has taken the *imitatio Christi* much further than Thomas à Kempis, John Tauler, or any other of the German mystics; but, nevertheless, it is from this theological standpoint that Müntzer makes his call for a reform of the rite of baptism. Müntzer, as the Anabaptists who follow him, is attacking the Reformers' Augustinian soteriology as much as their practice of baptism. In Müntzer's distinction between the inner word and the outer word, he moves from the authority of Scripture understood by the disciplines of history and grammar to a very subjective mystical illuminism. Müntzer is not a radical Protestant. His call for the reform of baptism is not a radical application of the basic principles of Protestantism, nor is he to be explained as one who simply applied the basic principles of Protestantism more consistently than the classical Protestant Reformers. Thomas Müntzer was indeed an amazingly creative thinker, but he is not to be numbered among the Reformers of classical Protestantism. He was the prophet of an entirely different approach to church reform. It was his combination of radical social revolution, ecstatic personal religious experience, illuministic exegesis, and Joachite millenarianism which was the furnace of religious power which ignited kindred spirits from all over Europe and from which eventually came a unique type of Christianity.

14. In the Middle Ages, it was from the faith of the sponsors that infant baptism was defended. Gratian's *Decretals, MPL* 187, pp. 1845-46; Lombard's *Sentences, MPL* 192, pp. 854-55; Thomas Aquinas, *Summa Theologica* 3.68.8-9.

15. Hans Hillerbrand, "The Origin of Sixteenth-Century Anabaptism: Another Look," *Archiv für Reformationsgeschichte* 53 (1962): 152-80; Walter Klassen, *Anabaptism: Neither Catholic nor Protestant* (Waterloo, Ont.: Conrad Press, 1973).

16. Goertz, *Innere und äussere Ordnung,* pp. 121-32.

Sources of Anabaptism in Strasbourg

In Strasbourg we find a similar combination of ideas espoused by a group of lay preachers as early as the summer of 1522. Karsthans Maurer, a strong supporter of the *Bundeschuh*, began to oppose the clergy, the civil authority, and the sacraments. Hans Wolf, a lay preacher from Benfeld, was another prophet of social justice; he predicted the return of Christ for the year 1533. He was particularly irritated by the professional clergy, regardless of how they felt toward the Reformation. To him the sacraments were mere externalities, and he, too, was strongly opposed to infant baptism, which he regarded as imposing "on little children an engagement of which they were not capable."[17] What is interesting here is the appearance of a resentment against institutional religion. We will find this strand appearing again and again in Strasbourg.

Clement Ziegler, another lay preacher, began about the same time to oppose the Mass, the use of images, and infant baptism. He was strongly millenarian and, although a pacifist, he was deeply committed to the cause of the peasants. Ziegler was a member of the gardeners' guild. This guild was the most proletarian of the guilds and had a strong pietistic bent. Part of the guild's activities included regular Bible study. The guild had a special connection with St. Aurelia's Church, whose pastor beginning in 1523 was none other than Martin Bucer. We can concentrate our attention on Ziegler because he has left us a significant writing stating his opinions: *Von der wahren Geniessung beider Leibs und Bluts Christi und von der Taufe.*[18]

Clement Ziegler's treatise was written sometime between April and August of 1524. It comes several months after the principal writings of Thomas Müntzer and yet shortly before the earliest writings of the Swiss proto-Anabaptists. Carlstadt had not yet visited Strasbourg; however, his ideas had surely reached the city by this time. The Reformers of Strasbourg had already begun to baptize in the German language, but still the rite they used was a translation of the old rite of the medieval diocese of Strasbourg. The Reformers of Strasbourg had not decided on the question of infant baptism. Capito had not yet published *Wass man*

17. *Quellen zur Geschichte der Täufer,* vol. 7, *Elsass, 1. Teil, Stadt Strassburg, 1522-1532,* eds. Manfred Krebs and Hans Georg Rott (Gütersloh: Gerd Mohn, 1959), p. 53. See also George H. Williams, *The Radical Reformation* (Philadelphia: The Westminster Press, 1962), p. 248. The *Quellen zur Geschichte der Täufer* will be abbreviated as *QGT* 7, while Williams's study will be cited as *The Radical Reformation.*

18. The original title reads, *Von der waren nyessung beid leibs und bults Christi . . . und von dem tauff, wie man den sonder allen zusatz öl, saltz oder beschwerung handeln sol, durch Clement Zyegler, gartner zu Straszburg* (Strasbourg: J. Schott, 1524). On Ziegler, see *QGT* 7, pp. 8-18 (nos. 6-8), and pp. 30-36 (no. 24).

halten soll, nor had Bucer published *Grund und Ursach.* At the time of Ziegler's writing, the question of infant baptism could conceivably have gone in either direction. The Reformers had not taken a firm stand on the matter. The work was also written before there had been any rebaptisms or the formal establishment of an Anabaptist Church.

Let us look at what Ziegler says in his work about baptism. When he gets down to the question of baptism, he begins by opposing the excessive liturgical forms with which baptism was celebrated.[19] John the Baptist used neither salt, nor bread, nor oil, nor chrism when he baptized Jesus. He only baptized in the name of Jesus, and this only in water. This baptism in itself is not really necessary; it is only an outer sign and indication of the true baptism of Jesus, without which no man can be saved. Baptism is only an outward sign, but that sign, Ziegler tells us, has been turned into a secondhand junk store of outer forms.[20] In words reminiscent of Thomas Müntzer, Ziegler tells us that these forms are nothing but human regulations, and they are carried on without our understanding or without our being instructed in their meaning.[21] On the other hand, Christ taught, "Go into all the world and preach the Gospel to all creatures," and again, "Whoever believes and is baptized will be saved." Baptism should, therefore, come only after believing. Ziegler goes on to say that the church of his day did not respect this order. Those who were baptized were not even old enough to speak. We do not find this in Scripture, Ziegler tells us. In fact, it is quite contrary to Scripture. For Christ says that we should first believe and then be baptized.[22]

Ziegler goes on to look at Philip's baptism of the Ethiopian and points to the fact that neither exorcised bread or salt was used in the baptism; nor, for that matter, did Philip use any kind of chrism, which Ziegler disparagingly calls "Schmalz." Deuteronomy 4:2 is cited to show that nothing is to be added to the law of God as delivered. This aspect of Ziegler's polemic may well have been learned from Bucer, who, it will be remembered, was Ziegler's parish priest. In regard to the supplementary rites, particularly the rite of giving exorcised salt and the rites of anointing, we find the same line of thought in Bucer's *Grund und Ursach,* published only a few months later in December of 1524. Ziegler comes out strongly against the rite of the consecration of the font. In fact, he even opposes the use of the font itself.[23] The use of godparents

19. *QGT* 7, pp. 12-13.

20. According to the editors, *QGT* 7, p. 18, this remark shows the influence of Jacob Strauss of Eisenbach.

21. *QGT* 7, p. 13.

22. *QGT* 7, p. 14.

23. *QGT* 7, pp. 16-17.

he condemns on the ground that oaths are unlawful.[24] The whole ceremony, with all its incantations and charms, he ridicules as merely mumbo jumbo.[25]

Ziegler goes on to charge that these additions are due to the commercial interests of the clergy. Next Ziegler attacks the exorcisms used in baptism. He makes use of 1 Timothy 4:1 and Matthew 24:22, and in another place Genesis 1:27, which says that God blessed man at the time of his creation.[26] Bucer, in the *Grund und Ursach,* does not specifically criticize the exorcisms. As the controversy develops, Bucer will give a very different argument for discontinuing the exorcisms. Ziegler complains that the new preachers are no better than the old. They may have translated baptism into German, but they still use the exorcisms and the baptismal anointings. Ziegler's work was indeed written in that brief period of about a year when the Strasbourg Reformers were using the German Mass and a baptismal form which was a simple German translation of the Latin baptismal rite. What is of particular interest at this point is that Ziegler is highly critical of the Reformers of Strasbourg because of the slowness with which they have made their reform. The Reformers had insisted, with reference to Romans 14 and 1 Corinthians 8, that they must have regard for the weaker brethren. Ziegler finds this intolerable. If these liturgical abuses are contrary to the Word of God, then they must be discontinued regardless of the weaker brethren.[27]

Ziegler now turns to asking how baptism is to be administered. In the first place, God must baptize with his Spirit and fire, just as we find in the prayer, "Come, Holy Spirit, and fill the hearts of Thy faithful ones; send on them the fire of Thy love. . . ." Where such a baptism takes place, one comes into the knowledge of Christ and the faith of the Holy Gospels.[28] From this, then, one comes into the fire of love and in such a passionate desire that one then desires the sign of outer baptism as a witness to one's faith in Christ. That the inner baptism must come before the outer baptism is essential to the position of Ziegler. When one has been baptized by God in such a manner, then the outer sign of baptism in water has the meaning of the fulfillment of faith. One can then suffer in the name of Christ. Like Müntzer, Ziegler insists that baptizing those who have not had this conversion experience is the root of all the other abuses in the Church.[29]

24. *QGT* 7, p. 17. See also *QGT* 7, pp. 6-7 (no. 4). The Reformers of Strasbourg were divided on the matter of godparents for some time. They would eventually discontinue the usage but for other reasons.

25. *QGT* 7, p. 16.

26. *QGT* 7, p. 17.

27. *QGT* 7, p. 15.

28. *QGT* 7, p. 15.

29. *QGT* 7, p. 16.

It is not yet clear whether Ziegler arrived at his position independently or whether he got his ideas from Müntzer or someone else. Contemporary research has not given too much attention to the sources of Ziegler's thought. He seems to have come to his ideas about the same time as the Zurich circle of proto-Anabaptists, but he does not seem to have gotten his ideas from Zurich. What we find in Ziegler's work is the same core of ideas about baptism which we found in Müntzer and which we will find in the Anabaptists who follow.[30] The emphasis is on inner baptism, which appears as a conversion experience. Outer baptism must follow this as a witness to the inner baptism. The ideas are not elaborated with anything like the clarity of Müntzer, Hübmaier, or Denck. In fact, it might be hard to understand these ideas of Ziegler's without the writings of Müntzer and the others. That his contemporaries understood him is probably due to the fact that much of the popular religious thought of the day had been largely influenced by the various strands of the Christian life and thought of the late Middle Ages. The German mystics, the nominalist theologians, and the Joachite millennial preachers had all made their mark on the folk religion of the early sixteenth century. At least for the present, Ziegler serves us best as an example of the sort of popular base on which Anabaptism was built.

Sources of Anabaptism in Zurich

In Zurich, too, there was a circle of proto-Anabaptists. As in Wittenberg and Strasbourg, the circle was made up of those who were impatient with the slowness and caution of those who were leading the Reformation. At the Second Zurich Disputation in October of 1523, Zwingli antagonized several of his followers because of his refusal to institute reforms until he had won the support of the city council. Zwingli was determined to work within the *de facto* structures of the Swiss Church. He wanted a constitutional reform of the whole Swiss Church. Conrad Grebel, Felix Mantz, Balthasar Hübmaier, and Louis Haetzer, who up to this time had supported Zwingli, saw no value in this. They wanted to move out and form a new church made up of those who were fully committed Christians. For these men the Second Zurich Disputation

30. Stayer et al., "From Monogenesis to Polygenesis," pp. 84-85, briefly mention Ziegler as an independent beginning of Anabaptism in Strasbourg, They are not too clear what is meant by this except that however close the attitudes of the Swiss circle of proto-Anabaptists may have been to each other, they cannot be shown to be dependent on each other. See also Hillerbrand, "The Origin of Sixteenth Century Anabaptism," pp. 177-78 (n. 123).

was a great disappointment. To them it made clear that Zwingli was compromising with the world. Several private attempts were made by the leaders of this circle to win over Zwingli. Sometime during the following year, 1524, those who had become dissatisfied with Zwingli began to hold services of worship in their homes. At first they were not much more than Bible studies or prayer meetings, but eventually they began to celebrate the Lord's Supper at these evening meetings. In the meantime, one of the most revolutionary young priests in Switzerland, William Reublin at Zollikon, a few miles up the lakeshore from Zurich, began to preach against infant baptism. In the spring of 1524, several members of his parish decided not to present their children for baptism. By this time the antipaedobaptism of the Zurich circle had become quite explicit. A good statement of the position of this circle is found in a letter written by Conrad Grebel to Thomas Müntzer a few months later, in September of 1524. Let us take a careful look at this letter.[31]

The letter begins by saluting Thomas Müntzer as the sincere and true herald of the gospel, and then, mentioning the two works of Müntzer's which the Zurich circle had read, *Von dem gedichteten Glauben* and *Protestation,* it confirms Müntzer's rejection of the evangelical preachers.

> Every man wants to be saved by superficial faith, without fruits of faith, without baptism of trial and probation, without love and hope, without right Christian practices, and wants to persist in all the old manner of personal vices, and in the common ritualistic and anti-Christian customs of baptism and of the Lord's Supper, in disrespect for the divine Word and in respect for the word of the anti-papal preachers, which yet is not equal to the divine Word nor in harmony with it.[32]

Like Müntzer, Grebel and his circle were at odds with the classical Protestant Reformers in regard to the doctrine of justification by faith. According to Grebel, the "superficial" or "artificial" faith preached by Zwingli and his colleagues is just as misleading as that preached by Luther. Grebel tells how for a long time he and his circle were misled by Zurich's evangelical preachers, but finally they took the Scriptures in hand, and, being instructed by the Scriptures, decided that the evangelical preachers had led them astray.

31. *Quellen zur Geschichte der Täufer in der Schweiz,* vol. 1, *Zürich,* eds. Leonhard von Muralt and Walter Schmid (Zurich: Theologischer Verlag, 1952), pp. 13-21 (no. 14). This volume will be abbreviated *QGT* 1. The English translation of the letter is available in *Spiritual and Anabaptist Writers,* ed. George H. Williams, The Library of Christian Classics, vol. 25 (Philadelphia: The Westminster Press, 1957), pp. 73-85. This translation will be cited as *LCC* 25.

32. *LCC* 25, p. 74; *QGT* 1, pp. 13-14.

Grebel complains about the patience of the Reformers. Their forebearance with the slower brethren is the root of the whole problem, a criticism we have already found in Clement Ziegler. "The cause of all this is false forebearance, the hiding of the divine Word and the mixing of it with the human. Aye, we say it harms all and frustrates all things divine."[33] As they were lamenting over the shortcomings of the evangelical preachers, Müntzer's book against false faith and baptism arrived and they were more fully informed.[34] Grebel then turns to exhorting Müntzer to preach only the divine Word, to set up only divine institutions, "to esteem as good and right only what may be found in pure and clear Scripture, to reject, hate and curse all devices, words, customs and opinions of men, including thy own."[35] With this, Grebel begins to set Müntzer straight on a few matters. First, he criticizes Müntzer on the use of church music. Singing in worship is not commanded in Scripture; therefore, it is forbidden. "Whatever we are not taught by clear passage or examples must be regarded as forbidden, just as if it were written: 'This do not; sing not.' "[36]

Next, Grebel begins to admonish Müntzer on the proper way to celebrate the Lord's Supper.[37] According to Grebel, the priesthood of all believers should be one of the major features of the service. Müntzer, who was a former priest, should not preside but rather someone from out of the congregation. Only those who are really brethren should participate. Backsliders are to be ignored and heed should not be taken of the slower brethren.[38] The Lord's Supper, as baptism, is for the spiritually mature. A few more words on the importance of church discipline, and Grebel returns to expressing his approval of Müntzer

33. *LCC* 25, pp. 74-75; *QGT* 1, p. 14.

34. Surely these lines make clear the extent to which the circle of Conrad Grebel was influenced by Thomas Müntzer. Grebel's letter shows that while his group was deploring the problems of the Church, they read the works of Müntzer and were more fully instructed on false faith and baptism. This should make it clear that what Müntzer taught Grebel and his friends was the error of Luther's doctrine of justification by faith and the mistake of baptizing children. Up to this point they were not proto-Anabaptists even if they were disillusioned with Zwingli. *LCC* 25, p. 75; *QGT* 1, p. 14.

35. *LCC* 25, p. 75; *QGT* 1, p. 14.

36. *LCC* 25, p. 75; *QGT* 1, p. 15.

37. Müntzer's German Mass was precisely that, a German translation of the Mass with most of the canon left out. Compared to other German Masses of the period, it was about what one would expect. Grebel would have been no more pleased with it than he was with the German translations of the baptismal rite by Luther, Jud, Osiander, and the Strasbourg Reformers. For the text of Müntzer's German Mass, see Julius Smend, *Die evangelischen deutschen Messen bis zu Luthers Deutscher Messe* (Göttingen: Vandenhoeck und Ruprecht, 1896), pp. 99-105.

38. *LCC* 25, p. 77; *QGT* 1, p. 16.

and his confidence that Müntzer will set all these things in order. Grebel also has kind words for Andreas Carlstadt and Jacob Strauss, whose writings have also been appreciated by the Zurich proto-Anabaptists.[39] Grebel regrets that Strauss and Carlstadt are not heard or heeded by the slothful scholars of Wittenberg or the pastors of Zurich. Everyone follows the evangelical preachers because they preach a sweet Christ rather than the bitter Christ. One of the things that Grebel shares with Müntzer is his emphasis on the bitter Christ.[40]

After treating briefly the problem of tithes and benefices, Grebel makes a statement of his stand for pacifism which closely connects it to baptism. "True Christian believers are sheep among wolves, sheep for the slaughter; they must be baptized in anguish and affliction, tribulation, persecution, suffering and death."[41] Here baptism is clearly a sign of the *imitatio Christi* for Grebel just as it is in Müntzer. Here we do see an important distinction between Grebel and Thomas Müntzer. Grebel, perhaps influenced by Zwingli, had gone much further in the direction of pacifism.

Grebel's letter finally comes to the matter of baptism. "On the matter of baptism, thy book pleases us well."[42] With this Grebel launches into his understanding of baptism.

> The Scripture describes for us thus, that it signifies that, by faith and the blood of Christ, sins have been washed away for him who is baptized, changes his mind, and believes before and after; that it signifies that a man is dead and ought to be dead to sin and walks in newness of life and spirit, and that he shall certainly be saved if, according to this meaning, by inner baptism he lives his faith. . . .[43]

For Grebel, baptism signifies. He tells us that baptism neither confirms nor increases faith, as the scholars of Wittenberg claimed, nor does it save, as the traditional church teaching claimed. One notices that for Grebel, the sacrament is far from being the Word of God made visible as it was for Augustine, and as the South German Reformers were coming more and more to understand

39. In a letter to Vadian as early as July 15, 1523, Grebel mentions having received "the most evangelical articles" of Jacob Strauss, *QGT* 1, p. 2. In a letter of October 14, 1524, Grebel wrote to Vadian about Carlstadt, *QGT* 1, pp. 21-23. Once again, we are not convinced by Bender and Yoder that the Saxon radicals had only a minimal influence on Grebel and the Swiss Anabaptists.

40. The theme of the sweet Christ and the bitter Christ was popular in late medieval German mysticism. See *The Theologia Germanica of Martin Luther*, ed. Hoffman (New York: Paulist Press, 1980), p. 82 (no. 16) and p. 84 (no. 18).

41. *LCC* 25, p. 80; *QGT* 1, p. 17.

42. *LCC* 25, p. 80; *QGT* 1, p. 17.

43. *LCC* 25, p. 80; *QGT* 1, pp. 17-18.

it. One notices that it is not a sign of what God will do in the life of the baptized, as Zwingli had understood it, but rather it is a sign of what the baptized has done already and will do in the future. It would appear that for Grebel baptism is not so much an act of God as an act of the one baptized. It is his or her confession of faith. Once he or she has decided this, Grebel's conclusions are, to be sure, quite understandable.

As short as this document is, it provides us with a clear picture of the basic concerns of the Zurich Anabaptists, Several things are clear. First, Grebel's circle did know Müntzer's work on baptism as they knew the works of Andreas Carlstadt and Jacob Strauss. It would seem rather hard to deny the influence of Müntzer and Carlstadt. One sees clearly that there are differences between the Zurich circle of proto-Anabaptists and the North German pioneers of the movement, but the letter tacitly admits the dependence of Grebel and his friends on Müntzer and Carlstadt. Grebel tells us that he and his friends were unhappy with the Reformers of Zurich before they read Müntzer, but Grebel clearly tells Müntzer his writings more fully informed them.

To be sure, one notices differences between the Zurich group and the North German group. Particularly noticeable in Grebel's work is an absence of millennialist and revolutionary social concerns. Another noticeable feature of Grebel's letter is the number of things Grebel specifically disapproves of in Müntzer's reform. Müntzer is at the time involved in what some have called the "magisterial reform."[44] He still uses a "liturgy." All this heightens the importance of their agreement on the subject of baptism. For the circle of Conrad Grebel, as for Müntzer, believer's baptism was the one key to the reform of the Church. If only those who gave evidence of a firm and mature faith were baptized, then the Church would be free from all kinds of impurities. Believer's baptism would be the effective sword used to separate the true Christian from Christendom. Believer's baptism was the cornerstone of this movement, because as Norman Cohn puts it, "The practice of rebaptism . . . was above all a means of expressing symbolically this voluntary separation from the unredeemed world."[45]

To the theologian, it is clear that there are wide divergences between the baptismal theologies implied by Grebel and Müntzer. Müntzer tends toward a spiritualist rejection of the outer sacrament of baptism by water. He points to the fact that neither the Virgin nor the apostles are recorded to have been baptized. Müntzer does not draw any conclusions from this, but Grebel picks this up in the postscript to his letter: "As for thy tracts and protestations I find thee without guilt, unless thou dost reject baptism entirely, which I do not

44. *LCC* 25, p. 75; *QGT* 1, p. 14.
45. Cohn, *The Pursuit of the Millennium*, p. 254.

gather from them."[46] Since Grebel was not a trained theologian, he might have had a hard time distinguishing between a sacramentarian and a spiritualist. Müntzer still speaks of baptism as initiation, a traditional concept which the Grebel circle had implicitly denied in insisting that one must have faith before baptism. But here the difference is an implication. It is not at all explicit on the level at which Grebel and Müntzer are treating the subject. To be sure, for the theologian, the influence of Zwingli on the one side is easily distinguished from the incipient spiritualism on the side of Müntzer. This the theologian cannot overlook; however, Grebel did overlook these differences. There was something so much more important by which Grebel felt himself at one with Müntzer that he did not notice some important theological distinctions. What was the root of the basic camaraderie?

First, it was the opposition to the practice of infant baptism. It was the practice itself rather than the theology of baptism which bothered the anti-paedobaptists. At least at this point they were more concerned with what they opposed than what they wanted to affirm. Müntzer does not affirm believer's baptism as clearly as Grebel affirms it, but that is evidently not as important to Grebel as the fact that Müntzer opposes infant baptism. Second, both Grebel and Müntzer attack the evangelical ministers' doctrine of justification by faith, and their opposition is quite evidently from the standpoint of an *imitatio Christi* soteriology. They both understand baptism as a sign of salvation by the imitation of Christ. While it may be true that the Saxons tend toward spiritualism and that Grebel has been influenced by Zwingli's sacramentarianism, it is also true that they both have common roots in the *imitatio Christi* mysticism of the Middle Ages. This is the most important thing to be noticed in a comparison between Grebel and Müntzer: in both there is a rejection of the doctrine of justification by faith and an acceptance of an *imitatio Christi* soteriology strongly influenced by medieval mysticism. Müntzer and Grebel were both heirs of Thomas à Kempis and William of Occam.

In December there were a number of private conferences between Grebel and his friends and the evangelical pastors of Zurich. In the middle of January 1523, a more formal discussion was held, the so-called First Baptismal Disputation. By this time it was clear to the evangelical pastors of Zurich that the question of baptism was the central concern of Grebel's circle.[47] At the end of the second session on January 17, Zwingli let it be known that he felt the matter had been discussed sufficiently. Unfortunately, Zwingli dismissed Grebel and his friends as troublemakers and from this point on had little interest

46. *LCC* 25, p. 83; *QGT* 1, p. 20.
47. See Felix Mantz's *Protestation und Shutzschrift,* in *QGT* 1, pp. 23-28 (no. 16).

in considering their ideas. On January 21, the city council took measures to disband the conventicles of separatists which were now calling themselves Brethren in Christ. That evening at a meeting in the home of Felix Mantz, Blaurock asked Grebel to baptize him. This action changed antipaedobaptism into Anabaptism. It founded the first Anabaptist church. For the next few days this first Anabaptist congregation carried on a brisk evangelization campaign. Working in Zollikon just outside Zurich, Grebel, Mantz, and Blaurock rebaptized some thirty-five converts. Interestingly enough, these baptisms were by pouring rather than immersion. In spite of the efforts to stop the growth of the newly founded Anabaptist church, the Zurich Brethren in Christ went throughout Switzerland to gather the true Christians into their new church. Mantz and Blaurock went to Graubunden, Grebel to Schafthausen and then to St. Gallen, and Reublin to Waldshut, where Balthasar Hübmaier was pastor.

Balthasar Hübmaier

Balthasar Hübmaier was one of those who were disappointed at the slowness of Zwingli's reform in Zurich. That Zwingli was moving too slowly became clear to Hübmaier at the Second Zurich Disputation held in 1523. When Balthasar Hübmaier returned home to Waldshut after the disputation, he was able to institute many of the reforms in his small city which Zwingli was as yet unwilling to institute in Zurich. Disillusioned by Zwingli, Hübmaier came more and more under the influence of Carlstadt. He began to preach against infant baptism. By the beginning of 1525, he persuaded his parishioners to postpone the baptism of their children and to have them dedicated instead. The town was ripe for conversion to Anabaptism by the time Reublin arrived, proclaiming the founding of the Brethren in Christ. At Easter, Reublin rebaptized Hübmaier and sixty others. Within a few days, three hundred were rebaptized in the public fountain, with Hübmaier using a bucket to pour water over them. In effect, the little city of Waldshut became Anabaptist for almost a year. Then the Austrian authorities captured the town and exiled Hübmaier.

Balthasar Hübmaier's *On the Christian Baptism of Believers* is the most serious attempt of any Anabaptist writer to give us a systematic presentation of his understanding of baptism.[48] The significance of this document is in-

48. *Von dem Christenlichen Tauff der glaübigen. Durch Balthasarn Hüebmör von Fridberg, yetz zu Waldshut, aussgangen* (1525), in *Quellen zur Geschichte der Täufer,* vol. 9, eds. Gunnar Westin and Torsten Bergsten (Gütersloh: Gerd Mohn, 1962), pp. 116-63. This volume will be abbreviated as *QGT* 9.

creased by the fact that its author was one of the few leaders of the movement who was a trained theologian. It is important at this point to make clear the nature of this theological training. Hübmaier earned his doctorate under Dr. John Eck, Luther's protagonist at Leipzig, the most renowned defender of the old Scholastic theology in Germany.[49] Hübmaier was trained in very conservative German Scholasticism. He was heir to the tradition of the "dark men of Cologne" who had resisted the philological studies of the Christian Humanists. The theological faculties of both Cologne and Ingolstadt, where Hübmaier had gotten his degree, had shown little interest for the study of Greek and Hebrew which the Christian Humanists had promoted as the key to a deeper understanding of Scripture.[50] The theological background from which Hübmaier came did not have any interest in the new methods of exegesis proposed by Jacques Lefevre d'Etaples or Erasmus. Particularly, the attention which Erasmus had given to the study of grammar and rhetoric as exegetical tools was looked on by conservative German Scholasticism as a frivolous innovation. Luther, Zwingli, Bucer, Oecolampadius, and Melanchthon, on the other hand, represented exactly the opposite theological tendency. They had been inspired by the Christian Humanists to take a new look at Scripture, and they had been prepared for their work by a thorough knowledge of the biblical languages as well as a deep appreciation for the grammar and rhetoric of Scripture. Hübmaier's theological training differed radically from that of the Reformers of classical Protestantism, and one of the places where this difference came out most clearly was the method in which Scripture was interpreted.

Another great difference between the theological education of Hübmaier and the theological education of the South German Reformers was that Hübmaier had been schooled in the Scholasticism of the late Middle Ages. This Scholasticism was thoroughly nominalist and thoroughly voluntarist.[51] The Scholasticism Hübmaier learned from Eck was an eclectic blend of *via antiqua* and *via moderna,* but it assumed the methods and interests of Scholasticism.

49. Torsten Bergsten, *Balthasar Hübmaier, seine Stellung zu Reformation und Taufertum, 1521-1582* (Kassel: J. G. Oncken, 1961). Bergsten tells us that Eck was quite eclectic in his use of both *via antiqua* and *via moderna.* He claimed to be specifically influenced by Bonaventure and Duns Scotus, but yet he was rector of the Nominalist Pfauenburse in Freiburg. Bergsten, *Balthasar Hübmaier,* p. 74.

50. Freiburg was more open to the new learning. While in Freiburg, Hübmaier probably studied a certain amount of Greek and Hebrew. Bergsten, *Balthasar Hübmaier,* p. 72. It is doubtful, however, that he ever gained a real mastery of these languages. Hübmaier himself claims that his theological education consisted chiefly of the study of Thomas, Duns Scotus, Gabriel Biel, Occam, and Gratian's *Decretals.* Bergsten, *Balthasar Hübmaier,* p. 75.

51. David C. Steinmetz, "Scholasticism and Radical Reform: Nominalist Motifs in the Theology of Balthasar Hübmaier," *The Mennonite Quarterly Review* 45 (1971): 123-44.

Hübmaier was steeped in the Scholasticism of William of Occam and Gabriel of Biel. For William of Occam and Gabriel of Biel, the decision of the human will was the central point of interest in the salvation of mankind.[52] While Hübmaier had been taught Scholasticism very uncritically, the High Rhenish Reformers had been taught Scholasticism very critically. In the theological education of Bucer, Zwingli, and Oecolampadius, the methods and interests of Scholasticism were no longer assumed. The Christian Humanists were trying to find a way out of Scholasticism. They had turned to the Church Fathers to find this way out. Jakob Wimpeling, who had been so influential in the Upper Rhineland, led an Augustinian revival. This Augustinian revival attempted to shift the focus of theology from the will of the individual to the grace of God. Augustine provided such a theology; consequently the Christian Humanists and even more their students turned to Augustine with increasing interest. To Hübmaier, on the other hand, this Augustinian revival was all quite foreign.

One more introductory remark should be made before we turn to an analysis of Hübmaier's work. For well over a year Hübmaier had been in conversation with Oecolampadius and Zwingli concerning his growing feeling that the baptism of children should be discontinued. These two Reformers did not give Hübmaier's questions anything like the attention they deserved, or anything like the attention he demanded. Zwingli and Oecolampadius doubtlessly had other things on their minds which they considered more important.[53] It was not until the end of May 1525, when there was an Anabaptist uprising in St. Gallen, that Zwingli finally got down to writing a short defense of the baptism of children, *On Baptism, Rebaptism and Infant Baptism.* It is to this work of Zwingli's that Hübmaier replies in his work *On the Christian Baptism of Believers.*

Hübmaier begins his work with an introductory chapter giving his canons of biblical interpretation.[54] He wishes nothing else than to baptize simply as

52. On the voluntarism of the Nominalist Schoolmen, especially Occam and Biel, see Heiko Oberman, "Some Notes on the Theology of Nominalism, with Attention to its Relation to the Renaissance," *Harvard Theological Review* 53 (1960): 47-76.

53. John Howard Yoder charges the Reformers with being unwilling to discuss the matter. John Howard Yoder, *Täufertum und Reformation in der Schweiz,* Part 1, *Die Gespräche zwischen Täufern und Reformatoren, 1523-1538* (Karlsruhe: H. Schneider, 1962), pp. 13-39, to be abbreviated *Täufertum und Reformation* 1. Part 2, *Dogmengeschichtliche Untersuchung der frühen Gespräche zwischen Schweizerischen Täufern und Reformatoren* (Zurich: EVZ-Verlag, 1968), to be abbreviated *Täufertum und Reformation* 2. It is probably more correct to say that the Reformers did not find the concerns of the Anabaptists very important or very interesting. It was not until the dissension began to cause the Reformers embarrassment that they were forced to deal with it.

54. *QGT* 9, pp. 118-21.

commanded by Christ and the apostles in numerous passages of Scripture. According to Hübmaier, the quibbling of the "rhetorical theologians" will be of no help in understanding baptism.[55] To discover what baptism is, one needs only to give oneself to the clear Word of God. Hübmaier concedes that occasionally for some obscure passage a knowledge of the original languages might be helpful; nevertheless, for the matter of whether children may be baptized, the Scriptures are as clear as day. Neither the original languages, nor the history of Christian worship, nor investigations of the history of doctrine, nor the opinions of the "big-name theologians" of the past will be of any help in deciding the question.[56] It is only necessary for the reader to judge with his own conscience according to the simple Word of God. If his reader will only do this, he can be well assured he will not err.

This introduction is quite clear on how Hübmaier intends to interpret the Scriptures. In repudiating the "big-name theologians," his break with Scholasticism is clear. For the Scholastic theologians, the quoting of the Fathers as well as the Schoolmen had authority. It was an important part of the Scholastic method of discerning truth. However, Hübmaier was also distancing himself from the classical Reformed theologians for whom the history of doctrine, the history of worship, and the study of the Fathers helped establish the historical context in which the Scriptures were to be interpreted. If Zwingli had not made much of the Church Fathers, Oecolampadius had made a great deal of the Church Fathers in his debate with Hübmaier.[57] Hübmaier's repudiation of the quibblings of the "rhetorical theologians" is the most significant remark of all. It is a repudiation of the exegetical method of Zwingli and Oecolampadius. For these two Reformers the study of the rhetoric and grammar used in Scripture was essential to understanding what these writings really intended to say. The historical-grammatical exegesis which the early Reformers had learned from the Christian Humanists was judged as valueless by Hübmaier. Hübmaier tells the reader that scholarship is of no use in deciding the matter. The Scriptures are so simple that the reader needs only to decide with his own conscience. Hübmaier trades on the medieval layperson's mistrust of the

55. "Aber es ist auch der grifflin eyns, das die Rhetorischen Theologen brauchen, wir erkennens bey jren grifflin. Darumb lieben frommen Christen, lassendt grifflin grifflin seyn, jr werdendt eüwer lebenlang auss dissen grifflin nit erlernen, was täuffen sey jnn dem nammen des Vatters vnd Suons vnd des heyligen geysts, sonder ergebendt eüch dem hellen wort Gottes, so ergreyffendt jr den rechten grundt der warheit." *QGT* 9, p. 120.

56. ". . . so thonds on alle anschawung der personen, der hohen nammen, des altenbrauchs, herkommens, auch gantz on alle anmuetigkeit, so eüch von der warheit abweysen möchte." *QGT* 9, pp. 120-21.

57. *Von der Kindertaufe, QGT* 9, pp. 256-69.

learned. He concludes by promising a sort of infallibility to the pious Christian who reads with a clear conscience: "Then judge in your own conscience and understanding according to the simple Word of God . . . and you can be well assured that you will not err."[58] This short sentence is a clear statement of Hübmaier's understanding of how Scripture is to be interpreted. Hübmaier rejects both medieval Scholastic exegesis with its great respect for tradition and the classical Protestant method of exegesis. In its place he puts a very private sort of personal illuminism.

The second chapter is devoted to the meaning of John's baptism.[59] Hübmaier tries in this chapter to refute Zwingli, who had offered a rather bold new interpretation. Zwingli had used John's baptism to show that baptism is to be understood as initiation. Zwingli claimed that the ministry of John was to introduce the ministry of Jesus. His baptism was true Christian baptism, just as the baptism of the apostles, because it introduced those who were baptized to "the Lamb of God who taketh away the sin of the world."[60] According to Hübmaier, John's baptism was a baptism of repentance, and of repentance only. It was not even a baptism for the forgiveness of sins. Before the Resurrection Christ alone could forgive sins, and only after the Resurrection could the baptism of the disciples be a baptism for the forgiveness of sins. Christian baptism could only be instituted, then, after the Resurrection, and Hübmaier finds himself taking the typical Scholastic position that Christian baptism was instituted in Matthew 28 over against the rather daring assertion of Zwingli. Hübmaier's understanding of John's ministry, however, is no less daring than Zwingli's. To him the baptism of John is "nothing other than a public witness, which a person receives and gives, that he recognizes and acknowledges, that in himself there is neither help nor good council . . . that all his righteousness is foul and condemned and he, therefore, renounces himself."[61] John's ministry,

58. "Darnach vrteylend in ewern conscientzen vnd gwissen nach dem einfeltigen worts Gottes. Dasselb alleyn lassend schlichter vnd richter sein, so werdent jr nit jrren. Hyemit syendt Gottbeuolhen." *QGT* 9, p. 121. While Hübmaier does not give a clear statement of illuministic exegesis, he is surely headed in that direction.

59. *QGT* 9, pp. 121-34.

60. *Of Baptism, LCC* 24, pp. 160-69; *Von der Taufe, CR* 91, pp. 258-68. See above, Chap. III, n. 39, regarding this treatise and its editions. Zwingli also found the theme of initiation in the words of the so-called baptismal formula, "baptizing them into the name. . . ." Zwingli pointed out that this was the actual reading of the Greek text rather than "baptizing them in the name," which had been the traditional translation ever since the Vulgate. Zwingli also found the theme of initiation in the sixth chapter of Romans. *Of Baptism, LCC* 24, pp. 144, 150, and 170-74; *Von dem Touff, CR* 91, pp. 235, 243, and 271.

61. "Auss dem eruolgt, das der wasser tauff Johannis nichts anders ist dann ein offenliche zeügnüss, die der mensch empfahet vnd gibt, darumb das er sich ein ellenden sünder schuldig gebe vnnd erkenne, der im selbs nit helffen noch radten möge, auch nichts

according to Hübmaier, was a ministry of penitential preaching. It was designed to bring people into fear of the law and terror of damnation. It was to bring people into the *Anfechtung* of which Thomas Müntzer and the late German mystics had spoken so eloquently. Hübmaier sums up: "God led through John into Hell and through Christ back up again."[62] That is, the ministry of John was to provide the crisis which would drive the sinner to conversion.

In the third chapter, Hübmaier turns to a long analysis of several passages of the New Testament which treat the ministry and baptism of John.[63] He is concerned to show that even in John's baptism there was always a sequence of five things: first, preaching the Word; second, hearing the Word; third, changing one's life or the confession of sin; fourth, baptism; and fifth, bearing the fruit of repentance.[64] It is very important that this sequence be maintained as Hübmaier sees it, and maintaining this sequence obviates the baptism of children. Next Hübmaier advances three arguments against Zwingli's point that baptism is initiation and therefore should be at the beginning of the life of a Christian. First, he attacks the close connection between John's baptism and Christian baptism which Zwingli asserts.[65] Second, he shows that even those who were baptized by John came to a conscious experience of repentance before they were baptized. Third, he denies that the baptismal formula implies that baptism is initiation.[66]

In the fourth chapter Hübmaier turns to consider the office of the apostles. It was the office of the apostles to lead people through the conversion experience. First, the apostles were to preach so as to move their hearers to

---

guots verbringe, sonder alle seine gerechtigkeyten seyen fuel vnd tadelhafftig, derhalb er an jm selbs verzage." *QGT* 9, p. 127.

62. "Jn summa: Gott fuort durch Johannem hynab inn die hell, vnnd durch Christam wider auffher." *QGT* 9, p. 127.

63. *QGT* 9, pp. 127-34.

64. Unfortunately Hübmaier's argument gets into trouble with his first example, Matthew 3:6. Hübmaier's German translation implied that they were baptized and then confessed their sins. Hübmaier comments, "while it is true that here the confessing of sin follows, in an outward way, the baptism, nevertheless in the heart it had indeed preceded it." The comment shows that Hübmaier either did not know the Greek text or did not understand it. "Merck hye, frommer Christ, wie die obangezeygte ordnung so eygentlich volget, wie wol die bekennung der sunden eüsserlich dem tauf nach stat, so ist sye doch im hertzen inwendig schon vorgangen." *QGT* 9, p. 128.

65. It is here that Hübmaier is at his strongest. Zwingli's interpretation of John's baptism was truly revolutionary. We later find this interpretation in most of the Reformers from Bucer to Melanchthon. Here, at least in relation to Zwingli's interpretation of Acts 19, Hübmaier does make Zwingli's use of rhetoric look artificial. *QGT* 9, pp. 131-33.

66. Hübmaier tries quite lamely to deny Zwingli's observation that to be baptized "into" the name implies that baptism is initiation. He never really addresses the grammatical question. *QGT* 9, pp. 131 and 137-38.

the confession of their sins.[67] The apostles were to do this in the same manner as John the Baptist. They were to reveal the accusation of the law, and bring about fear of judgment and a yearning for deliverance. Again we recognize in this the *Anfechtung* of the German mystics. To go through this experience was essential to the spirituality of Thomas Müntzer; as we shall see, it was essential to the spirituality of Hans Denck as well. It is, then, the first responsibility of truly apostolic preaching to bring people into the crisis experience. For Hübmaier, to enter the turmoil of doubt, anguish, and repentance is the first step on the road to salvation. Second, the apostles were to preach the grace of Christ and forgiveness of sins in such a way that the hearers would surrender themselves to God and inwardly commit themselves to God and to a new life according to the rule of Christ. In more contemporary terminology, the purpose of apostolic preaching was to bring about decisions for Christ. This is the conversion experience proper, the second step on the road to salvation. What is most striking here is that all this is understood in a thoroughly voluntarist way. It is the act of the human will which is decisive. It is "by the power of the inward 'yes' in the heart" that sins are forgiven.[68] Here we see with considerable clarity the reappearance of late medieval Nominalism.

It is only after this decision that one can have oneself baptized. Baptism is the third step on the road to salvation. It is emphasized repeatedly throughout Hübmaier's work that it was the office of the apostles to baptize only after they had brought about the conversion experience in their hearers. Since the decision for Christ is the decisive step on the road to salvation, Hübmaier feels obligated to explain why baptism is necessary at all. The answer is that one must make a public witness to the inner decision to be a disciple of Christ. This is the characteristic Anabaptist understanding of baptism. Baptism is an outward witness on the part of the believer to his or her own inner belief in the forgiveness of sins through Christ. Baptism is primarily something the Christian does rather than something that is done to him. That baptism is an act of God, done at his command by the apostles, does not enter into the discussion. Hübmaier sums up his position quite well: "In receiving water baptism, the one baptized publicly witnesses that he has surrendered to Christ and from now on obliges himself to live by the rule of Christ."[69] In his exposition of the apostolic office we have in effect the first three steps in the Anabaptist *ordo salutis,* or way of salvation.

67. *QGT* 9, p. 135.

68. ". . . sonder inn kraft des innwendigen Ja im hertzen. . . ." *QGT* 9, p. 137.

69. "Aber inn empfahung des Wassertauffs bezeügt der getäufft offenlich, das er sich ergeben hab, füan nach der Regel Christi zuleben." *QGT* 9, p. 145.

It is essential to the understanding of Hübmaier's argument that the steps of salvation must follow in the prescribed order. First, there must be hearing the Word; second, repentance and sorrow for sin; third, faith in Christ; fourth, baptism; and fifth, following Christ in doing good works. Here is really the heart of the Anabaptist objection to infant baptism. For the Anabaptist, salvation was gained neither by the medieval sacramental system nor by faith, but rather by the conversion experience. As Hübmaier understood it, one must go through the whole experience, one step at a time. For baptism to have any meaning at all, it had to fit into its proper place in the conversion experience. Baptism was not the conversion experience, but rather the public witness to the conversion experience which took place completely in the heart of the individual. The logic was quite clear. If the center of the Anabaptist *ordo salutis* is the inward "yes," the decision for Christ, then there is no place for the baptism of children. Baptism of children before they had had the crisis experience would tend to prevent the development of the crisis experience. The Anabaptists were voluntarists through and through. The important thing for them was the act of the will, the decision. For Zwingli, Oecolampadius, and their colleagues with their Augustinian theology, the emphasis was on grace. There is no problem reconciling infant baptism with such a theology, either in its Catholic or Protestant form. On the other hand, infant baptism simply could not be made to fit into the Anabaptist conversion experience and leave baptism any meaning at all. For baptism to fit into the conversion experience at all, it had to be believer's baptism. One thing must be said of Hübmaier: he did tenaciously insist that baptism must have a genuine function in the Christian life.

The fifth chapter is devoted to showing that numerous New Testament passages demonstrate this *ordo salutis.*[70] He begins with an interpretation of the closing words of the Gospel of Matthew. The translation he uses follows the Vulgate in reading, "Go and teach all nations, and baptize them in the name of the Father and of the Son and of the Holy Spirit, and teach them to observe all things which I have commanded you." He numbers the four steps of salvation and points out that since teaching must go before baptism and since infants cannot be taught before they are baptized, children may not be baptized. That, Hübmaier claims, "is as strong as a fortress wall."[71]

Since this passage is basic to his argument, let us look at it very carefully. It reveals much about his method of handling Scripture. The argument shows no interest in the meaning of the original Greek text.[72] Zwingli had already

70. *QGT* 9, pp. 146-51.
71. "Das ist vest wie ein mur." *QGT* 9, p. 146.
72. We have not yet been able to establish which German edition Hübmaier is quoting.

shown that the proper reading of the Greek text did not support the Anabaptist interpretation. Zwingli pointed out that the Greek does not say "teach all nations," but rather "make disciples of all nations." This is followed by two participles which tell how the apostles are to make disciples, namely by baptizing them and by teaching them. Zwingli then remarks that if one were to take the order of the text to imply that a certain sequence must be observed in making disciples, then obviously baptism should be administered before teaching; however, Zwingli says that the grammar should not be pressed that hard. The author probably did not intend to say that there should be a sequence, but only that both should be done.[73] For one who understands historical-grammatical exegesis, Zwingli has clearly cut the ground from under Hübmaier's argument. Why does Hübmaier repeat the argument, so badly damaged, without attempting to refute Zwingli's exegesis? Why does he still present it as the scriptural bulwark, "strong as a fortress wall"? The simple answer is that Hübmaier does not understand Greek well enough to be able to argue Zwingli's point.[74] All he can do is lambaste the new learning.

In similar fashion, Hübmaier tries to show that his four-point *ordo salutis* is to be found in about a dozen other passages of the New Testament. He goes through the baptisms on the day of Pentecost, the baptisms performed by Philip in the eighth chapter of Acts, the baptism of Cornelius, and the baptisms at Corinth and Ephesus. In each case he points out the same sequence: word, hearing, faith, baptism, works. Hübmaier's argument goes fairly well at this point. All of his examples have to do with first-generation Christians. We need to make this clear at this juncture in our presentation because we will want to pick it up further on. Hübmaier never deals with the question of whether the way the second-generation Christian comes to have faith might differ from the way one comes to Christian faith out of Judaism or paganism. The New Testament never tells us of how a second-generation Christian, that is, a child born and brought up in a Christian home, came to Christian faith. Hübmaier's hermeneutic leaves no room for approaching such a question.

Hübmaier's treatment of 1 Peter 3:21 also deserves our attention. The text says that baptism now saves us, "as an appeal to God for a clear conscience" (RSV). The German translation used by Hübmaier has, "but rather the conscious

73. Zwingli, *Of Baptism, LCC* 24, pp. 141-43; *Von dem Touff, CR* 91, pp. 231-34.

74. Here is another example of Hübmaier's laboring under his ignorance of the Greek text or having made serious mistakes because of his refusal to take the new learning seriously. In his interpretation of Mark 16:16, he forces a temporal sequence upon the text, "he who has believed and is baptized shall be saved." *QGT* 9, p. 146. But both "believe" and "baptize" are aorist participles and no time sequence between the two can be assumed.

confession of a good conscience with God."[75] It is on this passage of Scripture that the Anabaptists generally based their idea that baptism is a public witness of a previously existing faith. The German text supports this idea much better than the Greek text, once more suggesting that Hübmaier was not familiar with the Greek text. The Greek text is at this point far from clear. It must be admitted that Hübmaier's interpretation is far from being ruled out. If Hübmaier had known the Greek text, he might have been able to win a few points here.

Having given an exposition of his basic position, Hübmaier now devotes the sixth chapter to answering specific questions. Once more he takes up the subject of his approach to interpreting Scripture. For Hübmaier it is an essential principle that what is not commanded by Scripture is already forbidden.[76] He gives as his proof text: "Every plant which my heavenly Father has not planted will be rooted up" (Matt. 15:13). Conrad Grebel had appealed to the same principle. With this principle, Hübmaier tries to answer the objection that nothing in Scripture forbids the baptism of children. The principle of interpretation behind this objection is that what is not forbidden in Scripture is permitted. Hübmaier objects that if that principle of interpretation is used, then all those practices which the Reformation was trying to end could be justified. Idols, vigils, and masses for the dead would all be allowed in the Church. Baptizing mules is not forbidden either, but since it is not commanded we know it is forbidden. With arguments like these the Reformers would have to become more clear about how they understood *sola scriptura*.[77]

Hübmaier now turns to discussing the history of infant baptism. This he does in spite of the fact that in the introduction to his work he had announced that the study of church history was of no help in understanding the problem. The passage is interesting, nevertheless, because it reveals quite clearly the shallowness of his historical research. He has limited his investigation to a study of Gratian's *Decretals*. This was a perfectly acceptable practice for a Scholastic theologian, but the new learning of the Christian Humanists expected much more. With their new printed editions of the writers of Christian antiquity, such scholars as Zwingli and Oecolampadius delved into the source documents themselves rather than relying on collections of quotations of the

75. ". . . sonder die gewisse kundschafft eins guoten gewissens mit Gott." *QGT* 9, p. 150.

76. *QGT* 9, p. 151.

77. The principle of "what is not forbidden is allowed" as well as its opposite, "what is not commanded is forbidden," were equally unacceptable to the High Rhenish Reformers. They were determined to find a third principle, the reform of the church "according to God's Word." Oecolampadius spoke to this point in his answer to Hübmaier, *Antwort auff Balthasar Huobmeiers büchlein wider der Predicanten gesprach zu Basel von dem Kinder tauff* (Basel: Andreas Cratander, 1527), fol. G iiij r J iiij v.

Fathers, such as those made by Peter Lombard and Gratian. The Christian Humanists had for more than a generation taken a completely different approach to the study of Christian antiquity. Bullinger, Bucer, Hedio, Jud, Megander, and Pellikan had learned this new approach well. Hübmaier was in a different academic world, and his very old-fashioned attempt to reconstruct the history of infant baptism was not apt to impress his colleagues who had been so influenced by the new learning.

We have treated this document at considerable length because it reveals most clearly the concerns of the Anabaptists for the reform of the rite of baptism. It shows most clearly that the opposition to infant baptism arose primarily from an understanding of salvation radically different from that of classical Protestantism. But it also shows that the approach to Scripture of the Anabaptists was just as radically different from that of the Reformers. From this it should be quite clear why the programs of reform advocated by these two groups were completely unreconcilable.

Hans Denck

Hans Denck, having studied at both Ingolstadt and Basel, was one of the most capable of the early Anabaptist thinkers.[78] He had been exposed to both the Scholasticism of Eck and the Christian Humanism of Erasmus. While in Basel in 1523, he attended the famous Isaiah lectures with which Oecolampadius began the Reformation in Basel. It was the following year, however, while occupying a teaching position at St. Sebaldus school in Nuremberg, that Hans Denck began to advance toward Anabaptism. For several weeks in the fall of 1524, Denck was in close contact with Thomas Müntzer, who was in Nuremberg to see to the publication of his writings.

Hans Denck's *Nuremberg Confession* has three articles, "On Faith," "On Baptism," and "On the Lord's Supper."[79] The first of these articles gives us

78. G. Baring, "Hans Denck und Thomas Müntzer in Nürnberg 1524," *Archiv für Reformationsgeschichte* 50 (1959): 145-81; Werner O. Packull, "Denck's Alleged Baptism by Hübmaier: Its Significance for the Origin of South German–Austrian Anabaptism," *The Mennonite Quarterly Review* 47 (1973): 327-38; G. E. Rohrich, *Essai sur la vie des ecrits, et la doctrine de l'anabaptiste Jean Denk* (Strasbourg, 1853); Otto Eric Vittali, *Die Theologie des Wiedertauffers Hans Denck* (Offenburg: s.n., 1932); F. L. Weis, *The Life, Teachings, and Works of Johannes Denck 1495-1527* (Strasbourg, 1924).

79. "Bekenntnis für den Rat zu Nürnberg, 1525," *Hans Denck Schriften,* Part 2: *Religiöse Schriften,* ed. Walter Fellmann, *Quellen zur Geschichte der Taufer,* vol. 6, Part 2 (Gütersloh: C. Bertelsmann, 1956), pp. 20-26. This volume is to be abbreviated *QGT* 6:2. For a discussion of this document see G. H. Williams, *The Radical Reformation,* pp. 153-55.

an eloquent testimony of the struggles and anguish of a man seeking godliness. He tells us of the struggle within him between doubt and wretchedness on the one hand and the intimation of an unimaginable blessedness on the other.[80] Faith must be the dawning of the unimaginable blessedness. He wonders how the faith which one receives from one's parents, which one reads about in books or which people are always talking about, can be mistaken for the real faith. As for himself, he has to admit that he has not yet attained to this real faith. He sees himself struggling for it like Jacob wrestling with the angel. All he can say is, "Lord, I believe; help my unbelief."

Denck's statements on the significance of Scripture to the Christian life are of particular interest. The Scriptures are for him a lamp shining in the darkness, and there is indeed great darkness in his soul; but until the dawning of the Morning Star the darkness is not fully dispelled by the lamp.[81] Since he does not fully understand the Scriptures, how can he build on them? He must wait until God reveals the meaning of the Scriptures. Anything less only leads to fictitious faith.[82] Denck goes on to give a very clear statement of an illuminist or pneumatic approach to the Scriptures. He refers to the passage in 2 Peter which says that no Scripture is of private interpretation. He understands this to mean that it is the Holy Spirit who must interpret the Scriptures. This interpretation of the Spirit must be given consciously to each individual.[83] Denck is looking for a personal experience of illumination which will enable him to understand Scripture.

Next Denck addresses himself to baptism. He begins by stressing the primary importance of inner baptism as opposed to outer baptism. Human beings, he tells us, are by nature impure in both body and soul; therefore, outward washing is in vain unless it is begun from within.[84] It is the Word of God alone which enters into hardened hearts and changes lives. When this begins to happen, there is resistance. There is doubt, struggle, travail, and suffering because the unregenerate nature struggles against the beginning of the work of God.[85] This experience Denck compares, as Müntzer before him, to being overwhelmed by a great flood of water. What is particularly signif-

80. *QGT* 6:2, p. 20.

81. *QGT* 6:2, pp. 21-22.

82. Is "falschen galuben" (*QGT* 6:2, p. 22) an echo of Müntzer?

83. *QGT* 6:2, p. 22.

84. "Also auch der mensch, der von natur an leib und seel unrain ist, wirt von aussen vergeblich gewaschen, wo nicht von innen angefangen, erwaicht und gewunnen wirt." *QGT* 6:2, p. 23.

85. "Wo diss geschihet, do erhebt sich krieg im menschen, ehe sich die natur gibt, und verzweyfelung, also das er wenet, er müsse undergehn an leyb und seel, er möge das angefangen werck Gottes nicht erleyden." *QGT* 6:2, p. 24.

icant to notice here is the way Denck connects the sign of baptism with this experience of *Anfechtung* or struggling, this experience which is so important for the German mystics. One might say that for Denck it is the *res* of which water baptism was the *signum.* For Denck this is the real baptism, this inner experience. It is this baptism which, according to 1 Peter 3:21, saves us, not because it takes away the impurities of the body, but because of the covenant of a good conscience with God.[86] This covenant is the promise to die with Christ and to walk in Christ's way of life.[87] It is living the *imitatio Christi.* When this covenant has been entered into, then the Spirit of Christ comes and ignites the fire of love which burns away all remaining sin. If outward baptism takes place in this covenant, then it is of value; otherwise it is of no value.[88]

As one thinks over this document, several things stand out quite clearly. For Denck, as for the other Anabaptists we have studied, it is clear that salvation is achieved by going through an inner experience. Denck is not so much interested in the outward rite of baptism as baptism was administered in his day; it seemed to him a meaningless ceremony. The inner experience of baptism is another matter. Denck speaks of this inner experience of baptism in very mystical terms.[89] He is often called a spiritualist, and certainly one can see why. He has little to say about what Jesus did in history for his salvation. The center of the action is in his heart, not somewhere out in history. Hübmaier, on the other hand, is much less a spiritualist. He is much more concerned about the proper administration of outer baptism. One detects in Hübmaier little trace of the mystical. While both Hübmaier and Denck believed in salvation through experience, they had a different sort of experience in mind. For Hübmaier it was a crisis experience; for Denck it was a mystical experience. One can easily understand why both Denck and Hübmaier were so greatly offended by the Protestant doctrine of justification by faith.

Denck was consistent. His doctrine of Scripture and his doctrine of salvation were quite similar. It was only natural for Denck to insist that it was the inner interpretation of Scripture which was important. Just as he wanted a

86. "Gleichwie man wehnen will, wann ein grosses gewesser kompt, die erden müge nit bestehn, sonder müsse verschwembt werden. In solcher verzweyfelung sagt auch David: Herr Gott, hillf mir, dann das gewesser is mir biss auff mein seel gangen." *QGT* 6:2, p. 24.

87. "Diser bund ists, wer sich tauffen lesst, das ers thu auff den todt Christi, das wie er gestorben ist, auch diser sterbe dem Adam, wie Christus aufferstanden ist, auch diser in einem newen leben wandel Christo, wie zun Römern am VI." *QGT* 6:2, p. 24.

88. "Wo eüsserliche tauff in gemeltem bunde geschihet, ist sy gut. Wo nit, dienet sy niendert zu auss angezayter ursach." *QGT* 6:2, p. 24.

89. Steven Ozment, *Mysticism and Dissent: Religious Ideology and Social Protest in the Sixteenth Century* (New Haven, Conn.: Yale University Press, 1973), pp. 122-23.

salvation which was an inner experience, so he wanted a Scripture which was interpreted directly to him by the Holy Spirit.[90] Denck's inner interpretation of Scripture is indeed closely related to Hübmaier's demand for a simple interpretation of Scripture without the aid of the scholarly disciplines of language analysis and the searching out of historical context. Denck was perfectly capable of reading the Greek and Hebrew, unlike Hübmaier. That just was not what interested him. He sought a personal experience of its meaning, a mystical experience of revelation.

In 1525, Denck, having been exiled from Nuremberg, went to Augsburg, where he exercised an important role in the Anabaptist circle. In April, Hübmaier arrived in Augsburg after his exile from Switzerland. Denck and his circle were ready to take the step of establishing themselves as a truly purified church by accepting believer's baptism at Hübmaier's hand. While in Augsburg Denck baptized a great number of converts to the Anabaptist cause. More and more he developed a thoroughgoing voluntarist understanding of salvation. His denial of predestination and his espousal of free will were perhaps influenced by the humanist, Erasmus. One thing is clear, his tract "Whether God Is the Author of Evil" shows very little interest in the revival of Augustinianism.[91] He was obviously not treading the same path as Luther, Zwingli, Oecolampadius, and Bucer.

In November of 1526, Denck arrived in Strasbourg. There he was welcomed by Clement Ziegler, Michael Sattler, Louis Haetzer, and the thriving Anabaptist congregation. While he was enthusiastically received by the Anabaptists, the Protestants of the city were less than happy with his presence. In a short time he found himself in disagreement with Capito and Bucer, and after a very well-attended public debate with Bucer, Denck was asked to leave. Some months later in nearby Worms, Denck published his very influential *Von der wahrem Liebe.*[92] From this work we get a very clear picture of his fully developed understanding of baptism.[93]

Von der wahrem Liebe was published by Denck after two years of almost constant conversation with a variety of leaders of the Anabaptist movement. It represents the blossoming of his position. The first part of the work treats Christian love. He defines love as "a spiritual power through which one becomes

90. Ozment, *Mysticism and Dissent,* pp. 31-32, 121-23.

91. *Was geredt sey, das die schrifft sagt, Gott thue und mache guts und böses. Ob es auch billich, das sich yemandt entschuldige der sünden und sy Gott uberbinde* (Augsburg, 1526). *QGT* 6:2, pp. 27-47; *LCC* 25, pp. 88-111.

92. *Von der wahren Liebe* (Worms: Peter Schoffer, 1527). *QGT* 6:2, pp. 73-86. For the bibliographical details, see *QGT* 6:1, pp. 34-36.

93. Bucer answers this with his *Getreue Warnung, QGT* 7, pp. 91-115.

united, or desires to become united, with another."[94] This love is to be found as a little spark in every human being. In a way not unlike Meister Eckhart, Denck develops this idea of the *Funcklein*, or "little spark." This spark of love in every heart is God, who can neither make himself nor destroy himself but must love himself.[95] The spark of the divine in each human being naturally strives to reunite with what is divine. This love does not want to have anything to do with flesh and blood except where God is to be especially encountered in particular human beings who are called godly and children of God, in that they resemble or take after God as their spiritual Father. The stronger this spark in a person is, the more it is recognized and loved and the closer salvation comes. Therefore, it has pleased God to call the person in whom this love is most clearly recognized the savior of his people. This savior is Jesus of Nazareth, who was so fully united with God through love that all acts of God were the acts of this man, and all the suffering of this man was respected as the suffering of God. For Denck, "All those who are saved are one spirit with God."[96] Again we read, "All those who would be saved must be saved through Jesus; they must behold the perfection in spirit which is the one purpose which all those who are to be saved must see."[97]

Such a theology was, of course, miles apart from the theology of the Reformers. To be sure, one recognizes the influence of Neoplatonism. Whether it was the theology of Meister Eckhart or not is another matter, and a matter far afield from our primary concern. It can at least be understood as a popularization of the Rhineland mystics. Certainly one place where Denck would appear to differ with the German mystics was in his lack of insistence that all Christians had to be mystics in order to be saved. The primary point we want to make here is that the way of salvation taught by Denck was radically different from that of the classical Protestant Reformers. In his *Nuremberg Confession* Denck began by talking about salvation by faith, but made it quite clear that he did not accept the Protestant teaching on justification by faith. Now he is able to put much more directly his thought that salvation is by love.

Denck now turns to baptism. This time he presents us with a covenantal

94. "Liebe ist eyn geystliche krafft, dadurch man vereynet wirt, oder begert, vereynt zu werden mit eyenem andern." *QGT* 6:2, p. 76.

95. "Diser lieb spüret man in etlichen menschen je eyn füncklin, in eym mehr im andern minder, wiewol es leyder vast in allen menschen zu unsern zeiten erloschen ist; doch so ist es gewiss, dieweil die lieb geystlich ist, und die menschen alle fleyschlich seind, das diss füncklin, wie kleyn es in dem menschen ist, nit von den menschen, sonder von der vollkommenen lieb herkommen ist. Dise lieb ist Gott. . . ." *QGT* 6:2, p. 77.

96. "Alle, die selig werden, seind eyns geysts mit Gott." *QGT* 6:2, p. 78.

97. "Alle, so selig werden, müssen durch disen Jesum selig werden, die volkomenheyt im geyst zu betrachten, welche das eynig zil ist, auff welichs alle, die so selig werdern sollen, sehen müssen." *QGT* 6:2, p. 78.

baptismal theology.[98] Most interesting for our inquiry is the great distinction between what a covenant is in the Old Testament and what a covenant is in the New Testament. "The Old Law was a servitude; therefore, the sign of the covenant, which is circumcision, is given rather than desired, in order that all who come from Abraham's seed were responsible for upholding the law, whether they were in agreement or not. The New Law, however, is a sonship."[99] All those who are included are brought by the mercy of God alone; no other person may bring them. It must be the spark of the divine love from the innermost depths of their souls which brings them to God. The covenant sign of baptism should be given to those alone who have been divinely empowered by God; that is, to those alone who, recognizing true love, are drawn by that true love. Baptism is to be given only to those who desire that love and willingly follow it. He makes his point by a reference to Psalm 110:3, "Thy people will give themselves willingly."[100] It is interesting to notice that the voluntarism of Denck is joined to the Neoplatonic theme of the ascension of the divine spark within human beings to the divine source. As we have seen, the desire which moves the divine spark of love toward union with God is what brings one to salvation. It is this same desire which must bring us to baptism. Believer's baptism is valid and infant baptism invalid because only believer's baptism springs from a willing decision of the God-desiring spirit.

It is also interesting to notice how Denck regards the nature of the covenant relation. The covenant is understood not as the divine promise of grace, but rather as a contract between two consenting individuals.[101] Denck has taken over the Nominalist understanding of covenant. It was in terms of contract that the late Nominalists understood covenant.[102] For the Nominalists God had bound his absolute power by giving humans a covenant. It was then completely up to them as to whether he fulfilled the covenant. By this the Nominalists had seen a way of maintaining the absolute power of God and also insisting that humans must come to God by their own decision rather than by coercion. Once God had set up the system by which humans could be saved, the rest was left to them. The graciousness of God consisted in establishing a covenant, a covenant which gave God certain responsibilities and also gave

98. *QGT* 6:2, pp. 80-83.

99. "Darumb ist das alt gsatz nun eyn knechtschafft gewesen. . . . Darumb auch das bundzeychen, die beschneidung, gegeben ist, eer das man sein begeret hat, das alle, die von Abrahams somen kamen, dem gsatz verpflicht worden sind, sie weren willig oder nit. Das new gsatz aber ist eyn kindtschafft. . . ." *QGT* 6:2, p. 80.

100. *QGT* 6:2, p. 81.

101. *QGT* 6:2, pp. 80-81.

102. David C. Steinmetz, "Scholasticism and Radical Reform: Nominalist Motifs in the Theology of Balthasar Hübmaier," *The Mennonite Quarterly Review* 45 (1971): 135-36. See also Oberman's *The Harvest of Medieval Theology,* pp. 166-78.

humans certain responsibilities. God would be faithful to the covenant; the only question was, Would humans choose to enter the covenant? The decisive point, for the Nominalists, was the decision to enter into the covenant. Once people made this decision, it was God's responsibility to regenerate them. This theology of the covenant, as we shall see, is quite different from what the Reformed theologians meant by covenant theology.

At the end of 1527, sick and disillusioned, although still a young man in his late twenties, Hans Denck turned his back on the Anabaptists. He had served the Anabaptist cause passionately, but somehow the vision faded. He wrote to his old friend Oecolampadius, asking for a reconciliation. He wanted to return to Basel. Oecolampadius received him kindly, although he probably recognized that the basis of the reconciliation was Denck's disillusionment with Anabaptism rather than a conversion to classical Protestantism. Nevertheless, Denck probably recognized in Oecolampadius a genuine pastor to whom he could turn when his own vision had failed.[103] Shortly afterward Denck died of the plague.

Conclusion

Several things should be apparent from even this brief study of these Anabaptist leaders. Anabaptism was not simply the "Radical Reformation." Certainly it was not a radical reformation in the sense that it took the principles of the Protestant Reformation to their logical conclusions. It is far more a reaction against the Protestant Reformation. It is a very different approach to reformation than anything the classical Protestant Reformers had in mind. It was the taking of a different road than the Reformers, not simply going further along the same road.

As regards baptism, the Anabaptists proposed a completely new approach to the sacrament. It was not, of course, the reform of the rite itself which interested the Anabaptists. Strictly speaking, it was the discipline of baptism which interested them more than the rite. To them this reform of the discipline of baptism was the key to the reformation of the Church. The Anabaptist movement forced the Protestant Reformers of the Upper Rhineland to give far more attention to baptism than they might otherwise have given to the subject. The Reformers did not see baptism as the key to reform. The fact that the Anabaptists did force them to think more deeply about baptism could not help but affect the shaping of the Reformed rite of baptism. Now we must turn to the subject of how the Reformers answered the Anabaptists.

103. Ernst Staehelin, *Das theologische Lebenswerk Johannes Oekolampads* (Leipzig: M. Heinsius Nachfolger, 1939), pp. 392ff.

CHAPTER V

The Defense of Infant Baptism by the Earliest Reformed Theologians

The Reformers of the Upper Rhineland were rather slow in refuting the Anabaptist attack. Unlike Luther, who reacted quickly to Müntzer, Carlstadt, and others whom he regarded as *Schwärmer,* the Reformers of Strasbourg, Basel, and Zurich showed some initial interest in certain aspects of the Anabaptist proposals even if they were not ultimately convinced by the Anabaptist arguments.[1] Wolfgang Capito was the first to react. In the fall of 1524, he published an irenic work on the disagreements of Luther and Carlstadt in which it is evident that Capito had an open mind on the subject of whether children should be baptized.[2] Bucer, in his important liturgical work of December 1524, *Grund und Ursach,* has a wait-and-see attitude. He mentions the concern of some that the baptism of children should be discontinued, but he is not ready to decide on the question.

At the beginning Zwingli seemed positively inclined, or at least that is what the Anabaptists later claimed. Sebastian Hofmaister, then the Reformer of Schafthausen, does seem at first to have agreed with the proto-Anabaptists.[3] Oecolampadius hesitated when Hübmaier asked him to give him an opinion on the matter of baptizing children. After conferring with Zwingli by letter he answered in a rather noncommittal way.[4] By the end

1. On Luther's reaction to the Anabaptists see Mark U. Edwards, Jr., *Luther and the False Brethren* (Stanford, Cal.: Stanford University Press, 1975), esp. chaps. 2 and 3.

2. Capito, *Was man halten soll. . . .* See above, Chap. III, n. 3.

3. George H. Williams, *The Radical Reformation* (Philadelphia: The Westminster Press, 1962), p. 127.

4. Among the letters of Zwingli the following items refer to this discussion among the Reformers: Letter #352 (*CR* 95, pp. 251-53), Letter #353 (*CR* 95, pp. 291-93). Cf. also George H. Williams, *The Radical Reformation,* pp. 120-21 and John Howard Yoder, *Täufertum und Reformation in der Schweiz,* Part 1 (Karlsruhe: H. Schneider, 1962), pp. 58-59.

of 1524, however, Zwingli was more and more convinced that the proto-Anabaptists were wrong.

In January 1523, the first rebaptisms were held in Zurich. Within a few weeks Zwingli was embarrassed and annoyed to discover that the newly founded Anabaptist Church was carrying on a successful evangelistic campaign. The Anabaptist Church, or Swiss Brethren as they called themselves, spread rapidly through Switzerland. It was not until much later, however, when Vadian, leader of the Reformation in St. Gallen and brother-in-law of Grebel, desperately needed a statement, that Zwingli finally got something on paper. In May 1525, he published his first work defending infant baptism, to which he appended the baptismal rite which he had been drawing up for the Church of Zurich.[5] From this first baptismal service of Zwingli's it is clear what direction the Reformed Church would go in its reform of the rite of baptism. That children were to be baptized was clearly affirmed. The approach of Müntzer, Grebel, Carlstadt, Hübmaier, and other early Anabaptist leaders was not to be followed.

During the next ten years the High Rhenish Reformers produced a considerable literature in which they defended infant baptism against the attacks of the Anabaptists. Zwingli's first work, *Of Baptism,* was quite exploratory in nature. It is marred by a disdain for the Anabaptists as simple troublemakers. Zwingli has a tendency to ramble. The arguments are not fully developed. Nevertheless, much of the essential direction of the major Reformed defense is there. Zwingli's exegesis has broken loose the stones that Bullinger, Oecolampadius, Bucer, and finally Calvin would make into a very solid argument. In the next few months Zwingli wrote on the question several more times. His last work on the subject, *In catabaptistarum strophas elenchus,* was published in 1527.[6] To a large extent the work is a refutation of two different statements of the Anabaptist position, a tract probably written by Conrad Grebel, and a document commonly called the Schleitheim Confession.

In 1525 Oecolampadius published an account of a discussion between several of the reform-minded ministers of Basel and certain leaders of the local Anabaptist movement.[7] Two years later Oecolampadius wrote a reply to Hüb-

5. Zwingli, *Von dem Touff.* See above, Chap. III, n. 39.

6. *In catabaptistarum strophas elenchus, Huldreich Zwinglis Sämtliche Werke,* vol. 6, Part 1, *Corpus Reformatorum,* vol. 93, Part 1 (Zurich: Verlag Berichthaus, 1961), pp. 1-196. This edition will be cited as *Elenchus, CR* 93:1. An English translation, *Refutation of the Tricks of the Catabaptists,* is available in Ulrich Zwingli (1484-1531), *Selected Works,* ed. Samuel Macauley Jackson (Philadelphia: University of Pennsylvania Press, 1901 and 1972), pp. 123-258. The translation will be cited as *Refutation.*

7. *Ein gesprech etlicher predicanten zuo Basel, gehalten mitt etlichen bekennern des widertouffs* (Basel: Valentine Curione, 1525). To be cited as *Gesprech.*

maier, *Antwort auff Balthasar Hübmaier,* which was published in Basel in 1527.[8] His commentary on the articles of a certain Carlin, an Anabaptist lay preacher, is found in *Vnderrichtung von dem Widertauff,* also published in 1527.[9] The work of Oecolampadius is a good balance to that of Zwingli. Oecolampadius was a man of great maturity and insight, as well as a man of great learning. Although these are all popular works rather than theological treatises, they deserve careful study.

In 1531, the year in which both Zwingli and Oecolampadius died, Henry Bullinger published an important work refuting the principles of the Anabaptist movement, *Von dem vnuerschampten fräfel. . . .*[10] The young successor of Zwingli was only twenty-seven years old at the time, and yet one finds a growing clarity in his statement of the Reformed position; one might even say, a greater depth and maturity.

Bucer has left us a good number of writings dealing with the Anabaptists and their understanding of baptism. Many of them are in the form of unpublished reports written for the city council or minutes of hearings and interviews. Bucer was forced to deal with a great variety of Anabaptists. He took the arguments of some with considerable respect. His point-by-point refutation of Pilgram Marpeck is a serious theological discussion, although it was never published in the sixteenth century.[11] On the other hand, to cite but one example, Bucer dealt rather summarily with the more radical views of Jacob Kautz and Hans Denck in *Getrewe warnung der prediger,* published in July 1527.[12] His most important work for our purposes, however, was a Latin work which he addressed to Bernard Rotmann in 1533, *Quid de baptismate parvulorum . . . Sentiendum.*[13] Bucer recognized Rotmann as a serious theologian. Rotmann had recently become the

8. *Antwort auff Balthasar Huobmaiers büchlein wider der Predicanten gespräch zu Basel, von dem Kindertauff* (Basel: Andreas Cratander, 1527). This text will be cited as *Antwort.*

9. *Vnderrichtung von dem Widertauff, von der Oberkeit vnd von dem Eyd, auff Carlins N. widertauffers artickel* (Basel: Andreas Cratander, 1527). This text will be abbreviated as *Underrichtung.* It is also available in *Aktensammlung zur Geschichte der Basler Reformation in den Jahren 1519 bis Anfang 1534,* vol. 2, *July 1525, bis Ende 1527,* eds. Emil Durr and Paul Roth (Basel: Karl Werner, 1933), pp. 547-79 (no. 677). This edition will be cited as *AGBR* 2.

10. *Von dem vnuerschampten fräfel, ergerlichem verwyrren, vnnd vnwarhafftem leeren der selbsgesandten Widertöuffern, vier gespräch Bücher* (Zurich: Christoffel Froschour, 1531). This work will be abbreviated *Fräfel.*

11. *Bucers Widerlegung des Bekenntnisses von Pilgram Marpeck, QGT* 7, pp. 416-528 (no. 303).

12. "Getrewe warnung . . ." *QGT* 7, pp. 91-115 (no. 86). See above, Chap. IV.

13. *Quid de baptismate infantium ivxta scripturas Dei Sentiendum* (Strasbourg: Matthias Apiarius, 1533). This work will be cited as *Quid de baptismate.*

leader of the Reformation in the Westphalian prince-bishopric of Münster. Having begun as a Lutheran, Rotmann began to move in an Anabaptist direction. In the following year Bucer wrote a German work to the Church and city of Münster, *Bericht auss heyligen Schrift.*[14] Münster was at the time rapidly approaching the precipice of its millenarian tragedy. Bucer's warning was in vain. Breaking away from Rotmann, the true believers established a communist commonwealth which respected neither private property nor marriage. In 1535, the bishop of Münster retook the city, cruelly crushed the apocalyptic aberrations of the New Jerusalem, and held up the whole debacle as an example of Protestant degeneration. With this the first chapter in the discussion between the Reformers and the Anabaptists came to an end.

Let us now turn to the defense of infant baptism which we find in the literature we have just outlined. In this chapter we are not so much concerned to show the evolution of a position, or to show the distinctions between the ideas of the various Reformers. Others have already done this. We are much more concerned to find the central reasoning behind the position of a whole school of Reformers in order to understand the liturgical reforms which developed from this school.

The Argument from the Command of Christ and the Example of the Apostles

First, the Reformers defended infant baptism by claiming that ever since the days of the apostles, the Church had baptized the children of believers. They believed that even in New Testament times Christians had understood the commandment of Jesus to baptize all nations to have included the children of those whom they thus brought into the Church.[15] The Reformers were willing to admit that no passage in the New Testament expressly mentions the baptism of children.[16] That does not mean, as the Anabaptists claimed it meant, that no children were baptized in the New Testament Church, nor does it mean that children were not included in our Lord's command to baptize.

14. *Bericht auss der heyligen geschrift von der recht gottseligen anstellung und haushaltung Christlichen gemeyn, Eynsatzung der diener des worts, Haltung und brauch der heyligen Sacramenten* (Strasbourg: Matthias Apiarius, 1534). To be abbreviated as *Bericht.* This work is available in *Martin Bucers Deutsche Schriften,* vol. 5, ed. Robert Stupperich (Gütersloh: Gerd Mohn, 1978), pp. 119-258. This edition will be cited as *BDS* 5.

15. Bullinger, *Fräfel,* 63 r-v.

16. Zwingli, *Elenchus, CR* 93:1, pp. 48-54; *Refutation,* pp. 139-45; Bucer, *Quid de baptismate,* A iiij v to A v r.

Zwingli was the first to point out that it would not have been normal for the biblical writers to have made a special case of children. What they said in general terms would include men, women, and children. It was a matter of being sensitive to the way biblical writers used the language. Zwingli, being well versed in the study of ancient literature, suggested that the New Testament writers often used the rhetorical device of synecdoche.[17] It was because of this that one does not find the baptism of children expressly mentioned in the New Testament.

Zwingli first brought up the use of synecdoche in regard to the question of whether children were baptized on the day of Pentecost. After all, when the apostle Peter offered baptism to the people of Jerusalem he said, "Repent, and be baptized every one of you in the name of Jesus Christ for the forgiveness of your sins; and you shall receive the gift of the Holy Spirit. For the promise is to you and to your children and to all that are far off, every one whom the Lord our God calls to him" (Acts 2:38-39). Here, as Zwingli understood it, baptism was offered to men, women, and children. The Anabaptists replied that children could not have been included because Luke goes on to say that those who were baptized all participated in the apostles' teaching and fellowship, in the breaking of bread, and the prayers, and further that they all sold their possessions and distributed them to the poor. Infants could do none of these things; therefore, the Anabaptists argued, no infants were baptized on the day of Pentecost. Zwingli replied that the language could not be pressed that far. Luke was using a rhetorical figure called synecdoche. Synecdoche is when something is said of the whole which more exactly is true only of a part. When one has a sensitive understanding of the way language is used, as Zwingli understood it, one realizes that a careful interpretation of the text does not demand that all three thousand people baptized on the day of Pentecost did all of the things reported in the following lines. Surely, for example, there were those who were so poor that they had nothing to sell. It is understood that those who had goods to share shared them and that those who had the capacity to follow the teaching of the apostles did, and that those who had the time to enter into the daily prayer services did so. There is no reason to believe that infants were not included in that part of the life and worship of the primitive Church in which they could participate. If one recognizes Luke's use of the rhetorical figure of synecdoche, then, Zwingli tells us, there is no reason to insist that no infants were baptized on the day of Pentecost.[18]

17. Zwingli, *Elenchus, CR* 93:1, pp. 79-80; *Refutation,* pp. 166-67.

18. Zwingli, *Elenchus, CR* 93:1, pp. 96-103; *Refutation,* pp. 172-77. For a discussion of synecdoche, see John Yoder, *Täufertum und Reformation* 2, pp. 71-75.

But there were other passages of Scripture where the biblical writers used synecdoche in another way. This use of synecdoche was far more frequent, and explains very well why we have no explicit mention of the baptism of children, and incidentally only one example of the baptism of a woman. Not only does synecdoche take the whole for the part, it also takes the part for the whole. Bullinger defined the biblical use of synecdoche as follows:

> Now it is normal usage in Scripture . . . that when a man is spoken of, his wife and children are included so that with the heads of house are counted all who are part of the house. . . . This literary device is called synecdoche.[19]

In fact, it is quite normal in the biblical languages to speak of whole clans or even nations simply by mentioning the name of the tribal ancestor or ruler. Zwingli gives as an example the text, "Hear, O Israel, the LORD Thy God is one God. . . ." Israel, being the father of the twelve patriarchs, is the common ancestor of all the tribes of Israel. Under the name of the one man Israel, the whole nation is addressed.

On several occasions the New Testament records that a whole family was baptized. This is the case of the household of Cornelius, the house of Lydia, the family of the Philippian jailor, and the house of Stephanas in Corinth.[20] It seems likely that at least some of these families would have included children. One of the most obvious examples of synecdoche is to be found in 1 Corinthians 1:14, where Paul says, "I baptized none of you except Crispus. . . ." In the eighteenth chapter of Acts we read that Crispus believed with his whole house. Are we to say that Paul did not baptize the family of Crispus? It would seem all the more likely that the apostle did baptize the whole family of Crispus when we read further in 1 Corinthians 1:15 that he baptized the house of Stephanas. The divergence between the two passages is easily explained if we recognize that Paul is using synecdoche when he simply mentions baptizing Crispus. Zwingli's insight into the way the biblical writers wrote and thought cannot be denied.

One of Zwingli's most interesting passages is a reference to the Greek writer Plutarch.[21] The passage makes clear how in antiquity there was understood to be a corporate and psychic unity in family, tribe, and people. In today's language we would speak of corporate personality. For Zwingli, in the sixteenth

19. "Nun ist es ein bruch in der gschrifft . . . das man wyb und kind nit benamset, aber wol daryn verschlüsst, das wenn man den mann nempt oder den hussvatter, so wil man mit dem houpt alles verstanden und verschlossen haben. . . . Und heisst die art in der gschrifft ze reden 'syneckdoche'." Bullinger, *Fräfel,* 64 v.

20. Bullinger, *Fräfel,* 65 r.

21. Zwingli, *Elenchus, CR* 93:1, p. 159; *Refutation,* pp. 223-24.

century, to be aware of this distinctive feature of ancient peoples shows the depth of his penetration into the question of biblical language. What Zwingli had discovered by his attentive reading of the text of sacred Scripture was confirmed by his study of ancient classical literature. As a biblical philologist, Zwingli understood the importance of comparative literature.

Not only was it the case that the biblical languages spoke that way; it was also the case that the biblical peoples acted that way. The father of the family decided and acted for the family. This is shown very clearly in the story of the Philippian jailor, who was promised, "Believe in the Lord Jesus, and you will be saved, you and your household" (Acts 16:31). It was the faith of the father that was crucial, as is especially evident at the end of the story, where we are told that "he rejoiced with all his household that he had believed in God" (Acts 16:34). We assume that those of the jailor's family who were old enough to believe did believe, but if there were children too young to believe, they, too, were baptized; however, only the faith of the head of the family is mentioned. This is no more surprising in the New Testament than the Old Testament confession of faith, "As for me and my house, we will serve the LORD" (Joshua 24:15).

What Zwingli has done here is to insist that the biblical texts be heard in their historical context. He is amazingly clear-sighted as to his method of interpreting Scripture. He is in fact a pioneer in grammatical-historical exegesis. What Zwingli is saying is simply this: When the texts are heard in their historical context, one would expect that although children are not specifically mentioned the writers assumed them to be included.

The Anabaptists evidently missed Zwingli's pioneering insight into exegetical method. Not even Balthasar Hübmaier seems to have gotten the point. As we have already shown, Hübmaier was more influenced by late medieval Scholasticism than by the new learning with its emphasis on biblical philology. In regard to method of interpretation, he was definitely behind the times. He seems to have had some knowledge of the biblical languages, but normally worked with the Latin New Testament, or even simply the German.[22] The Anabaptists replied to Zwingli's argument with their usual scorn for university learning. As they understood it, Zwingli's grammar and rhetoric were nothing more than sophistry. Rhetoric and grammar could not be allowed to overthrow the "simple" understanding of the Word of God. Zwingli, Oecolampadius, Bullinger, and their colleagues, however, had learned from Erasmus and the Christian Humanists that the

22. Torsten Bergsten, *Balthasar Hübmaier, seine stellung zu Reformation und Taufertum, 1521-1582* (Kassel: J. G. Oncken, 1961), p. 360.

writers of antiquity had a highly developed rhetoric and that in interpreting ancient writers one must be aware of their rhetorical devices. Zwingli is not introducing sophistry; he is practicing grammatical-historical exegesis. This carried no weight with the Anabaptists because they were committed to pneumatic exegesis.[23] It was what the Holy Spirit revealed to their individual hearts that was the authoritative Word of God. With their strong tendency toward illuminism, which we have already noticed in the works of Müntzer, Hübmaier, and Denck, we should find it in no way surprising that the Reformers' arguments did not impress the Anabaptists. The root of the disagreement was a radically different approach to the interpretation of Scripture.

The Reformers believed that the command of Jesus to baptize included children as well as adults. The Reformers found evidence of this not only in the New Testament itself but also in the earliest Christian writers. In dealing with early Christian literature it is a matter of establishing the historical probability of how the texts of the New Testament are most likely to have been understood at the time they were written. Quotations from the Church Fathers gave evidence as to how the texts of Scripture were understood in classical antiquity. The Fathers were witnesses to the authority of Scripture.

It was Oecolampadius with his great wealth of patristic learning who first brought the patristic argument into play.[24] He was able to produce passages from Origen, Cyprian, and Augustine which indicated that the practice of infant baptism was very old. The passage in Origen claimed that the Church had baptized infants since the days of the apostles. Even Zwingli indicated that Origen's word on the matter was good evidence since he flourished about the year 200. The patristic argument did not constitute proof, but it indicated strong historical probability, which is what Oecolampadius, Zwingli, and Calvin were interested in. It did, however, refute the claim of the Anabaptists that infant baptism was the invention of the Pope.[25]

As we might expect, Oecolampadius had a rather nuanced approach to

23. Oecolampadius is well aware of this: "Ja auch etlich auss eüch die geschrifft als on nütz hindan legen, und auff yerem geist wöllen hindurch faren." *Antwort,* H iij r.

24. Oecolampadius, *Gesprech,* A ij r to A iij r. See also Williams, *The Radical Reformation,* pp. 146-47, and John Yoder, *Täufertum und Reformation* 1, pp. 63-65. On Hübmaier's use of the patristic argument see Bergsten, *Balthasar Hübmaier,* pp. 361-66. Cf. also Hughes Oliphant Old, "John Oecolampadius and the Patristic Argument in the Defense of Infant Baptism," paper read to the American Church History Society, Washington, D.C., 1979.

25. Zwingli, *Of Baptism, LCC* 24, p. 139; *Von der Taufe, CR* 91, pp. 228-29. See also Yoder, *Täufertum und Reformation* 2, p. 68.

the place of patristic literature in theology. He tells us that we should not lightly discard usages commended by the Fathers and Councils of the ancient Church which are also in accordance with the Scriptures. It is because their practice of infant baptism is in accordance with Scripture that we accept what they have taught concerning it. To be sure, if the Scriptures had forbidden it or if it were inconsistent with what the Scriptures taught about baptism, then whatever the tradition of the Church might have to say in its favor would not be able to establish the practice. Oecolampadius and his colleagues were convinced that infant baptism was in accordance with Scripture.[26] The practice of the Church of the patristic era had weight, then, in witnessing to the manner in which the Scriptures were to be heard.

The real question involved is how the Reformers understood the Bible as being the authority for liturgical reform. Oecolampadius discussed the hermeneutical principle advanced by the Anabaptists. They had appealed to the principle that what is not commanded by Scripture is forbidden by Scripture.[27] The Reformers, on the other hand, had appealed to the principle that worship must be "in accordance with Scripture." Had Oecolampadius contradicted this important principle to which the High Rhenish Reformers appealed when he brought the literature of the ancient Church into the argument? This, of course, he had been accused of doing, both from the Catholic side by John Eck and from the Anabaptist side by Balthasar Hübmaier. No, this is probably not the way we are to understand him.

Oecolampadius and his colleagues were trying to find a middle ground between two approaches to liturgical reform. The one was that what is not forbidden is therefore permitted, and the other was that what is not commanded is therefore forbidden. Obviously many liturgical practices fall in between the two. They are neither forbidden nor commanded. These things, Luther taught, were indifferent, *adiaphora*. About these the Church was free to do what seemed best, according to Luther. The High Rhenish Reformers, as Luther, found certain liturgical practices to be indifferent; for example, the question of whether baptism was to be administered by immersion or sprinkling. But on the other hand, there was much liturgical practice which was neither forbidden nor commanded and which should be decided on another principle. This principle was summed up in the phrase, "in accordance with Scripture." The High Rhenish Reformers believed that the question of whether children should be baptized or not needed to be decided according to Scripture. In other

26. Oecolampadius, *Antwort,* N iiij r.

27. Oecolampadius, *Antwort,* G iij r to G iiij v. Zwingli, *Elenchus, CR* 93:1, pp. 55-56; *Refutation,* p. 145.

words, the question ought to be, Was it a practice consistent with the teaching of Scripture? Unlike the Anabaptists, who had to find a specific proof text in Scripture, the High Rhenish Reformers recognized the importance of theological analysis. The weighing of ideas and the analogy between ideas becomes important to Reformed theology as well as the searching out of the specific commands and examples of Christ and the apostles. We shall see this demonstrated in the rest of this chapter. We shall see how the Reformers tried to demonstrate that the baptism of children was in accordance with Scripture.

By way of contrast, we can see what the Reformers meant by a practice being "in accordance with Scripture." The exorcism of children before baptism was a good example of a ceremony that was not in accordance with Scripture. To be sure, Jesus and the apostles did perform exorcisms, but not as a preparation for baptism. The Scriptures do not forbid us to exorcise before baptizing, nor do the Scriptures command us to exorcise before baptism. On the other hand, Scripture does tell us that the children of Christians are holy (1 Cor. 7:14). If children are holy, they do not need to be exorcised. The fact that the baptismal exorcisms can be demonstrated to be of great antiquity gives them no support because they are contrary to and inconsistent with a clear teaching of Scripture, that the children of Christians are holy.

It was indeed very important for the Reformers to know that their administration of the sacrament of baptism was in obedience to the command of Christ and in accordance with the example of the apostles. Particularly the Reformers found it important to carry out the command of Jesus found in Matthew 28 and to follow the example of the apostles in the book of Acts. In both cases they understood these passages to include children. They believed that when Jesus commanded the apostles to baptize, he intended them to baptize men, women, and children. When the apostles carried out that command, they did baptize men, women, and children.

The Argument from Typology

An important argument by which the Reformers defended infant baptism was the typological argument.[28] Two of the Old Testament types of baptism were

28. Calvin, in the following decade, that is, in the 1539 edition of the *Institutes*, develops the unity of the two covenants and the typological relation of circumcision and baptism into his major argument for the defense of infant baptism. He specifies, however, that between circumcision and baptism there is an anagogic relation. *Institutes* 4.16.1-8.

circumcision (Col. 2:11-17) and the passage through the Red Sea (1 Cor. 10:1-13). Circumcision was administered to children, so if circumcision is the type or pattern of baptism, then it would be appropriate to baptize children. In the same manner the passage through the Red Sea is a type of baptism, and here, too, the children of the Israelites were included with their parents.

One might well ask why the Reformers were willing to build up such an important argument on typology. For contemporary theologians typology is considered *complètement depassée.* The Reformers, however, were most aware that the New Testament writers themselves consistently interpreted their Scriptures in a typological manner.[29] It was the apostle Paul himself who saw in the Exodus a type of baptism and in circumcision a shadow of things to come. In fact, from the very earliest times baptism particularly had been explained in terms of the Old Testament types. In both the New Testament and patristic literature the meaning of baptism was to be found in the Old Testament types of baptism. One need read only Tertullian's *De baptismo,* Ambrose of Milan's *De sacramentis,* or Cyril of Jerusalem's *Mystagogical Catechisms* to see how important the baptismal typology has always been to baptism. One remembers that Hilary of Poitier's book on typology bears the title *Sacramentum futuri.* The sacraments are rooted in typology. Both typology and the sacraments stem from the same biblical approach to understanding. God speaks not only by means of words, but also by means of signs. As is well known, the baptismal prayers have down through the centuries been filled with allusions to typology. Reference to the Old Testament types of baptism even passed into the Reformation baptismal prayers in Luther's Great Flood Prayer. In the literature of the New Testament and in the literature of the Christian Church ever since, the understanding of the Old Testament types of baptism has been essential to understanding baptism.

Let us begin with the use the Reformers made of the passage through the Red Sea. It is found in its simplest form in a work of Oecolampadius.

> We find all the way through that the faith of the parents was profitably enjoyed by their children. In I Corinthians 10 the children also went through the Red Sea and participated in the faith of their parents. . . . At the time of the flood the children of the wicked perished with their parents. It was the same with

29. It is for this reason that typological exegesis belongs to grammatical-historical exegesis. Bucer in his commentary on the Psalms gives us an excellent example of the use of typological exegesis in the context of historical-grammatical exegesis. Allegorical exegesis was very popular in the interpreting of the Psalms. Bucer, however, embarked on a pioneer work of interpreting the Hebrew text in a grammatical-historical fashion using the works of Rabbis David Kimchi and Jbn Abraham. His work, however, carefully employs the interpretation given certain Psalms by New Testament writers.

> Sodom and Gomorrah; the children suffered with their elders. Through the disobedience of their parents children were led off as captives to Babylon and then again children were delivered from Babylon because of the faith of their parents. For children are in the same covenant with their parents. It is just as in Psalm 115:14. The Lord blesses the parents with their children.[30]

At first look one might imagine that the Reformers in their use of the typological argument were in reality arguing from the Hebrew concept of the solidarity of the family. Certainly that is involved, but there is more to it than that. The whole idea behind any typological argument is that God works with human beings in orderly, consistent patterns. This idea is a natural corollary to the concept of God as Lawgiver. Just as in the works of creation there is an order which corresponds to the order of divine Law, so there is an order or pattern in God's works of providence which corresponds to the Law of God. This is expressed with particular clarity in Psalm 19, where the order of creation is seen as a reflection of God's Law. If God works in patterns, then in recognizing a series of patterns we come to an understanding of how God works. To fully understand typology is to deal with the very nature of biblical language. It is to perceive a uniquely biblical way of communicating meaning. In the passage we have just quoted, Oecolampadius shows us a series of Old Testament types of redemption and judgment.[31] We see that children are always included. He even refers to a psalm which gives expression to the same principle. "May the LORD give you increase, you and your children!" (Ps. 115:14). The pattern which Oecolampadius finds is that in God's works of redemption the children of the faithful are redeemed with their parents. One should particularly note that the passage through the Red Sea is recognized as

30. "Wir finden allweg, das der glaub d'elter hatt der massen such den kinden genutzet. i. Cor. x. sein die kind auch durch das rot meer gangen und han genossen des glaubens yrer elter. . . . Im sindtfluss ertrancken der ongleübigen kinder mitt den alten, des gleichen zuo Sodoma und Gomorrha, litten sie such mitt den alten, Durch den onglauben der alten seind sie auch gefürt geen Babel, durch den glauben der alten seind sie auch aussgefürt. Dann sie in einem bundt mitt den alten, darumb auch im cxv. psalm steet, der herr hatt gesegnet die grossen mitt den kleinen." Oecolampadius, *Antwort,* K ij v.

31. It is only the passage through the Red Sea that Oecolampadius treats as a type of baptism. The Reformers were extremely chaste in their use of typology. They disapproved of allegorical interpretation altogether, and as for typology they limited themselves to the typology expressly mentioned in the New Testament. This was not the case with the Anabaptists. Melchior Hofmann, for example, developed a whole baptismal theology on the figure of the wedding. In the Song of Solomon, Hosea, and the other prophets, he found nuptial types of baptism. Melchior Hofmann, *The Ordinance of God,* found in *Spiritual and Anabaptist Writers, Documents Illustrative of the Radical Reformation,* ed. George Huntston Williams, *Library of Christian Classics,* vol. 25 (Philadelphia: Westminster Press, 1957).

a type of redemption by faith. In the New Testament the passage through the Red Sea is specifically given as a type of baptism. Furthermore, in this type of redemption by faith, children are included.[32]

With Bullinger and Bucer we find a slightly different twist to the same argument.

> The Apostles of the Lord always established their usages on the principles, patterns and examples of the Old Testament. That we can see in all four Gospels, the Acts, and Paul's letters. . . . Therefore we can be quite sure that they set up baptism according to the figure, principle, and meaning of the Old Testament. Now, however, the passage through the Red Sea is just such a pattern or type of baptism. This is shown by the Apostle Paul in I Corinthians 10. Certainly children are included in the figure, for truly those men pass through the sea with wives and children.[33]

Bullinger's argument here is most interesting. It is simply that the apostles and the ancient Church would have developed their rites in dependence on what was to them the Scriptures, that is, the Old Testament. A particularly striking example is Paul's defense of paying the ministry of the Word through reference to the manner of paying the Old Testament priests (1 Cor. 9:13-14). Bucer develops the same idea and gives several examples of how Jesus or one of the apostles established a New Testament practice.[34]

But an even more important type of baptism, at least for the discussion of infant baptism, is circumcision. In the New Testament we find the apostle Paul explaining baptism in reference to this Old Testament type (Col. 2:11-12). The apostle's perception of the nature of typology is found particularly in verse 17, where he says of certain aspects of the ceremonial law, "these are only a shadow of what is to come; but the substance belongs to Christ." This argument from circumcision soon became far more than a typological argument. It became what today we call covenant theology. Let us now turn to a consideration of covenant theology.

32. The Reformers were particularly fond of the apostle Paul's typological interpretation of the Exodus in 1 Corinthians 10 because he so clearly opposes a magical understanding of the sacraments and so clearly puts the sacraments in relation to faith.

33. "Die Apostlen des Herren habend jre händel alle zyt gerichtet uff den anlaass, grund, und vorbyld des Alten Testaments: Das zeygend wir an mit allen vier Evangelisten, mit den Gschichten der Botten, mit dem Paulo. . . . Darumb ist es ouch urgezwyflet, das sy den Touff ouch nach der figur anlaass und inhalt des Alten Testaments gerichtet habend. Nun aber so ist der durchgang durch das rodt Meer ein byld gewäsen des kunfftigen touffes. Bewär ich mit Paulo I Cor. 10. Und die kind sind ouch in der figur gewasen: Dann sy ye mit wyb und kind hindurch giengend." Bullinger, *Fräfel,* 64 v-r.

34. Bucer, *Bericht,* K iiii v to L i r; *BDS* 5, pp. 174-75.

Covenant Theology

In his first work *On Baptism,* Zwingli had said little about baptism being a covenant sign and even less about the nature of the covenant. He did say in this first work that just as circumcision was a sign of the covenant in the Old Testament, so baptism in the New Testament is a covenant sign.[35] During the year 1525, he was preaching through the book of Genesis, and this gave him the opportunity to deepen his understanding of the covenant. He began to appreciate the great importance of the concept of covenant to the whole of biblical theology. He saw that it was in terms of the covenant that the whole relation of God to his people had been thought out not only in the Old Testament, but in the New Testament as well. It was at this point that Zwingli began to discover from his study of Scripture that a covenant is far more than a contract between mutually consenting parties, but rather a promise of divine grace. In granting the covenant to his people, God had chosen them for himself. The covenant was a matter of election.

In July 1527, Zwingli published his *Elenchus* or, as it is translated into English, *Refutation of the Tricks of the Anabaptists.* Here he explores at length the doctrine of the covenant. He tells us of the establishment of the covenant with Adam and Eve, then the renewal of the covenant with Noah. In each case there are different provisions in the covenant. Again with Abraham the covenant is renewed, clarified, and confirmed with the sign of circumcision.[36] God, being faithful to the covenant, provided Abraham with numerous descendants and made him the father of a great nation. Here Zwingli insists on the graciousness of the covenant. As Zwingli sees it, the covenant is a matter of God's free choice of Abraham and his descendants to be his peculiar people. It is a matter of election, which is the freedom of God, and a matter of grace, which is the goodness of God. He goes on to point out that when this people was brought out of Egypt he appointed them to be a kingdom of priests and a holy race, giving them the Law, the worship, and the promises.[37] All this is given to the whole people, including the children. It is into this same covenant that Christians are now called. "Therefore, the same covenant which he entered into with Israel he has in these latter days entered into with us, that we may be one people with them, one church, and may also have one covenant."[38]

At this point Zwingli turns to the interpretation of the covenant found in the New Testament. Zwingli shows from numerous New Testament passages

35. Zwingli, *Of Baptism, LCC* 24, p. 138; *Von der Taufe, CR* 91, p. 227.
36. *Refutation,* p. 221.
37. *Refutation,* pp. 222-27.
38. *Refutation,* p. 229.

that through Christ the Gentiles have become heirs of the same eternal covenant.[39] Of particular interest is Zwingli's treatment of Acts 2:38-39, "Repent, and be baptized every one of you in the name of the Lord Jesus Christ for the forgiveness of your sins; and you will receive the gift of the Holy Spirit. For the promise is to you and to your children and to those who are far off, every one whom the Lord our God calls to him." For Zwingli this text makes quite explicit that the covenant has been opened up to the Gentiles. It is the one eternal covenant to which the Gentiles have been called, and yet it is also a new covenant in that it is a renewal of the eternal covenant. As Zwingli sees it, the inclusion of the Gentiles is one of the differences between the old covenant, that is, the version of the covenant as it was revealed to Abraham, and the new covenant revealed in Christ.[40] Just as the old covenant as stated in Genesis 17 had made explicit that the promise was to Abraham and to his children, so now in the words of Peter at Pentecost it is made explicit that the new covenant is with Christians and their children.[41] With the coming of Christ, as Zwingli sees it, the covenant made with Adam and Eve has been fulfilled. Christ in his death and resurrection has crushed the head of Satan. So the covenant, as it was renewed to Abraham, was fulfilled when Jesus was revealed as the true Isaac, the son in which the patriarch rejoiced (John 8:56). Yet with the coming of Christ, the eternal covenant was not only fulfilled but opened up to the Gentiles. Even in the statement of the covenant in Genesis 12, God had provided that in the seed of Abraham all peoples would be blessed, and so in the preaching of the apostles that began to come about. The covenant was now being opened up so "that in Christ Jesus the blessings of Abraham might come upon the Gentiles" (Gal. 3:14).

In the death and resurrection of Jesus, and in the pouring out of God's Spirit, once again the eternal covenant was renewed. In the gospel the fullness of the covenant is revealed with a clarity unknown under the Law.[42] As Zwingli saw it, that was another of the distinctions between the old covenant and the new. The old covenant was revealed in shadows and types, but as he found in Colossians 2, the substance only became clear in Christ.[43] This new clarity entailed, therefore, new signs of the covenant. When the eternal covenant which had been revealed to Adam and Eve was renewed to Noah, the rainbow was given as the sign of the covenant. When it was renewed to Abraham, circumcision was given as the sign of the covenant. When the covenant was

39. *Refutation,* pp. 228-32.
40. *Refutation,* p. 235.
41. *Refutation,* p. 232.
42. *Refutation,* p. 235.
43. *Refutation,* p. 235.

renewed in Christ, baptism was then given as the sign of the covenant.[44] Having given this long exposition of the biblical teaching on the covenant, Zwingli argues as follows. Children were specifically included in the eternal covenant as it was given to Abraham, and God specifically commanded Abraham, to give circumcision, the sign of the covenant, to his children. On the day of Pentecost, the apostle Peter proclaims the renewal of the eternal covenant in Christ. He specifically mentions that the children of believing Jews and Gentiles are to be included in the covenant. Therefore, since children are included in the covenant, they should receive the sign of the covenant.[45]

This theology of the covenant outlined by Zwingli was quickly picked up and developed by Zwingli's colleagues. Bullinger begins to point out that in a sign, particularly a covenant sign, there is an element of promise. Then, commenting on Genesis 17, Bullinger says,

> When God established the eternal covenant with Abraham, he made it clear that children were to be included in it saying: I shall be your God and the God of your children. It is therefore that children when they are eight days old are to be marked with circumcision as a sign of the covenant. From this it follows that today God is not only the God of adults who are able to come to him in faith and make a confession of faith, but also the God of their children as well. From the standpoint, therefore, of grace and the promise of God they ought to be included in the number of believers.[46]

Bullinger sees in the covenant made with Abraham a strong element of promise for the future; much of it would not even begin to be fulfilled until the coming of Christ and the gathering in of the Gentiles. The idea is beginning to develop that the sign is a sign of God's promise. Baptism is a sign of God's gracious promise to the child that the cleansing signified by the sacrament will be accomplished inwardly by the Holy Spirit. While the Anabaptists spoke of baptism as a sign of a faith that was already present, the Reformers more and more speak of it as a sign of God's promise to give faith by uniting the child to Christ.[47] It made sense to the Reformers to include children in the covenant because they understood the covenant primarily as a gracious promise given

44. *Refutation,* p. 237.

45. *Refutation,* p. 236.

46. "Als Gott den eewigen pundt mit Abrahamen uffrychtet, verfasst er besonders die kinder dryn, und sprach: Ich wil dyn Gott syn unnd dynes somens Gott. Heisst ouch darumb das achttägig kindle mit der bschnydung, als mit dem pundts zeychen, bezeychen. Daruss volgt, das yetzund Gott, nit allein der alten Gott sye, die im jn glouben könnend und den glouben verjähend, sunder ouch der kinden Gott verrächnet werdend, under die zal der glöubigen." Bullinger, *Fräfel,* 55 r-v.

47. Bullinger, *Fräfel,* 60 r.

by God, while the Anabaptists, on the other hand, understood the covenant as a contract entered into by mutually consenting parties.

The strength of the argument from covenant theology becomes even more apparent when one realizes that both circumcision and baptism are signs of the same thing. Bucer tells us,

> It is for this reason that God commanded men of old to circumcise not only all their children, but also their servants . . . and to bring them into the covenant of grace (Genesis 17). For circumcision also means a dying to sin just as baptism. That explains why St. Paul is able to treat these two sacraments in the same way. That is why he can say that he who is baptized should not let himself be circumcised, because by virtue of his baptism he is already circumcised; that is, he has the inner reality of the sacrament, or in other words, he has the most important part of the sacrament, namely, the putting away of the body of sin, the putting off of the flesh through the circumcision of Christ. It is also to this end that they are buried with Him in baptism.[48]

Bucer has gotten to the heart of what Paul said about the relation of circumcision and baptism in Colossians 2. He who had been buried with Christ in baptism and also raised by him through faith had received the reality of which circumcision was the sign. One notices with great interest that Bucer has a very high understanding of the spiritual value of the Old Testament sacraments.[49] They are not merely outward forms or ceremonies. They were ordained of God as signs of an inward and spiritual reality. Bucer did not reject the Old Testament ceremonies on the same principle that he rejected many of the medieval ceremonies of the Church. He did not consider them empty,

48. "Daher ists, das er den alten gebotten, nit allein ire kinder, sonder auch irer leibeigen knechten . . . zu beschneiden und in seinen gnadenpundt auffzunemen, Genes. 17. Nun hatt die beschneidung gleich so wol das absterben der sünden bedeutet als der tauff, daher auch der heylig Paulus dise zwey sacrament in demselbigen so gleich haltet, das er darauss beweret, wer tauffet ist, der darffe sich nit beschneiden lassen, er sey schon beschnitten, das ist, habe rem huius sacramenti, das furneme in disem sacrament, nemlich die ausziehung des leybs der sunden, des fleysches durch die beschneidung Christi, so sy mit ihm im tauff begraben sind. . . ." Bucer, *Bericht,* K iiij r; *BDS* 5, p. 173.

49. The Anabaptists generally taught that circumcision was only a carnal sign with carnal promises. This is particularly worked out by Pilgram Marpeck. Jan J. Kiwiet, *Pilgram Marpeck, ein Führer in der Täuferbewegung der Reformationszeit,* 2nd edn. (Kassel: J. G. Oncken, 1958). Balthasar Hübmaier, who led a persecution of the Jews in Regensburg in 1519, never could feel positively about the religion of the Old Testament. On the development of an Anabaptist Covenant Theology, see Yoder, *Täufertum und Reformation* 2, pp. 33-43. See also Calvin's criticism of the Anabaptist estimate of Old Testament religion: "They depict the Jews to us as so carnal that they are more like beasts than men." *Institutes,* 4.16.10.

meaningless ceremonies of merely human invention. The sacraments of the Old Testament were truly sacraments because they were divinely given. For Bucer, the problem with the medieval ceremonies was that they were not commanded by God. It was often the case that Anabaptists of a spiritualist tendency would find the difference between circumcision and baptism to be that circumcision was outward and physical while Christian baptism was inward and spiritual.

This line of thought becomes even more fully developed by emphasizing the unity of the two covenants. In Christ the Christian participates in the blessings of the Old Covenant, which is also the eternal covenant. If the two covenants are really one, then the fact that children could participate in the Old Covenant suggests that they could participate in the New Covenant as well. In the following passage Bucer shows how the apostle Paul linked the Old and New Covenants together as the one eternal covenant.

> Augustine, and with him the whole Church, places it (i.e., baptism) in the general category of signs or symbolic actions by which the divine good will is commended to us. With this we are in agreement. The Word of God itself leads us to this approval. Indeed, Paul, in Colossians 2, makes baptism and circumcision belong to the same category, when he tells us that we, through baptism, are circumcised. God himself in Genesis 17 calls circumcision a sign of the covenant. The covenant was the promise by which God promised to Abraham that he would be his God, the God of his seed, that is, he would be to them a savior and the grantor of eternal life. This is, to be sure, found in this promise. For it is from this same promise that our Lord demonstrated that Abraham, Isaac, and Jacob were participators in eternal life and even the resurrection itself. By the covenant or testament is correctly to be understood the promise of divine favor, as is evident from Galatians 3 where it is explained that through Christ the covenant promises made to Abraham are inherited by us. It is evident, therefore, that baptism is a sign of the promise of divine favor.[50]

50. "Augustinus, et cum hoc tota Ecclesia, illud ponit in genere signorum, uel actionum symbolicarum, quibus divina nobis beneuolentia commendatur. Huic nos assentimur. Verbum Dei, quo hic adsensus nostra nititur, est. Paulus Coloss ij. Baptisma et circumcisionem, adeo eiusdem generis facit, ut dicat, nos per baptismum circumcisos. Iam circumcisio signum foederis uocatur, ab ipso Deo, Genesis xvij. Foedus uero erat, promissio, qua Deus promittebat Abrahae, se futurum illi et semini eius, Deum, hoc est, seruatorem, ac uitae aeternae largitorem. Id enim est in hac promissione. Unde ex ea Dominus probauit Abraham, Isaac, et Iacob aeternae uitae esse participes, ac ideo resurrecturos. Per foedus, uel testamentum recte intelligi diuine beneuolentiae promissionem, liquet ex Gal. iij, ubi promissiones et facta διαθηκή Abrahae, pro eoden accipuntur. Liquet igitur baptisma esse signum promissionis diuinae benevolentiae. . . ." Bucer, *Quid de Baptismate,* A vi r-v.

From this passage we gather that the Reformers were beginning to see a strong continuity between the Old and New Covenant. Since so many of the Reformers were so well versed in St. Augustine, this is in no way surprising. By bringing Galatians 3 into the discussion the Reformers were willing to speak of the promise given to Abraham in Genesis 17 as the eternal covenant, the blessings and promises of which even the Gentiles now inherit in Christ.[51]

The unity of the two covenants is further demonstrated by the fact that both covenants require faith. Bullinger carefully goes over Paul's interpretation of the covenant found in the book of Galatians. Paul, of course, emphasizes that by faith even the Gentiles are children of Abraham. Paul tells us that in the covenant given to Abraham in Genesis 17, God preached faith to Abraham. Furthermore, the apostle Paul tells us that it was by faith that Abraham was justified. Abraham believed the promises. Now the sign of these promises was circumcision, which Abraham received as an adult believer but his descendants were to receive as infants. They were to be justified by faith, by believing the promises. The sign of these promises they were to receive as children. Faith was required of the children of Abraham no less than it is required of Christian children. Yet the sign of the covenant, circumcision, was given to them as infants. Even though circumcision was a sign of a covenant which rested on faith, it was to be given to children before they had intelligent faith. Since in reality the two covenants are one, why should it be different with baptism, the sign of the New Covenant?

It was from this understanding of the pattern of God's gracious gift of salvation, not only to parents but also to their children, that the Reformers were able to understand a number of New Testament passages. From this standpoint they now were able to understand the words of Jesus, "Let the children come to me, and do not hinder them; for to such belongs the kingdom of heaven" (Matt. 19:14). According to the Reformers, this text makes it clear that the Kingdom of God is not limited to adults.[52] Bullinger followed Zwingli in his understanding of Peter's sermon at Pentecost, "Repent, and be baptized every one of you in the name of Jesus Christ for the forgiveness of your sins; and you shall receive the gift of the Holy Spirit. For the promise is to you and to your children and to all that are far off . . ." (Acts 2:38-39). When Bullinger saw the connection of these words to the seventeenth chapter of Genesis, then he understood that they were indeed an offer of baptism to children.[53]

51. Bullinger, *Fräfel,* 55 r.
52. Bullinger, *Fräfel,* 55 v.
53. Bullinger, *Fräfel,* 65 r.

The Argument from Christian Nurture

The fourth reason for baptizing children which was advanced by the Reformers was that Christian parents had the responsibility, according to the teaching of the apostle Paul, to bring up these children "in the nurture and admonition of the Lord" (Eph. 6:4). As the Reformers understood it, children of believers are to be brought up inside the Church, not outside the Church.

One of the things which the Anabaptist argument really never took into consideration is that all of the baptisms recorded in the New Testament involve first-generation Christians. The Scriptures provide us no example of how someone born of Christian parents became a Christian. As has been indicated earlier, the Anabaptist hermeneutics was faced with a real problem when it had to deal with moving from the New Testament situation, where to become a Christian was to be converted from either Judaism or paganism into the Christian faith, to the situation of the sixteenth century, where to become a Christian was to believe the faith one's parents already believed.

There was another aspect to this matter. The Anabaptists found it difficult to believe that Christendom was really Christian. As the Anabaptists saw it, there was only a very small number of real Christians in the world. The Church, by the intention of Jesus, was to be made up exclusively of a small number of real Christians. This went hand in hand with their millenarianism, whether in its more revolutionary interpretation offered by Müntzer and Hoffman or its more pacifist interpretation presented by Grebel and Denck. It was not only that their hermeneutic could not deal with the problem of how to make Christians of the children of Christians. It was just as much that their eschatology ran counter to the idea that the whole of society should embrace the Christian faith and look to the Christian Church for salvation. By denying the validity of infant baptism, the Anabaptists were able to understand why they were such a small and misunderstood group. All those baptized people who claimed to be Christians were not really Christians after all. Because they had been baptized in infancy, their baptism was invalid. Müntzer and Denck particularly had made it clear that the root of the problem was the idea that one could bring up a child in the Christian faith. The Anabaptists were not interested in how children were to be brought up "in the nurture and admonition of the Lord."

From the very beginning, Zwingli pointed out that baptism is a sign of entrance into the Church. The Anabaptists usually began their argument by explaining that when Christ instituted baptism, he commissioned his disciples to "make disciples of all nations, baptizing them in the name of the Father and of the Son and of the Holy Spirit . . ." (Matt. 28:19). From this, they said, it is clear that one should teach first and then baptize. Zwingli, returning to the

Greek text, said that a strict reading of the text does not support this interpretation. If one follows the word order strictly, one learns that the apostles were commissioned *to make disciples* of all nations, and the way they were to do this was by "baptizing them. . . , teaching them to observe all things that I have commanded you" (Matt. 28:19-20).[54] The standard translations of the day had ignored two important details in the original Greek text. The Greek verb μαθητεύσατε is not correctly translated by *teach,* but by *make disciples.* The two participles βαπτίζοντες (baptizing) and διδάσκοντες (teaching) modify μαθητεύσατε (make disciples). That is, these two participles explain that disciples are to be made by baptizing and teaching. If the sequence of the words were to imply a temporal ordering of the two things, then that would imply that first new Christians are to be initiated by baptism and then taught; however, Zwingli, quite correctly, does not think that one can press the word order that far; there is no reason that the teaching could not be before baptism or after baptism, just as long as there is both teaching and baptism.

Zwingli continues to build up his argument that baptism should be understood as initiation.[55] Next he turns to the sixth chapter of Romans, "For as many of you as have been baptized into Christ have been baptized into his death."[56] Zwingli discusses the difference between being baptized in Christ and being baptized *into* Christ.[57] It is not those who are already in Christ who are baptized, but rather through baptism those who are outside of Christ are brought into his body. While the name of Tertullian is not explicitly mentioned, Zwingli uses Tertullian's comparison of baptism to the *sacramentum,* or pledge of allegiance, made by the soldier when he is enrolled in military service.[58] For Zwingli, baptism is the sacrament of initiation and therefore should be administered at the beginning of the Christian life. For the children of believers this is indeed at the very beginning of life itself. Zwingli's argument opened the way for understanding that there is a place for teaching the faith from inside the fellowship of the Church.

54. Zwingli, *Of Baptism,* pp. 143-44; *Von der Taufe,* pp. 234-35. Calvin, too, takes special care in showing that this key passage in the Anabaptist argument simply does not read the way they thought it did. Unfortunately the Anabaptists had relied on the Vulgate text, "Euntes ergo docete omnes gentes," rather than on the Greek text. The Vulgate might be translated "go teach all nations" rather than "go make disciples of all nations," as the RSV translates the Greek. *Institutes* 4.16.27.

55. See Thomas Müntzer, *Protestation,* who is willing to speak of baptism as initiation, and Grebel, *Programmatic Letters,* who insists that one must have faith both before and after baptism. Hübmaier.

56. Oecolampadius draws the idea that baptism is initiation from Acts 2:41; *Antwort,* K ij v.

57. *Of Baptism,* p. 150; *Von der Taufe,* p. 243.

58. *Of Baptism,* p. 147; *Von der Taufe,* p. 240.

Oecolampadius in his reply to Balthasar Hübmaier stresses that by making the child a member of the Church he is planted in the field of God's grace where, as it were, one can expect the cultivation of the Holy Spirit. In the fellowship of the Church the children are gathered about the fountain of God's grace.[59] It is from that fountain of God's grace that we can expect faith to come. In the fellowship of the Church God's Spirit can use the faith of other Christians to work faith in the heart of the child.[60] The key to the position of Oecolampadius is his strong doctrine of the sovereignty of God. In the last analysis the basis of our salvation is God's grace. It is because of God's grace toward us that he gives us faith. For Oecolampadius "the grace of Christ reaches farther than the sin of Adam."[61] In his answer to Carlin he tells us that baptism is a door and an entrance and that it is the job of the porter to let in everyone for whom there is hope that he will be taught.[62]

Oecolampadius, as one of the great patristic scholars of his age, was well aware of the fact that the Church Fathers often spoke of baptism as illumination. This tradition goes back to the book of Hebrews, where baptism is referred to as illumination (Heb. 6:4). Oecolampadius knew that many of the Fathers left much of the essential catechetical instruction until after baptism because they believed that without the enlightenment of baptism one could not be taught the deepest mysteries of the Christian faith. For the Church Fathers the healing of the blind man in the ninth chapter of the Gospel of John was usually interpreted as pertaining to baptism and the meaning they took from it was that there was much in the Christian faith which could only be learned from inside the faith.[63]

Bullinger, still pressing the typological relation between baptism and circumcision, makes the point that when we baptize children we take upon ourselves the responsibility of teaching them. Just as outward circumcision imposed the responsibility of being circumcised of heart (Jer. 4:4; Deut. 10:16; Rom. 2:25-29), so one's children are part of the covenant: "And these words which I command you this day shall be upon your heart; and you shall teach them diligently to your children . . ." (Deut. 6:6-7). It was after their circumcision that the children were taught what it meant. So also in the New Covenant

59. Oecolampadius, *Antwort,* K r.

60. Oecolampadius, *Antwort,* J iiij v.

61. ". . . die verdienst der gnaden Christi weitter reichen, dan die schuld Ade. . . ." *Antwort,* K r.

62. Oecolampadius, *Underrichtung,* C v; *AGBR* 2, p. 557.

63. Oecolampadius, *Underrichtung,* B iii v. Obviously the Reformer does not think of either illumination or the anointing of the Holy Spirit in a magical way. Cf. also *Underrichtung* D iiij r. *AGBR* 2, p. 564.

we are responsible to teach our children the meaning of the sign, and to introduce them to the knowledge of the true gospel.[64] It is the reasoning which explains the appearance in Reformed baptismal rites of vows taken by the parents to bring the child up "in the nurture and admonition of the Lord."

Another aspect of this argument which one frequently finds in the writings of the Reformers is the idea that baptism is the presentation or dedication of children to God.[65] In the Old Covenant it was part of the covenant responsibility to offer one's children to God. This was made clear in the commandment to teach the children the covenant (Deut. 6:6-7; Ps. 78:5-7), as well as in many stories such as Hannah's dedication of Samuel and the presentation of Jesus in the temple. As the Reformers understood it, this covenant responsibility to bring one's children up in the faith was behind the words of the apostle Paul in Ephesians 6:4. It was the responsibility of Christian parents to offer their children to God by bringing them up "in the nurture and admonition of the Lord." Bucer puts this interpretation on the house baptisms in Acts. It was the responsibility of the parents in their being baptized to offer their children to God as well.[66] This seems strange to us, perhaps, but it is a very biblical concept — particularly when it is seen over against the idea as often encountered today, that one should not prejudice children by indoctrinating them with religion before they have developed the critical facilities to think for themselves.

Argument from the Work of the Holy Spirit

A fifth argument to support infant baptism which the Reformers presented was that children should be baptized because the Holy Spirit is at work with children of believers from the very beginning of life. Christ begins his work of redemption in their hearts even before they have the power of reason. The Anabaptists had claimed that infants could not have the Holy Spirit until they had the power of reason. A person had to pass through a conversion experience before he or she could receive the Holy Spirit. A person had to make a decision for Christ before the Holy Spirit began to work in his or her heart.

Zwingli denied this, calling on the examples of Jeremiah (Jer. 1:5) and John the Baptist (Luke 1:41) to show that even in unborn infants God was already at work.[67] Luther, of course, in his teaching on the faith of infants,

64. Bullinger, *Fräfel,* 60 r-v.
65. Oecolampadius, *Underrichtung,* B r; *AGBR* 2, p. 551. Calvin, *Institutes* 4.16.32.
66. Bucer, *Bericht,* P iij r-v; *BDS* 5, p. 197.
67. Zwingli, *Of Baptism,* p. 149; *Von der Taufe,* p. 242.

fides infantium, had developed this theme at great length.[68] With Zwingli we find only a very modest development of the theme.

Bullinger, on the other hand, develops this position further than Zwingli. He denies the Anabaptist claim that children cannot have the Holy Spirit.

> Now even the children are cleansed by God; therefore, they have the Spirit of God. If they have the Spirit of God, then they are God's and they should have baptism as well.[69]

The key passage of Scripture here is 1 Corinthians 7:14, where the apostle Paul says that the children of believers are not unclean, but rather holy. The confidence that the children of believers were holy and had already the Holy Spirit at work in their hearts is the reason the Reformed Church has never exorcised infants as part of the baptismal rite.

From here Bullinger goes on to show from the story of Jesus blessing the children in Mark 10 and Matthew 19 that God does bless children.[70] What did Jesus do when he laid his hands upon them and blessed them? Was it a merely physical blessing? Bucer puts the same point even more forcefully:

> Are we to imagine that Christ's blessing of these children with the sign of the laying on of hands was more than mere words about salvation? Those who brought the children to him wanted him to pray for them. What for? Undoubtedly that they receive the grace of God, that is, for that same salvation that our savior won for us through his death, for it is through him that all the grace of God comes. . . . What else could this blessing mean than that Jesus prayed for and promised to these children all the good gifts of God.[71]

68. On Luther's understanding of the faith of infants see Lorenz Grönvik, *Die Taufe in der Theologie Martin Luthers,* Acta Academiae Aboensis, series A: *Humaniora,* vol. 36, no. 1 (Abo: Abo Akademi, 1968), pp. 154-72. Grönvik, after a careful study of the long discussion about this aspect of Luther's baptismal theology, concludes that Luther's teaching on the faith of infants is quite consistent with his teaching on the nature of faith. It is by no means to be regarded as an artificial construction developed purely for polemical purposes.

69. "Nun sind aber die kinder von Gottes gereyniget, darumb habend sy ouch den geist Gottes. Habend sie nun den selben, so sind sy Gottes, und hört jnen ouch der Touff." Bullinger, *Fräfel,* 57 v.

70. Bullinger, *Fräfel,* 57 v to 58 r.

71. "Mag nun diss segnen Christi diser kindlinen nit dem sacrament dess hendaufflegens, auch etwas anders sein, dann vertroestung seiner erloesung? Die die kindlin jm zubrachten begereten, je das er für sie betten solte. Waram? on Zweifel vmb die gnad Gottes . . . darumb wurt er ja für dise kindlin gebettet haben, Dann das er sy gesegnet hat, was kan dz doch anders sein, dann das er hatt jnen vom vatter alles guots gebetten, vnd zugesagt?" *Bericht,* f i v.

The early Reformed theologians were all in agreement that even before the children of believers made a confession of faith, even before they were old enough to make a decision, the Holy Spirit was at work within them applying to them the benefits of redemption in Christ. As Oecolampadius put it, "Christ washed us from our sins by his blood and in this grace our children also participate."[72]

What is at issue here is a sort of religious anthropology. Are children religious nonentities until they reach the age that they can make a reasonable decision? It is interesting that the Anabaptists denied that the Holy Spirit could be at work within a child until he matured. Did it mean that they were rationalists? Did it mean that faith had to be built on reason and that until there was reason there could be no faith? The Reformers, following Augustine and Anselm, gave primacy to faith over reason. They were thoroughly committed both to *fides quaerens intellectum* and to *credo ut intelligam.* The Reformers were quite willing to admit the existence of faith in children before the development of understanding. The story of Christ blessing the children is not irrelevant to the question of infant baptism. That simple childlike trust which children have before the age of reason is precisely the kind of faith which Jesus held up as exemplary to his disciples (Matt. 18:2-5; Mark 10:15; Luke 18:17). Before children are able to make a reasonable judgment or even a conscious decision, they can have faith as a gift from God. This faith is a trusting and loving inclination toward God. Faith is something deeper than either the reason or the will. It is something which, by the grace of God, the Spirit plants within us. Both obedience and understanding proceed from it. It is that election which Jacob received in his mother's womb, that consecration which Jeremiah received before he was born, that joy in the things of God with which John leaped in the womb of his mother Elizabeth. It is on the gracious act of God that our salvation rests, not on an act of the will or a perception of the mind; "So it depends not upon man's will or exertion, but upon God's mercy" (Rom. 9:16).

The Anabaptists were, to be sure, not so much rationalists as they were voluntarists. That is, they believed that we receive salvation through an act of the will. The Anabaptists often emphasized that only an adult could make the kind of conscious decision required to become a Christian. Children could not have the sort of experience described in the sixth chapter of Romans. Only adults could experience the feeling of being buried with Christ and rising with

72. ". . . das Christus uns mit seim blüt abgeweschen hab von unsern sünden, welcher gnaden auch die kind teilhafftig sein. . . ." Oecolampadius, *Underrichtung,* C iiij v; *AGBR* 2, pp. 561-62; and D ij r; *AGBR* 2, p. 564.

Christ. The Reformers believed the nature of saving grace was such that it could be received by children, and they were confident that God would be faithful to their children just as he had been to them.

Argument from the Primacy of Grace

Another insight with which the Reformers came more and more to defend the practice of infant baptism was that baptism is primarily an act of God. The fact that baptism is primarily an act of God rather than of the one baptized is, of course, clear from the very grammatical usage of the word. The word is used in the passive voice: such and such a person is baptized. Baptism is something done to a person, not something the one baptized does himself. It is the same way with the meaning of the sacramental action. One is washed; one does not wash oneself. The Reformers did not come to this position immediately. At the beginning of the discussion, Zwingli was nowhere near saying this, and in the end of the segment of the discussion which we are studying it is Bucer who has come most clearly to the position; nevertheless, as the discussion goes on, it will become an important line of thought.

Zwingli makes a radical distinction between outward baptism and inward baptism. Outward baptism is done by human beings and inward baptism is done by God. The disciples "could not baptize with the Spirit, for God alone baptizes with the Spirit, and he himself chooses how and when and to whom that baptism will be administered."[73] Zwingli can speak of baptism as an outward confession of faith. In his first work against the Anabaptists he compared it to the insignia worn by the Swiss to show that they are indeed Swiss. Surely, one of the outward aspects of baptism is that it serves as a public profession of faith, but this is a secondary aspect. As we shall see, Calvin will also speak of baptism as an outward profession of faith made by the one baptized, but it is by no means one of the things primarily signified by the sign of washing.[74]

Oecolampadius stood very close to Zwingli; nevertheless, he begins to overcome Zwingli's radical distinction between outward baptism and inward baptism by insisting that the sign of baptism is to be trusted. It is not a lying sign.[75] In his understanding of baptism Oecolampadius put the emphasis on what the Holy Spirit does in the heart of the Christian. It is the Holy Spirit who is the seal of our salvation. It is the inner anointing of the Holy Spirit

73. Zwingli, *Of Baptism,* p. 133; *Von der Taufe,* p. 221.

74. Calvin, *Institutes* 4.15.1 and 13.

75. Oecolampadius, *Underrichtung,* D i r; *AGBR* 2, p. 562.

which is the real guarantee of our inheritance. It is Christ himself who regenerates us and unites us to himself.[76] Oecolampadius is confident that God is working in the hearts even of very young babies. There is no reason Christian parents should not be confident that God has called their children to himself as well as he has called adults.

> O that they would realize and learn, that we who are called Christians are destined to eternal salvation, that is if we follow our calling, and also we hope that we not alone, but joined . . . to our children, through the gracious will of God, will partake of God's grace. Why then should we not rejoice in this our sign, which Christ with his baptism began before us and our children.[77]

Here baptism is presented as a sign which Christ has given us and our children. Christ in his baptism began the sign. By calling attention to the institution of baptism by Christ, he makes it clear that baptism is a divine work.

> What a good assurance this sign is, that in so far as the Lord enlightens them with his grace, the children with this sign are indeed counted to be joined with us, and when they come to the exercising of their reason the Lord will give them the foundation and the motivation to follow on with their religion.[78]

Since the sign of baptism is a divinely given sign, then there is no reason to doubt it. God will bring about what he has signified in the sign of baptism. Baptism is a work of God because God uses it to awaken faith in human beings.

> Not that there is any power in the sign itself, but rather in so far as God uses the sign, so far then does baptism have its effect.[79]

So then, not only is baptism a work of God because he instituted the sign of baptism in the first place, but also because God uses the sign to bring about

76. Oecolampadius, *Underrichtung,* C iiij v; and D i r; *AGBR 2,* pp. 561-62.

77. "Ach, das sie gedächten oder lerneten, das wir so Christen genant werden, all verordnet sein zum ewigen heil, wo wir anders unserer berüffung nachuolgen, hoffen auch das wir nit allein, sonder auch unser frucht und kinder auss gnadigen willen Gottes der gnaden theilhafftig werden. Warumb freüwten dann wir uns nit unsers zeichens, das Christus mit seinen tauff angefangen hat vor uns und die kind?" *Underrichtung,* D ij v to D iij r; *AGBR* 2, p. 564.

78. ". . . wie ein güte züversicht, das, so der Herr die gnad verleücht, die kind mit dem zeichen uns zügezelt werden, so sie zü übung der vernunfft kämen, der Herr werd jn auch vyl ursach und avreitzung geben, das sie jrer religion weiter nachtrachten." *Underrichtung,* D iij r; *AGBR* 2, p. 564.

79. ". . . auss der würckenden krafft Gottes, nit das die in jn sey, aber so sie Gott braucht, so hat der tauff auch solche würckung." *Underrichtung,* C iiij v; *AGBR* 2, p. 561.

what the sign signifies. For Oecolampadius a sign is clearly not useless. God does indeed use signs. Oecolampadius, without losing Zwingli's basic insights into the exegetical realities of what baptism is not, has nevertheless been able to add some very positive insights. He emphasizes that it is God who, in the person of his Son, initiated the sign of baptism and that it is God who, in the person of his Spirit, uses the sign to bring about that which it signifies.

Bullinger brings out still another complimentary thought. The sign of baptism is a sign of what God will do through his Spirit in the one who is baptized. Just as water washes the body, so God by his grace will wash the one baptized from his sins. Whereas the Anabaptists saw baptism as a sign of the believer's confession of sin and his promise to live a new life, Bullinger sees it as a sign primarily of God's activity in cleansing the baptized of sin.[80] For the Anabaptist baptism was a sign given by the one baptized of a decision he had made. It was a human sign of a human act. The contrast between the voluntarist approach of the Anabaptists which puts the emphasis on the decision of the convert and the Reformed emphasis on grace which sees salvation primarily in terms of God's saving act toward humankind becomes very evident here. As Bullinger saw it, it is God's action which is the inward reality toward which the outward sign points.

> . . . for us as the water washes away all the dirt of the body, the stains and spots and any kind of impurity, so also the one over whom the baptismal waters have been poured, is received by God's grace, washed by the blood of Jesus and obligated to live a new life.[81]

With Bucer, the action of God in baptism becomes most evident; he says, "Baptism is a divine action of the Church of Christ."[82] It is because baptism is an act of God carried out by the ministry of the Church that the minister must baptize according to the Word of God. Baptism is a divine action because of the divine institution of the sacrament, the divine promises behind the sacrament, and the divine empowering of the ministry. Here Bucer shows us that he is very clear about the part which the minister of baptism plays in the

80. Bullinger, *Fräfel,* 59 v to 60 r. Oecolampadius implies the same thing in *Underrichtung,* C iiij r-v; *AGBR* 2, p. 561. For a rather negative evaluation of this view see Johann Usteri, "Oekolampads Stellung zur Kindertaufe," *Theologische Studien und Kritiken* (1883): 167.

81. ". . . das wie dz wasser alle mosen des lybs, befleckung, und unreinikeyt, abwäscht: also werde ouch der begossen, uss gnaden ufgenommen, und mit dem blüt Jesu gewäschen, und geplichtet zü einem nüwen läben." Bullinger, *Fräfel,* 60 s.

82. "Der tauff ist ein Göttliche handlung der kirchen Christi." Bucer, *Bericht,* P r; *BDS* 5, p. 195.

sacrament. He baptizes not in his own name but in the name of Jesus.[83] The minister performs the sacrament at the bidding of the risen Christ (Matt. 28:18) and in obedience to him. It is, of course, for this same reason that the shaping of the baptismal rite must be according to God's Word. The sign of baptism is an act of God because God has given it. The giving of exorcised salt and the anointings with oil and chrism were not divinely given, and they have no divine promise behind them. It is precisely because of the divine institution of baptism that we can be sure that it is not an empty sign. It is the promise of God behind the sign which makes it a true sign. The minister as the servant of Christ baptizes, but it is in reality Christ who baptizes, because the action of a servant which is done in the name of and in obedience to the master is credited not to the servant, but to the master. In the most profound sense, then, it is neither the one baptized nor the minister of baptism who baptizes, but Christ himself. With the *First Helvetic Confession of 1536,* this position was adopted by the earliest Reformed Churches. We find in article 21, "According to the institution of the Lord, baptism is a bath of regeneration which the Lord offers and presents to His elect with a visible sign through the ministry of the church. . . ."[84] It is the risen and ascended Christ who in his death and in his resurrection makes us one body with himself. It is the glorified Christ who through his Holy Spirit produces in us the fruit of the Spirit, love, joy, and peace. It is Christ who through his indwelling Spirit brings about the new birth. Paraphrasing John 3:3, Bucer says, "Is it not from above that the new birth comes to us?"[85]

At the very heart of the Protestant Reformation was the revival of Augustinian theology with its strong emphasis on the primacy of grace. The Reformers believed that God took the initiative for humankind's salvation. In the light of such a strong doctrine of grace the baptism of infants was quite understandable. In fact, the baptism of infants demonstrated very powerfully that our salvation rests not on any knowledge or work or experience or decision of our own, but entirely on the grace of God.

One might do well to make clear at this point that for anyone who understands baptism as primarily a human act by which the Christian signifies his faith toward God and before the world, the question of the shaping of the rite of baptism takes on a very different nature. If baptism is a human sign,

83. Bucer, *Bericht,* fol. P r-v; *BDS* 5, p. 195.

84. For an English translation of the *First Helvetic Confession of 1536* see Arthur C. Cochrane, *Reformed Confessions of the 16th Century* (Philadelphia: Westminster Press, 1966), p. 108.

85. "Diss begraben in todt Christi, ist ja die newgepurt, kommet aber uns die nit oben herab?" Bucer, *Bericht,* O iiij V; *BDS* 5, p. 194.

then surely anyone is completely free to make that sign in any way he or she wishes. The fact that the Reformers insisted on shaping the rite of baptism according to God's Word was closely connected with the fact that they considered baptism a divine act. In the history of Christian worship it is again and again when the theology of grace is forgotten that new and more meaningful liturgical forms have to be invented. For example, the fourth- century baptismal rites, as splendid as they were, rested on a baptismal theology which demanded three years of preparation and scrutiny before one was baptized. Essentially one had to prove one was a Christian before one was baptized. This hardly tallied with the baptism of the Ethiopian eunuch or the Philippian jailor. The practice of the primitive Church was to baptize immediately. If in the fourth century one had to prove one was a Christian before one was baptized, no wonder Pelagianism developed! Side by side with these elaborate baptismal rites Donatism developed as well. Donatism could only develop because too much attention was given to the rite of baptism as a human work. The Church needed a stronger emphasis on grace when Augustine appeared on the theological horizon at the end of the fourth century!

Calvin's Adoption of the Argument

Up to this point we have not spoken of Calvin's response to the Anabaptist position.[86] Calvin's response has been left for separate consideration for several reasons. Calvin wrote four years after the fall of Müntzer, which marked the end of the first phase of the movement. Calvin wrote on the subject after the main position of the earliest Reformed theologians had been developed. There have been those who have argued that he did not really oppose the Anabaptist movement in the same way the earlier Reformers had. It is somehow imagined that Calvin merely followed along with his colleagues in Strasbourg, Basel, and Zurich, or that infant baptism was not really a live issue for him. In order that there be no confusion in this matter, Calvin's position will be presented separately.[87]

In 1539, while Calvin was pastor of the French Church in Strasbourg, he published his second edition of the *Institutes,* which included a chapter

86. On the subject of Calvin's understanding of the baptism of infants see L. B. M. Alting von Geusau, *Die Lehre von der Kindertaufe bei Calvin* (Bilthoven, The Netherlands: Uitgeverij H. Neilssen, 1963).

87. On Calvin's relation to the Anabaptist movement see the excellent work of Willem Balke, *Calvin and the Anabaptist Radicals* (Grand Rapids, Mich.: William B. Eerdmans, 1981).

devoted to the defense of infant baptism. In no city in Europe would he have been more close to the whole breadth of Anabaptist thought. Most of the Anabaptist leaders had passed through Strasbourg in a vain attempt to make it the Antioch of Anabaptism. Carlstadt, Sattler, Marpeck, Denck, and even Servetus had all entered into the theological discussions which characterized the city. Melchior Hofmann, whose apocalyptic prophecies did so much to provoke the siege of Münster several years before, was still railing behind the bars of a Strasbourg prison. Calvin even before his Strasbourg ministry had debated with the Anabaptists in the priory of Rive in Geneva. In Strasbourg he was instrumental in the conversion of a number of prominent Anabaptist leaders. In fact, Calvin married the widow of one of these converts from the Anabaptist movement. There is some evidence that Calvin gained a number of insights from Idelette de Bure herself.[88] Calvin knew the discussion and was well equipped to write on it.[89]

What Calvin did was to synthesize the basic arguments of the earlier Reformers into one consistent line of thought. It is the argument from covenant theology which forms the basis of Calvin's position. Calvin speaks of the typological or, as he calls it, the "anagogic" relation of the two covenants. He affirms that there is one eternal covenant embracing the Old and New Testaments, making them one people of God. The Old Covenant included children in the people of God, as is evident from the fact that children were circumcised. Calvin asks, Should we expect God to be less gracious to the children of Christians than to the children of the Jews? In fact, we have the word of Jesus that children do belong to the Kingdom of God (Matt. 19:14), and the word of the apostle Paul that children are included in the sanctifying work of the Holy Spirit (1 Cor. 7:14). Calvin goes on to say that there is no evidence that

88. Idelette de Bure's first husband, Jean Stordeur, had been a leader of the Anabaptist movement in Liege before being exiled in 1533. It was six years later that Calvin converted him. In 1540 Stordeur died of the plague. The little evidence which has been preserved would indicate that Idelette de Bure was a woman of strong personal faith who would have understood the Anabaptist position quite well. Cf. Willem Balke, *Calvin and the Anabaptist Radicals,* pp. 133-38.

89. See G. H. Williams's chapter "Calvin and the Radical Reformation," in *The Radical Reformation,* pp. 580-614. We find ourselves in disagreement with a number of points in the chapter. The fact that Calvin wanted a church independent from the government of Geneva is not an indication that he had been influenced by the Anabaptists. It indicates rather a basic weakness in the theory of Williams that the dependence of the Church on the state was of the essence of what he calls the "Magisterial Reformation," that is, the Reform of Luther, Zwingli, Bucer, and Calvin. The position of Bucer and Calvin simply indicates that classical Protestantism is not essentially "magisterial." By the same token, the fact that Hübmaier and Hoffmann were willing to go along with a magisterially supported reform did not mean that they were any less true Anabaptists than Grebel and Denck.

children were not baptized in the New Testament Church, nor is there any evidence that it was invented at a later period in the history of the Church. This, then, is the argument that he presents in the opening sections of his chapter on infant baptism.[90] In the second part of this chapter, he turns to answering Anabaptist arguments against the unity of the covenants and the typological relation between circumcision and baptism.[91] Next he defends the idea that the Holy Spirit is actively bringing children to Christ even in infancy.[92] More briefly he defends the historical argument in much the same way Zwingli had advanced it. The word "synecdoche" is not mentioned, but the principle is clearly affirmed.[93] Calvin, as Zwingli or Oecolampadius, believed the New Testament Church had baptized infants. The chapter is concluded by the study of various texts of Scripture which the Anabaptists had advanced to support their position.[94]

What is very clear is that Calvin has basically adopted the arguments of Zwingli, Bullinger, Bucer, and Oecolampadius. There is nothing mechanical about his adoption; Calvin has thought through these arguments and presented them in a clearer and more forceful way than any of his predecessors. The way Calvin has ordered and balanced the arguments shows his genius as a systematic theologian. When one compares Calvin's defense of infant baptism to those of Zwingli, Bucer, Oecolampadius, and Bullinger, it is hard to imagine that Calvin only went along with infant baptism to keep peace with his colleagues in Zurich, Basel, and Strasbourg. Calvin was obviously just as much concerned to maintain the practice of infant baptism as his colleagues were.

Conclusion

Having looked at the way the Reformers defended infant baptism, we are in a much better position to understand the development of their baptismal rite. The Reformed baptismal rite was developed not only as a reform of the Latin baptismal rite of the late Middle Ages, but it was also developed over and against the Anabaptist movement. One might say that the Reformers developed

90. *Institutes* 4.16.1-9.

91. *Institutes* 4.16.10-16.

92. *Institutes* 4.16.17-20.

93. *Institutes* 4.16.21-22.

94. *Institutes* 4.16.25-30. In a later edition of the *Institutes,* Calvin added a section to the chapter in which he refuted the arguments of Servetus, whom Calvin regarded as an Anabaptist. Calvin naturally recognized that Servetus was not the usual sort of Anabaptist, as his opening remarks to the new section indicate. *Institutes* 4.16.31.

their liturgical practice while thinking on two fronts at the same time. On the one side were the old Latin rites they had inherited and on the other side was the practice of the Anabaptists. This gave their work a far greater balance than it might otherwise have had. It made them think more deeply into what they meant by the importance of worship being "according to Scripture." Although they believed that the earliest Christians baptized infants, they admitted that there was no specific command or clear example of infant baptism in the New Testament; but the Reformers nevertheless believed that infant baptism was according to Scripture. It was according to scriptural principles.[95] In the same way it was the controversy with the Anabaptists which led the Reformers to delve more deeply into the theology of the covenant, and from this new appreciation of covenant theology many of the most profound insights of Reformed sacramental theology have developed. The controversy over infant baptism was an important stimulus to the maturing of Reformed theology, and this was particularly the case in regard to worship.

One thing which has come out quite clearly in this study is that the Reformers did not simply take over their defense of infant baptism from others. They worked it out for themselves. The sixteenth century was not the first time infant baptism had been called into question. Augustine had had to defend infant baptism in the fourth century, and in the Middle Ages Bernard of Clairvaux, Thomas Aquinas, and Bonaventure had had the same task. Their defense of the practice was based on the vicarious faith of the godparents.[96] The argument of Bernard was particularly solid. Although this defense was well known to the Reformers, the Reformers developed their own defense. If the Reformers continued to baptize infants, it was not simply because of the force of long tradition.

Another matter which should be equally clear from this study is that the position of the Reformers in regard to infant baptism was an integral part of their whole theology. It is not as though the baptizing of very young children was a strange inconsistency which was perpetuated out of habit. It is not as though here was a place where the Reformers strangely neglected to apply their usual principles of reform. The recovery of biblical Hebrew was one of the formative elements of the High Rhenish reform. Before the Anabaptists

95. On the way the Reformers worked out the principle that the Church is to be reformed "according to Scripture." See Hughes Oliphant Old, "John Oecolampadius and the Patristic Argument in the Defense of Infant Baptism."

96. On the Reformers' knowledge of the Scholastic defense of infant baptism see Hughes Oliphant Old, "Bullinger and the Scholastic Works on Baptism," *Heinrich Bullinger, 1504-1575, Gesammelte Aufsätze zum 400. Todestag.* 2 vols. (Zurich: Theologische Verlag, 1975), pp. 191-207, esp. pp. 203-4.

came on the scene, Zwingli, Capito, Pellikan, Oecolampadius, and Bucer were all engaged in a fresh study of the Hebrew text of the Old Testament. There is nothing at all curious about the fact that they should develop an argument largely based on the Old Testament. Reformed theology has consistently recognized the greatest possible value of the Old Testament for Christian faith and life. Besides that, the Reformers' appeal to the Old Testament doctrine of the covenant was quite consistent with their Augustinian theology. Augustine, too, had stressed the continuity of the two testaments, the unity of the one Church from Adam and Eve down to our own day. The baptism of infants was a logical corollary to *sola gratia,* for it clearly demonstrated prevenient grace. It was the same way with the doctrine of the Holy Spirit. The doctrine of the Holy Spirit was fundamental to Reformed liturgical theology. Far from being a failure to carry through their reforming principles to their logical conclusions, the Reformers' position on infant baptism was thoroughly consistent with their whole program of reform.

Even more must be said. It is precisely in this question that the High Rhenish Reformers clarified for themselves some of their most basic insights. It was in regard to this question that they really worked out covenant theology, and it was here that they worked out so much in regard to their method of interpreting Scripture. The difference between illuministic exegesis and grammatical-historical exegesis became clearer as Zwingli and Oecolampadius argued with Hübmaier, Denck, and Grebel. It was here that they had to work out their strong doctrine of the ministry. One must surely say that Reformed theology would never have become what it did apart from the controversy with the Anabaptists. Much of Reformed theology took shape during the controversy over infant baptism.

CHAPTER VI

Further Development and Revision of the Reformed Baptismal Rite, 1526-42

The first attempts to produce a baptismal rite that was "reformed according to the Word of God" produced three different baptismal rites in Zurich, Strasbourg, and Basel. These rites were produced out of the concern to reform the Latin baptismal rites of the Middle Ages. This concern for reform was largely inspired by Rhenish Christian Humanism and its desire to restore the purity of early Christian practice. The earliest Reformed rites, which we studied in Chapter III, were not significantly affected by the Anabaptist demand for reform, but beginning in 1526 the Reformed baptismal rites began to be affected by the controversy with the Anabaptists.

The first Reformed rites of Strasbourg, Zurich, and Basel were used as patterns by a number of other churches which began to follow these three cities in the path of reform. There was a considerable amount of cross-pollination between these three rites; thus we find in Bern, Ulm, Neuchâtel, Augsburg, and Geneva elements from all three of these earliest attempts.

In the period from 1526 to 1545, the Reformed baptismal rites were quite flexible. This was not only the case with the new rites developed in Bern, Ulm, Neuchâtel, Augsburg, and Geneva but it was also the case in Zurich, Basel, and Strasbourg, where there were several revisions of the rites. Let us look at the Reformed baptismal rites which were produced after the first attempts of 1525 and see what development we find in them.

Revision of the Baptismal Rite in Zurich

When Zwingli published his first work against the Anabaptists, the effect was not to put an end to the controversy, but rather to give it increased impetus. It was like burning autumn leaves. Zwingli tried to smother the controversy by heaping on it a pile of hastily gathered scholarly observations. Rather than smothering the Anabaptist controversy with his learning, he only gave it more fuel.[1] Zwingli's essay *Of Baptism,* published in late spring of 1525, was quickly answered by Balthasar Hübmaier's *From the Christian Baptism of Believers.*[2] This made it clear to Zwingli that the fire was still burning, and he was forced to publish yet another refutation of the Anabaptist position, *An Answer to Balthasar Hübmaier's Baptismal Book.* This second work Zwingli finished at the beginning of November that same year.[3] Zwingli was annoyed that he had to become involved in the controversy. For him it seemed quite beside the point. As he saw it, the major concerns of the Reformation were in a quite different direction. The defiance of civil authority which had become a feature of the Anabaptist movement made it more difficult for the Reformation to accomplish its ends. The fire of the Anabaptists only heated the resistance of those who opposed the reform. Nevertheless, Zwingli and his colleagues were now forced to turn their attention to the Anabaptist challenge. They knew that unless that blaze was brought under control it would bring to ashes their whole vision of reform. As reluctantly as they may have gotten involved in the controversy, they were now involved.

From this point on the Zurich baptismal services were bound to be affected by this controversy. It was probably at the very beginning of 1526 that the *Order of the Christian Churches of Zurich* was published.[4] This

1. G. H. Williams, *The Radical Reformation* (Philadelphia: Westminster Press, 1962), pp. 131-34, and John Howard Yoder, *Täufertum und Reformation in der Schweiz,* Part 2 (Zurich: EVZ-Verlag, 1968), pp. 33- 43.

2. On this document, see above, Chap. IV, n. 48.

3. *Ueber doctor Balthazarz touffbüchlin waarhaffte, gründte antwurt durch Huldrychen Zuinglin* (Zurich: Ch. Froschauer, 1525), in *CR* 91, pp. 585-642.

4. *Ordnung der christenlichenn kilchenn zuo Zürich. Kinder ze touffen. Die ee ze bestäten. Die predig anzefahen und zuo enden. Gedächtnus der abgestorbnen. Das nachtmal Christi zuo begon* (Zurich: Ch. Froschauer, n.d.), in *CR* 91, pp. 670-94. To be abbreviated as Zurich *Ordnung, CR* 91. The *Corpus Reformatorum* gives the date as sometime after Easter of 1525. As we shall see, Zurich *Ordnung* depends on either the *Strasbourg Church Service* (E) published in May 1525 or the *Strasbourg Psalter of 1526* (F). Unfortunately, the single existing copy of the earlier document was destroyed in 1870. It is quite possible that the Zurich *Ordnung* was published as early as June 1525, but since it is not possible to be sure whether the Zurich *Ordnung* is dependent on the earlier Strasbourg document it seems more prudent to assign to the Zurich *Ordnung* the date 1526.

liturgical book included the full range of services used in the Church of Zurich. It contained not only the baptismal service but the service for the Lord's Supper, the preaching service, and the marriage service. This book had a predecessor in Leo Jud's *Baptismal Book* of 1523, which also contained several other liturgical forms besides the baptismal rite.[5] Nevertheless, with the publication of this service book, the leaders of the Protestant Reformation in Zurich spread before the world the liturgical reforms which they proposed. To do this was both a challenge to the old traditions which they sought to reform and a defense against the challenges leveled at them by the Anabaptists.

A recent attempt has been made to show that this service book was published no earlier than 1529.[6] Unfortunately, the book does not carry a date of publication. There are good reasons to prefer the earlier date of 1526 than the later date of 1529. Leo Jud's *Baptismal Book of 1523* was out of date by the spring of 1525 when Zwingli published *Of Baptism* and appended the baptismal service which was then in use. Hübmaier's answer to Zwingli's attack led the Zurich Reformers to revise their baptismal rite still further in the months to follow. It is this revision which we find in the *Order of the Christian Churches of Zurich*.

As has already been said, the publication of these liturgical formularies was an important part of the Zurich Reformers' defense against the attacks of the Anabaptists. The Anabaptists were demanding radical liturgical reform. They were very critical of the slowness with which the evangelical pastors were moving. As long as the Reformers hesitated to institute their proposed reforms, the Anabaptists were able to capitalize on the slowness of the Reformers and were able to organize their own churches with so much more justification. Once the worship was actually changed and the liturgies published, half the logs, as it were, had been pulled from the fire.[7] It would seem quite logical, then, that Zwingli and his colleagues would have made all haste to publish this revision which the Anabaptist controversy had occasioned. To wait until 1529 to publish these liturgical texts would have been a great tactical blunder!

This new order for the celebration of baptism contains three major revisions. The first of these is the addition of a Baptismal Exhortation. This

5. See above, Chap. II, n. 14. While this is commonly called a baptismal book, it also included a number of other liturgical forms such as a General Confession, a Prayer of Intercession for the Sunday morning service, a memorial for the dead, and a set of wedding prayers.

6. Fritz Schmidt-Clausing, "Die Neudatierung der liturgischen Schriften Zwinglis," *Theologische Zeitschrift* 25 (1969): 252-65.

7. Zwingli was well aware of the apologetic value of publishing the liturgical texts. It was for apologetic reasons that he appended the baptismal rite to *Von der Taufe* and the rite of the Lord's Supper to the apology he wrote to Francis I in 1531.

exhortation has been added directly after the opening invocation and the questions regarding the intention of the sponsors and the name of the child.

> Let us be mindful that God, our savior, wills that all men come to a knowledge of the truth, through the only mediator, Jesus Christ, who gave himself for the salvation of all men. It is also his will that we should pray for one another that we come to one and the same faith and knowledge of God's Son our savior.
>
> Therefore, let us pray God that this child receive faith and that the outward baptism be, through the work of the Holy Spirit, inwardly accomplished with the rich water of grace.[8]

Essentially, this text has been borrowed from Strasbourg. It has been shortened and much of the Strasbourg material deleted; nevertheless, everything in it is also found in the *Strasbourg Psalter of 1526* (F).[9] Its theological insights, then, are those of the Strasbourg Reformers rather than the Zurich Reformers. Somehow those who have studied the baptismal orders of Zurich up to this point have overlooked this.

In studying this Baptismal Exhortation, as it is found in the Zurich rite, several things are to be observed. It begins by making a clear statement of God's redemptive volition. This is obviously intended to guard against the voluntarist interpretation of the question for the intention of those bringing the child to be baptized.[10] Just so there is no misunderstanding on the matter, the exhortation alludes to 1 Timothy 2:3-6, ". . . God our Savior . . . desires all men to be saved and to come to the knowledge of the truth. For there is one God, and there is one mediator between God and men, the man Christ Jesus, who gave himself as a ransom for all. . . ." This passage of Scripture teaches us the priority of God's saving intention. It is an affirmation of the doctrine of prevenient grace and a tacit

8. "So gedeckend, das gott, unser heyland, wil, das alle menschen zuo erkantnuss der warheit kommind, durch den einigen mitler Christum Jesum, der sich geben hat für yederman zuo erlösung. Er wil ouch, das wir für einandren bittind, damit wir zuo einerley glouben kommind und erkantnuss des suns gottes, unsers erlösers.

"Darumb lassend unns gott bitten disem kind umb den glouben, unnd das der usserlich touff innwendig durch den heiligen geist mit dem gnadrychen wasser beschehe." Zurich *Ordnung, CR* 91, p. 680. This exhortation is a condensed form of one found in the *Strasbourg Psalter of 1526* (F). Friedrich Hubert, *Die Strassburger liturgischen Ordnungen in Zeitalter der Reformation* (Göttingen: Vandenhoeck und Ruprecht, 1900), pp. 38-39.

9. There is always the possibility that Zwingli actually got this text from the *Strasbourg Psalter of 1525* (E). Unfortunately, this earlier edition of the *Strasbourg Psalter* has been lost.

10. Balthasar Hübmaier had pleaded a voluntarist interpretation of the questions to the sponsors "Do you will this child to be baptized?" in his *The Christian Baptism of Believers* in the summer of 1525. *QGT* 9, p. 136.

argument against voluntarism. Not only does this quotation of 1 Timothy make clear that God's will for our salvation precedes our intention that our children be saved; but this passage also makes clear God's intention that all human beings be saved. This is by no means an expression of a tendency toward universalism on the part of Zwingli; rather, it parries the exclusiveness of those who were convinced that most of Christendom was lost. As Conrad Grebel and his circle saw it, only a very few tried and tested mature Christians would finally enter the Kingdom of God. This premillenarian attitude was far too pessimistic for the Reformers, who were more inclined toward believing that a great number of people would receive salvation.

The exhortation, still following 1 Timothy 2:1-8, calls the congregation to prayer. The prayer of the congregation is to ask God that what the sign of baptism signifies be truly accomplished in the life of the child. Here we discover the line of thought which the Reformed theologians would follow in attempting to overcome the separation between the outward baptism with water and the inward baptism of the Holy Spirit.

We have already seen how Bucer, Oecolampadius, and the other High Rhenish Reformers tried to overcome the strong separation which Zwingli made between the outward sign and the inward reality of the sacrament. One of the ways they attempted to do this was to emphasize the epicletic nature of baptism. Here we see how Zwingli has incorporated Bucer's insights into his own baptismal rite. Zwingli did take seriously the insights of his colleagues in Basel and Strasbourg. It is becoming more and more clear that for the earliest Reformed theologians the Baptismal Invocation carried great theological weight. Essential to the Reformed rite of baptism is the prayer that the Holy Spirit bring about an inner washing with the water of grace.

This phrase "the water of grace" has sounded strange in the ears of theologians who know the language of Zwingli. Indeed, the phrase does not come from Zwingli. It comes from Bucer. It emphasizes the fact that the washing away of sins is the gracious work of the Holy Spirit in the heart of the Christian. While the phrase is Bucer's, it was obviously acceptable to Zwingli. The strongest argument in favor of dating this revision of the rite of baptism as late as 1529 is that Zwingli must have borrowed the phrase from a work of Luther's which first appeared in 1529.[11] Now that it is clear that the phrase has been borrowed from Strasbourg the most compelling argument for dating the document in 1529 has been removed.[12]

11. Fritz Schmidt-Clausing, "Die Neudatierung," argues that this phrase can only come from Luther.

12. Hubert, *Ordnungen*, p. 39.

The second important revision of the Zurich rite is the addition of an admonition to the parents. This admonition follows the reading of the Gospel story of Jesus blessing the children:

> Having now heard that it is the will of our Lord that little children should be brought to him — for indeed he is also the savior of children — so it is that we want to bring to him this child, in so far as we may; that is, in baptism we receive him into the congregation and give him the sign of the covenant and the People of God. May God grant his grace to this end; that this might happen let each one pray the Our Father and confess The Faith.
>
> The minister says to the godparents:
>
> You have consented to bring this child to baptism and in so doing to become joint fathers and mothers in regard to those things which pertain to a godly life. So I admonish you to consider that our God is a God of truth and that he wills that man serve him in truth. And as you have here before others taken responsibility for this child, so likewise after this, as the necessity appears, you should according to your ability help bring up this child to the glory of God to whom we now offer up this child.[13]

This admonition to the godparents contains a considerable amount of apologetic against the Anabaptist movement. It is done in the context of a commentary on the Scripture lesson always read at the baptismal service. The lesson tells the story of parents presenting their children to Jesus. The minister comments that the godparents are to help the parents bring their children to Christ. They are to pray for the salvation of the child, and set an example of serving God in truth and leading the child in a godly life. Just as it was proper to bring children to Jesus in the Gospel story, so it is still proper to present children to their savior. One does not have to wait until the children reach the age of reason. Bringing up children in the nurture and admonition of the Lord begins in earliest childhood. Children are given the sign of the covenant because they are brought up inside the covenant community, for indeed Christ Jesus is the

13. "Diewyl ir hie ghört habend, das der herr wil, das man imm die kindlin zuobringe — dann er ouch der kinder heylland ist —, so wellend wir im dises kindlin, so vil wir mögennd, zuobringen, das ist: mit dem touff in sin gemeind ufnemmen unnd im das zeichen des pundts und volck gottes geben. Gott gebe sin gnad darzuo, sölchs zuo erwäben, bätte ein yetlichs ein 'vatter unser' und verjehe den glouben."

"Der diener spreche zuon gfätteren:

"Ir habend üch erbetten lassen, dises kind zum touff ze bringen als die nun zuo göttlichen leben sine mitväter und -muetren sin wöllend. So erman ich üch, ir wöllind betrachten, das unser gott ein waarer gott ist und wil, das man im in der warheit diene. Und wie ir üch dises kinds hie vor andren annemmend, das ir sölichs hernach, so es die not erhöuschet, thuon wöllind, üwer vermögens, und helffen, das diss kind zuo der eer gottes, dem wir es yetz ufopfferend, erzogen werde." Zurich *Ordnung, CR* 91, p. 682.

Savior of children as well as of adults. In this admonition the polemic against the Anabaptists is clearly discernible.

The third revision is the addition of the two catechetical pieces, the Lord's Prayer and the Apostles' Creed. The pieces were placed in the midst of the admonition to the godparents. These catechetical pieces have a very clear function in this revised rite.[14] The saying of the Creed and the Lord's Prayer reveal the parents and godparents of the child as being Christians. In saying the Creed they make the covenant vow. The Zurich Reformers knew well Tertullian's explanation of the Creed as the *sacramentum* of the Christian. According to Tertullian the Creed was the *sacramentum* or vow by which a Christian enlisted in the Church. If baptism was to Zwingli the sign of the covenant, then reciting the Creed was the vow of the covenant. By reciting the Creed those present manifested that they were the Church. In the same way the congregation demonstrated itself to be the family of God by praying the Lord's Prayer. According to the apostle Paul, ". . . because you are sons, God has sent the Spirit of his Son into our hearts, crying, 'Abba! Father!' " (Gal. 4:6). Now that the Church has thus manifested itself to be the covenant people of God, the admonition continues, telling the godparents that they are to help bring the child up to the honor of God.

Another thing should be noticed here. The Church of Zurich was making progress in establishing genuine catechetical instruction. We will have more to say about this later, but for now it is sufficient to notice that the pastors of Zurich have in mind not so much that the parents and godparents simply teach the child the Creed and the Lord's Prayer. They have in mind a much broader concept of Christian education. A part of that Christian education was the regular catechetical instruction recently instituted by the Church of Zurich.

In 1528, another revision of the Zurich baptismal rite appeared, the *Zurich Service Book of 1528.*[15] This order indicates a simplification of the rite both over and against the service found in the appendix of *Of Baptism,* published in 1525, and the service found in the *Order of the Christian Churches of Zurich,* published in 1526. The Baptismal Exhortation has disappeared; so has the benediction at the end of the service. The admonition to the parents

14. Surely one of the reasons for believing that that document was produced late in 1525 or early in 1526 is that in 1526 Zwingli wrote to Johann Fabri saying that both the Lord's Prayer and the Apostles' Creed were used in the Zurich baptismal rite. *CR* 92, p. 50.

15. *Eine kurtz allgemeine Form, kinder zu taufen, die Ehe zu bestautigen, die Predigt anzufangen und zu unden, wie es zu Zürich gebraucht wird.* This original has not been available for this study. The text used is a modern German version in Fritz Schmidt-Clausing's *Zwinglis liturgische Formulare* (Frankfurt am Main: Otto Lembeck, 1970), pp. 43-50. See n. 24 below.

and godparents has been replaced by a rubric that there should be such an admonition but without providing the text. The rubric provides for the saying of the Lord's Prayer and the Ave Maria rather than the Lord's Prayer and the Apostles' Creed. The 1528 service has made a good number of stylistic changes over the two earlier baptismal rites.[16] This *Zurich Service Book of 1528* is rather puzzling because it seems to have been bypassed in the liturgical evolution in Zurich. Succeeding orders followed the forms developed in 1525 and 1526, completely ignoring the *Zurich Service Book of 1528.* If the 1528 revision was bypassed by Zurich, it was not bypassed completely by liturgical history. The Reformers of Bern adopted it for use in their first liturgical book, published in 1528.[17]

The Berner Taufbüchlein of 1528

With the Reformation Edict of February 7, 1528, the Church of Bern officially set about the reform of worship. The *Bern Service Book of 1528* was published a few weeks later, on February 21, by the Zurich printer Christoffel Froschauer.[18] The reformation of the city and canton of Bern had been a very festive affair.[19] A public disputation was arranged to which the bishops of Basel, Chur, Constance, and Lausanne had been invited, along with recognized leaders of the reform from over a large area. The bishops declined the invitation, but not the leaders of the reform. Bucer and Capito came from Strasbourg, Oecolampadius came from Basel, Konrad Sam from Ulm, and a number of ministers came from Augsburg, Schaffhausen, and Zurich. Johannes Zwick and Ambrosius Blarer came from Constance. William Farel, destined to be the Reformer of French-speaking Switzerland, was on hand. It was a gathering which represented a great number of churches throughout South Germany, Alsace, and Switzerland. To call it the first synod of the Reformed Church

16. The stylistic variations between the baptismal rite appended to Zwingli's *Of Baptism,* the *Third Zurich Service Book of 1525,* and the *Zurich Service Book of 1528* should make clear that the 1528 effort is a revision of the 1525-26 version, and not vice versa. Until such a time as a critical edition of the 1528 service is available, one hesitates to speak too confidently about these stylistic changes.

17. Cf. n. 24 below.

18. *Ein kurtz gmeine form, kinder zetouffenn, Die Ee ze bestäten, Die Predig anzefahen und zuo enden, wie es zü Bernn gebrucht wirdt* (Zurich: Ch. Froschauer, 1528).

19. Richard Feller, *Geschichte Berns,* vol. 2. *Von der Reformation bis zum Baurnkrieg 1516-1653* (Bern, 1953), esp. pp. 155-61. See also "Berner Disputation," *Realencyklopädie für protestantische Theologie und Kirche,* 3rd edn., vol. 2 (Leipzig: J. C. Hinrich, 1895-1913), pp. 614-19.

might be a bit anachronistic, but in fact it was a gathering which was trans-territorial if not international. In effect it was the first opportunity to gather together pastors of churches which had grown to have a feeling of a common bond and a very similar approach to reform.

It had been the intention of the local reform-minded priests, Berchtold Haller, Niklaus von Wattenwyl, Peter Cyro, and Franz Kolb, to carry out the reform of their rather large territory with the advice of other churches which had already embarked on the reformation. It is rather surprising, then, that the baptismal service published in the *Bern Service Book of 1528* is an exact copy of the *Zurich Service Book of 1528.*[20] While the Bernese Reformers were to produce a communion liturgy in the following year, that is, in 1529, in which elements from a number of different services were arranged together, the Reformers of Bern took over the baptismal practices of Zurich whole and unchanged.[21]

One wonders why the Bernese Reformers simply copied the Zurich baptismal rite. It seems to be best explained by haste. The *Bern Service Book of 1528* appeared, bearing the arms of the city, two weeks after the Reformation edict.[22] Perhaps the leaders of the reform in Bern feared that delay in sending out an official rite would encourage pastors in the various towns of the canton to develop their own services. This the authorities of Bern would have regarded quite negatively. For a good many years the city council of that vigorously expanding republic was quite insistent on liturgical uniformity within its domains.[23] Perhaps the city council was moved to act quickly because of the growing success of the Anabaptist movement, particularly in the outlying towns and villages of the canton. Whatever reasons may have been behind it, it would appear that in regard to the rite of baptism, the Church of Bern took over the rite of Zurich. The rites of Basel and Strasbourg seem to have had no influence.[24]

20. *Ein Kurtze gmaine form, kinder zetouffenn, Die Ee zebestäten. Die Predig anzefahen vnd zü enden, wie es zü Bernn gebrucht wirdt* (Zurich: C. Froschauer, 1528). The edition used for this study is found in A. Fluri, *Das Berner Taufbüchlein von 1528* (Bern: E. Baumgart, 1904), pp. 15-25.

21. On the composite nature of the Bernese communion liturgy, see Hughes Oliphant Old, *The Patristic Roots of Reformed Worship* (Zurich: Theologischer Verlag, 1975), pp. 1-53.

22. According to A. Fluri, the Bernese authorities considered the publication of Froschauer a bit premature but nevertheless sent his work out to all pastors for their immediate use. *Das Berner Taufbüchlein von 1528,* pp. 6-7.

23. This was also the case with the use of the baptismal font, which even today is characteristic of the churches of Zurich and Bern. These enormous baptismal fonts, prominently placed in the center of the church, are usually large enough to immerse the child. Covered over with a flat board, they were also used as the table for celebrating communion. The use of this characteristic font was often insisted upon by Bernese authorities.

24. It has already been stated that the *Zurich Service Book of 1528* is rather puzzling

The Baptismal Rite of the Strasbourg Psalter of 1530

As has already been mentioned, the Strasbourg Reformers regarded the baptismal rite which they developed in 1525 and 1526 as not completely satisfactory; however, it was not until 1530 that they produced another revision of their baptismal order. These changes were not extensive.

The introductory rubrics have been expanded. One of these explains that the ministers have begun to admonish the people to bring their children to be baptized on Sundays rather than other days. The reason given is that in baptism children are presented to the fellowship of God's people and are initiated into the Church. It is therefore appropriate that children be baptized at a regular service of worship when the whole congregation is present and the whole Church may earnestly and devoutly pray for them.[25]

Another rubric directs that the minister of baptism, after having preached to the assembled congregation, is to speak to the congregation in the following or similar words:

> Let us remember that it is the will of God our savior that all men be saved and come to a knowledge of the truth through the only mediator between God and man, namely through the man, Jesus Christ, who has given himself for every man for a redeemer, and that we should pray for one another for the sake of a common faith and knowledge of the Son of God, our savior.[26]

---

because it seems to be outside the mainstream of the development of the Zurich baptismal rite. One possible explanation of this would be that the Bernese baptismal rite is not in fact a copy of a previously existing rite used in Zurich but rather it was developed independently by the Bernese Reformers. The Bernese were, to be sure, greatly influenced by the Zurich pattern, but nevertheless they made a number of adaptations of their own. Since it was being printed in Zurich, the Zurich printers may have run off a few extra copies, without the Bernese coat of arms, for use in Zurich. If this is indeed the case, a comparison of the original documents should make this clear. Unfortunately, this study has had to be content with reprints of these documents.

25. ". . . haben sie das volck vermanet, alleyn auf den sontag jre kinder zum tauff ze bringen, auf das auss vnglauben nit zum wasser geeilet vnd das der tauff dess kinds aufopferung vnd ergebung inn die gemeyn sampt dem gebett für das kind mit rechtem ernst vnd andacht inn beisein der gemeyn gottes beschee." Hubert, *Ordnungen,* p. 38.

26. "Der täuffer, auff das bey der versamlung das wort getriben werde, diss oder dergleichen ermanung saget: 'so gedencken, das gott vnser heylandt will, das alle menschen genesen vnd zur erkantnuss der warheit kommen durch den einigen mitler zwischen gott vnd dem menschen, nemlich den menschen Christum Jesum, der sich selbs geben hat für yederman zuo einer erlosung, vnd das wir für einander bitten, vnd alle einer dem anderen die handt reichen sollen zuo einerley glauben vnd zuo der erkenntnüss des suon gottes, desselbigen vnsers erlösers.' " Hubert, *Ordnungen,* p. 38. This baptismal exhortation also appears in the *Strasbourg Psalter of 1526* (F).

After this the minister is to direct the people to pray for the child. They are to pray that God grant to the child the gift of the Holy Spirit so that as the child grows he or she might receive all the gracious gifts of God, the washing away of his sins, and strengthening in every good work. They are to pray that the child be buried with Christ and so die to the works of the flesh; that he rise with Christ and so walk in newness of life.

After this prayer the Creed is introduced. Then the minister is to recite the Creed as a prayer for faith not only for the child, but also for the congregation. This is followed by the Baptismal Invocation which had appeared in the earlier services, although there have been some changes in the text of the prayer. The rest of the service follows in essentially the same order as the earlier services except that the admonition to the godparents has been moved from before the actual baptism of the child to after it. There are some other variations to which we need not direct our attention at this point.

Let us analyze these revisions. Several characteristics stand out. We notice with particular interest the rubric which recognizes Sunday as the preferred day for the celebration of baptism. The ministers are to admonish the people, "On Sunday alone to bring their children to baptism."[27]

The most obvious reason for administering baptism on Sunday is not suggested in the rubrics; nevertheless, we can be sure that the Reformers of Strasbourg had it in mind. Bucer and particularly Capito were interested in recovering the biblical sign of the Old Testament Sabbath and the New Testament Lord's Day. The Strasbourg Reformers were surely aware of the patristic paschal baptisms. The custom was well attested in the patristic works most familiar to the High Rhenish Reformers. Surely they saw the point of Easter baptism as a means of making very clear that in baptism we are joined to Christ in his death and in his resurrection. It seemed reasonable to the Reformers that the same point could be made by reserving baptism to the Lord's Day. This seems a particularly likely line of reasoning for them to have made when one remembers that the Strasbourg Reformers put a much greater emphasis on the weekly celebration of Christ's resurrection than they did on the yearly Easter. It was from the Church Fathers that the Reformers had learned about the relation of the sign of the Lord's Day to the sign of baptism. The deeper insight which the High Rhenish Reformers had into the Old Testament also helped them understand that just as circumcision was administered on the eighth day after natural birth, so the Christian was baptized on the Lord's Day, which is also the eighth day. It is the eighth day of the old creation and the first day of the new creation.

27. ". . . haben sie das volck vermanet, alleyn auf den sontag jre kinder zum tauff ze bringen. . . ." Hubert, *Ordnungen,* p. 38.

In addition to this more obvious reason for baptizing on Sunday the rubric explains that when the child is baptized he or she is baptized into the congregation, and therefore the child should be baptized in the presence of the congregation. While this reason is perhaps less obvious, it carries more theological weight in the argument the Reformers were waging. The Reformers were very much aware of the tension which had developed between private baptism and church baptism. They were determined to get baptism back into the church and to make it part of the public worship of the congregation.

A second very significant revision found in the *Strasbourg Psalter of 1530* is the removal of the question regarding the intention of the sponsor. The earliest Reformed baptismal rites of Strasbourg had taken over this question from the old Latin rites. The celebrant was to ask the sponsors, "Do you will the child to be baptized?" The question relating to the intention to baptize had been very important to the late Middle Ages. The Nominalists interpreted it in a quite voluntarist way. The voluntaristic interpretation of it had been made clear by Balthasar Hübmaier in his reply to Zwingli's *Of Baptism.* No doubt it was for this reason that the Strasbourg Reformers now deleted it. With this question left out, the Strasbourg rite now begins with the Baptismal Exhortation. The minister, alluding to the text of 1 Timothy 2, assures the congregation that "it is the will of God . . . that all men be saved and come to a knowledge of the truth through the only mediator between God and man, namely through the man Jesus Christ. . . ."[28] Where the Latin rite had stressed the role of the will of the one being baptized, or more exactly the will of the baptismal sponsors, the Reformed rite of Strasbourg puts the emphasis on the will of God to save his people. Here the Augustinianism of the Reformers reveals itself in the clearest possible light over against the Nominalistic voluntarism of both the old Latin rites and the Anabaptists.

There is a theological concern here that needs to be pointed out. The Strasbourg Reformers have in mind that the number to be saved is greater rather than smaller. The Strasbourg Reformers, for all their devotion to predestination, consistently make 1 Timothy 2:1-8 one of the touchstones of their liturgical concern. In every service of worship the Church of Strasbourg interceded for the salvation of all people, paraphrasing 1 Timothy 2:1-8, and now the service of baptism begins with a proclamation of God's redemptive intention based on the same passage.

A third significant revision is found in the rubrics regarding the Baptismal

28. "So gedenken, das gott vnser heylandt will, das alle menschen genesen vnd zur erkantnüss der wahrheit kommen durch den einigen mitler zwischen gott vnd dem menschen, nemlich den menschen Christum Jesum." Hubert, *Ordnungen,* p. 38.

Invocation. At this point the rubrics are not particularly clear. "After one has prayed the minister explains something from the Creed . . . in order that the congregation might pray all the more earnestly for the child. . . . After which the minister says, 'Say with me in your hearts,' or, 'Let us pray together in common.' "[29] From reading the rubrics of the *Strasbourg Psalter of 1530,* one gets the impression that the evangelical pastors of Strasbourg are trying very hard to develop a deeper sense of congregational prayer. For the Strasbourgers the Baptismal Invocation has a crucial liturgical function, and the Reformers are concerned that this prayer be the prayer of the whole Church. Perhaps the vagueness of the rubrics reflects the fact that different pastors were trying different ways of leading the people in prayer. From Johann Ulrich Surgant's *Manuale curatorum,* we get a good picture of how much use was made of the bidding prayer in Southern Germany at the end of the Middle Ages. It was regarded as a good way of engaging the people in prayer.[30] The second half of the Baptismal Exhortation seems to be as much a bidding prayer as an exhortation or admonition to prayer. The rubrics suggest that there is still considerable confusion as to how the Creed is to function in the baptismal service. Is it to be recited or is it to be prayed? There is still a comprehensive Baptismal Invocation which appears in the rite. The minister is to lead in prayer, asking the congregation to pray with him, "Let us continue to pray in common, speaking with me in your hearts. . . ."[31] In time the Strasbourg Reformers will develop a sizable collection of well-formulated prayers for leading the congregation in prayer; but for the present the different pastors seem to be struggling with the problem of how they can best lead their people in prayer. What appears to be happening in this "season of prayer" is that first there is a bidding prayer in which the minister suggests the subjects of prayer while the people pray silently, then there is the reciting of the Creed as a prayer for faith, and finally there is a concluding collect or, more precisely, the Baptismal Invocation led by the minister. The rubrics specifically tell us that different ministers may do it a bit differently in their own churches or may vary it according to the situation.[32]

Finally, we want to point out that the *Strasbourg Psalter of 1530* shows

29. "Nachdem man gebettet, erzelet der diener vnd teuffer ettwa den glauben . . . damit sie auch dest ernstlicher fuer es bitten. . . . Demnach sagt der diener: Sprechend mit mir inn ewern nerteen oder: lasst vnss weiter inn gemeyn bitten." Hubert, *Ordnungen,* p. 40.

30. Johann Ulrich Surgant, *Manuale curatorum* (Basel: Michael Furter, 1503). See particularly chap. 4, "De exhortatione ad orandum pro omni statu ecclesie."

31. "Demnach saget der diener: 'sprechend mit mir inn ewern hertzen', oder 'lasst vnss weiter inn gemeyn bitten. . . .' " Hubert, *Ordnungen,* p. 40.

32. "Disse ordnung des tauffs ist bey jn gemeyn, aber etwan nach gelegenheit der personen würt mer oder minder geredt. . . . Dann christlich freyheit wöllen sye nyendert anbiden. . . ." Hubert, *Ordnungen,* p. 43.

a very definite theological development. One of the most interesting of these developments is to be found in these words which we read in the introduction to the service.

> The minister should aim much more at directing the people to live a Christian life through true faith, than an exaggerated concentration on the sign of baptism itself, for the power of baptism comes from the mystery or secret. The more one approaches the great secret, Christ Jesus, the nearer and more properly one can use the sign.[33]

Here the Strasbourg Reformers are beginning to think more deeply into the concept of sacrament. Knowing that the Greek Church used the word μυστήριον for sacrament, they have obviously looked into the meaning of the word in the New Testament and have discovered that the true mystery or secret is Christ himself.[34] There are several other ways the New Testament writers used the word μυστήριον. Earlier the Strasbourg Reformers had been heavily influenced by Tertullian's explanation of *sacramentum* and the implications of this for their understanding of sacrament. Now, faced as they are by the Anabaptists, they are beginning to consider the meaning of the sacraments in terms of the biblical concept of μυστήριον.

In the five years since the first attempt to produce a rite of baptism which was reformed according to Scripture, the Strasbourg Reformers have obviously grown considerably in their understanding of baptism. The controversies with the Anabaptists have evidently forced them to think through the meaning of baptism much more deeply. Nevertheless, their thinking is still in the process of development; and we shall see yet a further development in the baptismal rite of the *Strasbourg Psalter of 1537*.

The Baptismal Rite of Neuchâtel

The Principality of Neuchâtel was one of those French-speaking areas between the Swiss Confederation and the Kingdom of France which, because

33. "Vnd treiben also vil meer uff eyn christlich leben durch eynn waren glauben, dann uff überflüssig betrachten der zeychen an jn selbs, so all jr vermögen alleyn auss dem mysterio vnd geheymnuss heben. Darumb, ie meer eyn ieder die gross geheymnuss, Christum Jesum, erlanget, ie neher vnd eygentlicher er der zeichen geprauchen mag." Hubert, *Ordnungen,* p. 37.

34. On the appreciation of the Lord's Supper as μυστήριον by Oecolampadius, see Old, *Patristic Roots,* p. 47. Recent Roman Catholic theology has explored at some length the idea of Christ as the fundamental sacrament. Cf. Edward Schillebeeckx, *Christ, the Sacrament of the Encounter with God,* trans. Paul Barrett (New York: Sheed and Ward, 1963).

of its geographical location, was destined to play an intermediary role between the High Rhenish Reformation and the reform movement of French Christian Humanism.[35] William Farel, the Reformer of Neuchâtel, started his reforming career as a member of the circle of Meaux. As a student in Paris, he had been influenced by the revival of classical learning and the Christian Humanist revival of biblical studies. Guillaume Briçonnet, bishop of Meaux, had invited Farel to help reform his diocese. This diocese, lying not more than thirty miles east of Paris in the valley of the Marne, made up an important part of the Duchy of Alençon. The duchess of Alençon was Marguerite of Navarre, the sister of Francis I, a woman sincerely committed both to the deepening of the spiritual life and to the reform of the Church. She deserves to be recognized as one of the mothers of the Reformed faith. Briçonnet, on being consecrated bishop, welcomed to his cathedral city an impressive company of Christian scholars. Some of the best-known Christian Humanists of France were gathered. François Vatable, who introduced France to the study of biblical Hebrew, joined the circle of Meaux, and so did the venerable Jacques Lefèvre d'Étaples. Lefèvre had won great acclaim for his new editions of Aristotle and the Fathers of the ancient Church. His French translation of the Bible had won him even greater renown. Lefèvre and Vatable were only the most distinguished members of the circle. Farel joined these men in their attempt to bring about reform within the existing structures of the French Church. For some time the attempted reform seemed to be working, but then the forces which opposed the attempt won out and the circle of Meaux was disbanded. Several of the Meaux reformers took refuge in Strasbourg or in Basel, cities close to the French border which over the centuries have sheltered refugees from the vicissitudes of French politics. Farel particularly came under the influence of Bucer and Capito in Strasbourg and then Oecolampadius in Basel. For several years Farel served as the missionary of High Rhenish Protestantism, establishing the reformation in the French-speaking cities of Montbéliard, Aigle, Neuchâtel, and finally Geneva. He was a remarkable man, red haired and energetic; putting his cause above all, he is usually regarded as a man of action; nevertheless, as we shall see, he was a perceptive thinker as well.[36]

Farel's *French Evangelical Service Book of 1533* was aimed at a far

35. For a more thorough study of the background of the beginnings of French Reformed worship, see Old, *Patristic Roots,* pp. 68-79, particularly on the circle of Meaux, and the missionary work of William Farel. Further bibliographical details are given there.

36. Elfriede Jacobs has recently done much to recover the theological profile of Farel. This pioneering study demands a careful re-evaluation of the theology of Farel. *Die Sakramentslehre Wilhelm Farels* (Zurich: Theologischer Verlag Zurich, 1977).

wider audience than the Church of the Comté de Neuchâtel.[37] It was aimed at French-speaking Churches who accepted the reform over a large area; Neuchâtel, Aigle, Montbéliard, Lausanne, and Geneva were already in the process of accepting the Reformation. Ostensibly it is a translation of the *Bern Service Book of 1529,* but Farel has made a number of changes and additions incorporating features of the *Strasbourg Psalter* and the *Basel Service Book of 1526.*[38] Farel's translation, which is always rather free, frequently brings to the liturgical texts subtle shifts of meaning. Farel has a number of his own theological insights, which are clearly discerned in the baptismal rite of Neuchâtel. Farel was far from being merely a French-speaking Zwinglian. He was a French Reformer who brought to his work the unique character of French Christian Humanism.

The preface to the *French Evangelical Service Book of 1533* gives us an instructive statement on the reform of the rite of baptism as Farel understood it.

> Let no one then search here for the sacerdotal exorcisms and conjurations which adjure the devil; as though the devil possessed the infants, or as though our children were demon possessed, for the Son of God did not receive children in such a manner (Matthew 19). In the same way one should regard the exorcised and enchanted water upon which the priests blow, entreating that the Holy Spirit descend into the font. For the Holy Spirit does not dwell in the water (I Corinthians 3); but rather in the hearts of the faithful. The salt, the spittle and the oil are not to be found in this rite: but after devout prayers and teaching one baptizes with pure and simple water as the Savior was baptized and as the Apostles baptized.[39]

Here we recognize the same kind of concern for liturgical reform which we found particularly in the writings of Capito and Bucer. The remarks of Farel

37. *La manière et fasson quon tient en baillant le sainct baptesme en la saincte congregation de dieu* . . . (Neuchâtel: Pierre de Vingle, 1533). References are to the edition by Jean-Guillaume Baum, *Manière et fasson* (Strasbourg and Paris, 1859).

38. This use of features of the liturgies of Strasbourg and Basel, in addition to the features of Bern and Zurich, has been studied in regard to the eucharistic liturgy in Old, *Patristic Roots,* pp. 74-76. It is the *Bern Service Book of 1529* which Farel used rather than the edition of 1528.

39. "Donc personne ne cherche icy les adjuremens et conjurations des prestres, desquelz ilz adjurent le diable: comme sil possedoit les enfans, et quilz fussent demoniacles, veu que le filz de dieu ne les a receu en telle maniere. Ainsi fault entendre de leaue adjuree et enchantee, sur laquelle les prestres soufflent, disans que le sainct esperit descende en la fontaine dicelle eaue. Car le sainct esperit na son lieu ne habitation es eaues; mais au cueur du fidele. Le sel, crachantz et heyle ne sont icy: mais apres la saincte priere et enseignement lon baptise deaue pure et nette, comme le sauueur a este baptise, et les apotres ont faict." *Manière et fasson,* pp. 9-10.

show a contempt for what he clearly regards as the superstitious nature of many of the rites in the baptismal service.[40] For Farel as for Bucer, it was clear from Scripture that the children of Christians are holy (1 Cor. 7:14). It was because they are holy that they were to be baptized. The apology against the Anabaptists had put great emphasis on this. It was one of the Reformers' strongest arguments. For the Reformers then to turn around and exorcise children before baptism would be inconsistent.

Farel, like Bucer, argues for baptizing children at a regular service of worship rather than at a private service. "It is in the midst of the full congregation that one gives baptism."[41] The reason is that the whole congregation should be present to receive the child as a member of the Church. Farel also believes that there is great spiritual value in attending the baptism of another because that baptism can serve to remind all those present of the end to which they, too, have been baptized.[42] In watching a baptism, the Christian is exhorted to die unto sin and to walk in newness of life. It is important that the whole congregation be present in order that all may pray together that the promises displayed by the sign of baptism be realized in the life of the child. It is also important that each member of the congregation, seeing that sign performed, pray that the grace signified be increased in his or her own life.[43] Once again we see that the struggle against the privatizing of the rite of baptism was one of the most important themes of reform.

The baptismal service proper begins with the Invocation. "Our help is in the name of the Lord who made heaven and earth. Amen."[44] The traditional questions follow, "Do you present this child to God and to his holy Church and congregation asking that he be baptized? Answer, yes."[45] The question has been reformulated in such a way that it is much more consistent with Reformed theology. The Baptismal Exhortation follows. It is a free translation of the one found in the *Third Zurich Service Book of 1525* and the *Strasbourg Psalter of 1526* (F). This Exhortation begins with

40. Jacobs points out that for Farel it was a great relief to be able to leave aside the baptismal exorcisms. It was not a matter of a biblical legalism, namely that the New Testament accounts of baptisms do not report exorcisms, therefore the church may not use them. *Die Sakramentalslehre Farels,* pp. 102-3.

41. "Cest quen plaine congregation des fideles lon donne le baptesme. . . ." *Manière et fasson,* p. 14.

42. *Manière et fasson,* p. 15.

43. *Manière et fasson,* p. 15.

44. "Nostre ayde soit au nom de Dieu qui a faict le ciel et la terre. Amen." *Manière et fasson,* p. 15.

45. "Presentez vous cest enfant a dieu, et a sa saint eglise et congregation, demandans quil soit baptise. Respondent: Ouy." *Manière et fasson,* p. 16.

the words of the apostle Paul telling us to pray for the salvation of all people (1 Tim. 2:1-8). It urges the congregation to pray that "God grant to this infant a true and living faith, that the baptism visible and exterior be to him a true sign of the baptism that is invisible and interior, and that this from his grace might be given through his Holy Spirit."[46] Here we have one of those subtle shifts of meaning which mark the liturgical texts of Farel. While for Zwingli at the beginning of the Reformation water baptism was a *mere* sign, for Farel it was a *true* sign. In this Farel was much closer to Oecolampadius and Bucer than to Zwingli.

This leads to the saying of the Lord's Prayer, after which the minister leads the congregation in the Baptismal Invocation.

> God Almighty, Father Eternal, full of all mercy, who of your goodness have promised to be our God and God of our children, just as you were the God of Abraham and of his children, we humbly pray you and ask that you give to this infant your Holy Spirit, receiving him in the covenant of your mercy, according to the ordaining of your unchanging purpose, to the end that at the time you have planned, this child recognize you as his God, that he worship and serve you alone, living and dying in you, so that our act of baptism and our receiving of him into your holy assembly, be not in vain, but that he be truly baptized in the death of your Son, in the renewal of life, pleasing thee and being acceptable to thee through the same Jesus Christ your Son, our Savior. Amen.[47]

This prayer is an original composition of Farel's, although it is quite similar to the Strasbourg Baptismal Invocation. It is particularly noteworthy for its remembrance of Abraham and its reference to the covenant promise to be not only Abraham's God but also the God of his descendants. Here Farel has not used Zwingli's version of the Great Flood Prayer with its references to the typology of the Flood and the crossing of the Red Sea, but rather he has built

46. ". . . que Dieu luy doint vraye et viue foy, et que le baptesme visible et exterieur luy soit vray signe du baptesme inuisible et interieur, lequel de sa grace lui plaise donner par son sainct esperit." *Manière et fasson,* pp. 16-17.

47. "Diu tout puissant, pere eternel, plain de toute misericorde, qui de ta bonte nous a promis destre notre Dieu et de noz enfans, ainsi que de Abraham et des siens, nous te prions et humblement requerons, que tu donnes a cest enfant ton sainct esperit, le receuant en laliance de ta misericorde, selon lordonnance de ton propos immuable, affin que au temps que tu as ordonne, il te congnoisse comme son Dieu, te adorant et seruant toy seul, viuant et mourant en toy, tellement que nostre baptesme et reception en ta sainct assemblee, que nous faisons, ne soit en vain, mais quil soit vrayement baptise en la mort de ton filz, en renouuellement de vie, te plaisant et estant aggreable par iceluy Jesuchrist ton filz, nostre sauueur. Amen." *Manière et fasson,* pp. 17-18.

a prayer on the typology of circumcision. The *Strasbourg Psalter of 1537* will do the same thing.[48] For Farel the saving volition of Christ is in the end the basis on which children are baptized; it is the will of Christ to be the Savior of infants as well as of adults. Elfreide Jacobs has brought this out with particular clarity.[49] Once again the parents are asked if they bring their child to be baptized. The minister then asks those who have brought the child to be baptized "to promise to teach the child in the holy doctrine of our Lord, his holy law and faith, teaching him the commandments of God. . . ."[50] Then the Ten Commandments are recited. The minister continues, "And also teach him the faith and creed of true Christians. . . ."[51] The Apostles' Creed is then recited. The minister continues, "Teach the child also to put his whole confidence in God, to honor and serve him alone, to love him with all his heart, soul, ability and understanding and to love his neighbor as himself, and as a true Christian renounce himself abandoning all to follow Jesus, bearing his cross. . . . Do you so promise?"[52] In none of the Reformed baptismal rites we have studied up to this point have the catechetical pieces so clearly functioned as catechetical pieces. To be sure, it is the Creed and the Ten Commandments which are used rather than the Creed and the Lord's Prayer. Nothing is said about godparents, and presumably it is the parents who are asked to make this promise. The Neuchâtel service has no hint that either parents or godparents make the baptismal vows for the child or confess for the child. The vows that are made are to give the child catechetical instruction, and the Creed is recited in the course of the promise to teach the child the Creed and the meaning of the Creed.[53]

For the third time the parents are asked if they request baptism for the child. On answering in the affirmative, the minister says, "Name the child." Obviously, for Farel, it is quite appropriate that Christian children be given their names at the time of their baptism. We will have more to say about this

48. According to Jacobs there are differences at this point between Bucer and Farel. She does not see Farel as accepting covenant theology. *Die Sacramentslehre Farels,* p. 159.

49. Jacobs, *Die Sacramentslehre Farels,* p. 150.

50. ". . . enseigner cest enfant en la saincte doctrine de nostre seigneur, en sa sainte loy et foy, luy enseignant les commandemens de Dieu. . . ." *Manière et fasson,* p. 20.

51. "Et aussi luy apprendrez la foy et creance des vrays chrestiens. . . ." *Manière et fasson,* p. 23.

52. "Lenseignerez aussi dauoir toute sa fiance en Dieu, ladorer et servir luy seul, laymer de tout son cueur, sens, puissance et entendement, et son prochain comme soy mesme, et comme vray chrestien quil renonce soy meme, abandonnant tout pour suyure Jesus, portant sa croix. . . . Et ainsi vous le promettez?" *Manière et fasson,* pp. 24-25.

53. To Farel, the importance of the baptismal vows was particularly great. See Jacobs, *Die Sacramentslehre Farels,* p. 149.

in regard to the Genevan rite. The name of the child is given, and the minister baptizes the child with the trinitarian formula. A rubric directs that the minister is "to put plain and simple water on the head of the child."[54]

The service is concluded with a particularly striking benediction.

> Our Lord God by his grace and goodness grant that this infant, whom he has created and formed according to his image and likeness, be a true member of Jesus Christ his son, bearing fruit worthy of a child of God. Amen. Go in peace. Our Lord be with you all. Take good care of the child.[55]

One notices that there is both a benediction of the child and of the parents. For Farel these benedictions are characteristic. His marriage service also contains several original benedictions. In this benediction we find, as we shall find in one of the prayers of Bucer, a concern to relate the two themes of creation and baptism by a reference to the fact that God had created the child in the image of God. This was an important theme for Farel as it had been for his teacher, Jacques Lefèvre d'Etaples.[56] It is quite possible that the benediction of the child was accompanied by the laying on of hands, but there is no rubric to that effect.[57]

Liturgical Revision in Strasbourg, 1537

In 1537, more than a decade after the first Reformed services of worship had been attempted in Strasbourg, an important revision of the worship of the Church of Strasbourg was undertaken. This revision was to a large extent the fruit of the deepening theological insights of the Strasbourg Reformers themselves, but it was also the fruit of the discussion which the Strasbourg Reformers carried on with their colleagues in Basel, Zurich, and elsewhere. This revision reflects the common mind of the High Rhenish school of liturgical reform.

The rite of baptism as we find it in the *Strasbourg Psalter of 1537* has the following parts:

54. "Puis luy auoir mis sur la teste avec la main deaue pure et nette, sans sel ne huyle, ne crachatz, dit en ceste maniere." *Manière et fasson,* p. 25.

55. "Nostre seigneur Dieu par sa grace et bonte faice que cest enfant, quil a cree et forme a son image et semblance, soit vray membre de Jesus Christ son filz, portant fruict digne comme enfant de Dieu. Amen. Allez en paix. Nostre seigneur soit avec vous. Faites bonne garde de lenfant." *Manière et fasson,* p. 26.

56. See Jacobs, *Die Sakramentslehre Farels.*

57. On the importance given to benedictions in the Reformed liturgical tradition and to the gestures which accompanied them, see Old, *Patristic Roots,* pp. 330-31.

- Baptismal Exhortation
- Baptismal Invocation
- Scripture Lesson
- Creed
- Admonition
- Baptism
- Baptismal Thanksgiving
- Benediction

The introductory rubrics once again take up the questions of the times at which baptism is to be administered. Sunday is still the preferred time, although other times are permitted. One feels a certain tension in the rubrics. Evidently the ministers were having difficulty convincing their congregations that they should wait until Sunday to have their children baptized.

The Baptismal Exhortation has been elaborated so that it is to contain four points: First, the minister is to take one of the classic texts on baptism such as the fourth chapter of John, the sixth chapter of Romans, or the third chapter of Titus and explain something of the meaning of the sacrament. Second, the congregation is to be reminded of the significance of baptism for themselves. Third, the reason for baptizing children is to be explained from either Genesis 17, 1 Corinthians 7, or Matthew 19. Fourth, the congregation is to be urged to pray that what is promised in the sign of baptism be fulfilled in the life of the child baptized. Essentially what is expected at the beginning of this service is a brief sermon on baptism.

The Baptismal Invocation follows. Since there has just been an exhortation to pray for the child, a time of silence is given so that each person may pray. Then the minister leads the congregation in one of two prayers provided. The first of these is the same prayer we found in previous editions of the *Strasbourg Psalter,* although the text has been expanded considerably. The second prayer is a new composition.[58]

The Creed has been moved from the prayers where it had previously been to a place of its own. It is introduced by the words, "So now profess with me our holy Christian faith and awaken thereby the earnestness that this child be truly brought up in this same faith."[59] As we have seen up to this point, the Reformers of Strasbourg were not too sure how the Creed was to function in the baptismal rite, although they were sure that they wanted to include it. The

58. These two prayers will be considered at length in Chap. IX.

59. "So bekennet nun mit mir vnseren h. christlichen glauben vnd erwecket euch damit inn demselbigen dapffer zuo wachsen dises kindlin zuo solchem glauben getrewlich vffzuoziehen." Hubert, *Ordnungen,* p. 50.

point of reciting the Creed now seems to be that by making this confession of faith the congregation manifests itself as the Church into which the child is to be received. It also serves to introduce the admonition to bring up the child in the Christian faith.

The admonition follows the Creed. It is clearly addressed to the whole congregation as well as to the parents and godparents. It is to this congregation which has just professed its faith in the words of the Creed that the child is to be joined by baptism. "Now to the fellowship of this faith we want to baptize this child."[60] The congregation is admonished to receive the child as a member and to help bring up the child in the Christian faith. The godparents are then addressed and told that they are spiritual parents of the child.[61] Particularly in Strasbourg there had been a long-standing uneasiness about the use of godparents. Clement Ziegler, it will be remembered, had objected to the use of godparents as early as 1524. Among the Protestant pastors of Strasbourg there were various opinions on the subject. What we have here appears to be a compromise. As the defense of infant baptism developed, the Reformers began more and more to argue that the children of believers were to be baptized because of the faith of their parents, rather than because of the vicarious faith of the godparents. It was the faith of the parents which needed to be expressed. This was one reason for reciting the Creed at this point. It made clear the faith of the parents. The godparents have not been left out of the service, but they do not make any vows, nor do they confess faith for the child. Their function in baptism is quite secondary to the function of the real parents. From this point on, we shall see that Reformed baptismal rites will put a strong emphasis on the role of the parents both in baptism and in the Christian education of their children. Here we also find the beginnings of that typically Reformed idea that the whole Church serves as the baptismal sponsors of the child in receiving the child as a fellow member.

The baptism itself is now administered by pouring water on the child three times, "N. I baptize you in the name of the Father and of the Son and of the Holy Spirit. Amen."[62]

For the first time we find the Strasbourg rite providing a prayer of thanksgiving after the baptism. The Basel rite had concluded with a thanksgiving psalm which expressed many of the ideas of the covenant thanksgiving found in the new Strasbourg prayer. The prayer is worthy of our careful attention.

60. "Nun zü gemeinschafft dises glaubens wöllen wir dises kind teuffen." Hubert, *Ordnungen,* p. 50.

61. ". . . als geistliche mitvätter vnd mütter. . . ." Hubert, *Ordnungen,* p. 51.

62. "N., ich teufe dich imm namen des vatters vnd des süns vnd des heiligen geists. amen." Hubert, *Ordnungen,* p. 51.

> Almighty God, Heavenly Father, we give you eternal praise and thanks, that you have granted and bestowed upon this child your fellowship, that you have born him again to yourself through your holy baptism, that he has been incorporated into your beloved Son, our only Savior, and is now your child and heir. Grant, most loving and faithful Father, that we in the whole course of our lives might prove our thankfulness for your great grace, faithfully bring up this your child through all the situations of life and that we with this child as well, might more and more die unto the world, and joined to the life of your Son, our Lord Jesus, daily grow in grace, that we might ever praise you and be a blessing to our neighbor, through our Lord Jesus Christ. Amen.[63]

The prayer is confident that the child has begun the Christian life by becoming a member of the Church. He or she has been incorporated into the body of Christ, born into the life of the children of God, and is now heir to all the promises of God. Baptism is not an empty sign. In this child surely God will work faith and the fruit of the Spirit. For this marvelous grace of God the congregation now gives thanks as the child will one day give thanks himself in a life of worship and Christian service.

The service ends with a benediction based on Matthew 18:10, "Go in peace! The Lord grant that a holy angel, who beholds his face in heaven, guard this child from all evil and lead him to all good. Amen."[64] Again there is no indication as to the gesture which should accompany this benediction.

The Baptismal Rite of Augsburg

The first rays of Luther's dawning reform were caught by many a spire and church tower in the Imperial Free City of Augsburg. The citizens of Augsburg watched the growing light with excitement. From the very beginning they

63. "Almechtiger got, himmlischer vater, wir sagen dir ewigs lob vnd danck, das du deiner gemeind dises kind gegeben vnd verliehen hast, das es dir durch deinen h. tauff widergeporen, deinem lieben suon, vnserem einigen heiland, eingeleibet vnd dein kind vnd erb ietz worden ist. Gib, lieber, getrewer vatter, das wir vns alle diser deiner so grossen genaden inn allem vnserm leben danckbar beweisen, dises nun dein kind zuo allem deinem gefallen getrewlich vffziehen, auch sampt disem kind vns selbs immer mehr absterben vnd imm leben deines suons, vnsers herren Jesu, täglich zuonemen, das du durch vns allezeit geprisen vnd der nechst gebesseret werde, durch vnseren herren Jesum Christum, amen." Hubert, *Ordnungen,* pp. 51-52.

64. "Vnd geht hin im friden! der herre gebe, dass eine heiligen engel, die sein angesicht sehen imm himmel, dis kind vor allem argen zuo allem guoten bewaren vnd fürderen, amen." Hubert, *Ordnungen,* p. 52.

heard Luther's call to reform. They were very interested. At the time the Reformation began their cathedral preacher was none other than John Oecolampadius. They respected the deep piety and broad learning of their cathedral preacher, and when Oecolampadius began to indicate his support for Luther, many of Augsburg's most prominent citizens were won to the cause of reform.[65]

Augsburg was a city of merchant princes. Here was the famous banking house of the Fuggers. Here, too, lived the distinguished gentleman scholar, Konrad Peutinger. The brothers Bernhard and Konrad von Adelmann were both patrons of classical learning and the arts. Nevertheless, it was not from this circle of patrician intellectuals that the first supporters of the Reformation in Augsburg came. The city council vacillated on the question of church reform, and in 1520 Oecolampadius discretely resigned his position and left the city. Urbanus Rhegius was chosen to succeed him. Since he was a disciple of Dr. John Eck, one had every reason to believe that Rhegius would be loyal to the Catholic cause, but within a year he, too, had been convinced by Luther and was turned out of that enviable pulpit.[66] The city was rapidly moving in the direction of reform, although there was no one at the helm of the ship. The city council still vacillated. In the episcopal palace there was no firm voice of leadership. Nor did any able preacher mount the pulpit to lead the reform. Finally, Urbanus Rhegius, by now a staunch Lutheran, returned to the city and became pastor of the Church of St. Anna; but although he remained there from 1524 to 1530, the spiritual helm of the city was not in his hands. In 1525 Balthasar Hübmaier and Hans Denck won a considerable following for the Anabaptist movement. Numerous preachers followed the lead of Zwingli. Michael Keller, a very popular preacher, was the most capable of these, but still none of these men was able to draw the various parties together.[67] When the Emperor entered the city for the Diet of Augsburg in 1530, he ordered all Protestant preachers to leave the city. The presence of the Emperor, his opposition to the Reformation on one side, and the presence of a number of leading Protestant Reformers on the other hand, only stimulated the concern of the city leaders to achieve a solution to the problem.

Bucer spent some time in Augsburg during the meeting of the imperial Diet and became fast friends with a number of civic leaders. The Reformer of

65. On the background of the Reformation in Augsburg, see Old, *Patristic Roots,* pp. 56-64.

66. Paul Tschakert, "Urbanus Rhegius," *New Schaff-Herzog Encyclopaedia,* vol. 10 (New York: Funk and Wagnalls, 1911), pp. 22-23.

67. Friedrich Roth, "Zur Lebensgeschichte des Meisters Michael Keller, Prädikanten in Augsburg," *Beiträge zur bayrischen Kirchengeschichte* 5 (1889): 149-63.

Strasbourg tried to help them organize a church in a city where Catholic, Lutheran, Zwinglian, and Anabaptist teachings all had enthusiastic supporters. Bucer was optimistic about finding a position that would be acceptable to both Zwinglians and Lutherans. Bucer recommended two of his Strasbourg assistants, Wolfgang Musculus and Bonifatius Wolfhart, as pastors for the city, and things began to improve. Again in 1537, Bucer was called to Augsburg to help draw up a service book or church order for the Church of Augsburg.[68] For this purpose Bucer remained in Augsburg from May 18 to July 9.[69] On July 12, the church order was presented to the city council, and the liturgical texts were published shortly thereafter.[70]

The Augsburg baptismal rite begins with a number of instructions on how the rite is to be performed.[71] First, it was observed that Sunday is the most appropriate time for baptism, although it is recognized the Lord himself did not designate any particular time. Second, family, friends, and neighbors should attend a baptism not only that they might help make it a festive occasion, but also that they might enter into the prayers for the child and that they might remember and give thanks for their own baptism. Third, we find a defense of the use of the baptismal font. Just as each church has a pulpit for preaching and a table for communion, so each church should have a particular place for baptism. The German word is *Taufstett,* literally, a "baptismal place." Bucer seems to have in mind the large stone baptismal fonts which were in use in South Germany at the time. Anabaptists were opposed to the use of these fonts.[72] From these remarks, it is clear that Bucer was not in agreement. There was a strong Anabaptist influence in Augsburg, and undoubtedly this explains the need for Bucer to speak about the subject.[73]

68. On Bucer's work with the pastors of Augsburg, see E. Sehling, *Die evangelischen Kirchenordnungen des XVI Jahrhunderts,* vol. 12, part 2 (Tübingen: J. C. B. Mohr, 1963), pp. 25-27. To be abbreviated as Sehling, *Kirchenordnungen* 12:2.

69. It is not clear whether the new order for baptism produced in Strasbourg this same year came after or before the baptismal order for Augsburg.

70. *Forma, wie von dem hailigen Tauf, und dem hailigen Sacrament des leibs und bluts Christi, und demnach vom Elichen Stand bey dem Einsegen der Eeleut, zu reden sei, Gestellt in die kirch und Gemaind Christi der Statt Augsburg* (Philipp Ulhard, 1537). Our study is based on the modern critical edition found in Sehling, *Kirchenordnungen* 12:2, pp. 72-83.

71. These instructions are in the part of the church order which was not published. Sehling, *Kirchenordnungen* 12:2, p. 63.

72. The issue does not seem to be immersion, for the Anabaptists at first baptized in public fountains using a wooden bucket to pour water over the one being baptized. Williams, *Radical Reformation,* p. 136.

73. Clement Ziegler opposed the use of baptismal fonts as well as the use of chrism and consecrated water. His idea seems to be that the baptismal font was a blessed or consecrated place. *QGT* 7, p. 16.

The actual baptismal rite consists of the following elements: First, we find the Baptismal Exhortation, which is in effect a brief sermon on baptism. Four alternatives are given. Each one treats a different group of texts on baptism. All four follow the lines set down in the Strasbourg rite of 1537. While the *Strasbourg Psalter of 1537* gave directions only as to what should be covered in the Baptismal Exhortation, the *Augsburg Service Book of 1537* gives a complete text.[74] Second, we find the Baptismal Invocation, of which four alternative forms are given.[75] One of these forms is taken from Strasbourg. The Baptismal Invocation is completed by the Lord's Prayer. Third, we find the Scripture lesson, Mark 10:13-16. Fourth, several rubrics are given concerning the baptismal washing. The deacon is to bare the head of the child, and the midwife is to hold the child while the child is being baptized.[76] The baptism is performed by pouring water on the child three times with the hand while repeating the words of Christ.[77] The child is then presented to the godparents, who are to lay their hands on the child. The deacon is to say, "Let us then all regard this child as a child of God and as our fellow member in Christ, faithfully commending him to his kingdom."[78] Fifth, the Creed is then to be sung in Luther's version. Sixth, a prayer of thanksgiving is to be offered by the minister, the text of which is not given. Seventh, the service is concluded by the benediction.

This baptismal rite of Augsburg is quite obviously far from being a copy of the rite of Strasbourg, however much Bucer may have influenced it. One notices that great pains have been taken to preserve a number of local customs. Some of these customs, such as the participation of the midwife, probably go back to pre-Reformation times. Others, such as the singing of the Creed, may reflect the practice of the earliest Protestant ministers of the city, being well established before Bucer's influence began to make itself felt in Augsburg. Specifying that the font is to be used and that the water is to be poured on the child three times may have more than one explanation. Perhaps these were

74. Sehling, *Kirchenordnungen* 12:2, pp. 72-77.

75. Sehling, *Kirchenordnungen* 12:2, pp. 77-78.

76. The notes in Sehling (p. 78) explain these as local Augsburg customs of long standing. It is tempting to try to translate "die hebamm" as something other than "midwife," but a study of the pertinent dictionaries leaves one to conclude that in Augsburg it was indeed traditional for the midwife to participate in the baptism.

77. Sehling, *Kirchenordnungen* 12:2, p. 78. Bucer was evidently convinced by this time that trine baptism was to be preferred because it was a more obvious sign of washing.

78. ". . . zu denen sprech der helfer: 'Lasset euch das kindlin als ain kind Gottes und unser aller mitglid in Christo getreulich zu seinem reich befolhen sein.' " Sehling, *Kirchenordnungen* 12:2, p. 78. The text refers to "der helfer," which early in the Reformation was used to refer to the deacon, while the minister was called "der Diener."

questions which had been discussed by the ministers of Augsburg and which were only now being decided. On the other hand they may be ideas of Bucer's which he had been unable to institute at Strasbourg. Whatever may be the explanation of these variations, the baptismal rite of Augsburg is an interesting example of how the Reformed baptismal rite might be adapted to a particular local church.

The Genevan Baptismal Rite

John Calvin, in his first edition of the *Institutes,* proposed the outline of a baptismal service.[79] It is here that we should begin our study of the Genevan baptismal order. According to this outline, first the child is to be presented to the congregation. Then the assembly is to pray for the child and offer him to God. The Creed, which eventually the child is to be taught, is then recited. The scriptural promises in regard to baptism are recounted and explained. With the Trinitarian formula from Matthew 28:19, the child is baptized, and the service concludes with prayer and thanksgiving.[80] This brief outline was proposed by Calvin in 1536, that is, before he began his work in Geneva. Clearly it is not a description of any of the baptismal orders which we have studied up to this point. We see this particularly in the arrangement of the various components of the service. The Baptismal Exhortation follows the Baptismal Invocation. This again becomes apparent in regard to the postbaptismal prayers. Until this time the only baptismal order to include any kind of postbaptismal prayer would have been Basel's use of Psalm 116 or perhaps Farel's benediction. Neither of these seems to fit Calvin's words completely. Although the benediction or prayer used in Zurich to accompany the clothing of the newly baptized child in white would probably have been understood in this way, this does not seem to be what Calvin has in mind either. It seems, then, that Calvin's remarks are by way of a proposal rather than a description of a baptismal order then in use. As we shall see, the baptismal orders which Calvin actually drew up in the years to follow departed from this early proposal quite considerably. Calvin obviously wanted to build on the foundations already set by the other Reformers.

During Calvin's first period in Geneva, the baptismal order which was

79. *Institutes* 4.15.19.

80. The Latin text of 1536 reads as follows, "At quanto satius erat, quoties baptisandus aliquis esset, in coetum fidelium ipsum repraesentari, et tota ecclesia, velut teste, spectante et orante super eum, Deo offerri? recitari fidei confessionem, qua sit instituendus catechumenus? enarrari, quae in baptismo habentur, promissiones? catechumenum baptisari in nomen patris et filii et spiritus sancti? remitti demum cum precibus et gratiarum acetione." *Opera Selecta* (hereafter *OS*), ed. Petrus Barth, vol. 1 (Munich: C. Kaiser, 1926), p. 160.

undoubtedly used was the order found in the *Evangelical Service Book of 1533.* Calvin himself may not have administered baptism at this time since his call was primarily to a teaching ministry. On this we can only speculate.

It was a different matter when Calvin became the pastor of the French congregation in Strasbourg. There as the shepherd of the flock he was responsible for administering baptism. It was for this little congregation that he produced the baptismal rite found in the *French Evangelical Psalter of 1542.*[81] Many of the liturgical forms found in that psalter were simply French translations of the forms used by the German-speaking churches of Strasbourg. This is not the case for the order of baptism. Calvin wrote his own baptismal liturgy. Much of the material he drew from Farel's order of 1533, and some influence of Strasbourg is clearly discernible, however much Calvin may have reworked it. After the usual invocation, "Our help is in the name of the Lord. . . ," there is a highly developed Baptismal Exhortation. This is Calvin's own composition, although it resembles the Baptismal Exhortation of the *Strasbourg Psalter of 1537.* This is followed by a Baptismal Invocation, which follows the pattern of Farel's prayer but which Calvin has generously elaborated. The admonition comes next. Again Calvin follows Farel closely. The only major deviation is that Calvin, instead of repeating the Creed, gives us a paraphrase of the Creed.[82] The Gospel story of presenting the children to Jesus is then read, and, following the Neuchâtel order, the parents are asked if they wish to have the child baptized. The child is then baptized, "in the name of the Father and of the Son and of the Holy Spirit." The service is concluded with the benediction.[83] Calvin's most significant additions to the work of Farel are the Baptismal Exhortation and the reformulation of the Baptismal Invocation. At the end of Calvin's life he claimed to have written the baptismal service himself. On the other hand, in a letter to the authorities of Bern he claimed that the baptismal liturgy of Geneva was essentially the liturgy which he had found when he came. As contradictory as the statements appear, they are both quite true.[84]

81. *La manyere de faire prieres aux eglises Francoyses. . . .* This edition is usually called the "Pseudo-Romana." It was undoubtedly printed in Strasbourg, but in order to get it over the border into France it bore the following, "Imprime a Rome par le commandment du Pape. par Theodore Bruss Allemant. . . ." It bears the date 1542. This is undoubtedly a second edition of a now lost first edition of 1540. On questions of the textual tradition see *OS* 2, pp. 5-7. For the text itself see *OS* 2, pp. 36-38.

82. This sort of thing was often done. Perhaps this is what is implied by the rubrics of the *Strasbourg Psalter of 1530,* ". . . erzelet der diener . . . ettwa den glauben." Hubert, *Ordnungen,* p. 40.

83. Farel's charge, "take good care of the child," has been omitted.

84. This apparent contradiction has been discussed at length. Emile Doumergue, *Jean Calvin: les hommes et les choses de son temps,* vol. 2 (Lausanne: G. Bridel, 1902), p. 499.

Calvin had taken Farel's service and rewritten it, elaborating it here and there, deleting a few things; it was still essentially Farel's service.

When Calvin returned to Geneva, the *Genevan Psalter of 1542* was published. It contained a baptismal rite which was a somewhat briefer version of the service Calvin developed for the French congregation in Strasbourg.[85]

The "Form for Administration of Baptism" begins with a rubric laying down the times when baptism is to be celebrated. "Either on the Lord's Day at the time of the catechetical service or on the other days at the time of the sermon, the reason being that since baptism is a solemn reception into the Church, it should take place in the presence of the assembly. The child is to be presented after the sermon has been finished."[86] Here we discern the influence of Strasbourg. Calvin, as Bucer, would no doubt have liked to insist on reserving baptism to the Lord's Day and to the morning service, but the rubric indicates that a judicious compromise has been made. There were too many people who were still uneasy about waiting that long to have their children baptized.

The service begins with Farel's invocation, "Our help is in the name of the Lord. . . ," which reflects the influence of Zurich. The parents are asked, "Do you present this child to be baptized?" To this they are expected to answer, "Yes." The minister then begins the Baptismal Exhortation, which Calvin composed for his congregation of French exiles in Strasbourg, following the outline of the *Strasbourg Psalter of 1537.* Beginning with the words of Jesus to Nicodemus, that one must be reborn to enter the Kingdom of God, the whole plan of redemption is outlined. The meaning of baptism is explained. "All these graces are conferred upon us when he is pleased to incorporate us into his Church by baptism. For in this sacrament he testifies to us the remission of our sins. And for this cause, he has ordained the sign of water, to signify that as by this natural element the body is washed of its bodily odors so he wishes to wash and purify our souls."[87] Here we clearly see that for Calvin the sign of baptism is not

---

For the passages which apparently contradict each other see *CR,* Calvin's *Opera* 9, p. 894 and 15, p. 538. See W. D. Maxwell, *The Liturgical Portions of the Genevan Service Book* (London: Faith Press, 1965), p. 48.

85. "La Forme d'administrer le baptesme," *La Forme des Priéres et Chantz ecclesiasticques,* in Calvin's *Opera Selecta,* eds. Petrus Barth and Dora Scheuner, vol. 2 (Munich: C. Kaiser, 1952), pp. 30-38. To be abbreviated as "La forme," *OS* 2.

86. "Il est à noter qu'on doit apporter les enfans pour baptiser, ou le Dimanche, à l'heure du Catechisme, ou les aultres iours au sermon, afin, que comme le Baptesme est une reception solennelle en l'Eglise, qu'il se face en la presence de l'Assemblee. Le sermon achevé, on presente l'enfant." "La forme," *OS* 2, p. 31.

87. "Toutes ses graces nous sont conferées, quand il luy plaist nous incorporer en son Eglise par le Baptesme. Car en ce sacrement, il nous testifie la remission de noz pechez. Et

primarily burial and resurrection, but rather washing.[88] Calvin goes on to say that we receive a double grace and benefit at baptism. "Here we have a sure witness that God wishes to be a loving Father, not counting all our faults and offenses. Secondly, that he will assist us by his Holy Spirit so that we can battle against the devil, sin, and the desires of our flesh, until we have victory in this, to live in the liberty of his kingdom."[89] Calvin explains baptism, as Farel and Oecolampadius, not as a *mere sign* but as a *true sign.* Baptism is a "sure witness" of both our justification and our sanctification. For Calvin, baptism is a sign of something which will go on through the whole of life.

The Baptismal Exhortation continues, ". . . those two things are accomplished in us, through the grace of Jesus Christ: it follows that the truth and substance of baptism is comprised in him. For we have no other washing than in his blood, and we have no other renewal than in his death and resurrection. But as he communicates to us his riches and blessings by his word, so he distributes them to us by his sacraments."[90] This is a good statement of the way Calvin understands the relation of the sacrament to the saving work of Christ. Our salvation was accomplished by Christ's death and resurrection there and then, but the benefits of that saving work are applied to us here and now by Word and sacrament.

The exhortation turns to the subject of the baptism of infants. Following the Strasbourg pattern, this is done by way of commentary on Genesis 17:7-9, 1 Corinthians 7:14, and Matthew 19:13-15. Here we find an unusual feature

---

pour ceste cause, il a ordonné le signe de l'eaue, pour nous figurer, que comme par cest element les ordures corporelles sont nettoyées: ainsi, il veult laver et purifier noz ames. . . ." "La forme," *OS* 2, p. 32.

88. Calvin goes on to say that the sign of baptism also represents renewal, which rests in the mortification of our flesh and the spiritual life which God produces and raises up in us. As is shown in the work of Benoît, Calvin is quite correct in seeing baptism first as a sign of washing and then renewal. It is not primarily a sign of burial or resurrection. This interpretation of the sign comes only in the third century with a misunderstanding of the sixth chapter of Romans. André Benoît, *Le baptême chrétien au second siècle; la théologie des pères,* Etudes d'histoire et de philosophie religieuses, vol. 43 (Paris: Presses Universitaires de France, 1953).

89. "C'est que nous y avons certain tesmoignage, que Dieu nous veult estre Pere propice, ne nous imputant point toutes noz faultes et offences. Secondement, qu'il nous assistera par son sainct Esprit, afin que nous puissons batailler contre le Diable, le peché, et les concupiscences de nostre chair, iusques à en avoir victoire, pour vivre en la liberté de son Regne." "La forme," *OS* 2, p. 32.

90. ". . . ces deux choses sont accompliees en nous, par la grace de JESUS Christ: il s'ensuit, que la verité et substance du Baptesme est en luy comprise, Car nous n'avons point d'aultre lavement, que son sang: et n'avons point d'aultre renouvellement, qu'en sa mort et resurrection. Mais, comme il nous communique ces richesses et benedictions, par sa parolle: ainsi il nous les distribue par ses Sacrements." "La forme," *OS* 2, p. 33.

of the Genevan order. The Gospel story of presenting the children to Jesus appears as part of the Baptismal Exhortation rather than later on in the service. It is quoted or paraphrased rather than read as a Scripture lesson. This is in contrast to the order of the French-speaking congregation of Strasbourg. The exhortation, as it was by this time the well-established custom in most Reformed Churches, leads to the Baptismal Invocation.

The Baptismal Invocation is the same as it was in Calvin's Strasbourg service except that it is followed by the Lord's Prayer.[91] The admonition follows the admonition of Farel's *Evangelical Service Book of 1533,* except for the recitation of the Ten Commandments.

A rubric follows, "After the promise has been made, the name is given to the child." Evidently Calvin has nothing against the idea that in baptism the child is given a name. Indeed, for Calvin, the giving of a name had considerable religious significance. This is indicated by the fact that the Church of Geneva felt the necessity of drawing up a list of appropriate and inappropriate names to be given children. That the choosing of the appropriate name for a child had a religious significance is a very biblical concept. With the strong relation between baptism and circumcision so heavily emphasized by the Reformers, it is not at all surprising that in the story of naming John the Baptist (Luke 1:57-64) as well as in the story of naming Jesus (Luke 2:21) they saw scriptural basis for giving names to children at baptism. We will have more to say about this in another chapter.

The minister then baptizes the child, putting pure and simple water on his head while saying, "In the name of the Father and of the Son and of the Holy Spirit."[92]

At the end of the service is another set of rubrics directing that "all this is to be said in full voice and in the common language of the people." Then the rubric goes on, "We are fully aware that besides this there are many other ceremonies, the antiquity of which we in no wise deny. . . . Be that as it may, since these other ceremonies have been invented apart from the Word of God . . . we have not found any difficulty in abolishing them. . . ." Finally, the rubric concludes, "At the least we have a form of baptism which was instituted by Jesus Christ, which the apostles kept and followed and which remained in force in the primitive Church. . . ."[93] These remarks are important because

91. "La forme," *OS* 2, p. 35.

92. "En apres le ministre le baptizera luy mettant de l'eaue pure et nette sur la teste en disant. 'Au nom du Pere, et du Filz, et du sainct Esprit.' " "La forme," *OS* 2, pp. 37-38.

93. "Le tout se dit à houlte voix, en language vulgaire: . . . Nous sçavons qu'on faict ailleurs beaucoup d'aultres ceremonies, lesquelles nous ne nyons pas avoir esté fort anciennes; . . . quoy qu'il soit, puis qu'elles ont esté forgées sans la parolle de Dieu, . . . nous

they make clear what Calvin understood to be the purpose of the liturgical reform of his day. The purpose of this liturgical reform is here particularly applied to the reform of the rite of baptism. Essentially Calvin sees the problem to be that although the basic core of the baptismal rite had remained intact, it had been incrusted by a number of superstitious rites which had obscured the basic sacramental action. To be sure, and Calvin recognizes this, the first reform which was needed was the translation of the service into the language of the people. Calvin has obviously understood Luther's point on the question of the *adiaphora,* for he expressly says, "Those matters about which we have no commandment of God are in our liberty"; however, Calvin goes further and says, "How much more true then, that which leads to stumbling and serves as an instrument of idolatry and gives rise to misleading opinions, ought in no way to be allowed."[94] For Calvin the problem faced by the Church in the reform of the rite of baptism was to free the rite from the elaborate anointings with oil and chrism, the consecration of the font, and the repeated exorcisms. To Calvin, as to the sixteenth-century Rhenish Reformers, all these supplementary ceremonies seemed more closely allied to witchcraft and magic than to Christianity. These symbolic rites had been invented by human beings rather than instituted by Christ. They bore no divine promise, and that was sufficient reason not to use them, but there was more. They misled the faithful. They made of the Christian sacrament an occult rite. They made it look like the mystery religions of ancient Greece and Rome. The rite needed to be freed from these accretions so that the full force of the baptismal sign of washing might appear in all simplicity and directness.

Conclusion

In this chapter we have seen how the Reformed baptismal rite developed over a period of some twenty years. It was shaped and developed by many hands. It was influenced by the theological insights of such diverse theologians as Luther, Zwingli, Capito, Bucer, Oecolampadius, Farel, and Calvin. It was

n'avons point faict difficulté de les abolir. . . . Pour le moins, nous avons telle forme de Baptesme que JESUS Christ a ordonnée, que les Apostres ont gardée et suyvie, que l'Eglise primitive a eu en usage." "La forme," *OS* 2, p. 38.

94. "Premierement, ce qui ne nous est point commandé de Dieu, est en nostre liberté; d'avantage tout ce qui ne sert de rien à edification ne doit estre receu en l'Eglise; et s'il avoit esté introduict, il doit estre osté. Par plus forte raison, ce qui ne sert que à scandaliser, et est comme instrument d'idolatrie et de faulses opinions, ne doit estre nullement toleré." "La forme," *OS* 2, p. 38.

adapted to the church life of a wide variety of cities and territories. The Reformation took very different forms in Zurich, Basel, Strasbourg, Bern, Augsburg, Neuchâtel, and Geneva, and the baptismal rites of these churches reflect these differences. There were, nevertheless, a number of common concerns and approaches which transcended the ethnic, linguistic, and cultural particularities of these different churches. One discerns quite easily a common approach to liturgical reform at work in these various churches.

This school of liturgical reform arose primarily from the need, so widely felt at the beginning of the sixteenth century, to reform the old Latin rites of the Middle Ages. It was largely inspired by Christian Humanism and its interest in returning to the sources of Christian antiquity. In the Upper Rhineland Christian Humanism developed into a new interest in biblical studies as well as a revival of patristic studies. It developed into a revival of Augustinian theology. With Luther and the beginning of the Protestant Reformation these disciples of the Christian Humanists were given the opportunity to reform the old Latin rites. This they began to do, and most of their reforms must be understood in terms of the attempt to reform the old Latin rites.

The Reformers had no more begun this reform than they found themselves confronted by the Anabaptist movement. The Anabaptists had a very different approach to baptismal reform. More and more the Reformers found that they had to defend themselves against the Anabaptists. The baptismal rites they were developing could not help but be affected by this polemic, although the general direction of the liturgical reform had already been set before the confrontation with the Anabaptists began. It was as a result of the controversy with the Anabaptists that the Reformers became increasingly interested in covenant theology and the importance of circumcision as a type of baptism. This emphasis had its effect on the Reformed baptismal rites. From this came the fact that the Reformers gave increasing importance to the parents rather than the godparents in baptism. It was the emphasis on covenant theology which at least in part gave them the reason for discontinuing the exorcisms. The polemic with the Anabaptists left its mark on the Baptismal Exhortation. The Baptismal Exhortation became very long and was characterized by much theological apologetic. One had to explain very carefully why children were being baptized. The controversy with the Anabaptists played a role in shaping the Reformed baptismal rite, but it was not the most important role.

Even in the face of the Anabaptist controversy the Reformers still held to the basic concerns of the reform which they began before the Anabaptists gained their attention. Still very basic to this school of reform was the need to overcome the tension between private baptisms and church baptisms. Long before the Anabaptists appeared, the Christian Humanists were intent on restoring the catechumenate. The restoration of the catechumenate became one of the most successful projects of the Reformation. Surely one of the fundamental motives of this school was the desire to overcome the dichotomy between water and the Holy Spirit which had developed with the emergence of the sacrament of confirmation. Luther's insight into the epicletic nature of baptism was taken up with considerable conviction. The Baptismal Invocation was essential to the Reformed baptismal rite. As the earliest Reformed theologians saw it, the rite of baptism must make clear that baptism with water is a sign and a promise of baptism by the Holy Spirit. Nothing in the rite should lead the faithful astray by suggesting that water is a sign of the washing away of sins and that something else, such as oil or the laying on of hands, is the sign of the giving of the Holy Spirit. Above all, the Reformers were devoted to celebrating baptism in such a way that the sacrament be a sign of the richness of God's grace. If the early Reformed theologians rejected the Anabaptist approach to reform it was above all because the Anabaptists had failed to appreciate the primacy of grace. An appreciation of the Augustinian doctrine of grace was one of the fundamental insights of classical Protestantism. It was this appreciation for grace which led the Reformers out of late medieval Scholasticism, and the Reformers were not about to be charmed back into it by the Anabaptists. The Anabaptists were Pelagian and just as voluntaristic as the late medieval Scholastic theologians. In continuing to baptize infants the Reformers were only confirming their original Augustinianism. The baptismal rites they developed bore witness to a strong doctrine of grace. They were confident that the God who had so graciously made them members of the covenant community would be just as gracious to their children, and so they baptized their children. It was not because of a superstitious belief that their children would be saved by some sort of magical ceremony, but out of faith in the covenant promises of God.

CHAPTER VII

Catechetical Instruction

Having traced the history of the Reformed baptismal rite from the first attempts of the High Rhenish Reformers to translate the Latin rite through a development of more than twenty years which finally culminated in the baptismal rite of the *Genevan Psalter* of 1542, we turn to a systematic presentation. In the next four chapters we will take up each of the main parts of the total baptismal experience. We will look at the rite systematically, studying its prayers, trying to understand why the sacramental action was developed as it was, and taking a look at the setting in which baptism was performed. We will see how the sign of baptism administered at the beginning of the Christian life entails Christian education, profession of faith, witness before the world, and the life of prayer. Of the essence of the Reformed understanding of baptism is the belief that it is a prophetic sign. It is a sign under which the whole of life is to be lived. Our baptism is always with us, constantly unfolding through the whole of life.

The Christian Humanists' Ideal of the Restoration of Catechetical Instruction

From the Christian Humanists the Reformers inherited a high regard for Christian education. When the Christian Humanists spoke of church reform, they gave the reform of Christian education a high place on the list of their priorities. This was only natural because many of the Christian Humanists were educators and teachers. It was out of a concern for Christian teaching that the Brethren of the Common Life inspired the establishment of a number of important schools in Northern Europe which combined a profound piety with serious scholarship.[1] One of the most important of these schools was the Collège Montaigu in Paris, where Standock and Erasmus had taught and where Calvin and Loyola had studied.[2] The Latin schools of Pfortzheim and Heilbronn were likewise centers of pious Christian Humanism in South Germany. Another such school was the Latin school at Sélestat, where Martin Bucer, Paul Phrygius, and Leo Jud had studied.[3] The founder of this school was Jakob Wimpfeling, an important leader of German Christian Humanism. His influence was made not only by his school but by an essay on Christian education, *Adolescentia.* This essay did much to arouse an interest in Christian education as well as to popularize the ideas on Christian nurture by other Christian teachers of the day, such as Sebastian Brandt, Pico della Mirandola, Rudolf Agricola, and above all Jean Gerson. It was in a school influenced by the Brethren of the Common Life that Erasmus himself had studied. Erasmus produced several works on Christian education. In 1514, his *Christiani hominus institutum* appeared.[4] This work was designed to be used by his friend, John Colet, in the newly founded St. Paul's School in London. These schools did much to encourage a reverent study of the classics of Christian antiquity. The schools of the Christian Humanists, however, were aimed at the production of an intellectual elite rather than providing for all the baptized the fundamentals of catechetical instruction.

1. On the educational activities of the northern Christian Renaissance, see the following works: Pierre Debongnie, "Dévotion moderne," *Dictionnaire de la Spiritualité,* vol. 3, pp. 727-47; Albert Hyma, *The Christian Renaissance, a History of the "Devotio Moderna,"* 2nd edn. (Hamden, Conn.: Archon Books, 1965); R. R. Post, *The Modern Devotion: Confrontation with Reformation and Humanism* (Leiden: E. J. Brill, 1968); Lewis W. Spitz, *The Religious Renaissance of the German Humanists* (Cambridge, Mass.: Harvard University Press, 1963), pp. 1-19.

2. On the influence of the Collège Montaigu, see Alexandre Ganoczy, *Le jeune Calvin: Genèse et évolution de sa vocation réformatrice* (Wiesbaden: F. Steiner Verlag, 1966), p. 43.

3. On the influence of the Latin school of Seléstat, see Ernst- Wilhelm Kohls, *Die Schule bei Martin Bucer in ihrem Verhältnis zu Kirche und Obrigkeit* (Heidelberg: Quelle und Meyer, 1963), particularly the chapter "Die überragende Bedeutung der Stadschule zu Schlettstadt," pp. 23-28. On the reform of Jakob Wimpfeling, see his *Adolescentia,* ed. Otto Herding with Franz Josef Worstbrock (Munich: W. Fink, 1965); Spitz, "Wimpfeling, Sacerdotal Humanist," chap. 3 of *The Religious Renaissance,* pp. 41-60; Staehelin, "Im Bannkreis der Wimpfelingschen Reformbewegung 1499-1512," chap. 2 of *Das theologische Lebenswerk Oekolampads* (Leipzig: M. Heinsius Nachfolger, 1939), pp. 15-54.

4. On the catechetical work of Erasmus, see Rudolf Padberg, *Erasmus als Katechet. Der literarische Beitrag des Erasmus von Rotterdam zur katholischen Katechese des 16. Jahrhunderts, Eine Untersuchung zur Geschichte der Katechese* (Freiburg: Herder, 1956). Between the catechism of 1514 and the catechism of 1533 the religious situation of Europe had changed drastically. The catechism of 1533 was in effect a controversial piece. The first of the two is of much greater interest in demonstrating the direction in which the Christian education of the day was headed before the Reformation began. See Padberg, *Erasmus,* pp. 124-33.

Jean Gerson, the renowned conciliarist and chancellor of the University of Paris, had a great influence on the teaching of the elementary principles of Christian faith and devotion to the simple and uneducated of his day. *L'ABC des simples gens* gained wide circulation with the coming of the printing press. Another work on the Christian education of children, *Tractatus de parvulis trahendis ad Christum,* was a manual for pastors. It is remarkable in that it recognizes the unique problems of the pastoral care of children. Gerson's most influential catechetical work was his *Opus tripartitum.* Unlike the catechetical instruction of the Reformation, which was preparation for Communion, Gerson's work understands catechetical instruction in terms of preparation for the sacrament of penance. The sincere piety of this extraordinary Christian leader is demonstrated by the fact that toward the end of his life (1409-12) he devoted his time to the Christian education of children at St. Paul's Church in Lyon.[5]

Many individual Christian Humanists made contributions to Christian education. One thinks particularly of the efforts of the Bishop of Basel, Christoph von Utenheim, to introduce regular catechetical preaching in all the parishes of his diocese.[6] By this was meant the classical catechetical preaching, that is, an explanation of the Creed, the Lord's Prayer, and the Ten Commandments. Perhaps added to this might be an explanation of the Ave Maria, the seven deadly sins, and an explanation of the Mass. From Johann Ulrich Surgant we learn something about his bishops' attempt at restoring catechetical instruction.[7] It was perhaps one of the best attempts made in that age, but it did not have anything like the desired success.

Another brilliant attempt at educating ordinary church members was that undertaken by the Bishop of Meaux, Guillaume Briçonnet. The bishop was a prominent member of the group of evangelically inclined intellectuals close to Marguerite of Navarre, the sister of Francis I. On becoming bishop he envisioned a reform of his diocese through biblical preaching and teaching. The circle of scholars which he formed to renew his diocese was indeed outstanding. Jacques Lefèvre d'Étaples, François Vatable, Gerard Roussel, and such young preachers as William Farel did much to increase a knowledge

5. On Gerson's dedication to the education of children see Louis B. Pascoe, *Jean Gerson: Principles of Church Reform* (Leiden: E. J. Brill, 1973), pp. 125-31.

6. On the Christian Humanist Reform work of the bishop of Basel, Christoph von Utenheim, see Staehelin, *Das theologische Lebenswerk Oekolampads,* pp. 20-22; Eberhard Vischer, "Utenheim, Christoph von," *Realencyklopädie für protestantische Theologie und Kirche,* vol. 20, 3rd edn. (Leipzig, 1908), pp. 370-76.

7. On the influence of the *Manuale curatorum* in the inner-church reform of the Christian Humanists, see Old, *Patristic Roots,* pp. 7-10.

of the Bible in the diocese of Meaux, but strictly speaking this was not catechetical instruction.[8]

Johann Geiler von Kaisersberg, often considered the most brilliant preacher of the late Middle Ages, did an outstanding work in developing the catechetical sermon. Geiler, who for years preached at the cathedral of Strasbourg, winning the admiration of Sebastian Brandt, Beatus Rhenanus, Jakob Wimpfeling, and the Rhenish intelligentsia in general, followed much in the tradition of Jean Gerson. He was very fond of preaching on the Christian basics. Geiler was a great example of the teaching-preacher. We have manuscripts of a good number of his catechetical sermons.[9]

It is without doubt Erasmus who had the most clear plan to restore catechetical instruction. Erasmus, as a patristic scholar, knew much about the catechumenate in the ancient Church. In his *Paraphrases on the Gospel of Matthew,* published in 1522, Erasmus proposed the restoration of the ancient catechumenate.[10] As he saw it, a revived catechumenate would need to be adapted to the situation of the church of the sixteenth century in which most people were baptized as infants. This would require giving the catechetical instruction after baptism rather than before baptism. When young people came to sufficient age to understand basic Christian teaching, they were to be instructed in the fundamentals of the faith. The vows which their sponsors had made for them at baptism would then be explained to them. Erasmus follows the ancient catechumenate so closely that he suggests that the classes be held in Lent. Finally, the young people are to be examined, and if it is found that they sufficiently understand their faith they are to renew their baptismal vows in a church ceremony. In the more official Roman Catholic circles, Erasmus' suggestion was treated with considerable hostility, and some charged that it would constitute a rebaptism.

The Reformers Begin Catechetical Instruction

If there were many who opposed the suggestion of Erasmus, there were also those who welcomed it. In the following year, 1523, both Luther and Zwingli

8. Guy Bedouelle, *Lefèvre d'Étaples et l'intelligence des écritures* (Geneva: Droz, 1976). See particularly the subchapters "Lefévre, un pédagogue," pp. 47-56, and "Le cercle de Meaux et l'initiation à la vie évangélique," pp. 90-103. On catechetical work at Meaux, see pp. 99-100.

9. E. Jane Dempsey Douglass, *Justification in Late Medieval Preaching: A Study of John Geiler of Keisersberg* (Leiden: E. J. Brill, 1966).

10. John B. Payne, *Erasmus, His Theology of the Sacraments* (Richmond, Va.: John Knox Press, 1970), pp. 171-80.

began to hold regular catechetical instruction for the youth of their respective churches. Following closely the suggestion of Erasmus, Luther's series of sermons continued for a period of two weeks before Easter, meeting at least four times each week. In July 1523, Zwingli announced in his *Usslegen und Gründe der Schlussreden* that recently the Church of Zurich had begun to gather the youth of the city together for catechetical instruction. Zwingli's comment is most enlightening in regard to the beginnings of catechetical instruction in the Reformed Church.

> . . . From ancient writers I have heard it said that those being confirmed were asked what their names were, and afterward whether they knew the Creed and the Lord's Prayer, and after this they were then anointed with oil or chrism. From these practices and from the fact that today one still asks the question concerning the name leads me to think that confirmation came into practice when it became normal to baptize infants, so that the father and mother affirmed the faith for them through the godmother and godfather. . . . I well know, for the ancient writers show this, that from early times children were occasionally baptized; nevertheless it was not by any means as common as in our day. More normally they were brought together and publicly instructed in the message of salvation when they came to the age of understanding. From this came the practice of calling them catechumens, that is, those being instructed. So when they had been given a strong faith in their hearts and confessed that faith with their mouths, they were baptized. This custom of teaching I would very much desire to have reinstituted for today; namely, that since the children are baptized so young they receive instructions as soon as they can understand and receive the word of God. . . . For this reason we have also begun here in Zurich for more than a year to call all the youth together twice each year and having them all there together we teach them the knowledge of God and of his will and his word, how they should treat their neighbor and how they should understand God to be their friendly and loving Father and how they should go to him in times of need for both body and soul.[11]

11. "Ich hab aber von den alten ghört, das man vor zyten den gfirmten gefragt hab, wie er heyss, und darnach, ob er den glouben und das vatter unser könne, und demnach gesalbet mit dem öl order krisem. Uss den brüchen und das man noch hüt by tag den namen erforscht, müss ich ye gedencken, das die firmung erst in einen bruch kummen sye, als man die kinder gemeinlich hat angehabt in der kindtheit, ja, so bald sy worden sind, touffen, damit inen der gloub, den vatter und müter für sy durch gotten und götinen verjehen habend, nit unbekant sye. Wiewol ich weiss, als die alten anzeigend, das man von alter har die kind etwan getoufft hat, ist es doch nit also gemein xin als zu unseren zyten, sunder man hat sy offenlich mit einandren gelert, als sy zu verstentnus kummen sind — dannenhar sy ouch katechumeni hand gheissen, das ist: die berichten —, das wort des heils. Und so sy dem vesten glouben imm hertzen ggeben habend und mit dem mund verjehen, hat man sy getoufft.

Several comments need to be made regarding this passage. First, we notice that for the Reformer of Zurich, catechetical instruction is an essential part of the sacrament of baptism. Second, we find that the beginning of catechetical instruction in Zurich is consciously an attempt to restore the catechetical instruction of the ancient Church. There is a problem here. While Zwingli evidently does know a certain amount about the catechumenate of the ancient Church, he has drawn some erroneous conclusions about it. He proposes the theory that when it became the regular practice to baptize infants, those who had been baptized in infancy were required to take the catechetical instruction once they were of sufficient age to understand it. He goes on to suggest that confirmation owed its origin to the need to have these young people make the profession of faith for themselves which their godparents had made for them when they had been baptized as infants. Zwingli was not the only one in the sixteenth century to have advanced this theory; nevertheless, it was quite erroneous. Third, we learn that the purpose of catechetical instruction is to present the gospel of salvation in such a way that young people are led to a public profession of their faith. Fourth, we are not too sure how much time was given to these sessions. Did they try to do this teaching in a single session, or did they have four sessions a week for two weeks as was the practice in Wittenberg? From Rudolf Stähelin we learn that shortly after this time the semiannual lessons were supplemented with a weekly children's catechetical service held at eleven o'clock each Sunday morning.[12]

Fifth, we are impressed by the fact that Zwingli emphasizes that the instruction is to be a public instruction carried out by the Church for all the young people together. What Zwingli has in mind is a distinct departure from what had been the practice of the medieval Church. The procedure of the Middle Ages was simply to leave the responsibility of catechetical instruction to the godparents or to the schools. For children of more privileged families

---

Welchen sitten der leer ich beger noch hüt by tag wider angenommen werden, namlich, das man, sydtenmal man die kinder so jung toufft, sy fürneme ze leren, so sy zuo sölchem verstand kummend, dass sy vernemmen mögend das wort gottes. . . . Uss welchem grund wir ouch zuo Zürich vor jaresfrist angehebt habend zwürend jm jar alle jugend berüffen und sy alda mit einandren leren gott erkennen unnd demnach sin wort und willen inen offnen, wie sy sich gegen im und dem nächsten halten söllend; ouch wie sy sich zuo im, als zuo eim früntlichen, lieben vatter, versehen söllind und zuo im louffen in aller not des lybs unnd des gemütes." *Usslegen und Gründe der Schlussreden, CR* 89, p. 123.

12. Rudolf Stähelin, *Huldreich Zwingli,* vol. 2 (Basel: Benno Schwabe, 1897), pp. 121-31. In the *Züricher Prädicantenordnung* of 1532, we find that the holding of catechetical instruction every Sunday was a regular responsibility of the pastors. A. M. Richter, *Die evangelischen Kirchenordnungen des sechszehnten Jahrhunderts,* vol. 1 (Weimar: Verlag des Landes-Industrie-Comptoirs, 1846), p. 171.

this was not much of a problem because the tutors which they hired were more often than not clerics and the schools to which they sent their children were more often than not operated by religious orders. In many places the schools were poorly attended so that the effect of leaving catechetical instruction to the schools would mean that only privileged children would receive it. Zwingli, on the other hand, did much to promote public education in Zurich. The public schools of Zurich were well attended, and, to be sure, they provided a considerable amount of Christian education. Even at that Zwingli wanted regular catechetical education in the Church.[13]

Zwingli's remarks in the *Usslegen der Schlussreden* leave us desiring more information on the content of catechetical instruction in those earliest days. That information is supplied by another document of the period, the so-called *Zurich Tafel-Katechismus.*[14] This single sheet of paper, which was meant to be hung on the wall, was published in Zurich in 1525 by Christoffel Froschauer. It is not completely clear who was responsible for its publication, but probably it was Leo Jud. He was the pastor of St. Peter's Church in Zurich and a close friend of Zwingli. The *Tafel-Katechismus* contains four catechetical pieces, the Ten Commandments, the Lord's Prayer, the Creed, and the Hail Mary. For several centuries the memorizing of these pieces had been considered the minimum Christian education, and thus it is understandable that it was here that the Zurich Reformers started.

Much the same thing was happening in Strasbourg at about the same time.[15] In the summer of 1526, we find that regular catechetical instruction was held in the parish churches of St. Pierre le Jeune, St. Pierre le Vieux, and St. Aurelia.[16] All the pastors were to take their turn at the weekly *Kinderbericht,* or catechism classes. It seems that the weekly *Kinderbericht* consisted primarily in explaining the Creed, the Ten Commandments, and the Lord's Prayer, and probably having the children recite these pieces as well. Perhaps there was a rehearsal of some sort of summarized form of the points treated. It would have been from such formulations that the catechism grew. Possibly much of the catechism developed in an oral tradition before publication. In 1527,

13. Willi Meister, *Volksbildung und Volkserziehung in der Reformation Huldrych Zwinglis* (Zurich: Zwingli-Verlag, 1939).

14. *Die evangelischen Katechismusversuche vor Luthers Enchiridion,* ed. Ferdinand Cohrs, vol. 1 (Berlin: A. Hofmann & Co., 1900), pp. 122-27. This collection is vol. 20 of the *Monumenta Germaniae Paedagogica,* which will be abbreviated *M. G. Paed.* Hence *M. G. Paed.* 20, pp. 122-27.

15. See August Ernst and Johann Adam, *Katechetische Geschichte des Elsasses bis zur Revolution* (Strasbourg: Friedrich Bull, 1896), p. 187.

16. *M. G. Paed.* 21, p. 85. See also Ernst and Adam, *Katechetische Geschichte,* p. 116.

Wolfgang Capito published his *Kinderbericht und fragstuck.*[17] Capito's *Kinderbericht* is essentially a prolonged explanation of the Apostles' Creed in a question-and-answer form. To the third article is added an explanation of the sacraments of baptism and the Lord's Supper. In succeeding years both Matthis Zell and Martin Bucer published catechisms which in all probability grew out of their catechism classes. These catechisms were published in order that children might practice answering the question both at home with their parents and at school with their teachers. In the schools, which due to Bucer's efforts were very well attended, one day each week was set aside for studying the catechism. Four times each year the pastors were to hear the catechism, the purpose of which was to check the progress of the children by having them recite what they had learned. When the children were able to satisfy the pastors that they understood the Christian faith, then they were to be admitted to the Lord's Supper.[18] The close connection between the sacrament of baptism and the catechetical instruction was made most clear in Bucer's catechism of 1534. This catechism begins with the following question and answer:

> Dear child, do you wish to lead a Christian life and to live according to the will of God our heavenly Father?
>
> Yes, dear father, for I have been baptized in the name of God, the Father, the Son and the Holy Spirit. . . .[19]

Strasbourg's plan of catechetical instruction, led by the pastors, its excellent public school system which had been entrusted to such capable men as Jean Sturm, Wolfgang Sapidus, and Otto Brunfeld, and its newly developing university, made the city a center of evangelical education.[20] For the Re-

17. *Kinderbericht und fragstuck von gemeynen puncten Christlichs glaubens* (Strasbourg: W. Köpphel, 1527). For a modern edition see *M. G. Paed.* 21, pp. 85-201.

18. F. Wendel gives a more thorough treatment. *L'église de Strasbourg, sa constitution et son organisation, 1531-1535* (Paris: Presses universitaires de France, 1942), pp. 216-20.

19. "Underrichter.

"'Liebs kind, du begerest dein leben Christlich und nach dem gefallen Gottes unsers himmlischen vatters anzustellen?'

"Kind.

"'Ja lieber vatter oder meyster, dann ich uff den namen Gottes, vatters, sons und heyligen geysts ge teuffet.'"

Quellen zur Geschichte des Katechismus-Unterrichts, vol. 1: *Süddeutsche Katechismen*, ed. Johan Michael Reu (Gütersloh: C. Bertelsmann, 1904), p. 25. To be abbreviated Reu, *Quellen*.

20. On Bucer and the educational system of Strasbourg, see Ernst-Wilhelm Kohls, *Die Schule bei Martin Bucer in ihrem Verhältnis zu Kirche und Obrigkeit* (Heidelberg: Quelle

formers of Strasbourg the whole system was based on the sacrament of baptism and Christ's command to "Go therefore and make disciples of all nations, baptizing them . . . and *teaching* them to observe all that I have commanded you" (Matt. 28:19-20). For these Reformers, it was likewise clear that their catechetical instruction was inspired by the catechumenate of the ancient Church.

We cannot, of course, be sure just exactly what the pastors of Strasbourg knew about the catechumenate in the ancient Church. That there was catechetical instruction in the ancient Church can, of course, be learned from many sources. From Eusebius, a favorite source of the Strasbourg Reformers, one can learn about the catechetical school of Alexandria. Since Hedio published a German translation of Eusebius's *Ecclesiastical History* in 1530, we can assume that this information was fresh in their minds. Augustine's *Confessions* would also have been a source. Just which of the different series of catechetical sermons which have come down to us from antiquity were known to the Strasbourg Reformers is not too clear. Certainly the *De sacramentis* of Ambrose and the catechetical sermons of Augustine were well known. There were plenty of places the Reformers could have learned about the catechumenate in the ancient Church.

The catechetical instruction developed by the Reformed Church of Constance deserves special attention. The Reformation of this city was guided by three particularly able men, Johannes Zwick and the brothers Ambrosius and Thomas Blarer. Zwick was regarded as one of the best catechists of his age.[21] He was well on his way to a distinguished career in law when he decided for the Reformation. After studies in Freiburg, Avignon, and Bologna, he received his doctorate in both laws at the University of Siena. He was a favorite pupil of the great Zasius, and, like Calvin, he had studied under the master of Italian Humanist jurisprudence, Andreas Alciati. He was fully educated in the Humanist tradition, but it was clearly the Italian Humanist tradition, and even in the Christian Humanism of Erasmus, rather than in the Christian Humanism of Jakob Wimpfeling or Jacques Lefèvre d'Étaples. Returning to Northern Europe, he settled at the University of Basel, where he taught law. There his old friend Bonifatius Amerbach introduced him to the circle of Erasmus. He won considerable acclaim for his teaching, and back in Constance he was

---

& Meyer, 1963). See also Allan H. Gilbert, *Martin Bucer on Education* (Urbana, Ill.: University of Illinois, 1919). Gilbert's pamphlet is a reprint from *The Journal of English and Germanic Philology* 18:3 (July 1919): 321-45.

21. Bernd Moeller, *Johannes Zwick und die Reformation in Konstanz,* Quellen und Forschungen zur Reformationsgeschichte, vol. 28 (Gütersloh: Gerd Mohn, 1961), to be abbreviated as Moeller, *Zwick.*

admired as the hometown boy who had made good. He was generally regarded as a very promising young man. While his career was beginning to blossom he found himself becoming more and more interested in the writings of Luther. In 1522, he met Zwingli and was won to the Reformation. Giving up his post in the faculty of law, he took the position of priest in the Swabian town of Riedlingen, not far from Constance.[22] It was there that he began his work of teaching the young people in his parish. It was, of course, this same year, 1522, that Erasmus had written his important exhortation for the revival of catechetical instruction.[23]

Two catechisms of Zwick have been preserved. One is a catechism on the Lord's Prayer, the other on the Apostles' Creed.[24] There may also have been a catechism on the Ten Commandments. These works seem to have been developed in the years at Riedlingen, perhaps as early as 1525 or 1526.[25] The printed editions which have come down to us, however, stem from 1529-30, after he had begun his pastorate in Constance.

Of even greater interest than these two catechisms are the catechetical hymns which Zwick composed.[26] Zwick composed these hymns as a method of teaching the children of his Church. He provided these young people with a version of the Creed, the Decalogue, and the Lord's Prayer. He also provided

22. On the subject of Zwick's conversion from Humanism to Protestantism, see the excellent treatment in Moeller, *Zwick*, pp. 46-51. The position at Riedlingen was open to him because of the death of his uncle, who had previously held the position. Zwick inherited the benefice but could not conscientiously turn it over to a vicar. That had come to be his conviction after reading the writings of Bucer. As Moeller ably reconstructs the story, Zwick interpreted this turn of events as a call into the ministry.

23. See above, n. 10.

24. *Das vatter vnser in frag vnd gebätts wyss, für jung vnnd einfaltig lüt* (Zurich: Ch. Froschauer, 1535); *Bekantnus der zwölff artickel, des Glaubens von Jesu Christo, quo dem Allmächtigen Gott in himel* (Konstanz: J. Spitzenberg, 1530); Moeller, *Zwick*, p. 281.

25. *M. G. Paed.* 23, pp. 56-57; Moeller, *Zwick*, pp. 128-32.

26. Philipp Wackernagel, *Das deutsche Kirchenlied von der ältesten Zeit bis zur Anfang des XVII Jahrhunderts*, vol. 3 (Leipzig: B. G. Teubner, 1870), pp. 603-17. "Herr Gott, din trüw mit gnaden leist" (p. 604, no. 674) is entitled a song for the beginning of the children's catechetical service. "Jetz und so bitten wir dich, herr" (pp. 604-5, no. 675) is given as a hymn for the end of the same service. Several other hymns are obviously intended for the catechetical service: nos. 676-78, 680, and 684 (pp. 605-7, 609). The last named is a long paraphrase of the Lord's Prayer, giving a long stanza to each phrase of the prayer. It is an excellent catechetical hymn! Number 685 (p. 610) is a long paraphrase of the Beatitudes, similar in construction to the paraphrase of the Lord's Prayer. In addition, Zwick produced two hymns on baptism, nos. 672 and 673 (pp. 603-4). Zwick's friend and colleague in the Reformation, Thomas Blarer of Constance, also produced some hymns for the children's catechetical service: "Globet sey der herre Gott" (no. 666, p. 600 in Wackernagel 3), which was written for the beginning of the service, and "Du hast uns lub und seel gespysst" (no. 667, p. 601), written for the end.

them with hymns for beginning and closing the catechetical service. Later these hymns appeared in a small hymnbook especially for children.[27] It is significant that this youth hymnal bore the title *Prayers for Young People.* For Zwick catechetical instruction was to take place in a context of worship. Obviously the catechetical services were conceived as services of worship. We will notice as our study proceeds that in both Zurich and Geneva this attitude was perpetuated. Children were not only to be taught about prayer, they were to be taught to pray as well.

Johannes Zwick, doctor of both laws, must have had a special fondness for children. Possibly it was because he and his wife Anna never had children of their own.[28] The particular devotion of this man for children is expressed in his carefully-worked-out program of Christian education, which some have regarded as the best of its time.[29]

In 1528, the Church of St. Gallen published a catechism borrowed from the Czech Brethren.[30] In the same year the Church of Ulm, under the guidance of its pastor, Konrad Sam, published a catechism, *Christliche underweysung.*[31] In the preface, the schoolmaster of Ulm, Michael Brothag, reminds his readers that "catechism" comes from the word used for Christian instruction in the ancient Church.[32] This catechism is the first to contain all three of the traditional catechetical pieces, the Creed, the Lord's Prayer, and the Ten Commandments. The second edition of 1529 added the fourth theme of the traditional Reformed catechism, an explanation of the sacraments.

In 1529, the city of Basel officially recognized the need for catechetical instruction. In the *Reformation Act of 1529,* we find the following provision:

> Besides this the young people are not to be forgotten by the pastors; rather the pastors are to bring them up in the fear of the Lord and in Christian discipline. To this end it would be fruitful if the pastors would take those between approximately the ages of seven and fourteen and gather them

27. *Gebätt für jung lüt, die man in Schuolen vnd inn Huss alltag vnnd durch die wochen sprechen man, wäm sölichs geliebt vnnd der nit bessers weisst* (Zurich: Ch. Froschauer, 1540). Moeller, *Zwick,* p. 288.

28. The fact that Zwick was married did not bar him from taking his uncle's parish in Riedlingen under the old regime of the bishop of Constance. Because he was married, however, he had to pay a fine to the bishop.

29. This is the evaluation of Ferdinand Cohrs, *M. G. Paed.* 23, p. 46.

30. For a short treatment of this catechism, together with the text of the Czech catechism, see Joseph Muller, *Die deutschen katechismus der Böhmeschen Brüder* (Berlin, 1887). Unfortunately this book has not been available for this study.

31. *Christenliche underweysung der Jungen, in fragszweis von dem Glauben, Vatter unser, und zehen Gebotten* (Ulm: Hans Gruner, 1528). *M. G. Paed.* 23, pp. 75-128.

32. *M. G. Paed.* 22, p. 93.

> together publicly in the church with the aid of the deacons. This should be done at four different times each year. They should be asked whether they can pray and whether they know the commandments of the Lord; and in an appropriate manner they should instruct them in the faith and in the love of God. Besides this the young people who have not yet received the sacrament of the Lord and now wish to receive the Lord's Supper are to be publicly instructed by the pastor and the deacon in what they should understand about the sacrament.[33]

From this document it is not quite clear how much catechetical instruction children received. It seems unlikely that they received only four sessions per year in each parish. Possibly there were several sessions at each of the four annual instructions, but this is not expressly stated. On the other hand, Ernst Staehelin tells us that catechetical instruction was handled for the most part by the schools. In both the German and Latin schools there were set times each week for catechetical instruction. Staehelin understands quarterly parish catechetical sessions as an opportunity for pastors to check the progress of the children who were learning the catechism either at home or at school.[34] One thing which stands out quite clearly in this document is that catechetical instruction is in Basel thought of primarily in terms of communicants class, that is, preparation to receive communion.

Another document of the Church of Basel which deserves our attention is the catechism written by John Oecolampadius.[35] Unfortunately, the oldest copy which we have comes from 1537, six years after the Reformer's death. When it first appeared, we do not know. Ferdinand Cohrs suggests that it appeared between 1525 and 1527, and therefore regards it as one of the oldest Protestant catechisms.[36] Ernst Staehelin, whose suggestions deserve the highest respect, would date the catechism in the same period as the *Reformation Act*

33. "Ausserdam sollen sie der Jugend nicht vergessen, sondern sie in Gottesfurcht und christlicher Zucht erziehen. Dazu wird es fruchtbar sein, wenn die Leutpriester die Kinder, ungefähr von siebten bis zum vierzehnten Jahr, alle Jahr viermal zu sich und ihren Helfern öffentlich in die Kirche kommen lassen, sie fragen, ob sie beten können und die Gebote des Herrn kennen, und sie darauf in geziemender Weise im Glauben und in der Liebe Gottes unterweisen. Dabei sollen auch die jungen Leute, die bisher das Sakrament des Herrn nicht empfangen und jetzt das Abendmahl des Herrn nehmen wollen, durch die Leutpriester und Helfer öffentlich in der Kirche unterrichtet werden, was sie von den Sakramenten halten sollen." From *Das Buch der Basler Reformation,* ed. E. Staehelin (Basel: Helbing & Lichtenhahn, 1929), p. 200.

34. Staehelin, *Das theologische Lebenswerk Oekolampads,* pp. 586-92.

35. *Frag und Antwort in Verhörung der Kinder der Kilchen zuo Basel. M. G. Paed.* 23, pp. 2-19.

36. *M. G. Paed.* 23, p. 6.

of 1529. While the catechism is quite short, it treats the Creed, the Commandments, the Lord's Prayer, and the sacraments. The brevity of this catechism alone leads us to believe that it was intended to be said at a service of worship like the one suggested by Erasmus. The suggestion of Erasmus does not seem to be the only inspiration of this catechism. Oecolampadius, with his wide knowledge of patristic literature, seems to have been inspired by the ancient rite of the tradition and reddition of both the Creed and the Lord's Prayer, as it was practiced in the fourth century. That Oecolampadius had this ancient practice in mind appears even more likely from a sermon of the Reformer of Basel which was preached on the occasion of admitting young people to the Lord's Table. This sermon is clearly modeled on the *Traditio symboli,* known to us from so many patristic sources.[37] Oecolampadius does not seem to have shared Zwingli's confusion about the origin of confirmation. For Oecolampadius the patristic practice which inspired his rite of reciting the catechism was the fourth-century rite of the *Redditio symboli,* not a supposed rite of confirmation.

The Growth of Catechetical Instruction, 1530-41

During the 1530s catechetical instruction became more and more popular. It also became more and more characteristic of those churches which had accepted the Reformation. This was as much true of the churches which looked to Luther for leadership as it was for the churches of the Upper Rhineland led by Bucer, Oecolampadius, and Zwingli. In 1529, Luther published both a larger and a shorter catechism.[38] These two works have remained classics in the Lutheran Church ever since. It was not until 1531 that the larger catechism reached its definitive form. Luther's catechetical works had the effect of standardizing the program of catechetical instruction for the Reformation. With these publications, the history of catechetical instruction entered a new phase. The experimentation which had followed the suggestion of Erasmus had proved very successful. Luther's publications had the effect of consolidating and institutionalizing these first attempts.

Whether in Wittenberg or in the Upper Rhineland, the program was essentially the same. Catechetical services were held each Sunday. At these

37. For the text of this sermon, see Karl Rudolf Hagenbach, *Johann Oekolampad und Oswald Mykonius, die Reformatoren Basels* (Elberfeld: R. L. Friderichs, 1859), pp. 284ff.

38. *D. Martin Luthers Werke: Kritische Gesamtausgabe,* vol. 30, part 1 (Weimar: Hermann Böhlau, 1891), p. 425, to be abbreviated *WA* 30:1.

services the catechetical pieces were explained by one of the ministers in a special catechetical sermon. Catechisms were published by the Church so that this catechetical material could be studied both at school and at home. When a child had mastered the material, the child was presented to be examined by the ministers at a service of worship held for that purpose. The saying of the catechism admitted the young person to Communion, which was held the following Sunday.

The main features of this program we see instituted in one place after another. In the *Ulm Reformation Act of 1531,* we find just such a program.

> On Sunday at midday a service is to he held in which the Ten Commandments, the Creed, and the Lord's Prayer are to be explained. The young people are to be exercised with questions at this time, and four times each year catechizing is to take place.[39]

In Augsburg we find *Kinderbericht,* established by the *Augsburg Church Order of 1537.* The Principality of Hesse adopted such a program in 1539.[40] In fact, the re-establishing of catechetical instruction became one of the most important projects of the Protestant Reformers.

Leo Jud, the minister at St. Peter's Church in Zurich, is another reformer who wrote significant catechetical literature at this time. We remember that it was Leo Jud, a graduate of Jakob Wimpfeling's Latin school in Sélestat, who in 1523 produced the first German baptismal rite for the Church of Zurich. In 1534, three years after Zwingli's death, Leo Jud published his *Larger Catechism.* Jud draws on the catechisms of Capito, Zwick, and Sam. He uses the traditional four-part schema: The Ten Commandments (which appear for the first time in the traditional Reformed numbering), the Apostles' Creed, the Lord's Prayer, and the teaching of the Church on the sacraments. Particularly interesting is the collection of prayers for use at the table and for use in the morning and the evening. Leo Jud also found that teaching the child to pray was an essential part of catechetical instruction.

As a larger catechism it is designed primarily for parents and others charged with giving religious instruction to children. This is to be noticed from the fact that the child asks the questions and the teacher gives rather complete

39. ". . . und an den Sonntagen zu Mittag werden die zehen Gebote, der Glaube und das Vaterunser erklärt. Das junge Volk soll zu Zeiten mit Fragen geübt, und jährlich viermal sollen mit ihm Catechisationen angestellt werden." Aemilius Richter, *Die Evangelischen Kirchenordnungen des sechszehnten Jahrhunderts,* vol. 1 (Weimar: Verlag-des Landes Industrie-Comptoirs, 1846), p. 157.

40. *Martin Bucers Deutsche Schriften,* vol. 7, *Schriften der Jahre 1538-1539,* ed. Robert Stupperich (Gütersloh: Gerd Mohn, 1960), pp. 281-82, to be abbreviated *BDS* 7.

answers. It is nevertheless, as the title indicates, a "Christian, clear, and simple introduction in the will and in the grace of God, whereby not only the youth, but also the parents may be taught."[41] A preface, written by Henry Bullinger, by this time Zwingli's successor, stresses the responsibility God has given parents to provide Christian instruction for their children.

The success of the book was enormous not only in Zurich but also in Bern, Schaffhausen, St. Gallen, Graubunden, and other parts of the Swiss confederation.[42] In 1541, at the request of the Zurich synod, Leo Jud set to work on a shorter catechism, this time with the teacher asking the questions and the children answering.[43] This catechism, too, has the fourfold subject matter which by then had become traditional. Again we find a collection of prayers appended to the catechism. Both from literary and theological points of view, Jud's work is well regarded as a clear statement of the faith of the Church of Zurich.

It was in the year 1534 that the pastors of Strasbourg published *A Short Scriptural Explanation.*[44] This work, which in fact was written by Bucer, actually contains two catechisms. The first is a rather full treatise on Christian doctrine directed to the parents, and the second is a summary intended for children. The catechism is divided into three parts: the Creed, the Commandments, and the Lord's Prayer. The sacraments are treated in the third article of the Creed. Bucer's catechism went through a number of editions and revisions in Strasbourg and elsewhere. The catechism of Matthis Zell, the preacher at the Cathedral of Strasbourg, should be mentioned, although it seems to have been primarily intended for his own congregation.[45] Almost all the Reformers tried their hand at a catechism at some time or another. As we have seen, the

41. *Christliche, klare, und einfache Einführung in den Willen und in die Gnade Gottes, womit nicht nur die Jugend, sondern auch die Eltern unterrichtet werden, wie sie ihre Kinder in den Geboten Gottes, im christlichen Glauben und um rechten Gebet unterweisen können.* Leo Jud, *Katechismen,* ed. Oskar Farner (Zurich: Max Niehaus, 1955), pp. 27- 239.

42. See the remark of Oskar Farner in the introduction to *Katechismen,* p. 19.

43. *Eine kurze christliche Unterweisung der Jugend in der Erkenntnis und in den Geboten Gottes, im Glauben, im Gebet und andern notwendigen Dingen, durch die Diener des Wortes zu Zürich in Fragen erteilt. Katechismen,* pp. 243-376.

44. *Kurtze Schrifliche erklärung für die kinder und angehende der gemeinen artickeln unsers christlichen glaubens, der zehn gebott, des Vatters unsers* (Strasbourg: Matthias Apiarius, 1534). For a modern edition see n. 19 above. The shorter catechism was revised three years later, *Der kürtzer Catechismus und erklärung der XII stücken Christlichs glaubens, des Vaters unsers, und der zehen gepotten. Für die Schüler und andere kinder zu Straszburg. Durch die Prediger daselbst gestellet* (Strasbourg: Wendelin Rihel, 1537). For a modern edition see Reu, *Quellen,* pp. 67-90.

45. *Frag vnnd Antwort vff die artikel des Christlichen glaubens. . . .* In Reu, *Quellen,* pp. 105-23.

number of catechisms produced in these early years is certainly impressive. One reason was simply that they were all engaged in catechetical instruction, and they all developed their own ways of formulating basic Christian teaching. But there was another reason. The re-establishment of the catechumenate was a reform that the classical Protestant Reformers considered very important.

Catechetical Instruction in the Church of Geneva

Already in the *Ecclesiastical Articles* of 1537, written during his first pastorate in Geneva, Calvin had proposed the reinstitution of catechetical instruction as it had been practiced by the ancient Church:

> The third article concerns the instruction of children, who, without doubt, owe to the Church a confession of their faith. For this reason it was the ancient practice to have a kind of catechism for the instruction of each child in the fundamentals of the Christian religion and which was a sort of formula which each person used for professing his faith, and particularly when the children had been taught this catechism it became the profession of faith before the Church which they had not been able to make at the time of their baptism.[46]

Several comments should be made here. This document makes a small number of proposals to the authorities of Geneva for church reform. The fact that the reinstitution of the ancient discipline of the catechumenate is mentioned on this list shows how important it was for Calvin. It is clear from this document that the purpose of catechetical instruction was to prepare young people to make a public profession of their faith before the Church. Calvin clearly understands this as the baptismal profession of faith. The more ancient practice had obviously been to make this at the time of baptism, but as Calvin saw it, since children are not able to make their own confession of faith at their baptism, they have to make it later. That is, Calvin understands the baptismal profession of faith to be postponed. One notices as well that Calvin has been

46. "Le 3e article est de linstruction des enfans, lesqueulx sans doubte doibuent a lesglise vne confession de leur foy. Pour ceste cause anciennement on auoyt certain catechisme pour jnstituer vng chascun aux fondemens de la religion crestienne, et qui estoyt comme vng formulayre de tesmoignage dont vng chacun usoyt pour declairer sa crestiente, et nommeement les enfans estoyent enseignez de ce catechisme pour venir tentiffier a lesglise leur foy dont jl nauoyent peu rendre tesmoignage a leur baptesme." "Articuli Ecclesiastici, 1537." *Opera Selecta*, ed. Petrus Barth, vol. 1 (Munich: C. Kaiser, 1926), p. 375, to be abbreviated *OS* 1.

inspired to institute catechetical instruction by the practice of the ancient Church. By that he evidently means the practice of the third and fourth centuries. The most interesting remark that we find in this passage is the reference to the catechism of the ancient Church. Calvin says, "For this reason it was the practice of the ancient Church to have a certain catechism for the instruction of each child." What did Calvin mean by "catechism" here? Surely Calvin was not thinking of little booklets like those we have today! No, Calvin, as Oecolampadius, has in mind the catechetical pieces, above all the Apostles' Creed. It was the Apostles' Creed which, as Calvin understood it, was the patristic prototype of the Reformed catechism. One clear evidence of this is that the catechism was recited in question-and-answer form, just as the Creed was put to the catechumen in the form of questions in so many of the ancient baptismal rites.

When Calvin returned to Geneva in 1541, the establishment of a regular program of catechetical instruction was one of his initial projects. When Calvin had been exiled from Geneva three years earlier, he recognized that the Reformation could never mature in Geneva as long as the Reformed Church of Geneva had no church constitution and was governed purely by the decisions of the city council. Geneva had been a prince bishopric, and at one time it was the bishop who had complete control of the city. Gradually the city council had wrested from their bishop more and more control. Bit by bit the city council had consolidated its control of the entire community, both civil and ecclesiastical. At the time the city council ran the bishop of Geneva out of the city, the bishop had had very little authority in the city. For us today it is understandable that he had very little political authority, but what we find hard to understand is that he had very little authority in what today we would call purely religious affairs. Once the bishop was gone and the city officially adopted Protestantism, it was the city council which exercised sole authority in the Republic of Geneva. This authority was exercised in both church and state. When Calvin arrived in Geneva the first time, the city had completely affected the transition from a state dominated by the church to a church dominated by the state. This transition had taken centuries, and Calvin would have a hard time restoring any kind of balance between the two. Calvin had in effect been exiled from Geneva because he would not tolerate a state-dominated church. Calvin agreed to return only on the condition that the church be allowed its own constitution. This constitution would need to establish certain basic reforms along the lines of the *Ecclesiastical Articles* of 1537. Calvin's demands were met by the adoption of *The Ecclesiastical Ordinances* at the end of November 1541. This document clearly provides for catechetical instruction. The next matter was for Calvin to provide the text of a catechism, which he did a short time afterward in the *Genevan Catechism.* Let us look at these two documents, first *The Ecclesiastical Ordinances* and then the *Genevan Catechism.*[47]

The *Ecclesiastical Ordinances,* in describing the times and places at which services were to be held, specified that every Sunday at midday catechism was to be held for children in all of the parish churches.[48] Reading further on into the document, we find a special section devoted to catechetical instruction. From the several paragraphs of this section we learn that all citizens and inhabitants were to send their children to the catechetical sermons on Sunday.[49] Furthermore, "there is to be a certain formulary as basis for their instruction."[50] By that we understand the catechism which Calvin would have to compose. Then "when a child was sufficiently instructed to be able to pass the catechism, he shall solemnly recite the sum of what it contains and in so doing make a profession of his Christian faith before the Church."[51] This was all fairly standard. It was the regular program of catechetical instruction which the German Reformers had started to work out almost twenty years before.

Whether the catechetical services included prayer and psalmody is not clear, but there is some evidence that they did. The Genevan Reformers were quite well aware of the pedagogical nature of psalmody. They understood psalmody to have great teaching value. Any good Christian Humanist was aware of how powerful an aid the right use of music could be in education.[52] A number of the psalms found in the *Genevan Psalter,* published at about the same time, would have been particularly appropriate to be sung at the catechetical services. The wisdom psalms would, of course, be the first choices: Psalm 1, Psalm 19, Psalm 37, a stanza from Psalm 119, or the first few stanzas of the 78th Psalm. From *The Ecclesiastical Ordinances* we learn that it was Calvin's plan to train the Church of Geneva to sing by first training the children to sing.[53]

47. For the text of *Les Ordonnances ecclesiastiques de l'eglise de Geneve* see *OS* 2, pp. 325-89. Note particularly the introduction to the text, pp. 325ff.

48. "A mydy quil y ait cathechisme, cest a dire instruction de petiz enfans en touttes les troys esglises, assavoir la magdelene, sainct pierre et sainct gervais." *Ordonnances ecclesiastiques, OS* 2, p. 337.

49. "Que touz citoyens et habitans ayent a mener ou envoyer leurs enfans le dymanche a mydy au cathechisme, dont il a este parle." *Ordonnances ecclesiastiques, OS* 2, p. 356.

50. "Quil y ait ung certain formulaire compose sur lequel on les instruyse." *Ordonnances ecclesiastiques, OS* 2, p. 356.

51. "Quant ung enfant sera suffisamment instruict pour se passer du cathechisme, quil recite solennellement la somme de ce qui sera contenu: et aussi quil face comme une profession de sa chrestiente en presence de lesglise." *Ordonnances ecclesiastiques, OS* 2, p. 356.

52. Charles Garside, *The Origins of Calvin's Theology of Music: 1536-1543* (Philadelphia: The American Philosophical Society, 1979), p. 29.

53. "Nous avons aussi ordonné d'introduire les chants Ecclesiastiques tant devant qu'apres le sermon, pour mieux inciter le peuple à louer et prier Dieu. "Pour le commence-

From the very beginning Calvin had seen the value of the re-establishment of regular catechetical preaching. Catechetical preaching was a very special kind of preaching. From the standpoint of literary form the catechetical sermon was quite different from the expository sermon. Rather than attempting to expound a specific passage of the Bible, the catechetical sermon took as its task the elucidating of a particular teaching or doctrine of the Church. These catechetical services were now established, and the weekly catechetical sermon became from that time on one of the features of the church life of those lands where the Reform was accepted.

The text of *The Ecclesiastical Ordinances* articulates with considerable clarity an essential point of the Rhenish school. The saying of the catechism is the making of a solemn profession of Christian faith before the whole Church. It is here that the baptismal vows are made which were omitted in the baptismal service of the infant child. The baptismal vows were not made by parents or godparents in place of the child. Rather, the vows were postponed until the child had received catechetical instruction. Then, having learned the catechism, the child, somewhere between twelve and fifteen years old, recited the catechism as his or her profession of faith.

Now let us turn to the second of these documents, the *Genevan Catechism.* Unfortunately, it was produced too quickly. Calvin wanted to have it ready so that it might reach port on the floodtide of acceptance and goodwill which had brought him back to Geneva.[54] The Reformer himself admitted that it had been written hastily. It is not one of Calvin's great accomplishments, and it reached nothing like the classic stature of either Luther's *Shorter Catechism* or the *Heidelberg Catechism.* To this day the *Heidelberg Catechism,* not the *Genevan Catechism,* remains the great Reformed catechism. With its 373 questions, the Genevan catechism is far too long to be memorized by the ordinary child. It misses the brevity of Luther's catechism. Unlike Luther's small catechism, which is so admirably adapted for use by children, Calvin's work often develops ideas which must have been hard for children to grasp.

One feature of Calvin's catechism deserves our particular attention. The catechism has at the conclusion a small collection of prayers. Together these prayers form a discipline of daily prayer. First there is a prayer to say in the

---

ment on apprenda les petitz enfans, puis avec le temps toute l'Eglise pourra suivre." *Ordonnances ecclesiastiques, OS* 2, p. 345. This text, which appears in lines 5-9 and again in lines 16-19, dates from 1561. But the project was well underway by then.

54. *Le Catechisme de l'Eglise de Geneve, c'est à dire le Formulaire d'instruire les enfans en la Chrestienté (1542) —Catechismus ecclesiae Genevensis, hoc est formula erudiendi pueros in doctrina Christi (1545). CR* 34, pp. 1-160. The Latin text is also found in *OS* 2, pp. 59-144.

morning on rising.[55] This prayer is prefaced with several verses from Psalm 143, one of the traditional morning psalms. Then follows a prayer to be said before beginning one's daily work.[56] This is prefaced by a few verses from Psalm 119. There are prayers for the beginning and ending of meals.[57] Finally, there is a prayer to be said before retiring at night.[58] From Calvin's chapter on prayer in the *Institutes,* we learn that this follows exactly what Calvin taught as the daily discipline of personal prayer which everyone should keep whether one was able to attend the daily prayer services held in the church or not.[59] The inclusion of these prayers in the catechism makes it clear that instruction in the disciplines of prayer was an important part of fundamental training in Christian faith. The devotional aspect of the Christian life needed to be trained as much as the intellectual and the moral.[60]

A study of the *Genevan Catechism* of 1542 leads one to ask exactly what the purpose of this catechism is. Is it a summary of Christian doctrine to be memorized by children and recited by them as a confession of faith? Surely it is too long to serve that purpose. One wonders if Calvin started out to produce such a document and then, once he started writing, could not stop and ended up producing something much longer than he had really intended. It gives much more the impression of being a manual for the catechist rather than a text for the catechumen. To use a contemporary term, it gives the appearance of being a curriculum for catechetical instruction. This catechism is the "catechism for the instruction of each child," mentioned in *The Ecclesiastical Ordinances;* however, it is not the "formula which each person used for professing his faith." It would seem that this catechism is not as much the profession of children before the congregation as it is the profession of faith

55. "Oraison pour dire au matin, en se levant," *Le Catechisme, CR* 34, pp. 135-38; *OS* 2, pp. 144-46.

56. The first edition of the catechism had a prayer to be said before beginning one's studies at school. In later editions, this was replaced by a more general prayer for beginning any kind of work. *Le Catechisme, CR* 34, pp. 137-40; *OS* 2, pp. 144-46.

57. "Oraison pour dire devant le repas" and "Action de graces apres le repas," *Le Catechisme, CR* 34, pp. 139-42; *OS* 2, pp. 147-49. The former begins with the quotation of a verse from Psalm 104 (compare the table grace in Luther's *Shorter Catechism*) and ends with "L'homme ne vit point de seul pain: mais de la parole procedante de la bouche de Dieu" from Deuteronomy 8. The prayer after the meal begins with a verse from Psalm 118. It is interesting how even in these short prayers there is this movement from scripture to prayer.

58. "Oraison pour dire devant que domir," *Le Catechisme, CR* 34, pp. 143-46; *OS* 2, pp. 149-50.

59. *Institutes* 3.20.50.

60. On the place of instruction in prayer in the catechumenate, see Pierre Lestringant, *Le ministère catéchétique de l'église* (Paris: Éditions "Je sens," 1945), pp. 145-65. J. A. Jungmann, *Handing on the Faith, A Manual of Catechetics* (New York: Herder & Herder, 1959), pp. 261-70.

of the Church of Geneva before the whole Christian Church. Calvin soon gave this larger catechism a Latin translation. The Latin translation, as we learn from the preface, has the intention of laying before other churches a summary of the teaching of the Genevan Church.[61]

This was not Calvin's first attempt at a catechism. This *Genevan Catechism* of 1542 had been preceded by a catechism composed for the French Church in Strasbourg.[62] This was a shorter catechism. In many respects it was similar to the catechism of Oecolampadius of 1525, and Luther's *Shorter Catechism* of 1529. Like these two catechisms, a great portion of the text which the child was expected to memorize was the actual text of the three catechetical pieces. Calvin used this shorter catechism, which he developed in Strasbourg, as the basis of the longer work he did for Geneva. Nevertheless in 1553, Calvin produced another shorter catechism. Here we have the "formula of testimony" which each person used to profess his faith. To use the words of *The Ecclesiastical Ordinances,* it is "the sum of what it contains." That is, this shorter catechism is the summary of the *Genevan Catechism* used as the "formulayre de tesmoinage." It is a profession of faith in question-and-answer form. It was intended to be memorized by children and then publicly recited. This second shorter catechism was intended for actual liturgical use in the Genevan Church. We will look at this catechism more thoroughly in the following chapter.

Conclusion

The development of a catechumenate for children who had been baptized in infancy was one of the most successful reforms of the sixteenth century. Its success can be measured in several ways. The Sunday afternoon or evening catechetical sermon became a characteristic of Reformed Church life throughout Europe. It quickly became something of interest to adults as well as to children. Within a generation or two this program of catechetical instruction produced a well-informed Christian public. The Reformers largely succeeded in getting the inhabitants of their cities and territories to follow the catechetical instruction they set up. The sacrament of baptism as understood by the Reformers entailed a lifelong study of Christian teaching. This was what it meant to be a *disciple,* to learn "all things that I have commanded you" (Matt. 28:20). At baptism the Christian is called to a lifelong discipline of study.

61. *Le Catechisme, CR* 34, pp. 5-8; *OS* 2, pp. 72-74.

62. *Institution purile de la doctrine chrestienne faicte par maniere by dyalogue. OS* 2, pp. 152-57. The only text of this catechism which has come down to us is the one in the *French Evangelical Psalter* of 1542.

Perhaps the greatest compliment this reform would receive was that of imitation. Before long Catholics began to recognize the value of this reform, too. Such reform-minded Catholics as John Gropper, George Witzel, and above all Peter Canisius produced excellent catechisms which were soon accepted in even the most conservative Catholic circles.[63] In effect, the catechetical reform became one reform in which Catholics soon joined Protestants.

63. Jean Claude Dhotel, *Les origines du catéchisme moderne, d'après les premiers manuels imprimés en France* (Paris: Aubier, 1967), pp. 50-82; Winfried Glade, *Die Taufe in den Vorcanisianischen Katholischen Katechismen des 16. Jahrhunderts im deutschen Sprachgebiet* (Nieuwkoop: B. de Graaf, 1979).

CHAPTER VIII

The Baptismal Vows

The second principal element in the baptismal rites of the earliest Reformed Churches was the making of vows. Basically two kinds of vows come into our consideration. There are, on the one hand, the vows of faith made by the person being baptized, and, on the other hand, the vows of the parents, to bring up the child in the Christian faith. In the Reformed baptismal rites the vows made by parents or godparents or other members of the family are not really understood to be the actual baptismal vows. It is only the vows of the one baptized, professing his or her own Christian faith, which are regarded as the real baptismal vows.

Vows and Admonitions Found in the Reformed Baptismal Services

As we have seen in previous chapters, the different baptismal rites of the Reformed Churches varied quite a bit in this matter. In the baptismal services of Zurich there are no baptismal vows at all. There is rather an admonition to the sponsors to bring up the child in the Christian faith. This admonition is not put in the form of a vow. As we have seen, some of the earlier Strasbourg services ask the godparents and other members of the congregation to agree to bring up the child in Christian discipline and in the fear of God. The *Strasbourg Psalter of 1537* drops even this simple vow and replaces it with an admonition, so that there are no vows in the actual baptismal service. Only in the baptismal liturgy of Basel do we find the ancient threefold renunciation of the devil and his ways, followed by the threefold confession of faith. Strictly speaking, these vows are the baptismal vows, even though they are made vicariously. In the tradition of the Latin baptismal rites of the late Middle Ages, these vows had been made by the godparents in the place of the child. In the rite of Basel, then, we find an exception to the usual pattern of early sixteenth-century Reformed baptismal rites. In Neuchâtel we find that while there are no baptismal vows, properly speaking, there were four vows which the parents were asked to make. These vows promise to bring up the child in the Christian faith.

In the order for baptism of the *Genevan Psalter* of 1542 the parents make four vows. The first is to instruct the child in Christian doctrine.

> Because this is a matter of receiving this child into the company of the Christian Church, do you promise that when he comes to the age of discretion that he will be instructed in the teaching which is received by the people of God as it is summarized in the confession of faith, which we all hold?[1]

The instruction in Christian doctrine is not simply left to parents nor to the sponsors, as had been the case in the Middle Ages. Official catechetical instruction had been set up by the Church of Geneva, and it was to this instruction that baptized children were expected to be brought. Zwingli had made this point quite early in the Reformation, and it was followed by the other Reformers faithfully. The vow is expanded by reciting the Apostles' Creed and a short explanation or paraphrase of it.[2] The second vow is to instruct the child in all that is taught in the Scriptures of the Old and New Testament as being the Word of God. The third vow is the promise to exhort the one baptized to live according to the law of Christ. This is understood as first Christ's summary of the Law and second as the Ten Commandments. That is, they are to teach the child "all that I have commanded you" (Matt. 28:20). Finally, there is the vow to instruct the baptized child to live as a true Christian, to deny himself, and to consecrate himself to live to God's glory and the service of his neighbor.[3]

1. "Puis qu'il est question de recevoir cest enfant en la compagnie de l'Eglise Chrestienne: vous promettez quand il viendra en eage de discretion, de l'instruire en la doctrine, laquelle est receue au peuple de Dieu, comme elle est sommairement comprise en la confession de Foy, que nous avons tous." "La forme," *OS* 2, p. 35. As above in Chap. VI, n. 85.

2. See Spital on the catechism of the sponsor. *Der Taufritus in den deutschen Ritualien* (Münster: Aschendorff, 1968), pp. 91-92.

3. "Vous promettez donques, de mettre peine de l'instruire en toute ceste doctrine, et generallement en tout ce qui est contenu en la saincte Escriture du vieil et nouveau Testament: à ce qu'il le reçoyvent comme certaine parolle de Dieu, venant du Ciel. Item, vous l'exhorterez à vivre selon la reigle, que nostre Seigneur nous a baillée en sa loy, laquelle sommairement consiste en ces deux poinctz: que nous aimions Dieu le tout nostre sens,

A number of comments need to be made about these Genevan vows. In the first place we notice that the vows are made by parents rather than by sponsors.[4] There was a very definite reason for this. The Reformers had defended the doctrine of infant baptism on the basis of the doctrine of the covenant. The children were baptized, to quote the Genevan Baptismal Invocation, because "God is not only our God, but the God and Father of our children." If this is the reason for administering baptism to infants, then it hardly makes sense to have baptismal sponsors present children for baptism. The institution of baptismal sponsors was not, of course, developed because of infant baptism.[5] Originally the baptismal sponsors were to be witnesses to the bishop that such and such a candidate for baptism did have faith. That the sponsors should vicariously take the vows for the baptized was a later development. Children are to be baptized, according to the Reformers, because they are the children of believers, not because a believer has vicariously confessed faith for them.

In the second place, we notice that the vows are not vows of faith on the part of the parents. The parents confess neither their own faith nor the faith of their children. These vows are obviously something quite different from the vows of the Latin rites. In the phrase traditional to Anglo-Saxon Reformed liturgies, the vows are to bring up the child "in the nurture and admonition of the Lord" (Eph. 6:4, KJV). We have to conclude, then, that in the strictest sense of the term baptismal vows are not made in the Genevan baptismal order of 1542.

In the third place, we notice that in these four vows the parents promise to instruct the child in the implications of the sign of the covenant. The Creed, the Law, and the Lord's Prayer are the responsibilities of the covenant into which the child has been brought. The Scriptures are the Scriptures of the Old and New Covenant and are therefore implied by the sign which has been graciously given. The sign is a sign of being washed from sin, a sign of new life, a sign of being born again, a sign of our union with Christ in his death and resurrection, and a sign of renouncing ourselves and walking in newness

---

nostre coeur, et puissance: et nostre prochain comme nousmesmes. Lenseignerez aussi comme vray Chrestien de renoncer à soymesme abandonnant tout pour suyvre Jesus on Filz, portant sa croix, c'est adire les tribulations et afflictions que nostre Seigneur ley envoyra, tellement que toute sa vie soit à l'honneur de Dieu et ledification de tous. Et pourtant l'exhorterez et admonesterez le corigeant ou il fauldra, ainsi que un chascun est tenu à son frere Chrestien en sorte quil soit nourry & enseigné en la saincte doctrine de Dieu. Et ainsi le promettez. Et ils respondent. Ouy." "Laforme," *OS* 2, p. 36.

4. "En apres demandera le ministre aux parens de l'enfant." "La forme," *OS* 2, p. 35.

5. On the origin of baptismal sponsors, see Michel Dujarier, *Le parrainage des adultes aux trois premiers siécles de l'Église* (Paris: Les Editions du Cerf, 1962).

of life. The obligation is to teach the child what all this means. The vows are not taken either for the child or by the child; nevertheless the vows are implied by the sign; in fact, one could even say that they are urged by the sign. Just as Israel is first given the covenant and having been brought out of the land of Egypt is then given the Law, so in Christian baptism the child is made part of the New Covenant people, the Church, and is therefore taught the implications of the New Covenant to which he or she has been called.

For the early Reformed Church it remained, nevertheless, quite clear that an important part of baptism was the making of vows. It was after all the meaning of the word *sacramentum.* From Tertullian the Reformers had learned that the *sacramentum* was the vow made by a soldier entering military service. This approach to sacramental theology, developed by the North African theologians Tertullian, Cyprian, and Augustine,[6] was a viewpoint the Reformers were not inclined to overlook, particularly because it fit so well into covenant theology. That Calvin understood baptism as a *sacramentum* or a vow is clear from the following:

> But baptism serves as our confession before men. Indeed it is the mark by which we publicly profess that we wish to be reckoned God's people; by which we testify that we agree in worshiping the same God, in one religion with all Christians; by which we openly affirm our faith. . . . Paul had this in mind when he asked the Corinthians whether they had not been baptized in Christ's name (I Cor. 1:3). He thus implied that, in being baptized in his name, they had devoted themselves to him, sworn allegiance to his name, and pledged their faith to him before men.[7]

The problem with this passage is that in the text of the *Genevan Baptismal Order of 1542,* there are no vows which make explicit this confession public. This can be understood, however, from the words of the apostle Paul which Calvin then quotes. The apostle does not appeal to vows which the Corinthians had taken in the course of the baptismal liturgy celebrated in Corinth, but rather to the actual fact of being baptized in Christ's name. The earliest baptismal celebrations of the apostolic Church probably had no vows or confessions of faith; nevertheless, the baptism itself implied a public confession. For Calvin as for the apostle Paul vows were implicit in the sign of baptism.

A passage in which this becomes much clearer is Calvin's commentary on the story of Jesus blessing the little children. The reading of this Scripture

6. On Tertullian's covenantal understanding of baptism and the development of the baptismal vows see Joseph Cretian, *Early Christian Baptism and the Creed* (London: Burns, Oates and Washbourne, 1950), pp. 96- 110.

7. *Institutes* 4.15.13. See also 4.14.19.

had been included in the baptismal service in Farel's *French Evangelical Service Book of 1533,* as well as Calvin's *French Evangelical Service Book of 1542.* His comments on this passage are particularly important because Reformed apologetics frequently used the passage to defend infant baptism. Showing, therefore, what this passage has to say about infant baptism, Calvin says:

> Infants are renewed by the Spirit of God according to the capacity of their age, till that power which is concealed within them grows by degrees, and becomes fully manifest at the proper time.[8]

Here is the pivotal point on which the reform of the baptismal liturgy was made. For a child of but a few days it is sufficient to mark the child with the sign of baptism to demonstrate that he or she belongs to the household of faith. At the proper time he will undergo catechetical instruction; he will learn to repent of sin, to call on God for his salvation, and to confess his faith. The implications of the sign, according to Calvin, will unfold throughout the whole life of the child. All this is implied by the sign of baptism and will at the proper time be expressed by the child.

The Baptismal Profession of Faith

The question now is, How and when does the child make this profession of faith? In regard to catechetical instruction, Zwingli was quoted above to the effect that the goal of catechetical instruction is a profession of Christian faith.

> In such a form it seems to me confirmation ought now to be practiced, that is, that those who have been baptized before the age of discretion should when they reach that age of understanding make an affirmation themselves of a faith which they have come to understand. That is, they should first do this after they have been instructed in the matter of salvation.[9]

It is clear from this that the object of catechetical instruction is to bring the child to make a confession of faith. How this is done and where it is done become evident from a study of the texts of the catechisms. The catechisms

8. ". . . renovari Dei spiritu pro aetatis modulo, donec per gradus suo tempore quae in illis occulta est virtus augescat, et palam refulgeat." *CR* 73, col. 535.

9. "Sölicher gstalt mein ich die firmung gebrucht sin, damit die, so vormals unwüssend getoufft warend, hernach, so sy zü vernunfft kommend, wüssenhaffter sach den glouben selbs verjehend, doch erst nachdem sy in dem handel des heils wol bericht warend." *Usslegen und Gründe der Schlussreden, CR* 89, pp. 123-24.

are themselves confessions of faith, particularly the shorter catechisms. Just as in the ancient Church there were confessions of faith in the form of questions and answers, so through questions and answers the young people of the Reformed Church confessed their faith by means of a public repetition of the catechism. Let us look at the catechism of Oecolampadius:

> Q. Are you a Christian?
> A. Yes, praise be unto God!
>
> Q. Do you wish to remain a Christian?
> A. Yes, by God's grace.
>
> Q. Even when Christians are persecuted, imprisoned, killed, and burned will you still remain a Christian?
> A. Yes, by God's grace. . . .
>
> Q. Who is a Christian and who is not a Christian?
> A. He who believes in his heart that the Son of God is become man, that through his suffering and death he has won for us the forgiveness of sin and eternal life. He who does not believe this is no Christian.
>
> Q. Does one need to believe anything else?
> A. He who believes this truly will also confess the articles of the Creed.
>
> Q. Then repeat the Creed for me.
> A. I believe in God, the Father, etc.[10]

Oecolampadius's catechism continues asking question after question, "Bist Du?" "Willst Du?" "Glaubst Du?" All these questions are asked in the second-person singular. Each child is personally and individually challenged to make a profession of faith and a commitment to live the Christian life. The catechism which the child repeated in public was a confession of faith, not simply a handbook on Christian doctrine.

Let us look at another example, Martin Bucer's shorter catechism of 1534.

10. "Frag. Bist du eyn Christ? Anwort. Ja, Gott sy lob. 2. Frag. Wilt du eyn Christ blyben? Antwort. Ja, mit der gnad Gottes. 3. Frag. Wenn mann aber die Christen wurde vertryben, fahen, töden, und verbrennen, wilt du dannocht eyn Christ blyben? Ant. Ja, mit der gnad Gottes. . . . 5. Frag. Welcher ist eyn Christ, und welcher ist keyn Christ? Ant. Welcher gloubt von hertzen, das der Sun Gottes ist war mensch worden, der do mit synem lydem und sterben uns erworben hatt verzyhung der sund und das ewig läben: Der es aber nit gloubt, ist keyn Christ. 6. Frag. Darff man sunst nüt glouben? Ant. Wer diss recht gloubt, wurt die ander Artickel des gloubens ouch bekennen. 7. Frag. So sag mir den glouben? Ant. Ich gloub in Gott vatter, etc." *Frag und antwort in verhörung der kinder, M. G. Paed.* 23, p. 13.

Q. You have been baptized in the name of the Father and the Son and the Holy Ghost. What is your faith then in God our heavenly Father, in our Lord Jesus Christ and in the Holy Ghost the one true God?

A. As I have been taught in the articles of the Christian faith.

Q. Repeat them.

A. I believe, . . .

Q. What do you mean by that little word believe, when you say, "I believe?"

A. To hold something for true and certain without doubting.[11]

Bucer's catechism is especially clear in showing the relation of baptism, Christian instruction, and confession of Christian faith. Baptism is the fact, Christian instruction is the explanation of that fact, and the saying of the catechism is its acceptance.

Calvin's Strasbourg catechism is similar:

Q. Are you, my son, a Christian in fact as well as in name?

A. Yes, my father.

Q. How do you know yourself to be?

A. Because I am baptized in the name of the Father and of the Son and of the Holy Spirit.

Q. What knowledge do you have of the Father and of the Son and of the Holy Spirit?

A. I have that knowledge which the principal articles of our religion teach, which we make our profession through individual confession.

Q. What is that confession?

A. I believe in God the Father Almighty, etc.

Q. And what do you confess by these words?[12]

11. V. . . . Was ist nun dein glaub vnd haltung von Gott vnseren himmlischen vatter, von unserem Herren Jesu Christo vnd von dem heyligen geyst, dem eynigen waren Gott, vff des namen du geteuffet bist? . . .

K. Wie die gemeynen artickel des glaubens inhalten.

V. Erzele die.

Ich glaub. . . .

V. Was heyst dir dz wortlin, "glauben"? Ich glaube, sprichstu?

K. Etwar steyff, vest, vnd ohn allen zweyffel für war halten." *Kurtze schrifftliche erklärung für die kinder vnd angohnden,* in J. M. Reu, ed., *Quellen zur Geschichte des Katechismus-Unterrichts,* vol. 1, part 1 (Gütersloh: C. Bertelsmann, 1904), pp. 25-26.

12. "Le maistre. Mon filz es tu chrestien de faict comme tu es de nom? Lenfant. Ouy

When Calvin returned to Geneva in 1542, he published another catechism, *The Genevan Catechism of 1542.* As we have noted in the preceding chapter, this *Genevan Catechism of 1542* was a "larger catechism," that is, one which was primarily intended for the teaching of adults. It was not at all suitable for the actual making of vows by young people in a public service of worship. For this purpose possibly, Calvin continued to use the shorter catechism which he had prepared in Strasbourg, or else he could already have used the catechism which we find first in an edition of 1553. Possibly this catechism could have been published well before 1553, even though no copies of an earlier edition have come down to us. This shorter catechism is of such a length that one could realistically expect children to memorize it. Furthermore, it does present Christian beliefs in the manner of a confession of faith rather than a doctrinal summary. *The Genevan Shorter Catechism of 1553* begins as follows:

> Q. In whom do you believe and in whom do you put your complete trust?
> A. I believe in God the Father and in Jesus Christ his Son and in the Holy Spirit and look to no other.
>
> Q. Father, Son and Holy Spirit; is that more than one God?
> A. No.
>
> Q. And what confession of faith do you make?
> A. That which the Christian Church has always made and which is called the symbol of the Apostles: I believe in God the Father, etc.[13]

---

mon pere. Le maistre. Comment le scais tu? Lenfant. Car ie suis baptise au nom du Pere et du filz et du sainct Esprit. Le maistre. Quelle foy et congnoissance as tu du Pere, du filz et du saint Esprit? Lenfant. Ie lay telle que les principaux articles de nostre religion nous enseignent, desqueux nous faisons profession avecques singuliere confession. Le maistre. Quelle est ceste confession? Lenfant. Ie croy en Dieu le Pere tout puyssant, createur etc. . . . Le maistre. Que confesse tu par ces parolles?" *Institution puerile de la doctrine chrestienne faicte par maniere de dyalogue, CR* 50, cols. 101-14. See also *OS* 2, pp. 152-57. The editors of the *Corpus Reformatorum* are not sure that this work is Calvin's; see "Catechismus aliquis anni MDXLII dubiae originis," *CR* 50, col. 1.

This catechism is included in the *French Evangelical Psalter* of 1542. Whether it was written by Calvin himself is not the main concern. Of more interest is that this catechism was used by Calvin's Church in Strasbourg. See Orentin Douen, *Clément Marot et le Psautier Huguenot, étude historique, littéraire, musicale et bibliographique,* vol. 1 (Paris: Imprimerie nationale, 1878), pp. 339-40.

On the *Genevan Shorter Catechism* of 1553, *La maniere d'interroguer, CR* 34, cols. 147-60, see below at n. 34.

13. "Et premierement le ministre demande: En qui crois-tu? et en que mets-tu toute la fiance de ton salut? L'enfant. Ie croy en Dieu le Pere et en Iesus Christ son Fils, et au sainct Esprit, et n'espere salut d'ailleurs. Le ministre. Le Pere, le Fils, et le sainct Esprit,

From these examples it should be quite clear that reciting the catechism before the Church was in fact making the baptismal vows.

Bucerian Confirmation

Having seen that the reciting of the catechism is in effect the giving of the baptismal confession of faith, we now turn our attention to the liturgical setting in which this confession of faith was made. In the previous chapter we saw how weekly catechetical sessions were established in Strasbourg, Zurich, Basel, Constance, Ulm, and Geneva. This was one of the most obvious and easily documented of all the sixteenth-century liturgical reforms. Now we want to focus our attention not on the instruction but rather on the service at which the baptized young people were examined as to their faith and then, even more importantly, made profession of their faith.

For the earlier days we have little information as to what actually happened at those services in Strasbourg, Zurich, and Basel. We simply know from some of those passages which were quoted above that four times a year, before the Communion services at Christmas, Easter, Pentecost, and the first Sunday in October, there was a public service of worship at which those who knew the catechism recited it before the Church and were admitted to Communion. We are not told exactly what happened at these services in terms of liturgical form, although clearly the essential thing was reciting the catechism as a profession of faith. As time went along, however, these services developed. First we shall look at the development of "evangelical confirmation" or, as it is sometimes called, "Bucerian confirmation." Then we shall look at a quite different approach, that which we find developing in Geneva. This approach puts the emphasis on making the vows of faith entailed by baptism and on admission to the Lord's Table.

Martin Bucer is generally recognized as being responsible for the development of "evangelical confirmation." Bucer did not develop his rite of confirmation for the Church of Strasbourg, but rather for the Church of Hesse.[14]

---

sont-ils plus d'un Dieu? L'enfant. Non. Le ministre. Et quelle confession de foy fais-tu? L'enfant. Celle que l'Eglise Chrestienne a tousiours faite, la quelle on appelle le Symbole des Apostres, qui est: Ie croy en Dieu (etc.)." *La maniere d'interroguer les enfans qu'on veut recevoir a la cene de nostre Seigneur Iesus Christ. CR* 34, cols. 147-49.

14. Walter Caspari's older work names Strasbourg, *Die evangelische Konfirmation, vornämlich in der lutherischen Kirche* (Erlangen und Leipzig: Andr. Deichart, 1890), p. 11. More recent research advances Hesse. Arthur C. Repp, *Confirmation in the Lutheran Church* (St. Louis: Concordia, 1964), pp. 30-31. Most recently René Bornert admits that the documentation is not sufficient to decide the question but is inclined to favor Strasbourg rather

Philipp, Prince of Hesse, had for some time been enthusiastic in his support of Bucer. The two men had become good friends in 1529, at the time of the Marburg Colloquy. Philipp was host to the colloquy, Marburg being a prominent city in Philipp's realm. The Prince of Hesse was particularly concerned for the success of the colloquy. While he was inclined toward the ideas of Zwingli, Philipp was determined to maintain the unity of Protestantism.[15] As the Anabaptist movement began to develop, Philipp became alarmed as he discovered the success of the Anabaptist preachers in Hesse, above all in Marburg. The concern of the Prince grew in 1536 as the Anabaptists set up their millennial reign in Münster, a city in neighboring Westphalia. The Anabaptist movement continued to prosper even after the fall of Münster. In November of 1538 Philipp invited Bucer, who was by this time the seasoned veteran of many a debate with the Anabaptists, to try to turn back the growing success of the movement. Bucer, after only three days of discussion, was able to convince several of the Anabaptist preachers of the legitimacy of infant baptism. One of the leaders of the Hessian Anabaptist movement, Peter Tesch, became a lifelong assistant and personal friend of the Strasbourg Reformer. It was a very friendly sort of settlement, and a month later a Synod of the Hessian Church held in Ziegenhain adopted a new church order which bore the mark of Bucer. It was a thoroughly presbyterian church constitution in many respects, and in this *Ziegenhainer Zuchtordnung* Bucer was able to establish his ideas on the ministry in a way he had not been able to do earlier. It is in this church order that we first find the proposal of an "evangelical confirmation." It is from this rite that Anglicans and Lutherans have derived their rite of confirmation.

A month later at a synod held in Cassel Bucer produced a set of liturgical texts for the Hessian Church called the *Kasseler Kirchenordnung.* The introduction starts out by reminding us of the words of the apostle Paul that all things are to be done decently and in order. *The Church Order of Cassel* is not so much a service book or a psalter as it is a directory for worship. Directions for conducting the service are given rather than actual formulations of the prayers and other liturgical texts. Nevertheless, in the appendix there is a complete text for an order of confirmation, "Order for Confirmation and the Laying On of Hands."[16] In the introductory rubrics we learn that the service

---

than Hesse. René Bornert, *La réforme protestante du culte à Strasbourg au XVIe siécle* (Leiden: E. J. Brill, 1981), p. 369.

15. On the relations of Bucer and Phillip of Hesse, see Hastings Eells, *Martin Bucer* (New Haven, Conn.: Yale University Press, 1931), pp. 238-42.

16. *Ordnung der Firmunge und der Hendt auflegen.* The German text will be cited from *Bucers Deutsche Schriften* 7, pp. 310-14, under the abbreviation *Ordnung der Firmunge,*

is to take place before the regular sermon on Easter, Pentecost, or Christmas. The ministers are to make sure during the preceding week that each of the young people can recite the whole catechism alone. A considerable point is made that each young person is to recite it himself before the minister and the elders. Then the young people are to partake of the Lord's Supper that day.[17] Presumably the communion service followed the sermon. On the days when confirmation was celebrated, the service was to start an hour early, and this should be announced beforehand.

The service begins with a short catechism of eighteen questions and answers,

> Q. Are you a Christian?
> A. Yes.
>
> Q. How do you know?
> A. Because I have been baptized in the name of the Father, Son and Holy Spirit.[18]

Then the Apostles' Creed is introduced and recited. There are questions on the meaning of the Creed. The minister proceeds,

> Q. Are you in the Church and fellowship of Christ?
> A. Yes.
>
> Q. How did you enter?
> A. Through holy Baptism.[19]

Several questions on the meaning of the sacraments follow. Both in regard to baptism and communion the ethical imperatives implicit in the sign are stressed. The young people promise to participate in the prayer of the Church,

---

BDS 7. It is also found in E. Sehling, *Die evangelischen Kirchenordnungen des XVI Jahrhunderts,* vol. 8 (Tübingen: J. C. B. Mohr, 1963), pp. 124-26. J. D. C. Fisher gives an incomplete and confusing presentation of the various Bucerian documents, *Christian Initiation: The Reformation Period,* pp. 174-81, 194-203. A good contemporary study of Bucer's work is found in A. C. Repp, *Confirmation in the Lutheran Church,* pp. 13-59.

17. "Diese sol geschehen auff Weihnachten, Ostern und Pfingsten gleich vor den gemeinen predigen, . . .

"... durch sein eigen mundt vor dem diener des worts und Eltesten. . . .

"Damit dann auch die kinder, denen man die hendt ufflegen, dasselbig tags auch zum heiligen Nachtmal Christi gangen." *Ordnung der Firmunge, BDS* 7, p. 310.

18. "Frag: Bistu ein Christ? Antwort: Ja. Frag: Woher weistu das? Ant.: Daher, das ich bin getaufft auff den namen Gottes, des Vaters, Sohns und heiligen Geistes." *Ordnung der Firmunge, BDS* 7, p. 310.

19. "Frag: Bistu auch in der kirch und gemein Christ? Antwort: Ja. Frag: Wie bistu darein kommen? Antwort: Durch den heiligen Tauff." *Ordnung der Firmunge, BDS* 7, p. 311.

give alms, and follow the pastoral leadership of the Church. The final question is, "Will you then hold to and do all this which you have confessed?" The young people answer, "With the help of our Lord Jesus Christ, yes."[20] All of the questions do not need to be asked of all the children separately during the actual service. After one has recited the whole thing it is sufficient to ask the others, "Do you believe and confess, will you also surrender yourself to the fellowship and obedience of the Church of Christ, as you have just heard. . . ?" Each answers, "Yes, through the help of our Lord Jesus Christ."[21] In the various Bucerian documents different solutions were attempted on how one could avoid having to go through all the questions for each young person and yet maintain some clear statement of faith on the part of each.[22]

When the catechism has been recited before the minister and the elders, the whole church being present, the minister is to admonish the congregation to pray for the young people. At the end of these prayers the minister is to draw the prayers together in a pastoral prayer.[23] The prayer is quite comprehensive. It thanks God for granting to the young people new birth and illumination, God's grace and every spiritual gift, and above all their redemption in Christ. God is asked to strengthen his work already begun in them, and to increase to them his Holy Spirit so that they might remain faithful members of the Church and be obedient to the gospel. One notices how clear the prayer is on this matter. The prayer asks for the strengthening and increase of the Holy Spirit who has been at work in the child since baptism. The prayer elaborates at some length on the gifts of the Holy Spirit. "So grant to them also, as we lay hands upon them in your name, the presence of your own gracious hand and your Holy Spirit, the Spirit of all strength and help. . . ."[24]

After this prayer the minister is to lay hands on the young people and

20. "Frag: Wiltu aber dieses alles also thun und halten, wie du es bekkenet hast? Ant.: Durch die hülff unsers Herren Jhesu Christi, Ja." *Ordnung der Firmunge, BDS* 7, p. 312.

21. "Gleubst und bekennestu, wiltu dich auch in die gemeinschafft und gehorsam der kirchen Christi begeben, wie du itzt gehöret hast, das dieses kindt glaubet und bekennet und sich der kirchen Christi begeben hat? Darauff sol gnug sein, das die andern kinder. Antwort: Ja, durch die hülff unsers Herren Jhesu Christ." *Ordnung der Firmunge, BDS* 7, p. 312.

22. See Friedrich Hubert, *Die Strassburger liturgischen Ordnungen in Zeitaltes der Reformation* (Göttingen: Vandenboeck und Ruprecht, 1900), pp. 134-39.

23. ". . . denn sol man die gantze kirchen zum gebeth für die kinder ermanen, und nach solchem gebet sol denn der Pfarherr das selbig mit solcher Collecten Summiren, wie volget. . . ." *Ordnung der Firmunge, BDS* 7, p. 312.

24. "So verleihe ihnen auch, so wir ihnen itzt in deinem namen die hend aufflegen und sie damit deiner gnedigen handt und deines heiligen geistes, des geistes aller sterk und hülff, zu recht Christlichem leben vertrösten. . . ." *Ordnung der Firmunge, BDS* 7, p. 313.

say, "Receive the Holy Spirit, shield and shelter from every evil, strength and help in every good, from the gracious hand of God, the Father, Son and Holy Spirit. Amen."[25] The service is ended by singing a hymn.

We sing thanks to thee, O God,
    for Jesus Christ, our Lord,
Who with his holy word
    has indeed enlightened us.
And has redeemed us, with his
    blood from the devil's power.
Him we all should praise
    together with his angels
Singing, one great host;
    Glory to God in the highest.[26]

What are we to say about Bucer's rite of confirmation? Certainly, it has confused more than one scholar. To get to the bottom of the confusion would demand a separate monograph and would take us far beyond the legitimate concerns of our subject. Two things need to be said, nevertheless. Bucer is usually presented as basing his rite of confirmation on an erroneous theory of the origin of confirmation. Put simply, this theory runs as follows. Confirmation was neither instituted by Christ nor practiced by the apostles. It originated centuries later when the ancient Church needed to provide a means for children who had been baptized as infants to make a profession of faith after completing their catechetical instruction. Furthermore, the theory stated that those who had been baptized as infants were required to take catechetical instruction, and that when they had completed the catechetical instruction they were then received into the regular membership of the Church with prayer and the laying

25. "Nim hin den heiligen geist, schutz und schirm vor allem argen, sterck und hülff zu allem gutem von der gnedigen handt Gottes, des Vater, Sohns, und heiligen geistes, Amen." *Ordnung der Firmunge, BDS* 7, p. 313.

26. "Danck sagen wyr all Gott unserm Herren Christo,
der uns mit einem word hat erleuchtet,
und uns erlöset hat
mit seinem blutte von des teuffels gwalt.
dem sollen wyr alle
mit seinen Engeln loben mit schalle
singend 'Preiss sey Gott ynn den höchsten.' "

Philipp Wackernagel, *Das deutsch Kirchenlied,* vol. 3 (Leipzig: B. G. Teubner, 1864-77), no. 599, p. 550. This hymn, by Amrosius Moibanus the Silesian reformer, appeared first in the *Erfurter Gesangbuch* of 1527. The Confirmation order of St. Nicholas Church in Strasbourg suggests "Erhalt uns, Herr, bey deinem wort," and the "Magnificat." Hubert, *Ordnungen,* p. 138.

on of hands. This theory with one variation or another was repeated by a number of sixteenth-century Protestant Reformers.[27]

Just how this theory originated is not at all clear.[28] There are those who have traced it to Erasmus, while others have traced it to the followers of Jan Hus in Bohemia or to the Waldensians.[29] This theory may well have much deeper roots, but that question we leave to others.

There is no doubt but that this theory, stated in the form we have just stated it, is quite incorrect. The theory is incorrect at two points. First, the ancient Church did not require those baptized in infancy to undergo the usual catechetical instruction held before Easter each year. Second, confirmation began to develop as a second sacrament not at the point when infant baptism became more regular than adult baptism, but rather at the point when the presbyter, rather than the bishop, became the normal minister of baptism. However wrong this theory may have been, it was certainly no further from the truth than the theory held by so many of Bucer's contemporaries, namely that the sacrament of confirmation went back to the time of Christ and the apostles.

Bucer's ideas on the subject seem to have changed over the years. The theory about the origins of confirmation seems to have been quite popular early in the Reformation, and yet neither Bucer nor any of his colleagues seem to have been the least bit interested in trying to institute a "Reformed confirmation."[30] Bucer, as others, may have repeated the theory, but for them the

27. Zwingli, *Usslegen und Gründe der Schlussreden, CR* 89, p. 123. Calvin, *Institutes* 4.19.4 and 13.

28. Cf. two more recent works on the subject: B. Hareide, *Die Konfirmation in der Reformationszeit,* German translation by K. Kvideland (Göttingen, 1971) and K. Frör, "Zur Interpretation der Kasserer Kirchenordnung von 1539," *Reformatio und Confirmatio, Festschrift für Wilhelm Maurer* (Berlin and Hamburg: Lutherisches Verlagshaus, 1965), pp. 161-79.

29. Caspari, *Die evangelische Konfirmation,* pp. 20-22. J. D. C. Fisher, *Christian Initiation: The Reformation Period* (London: S.P.C.K., 1970), pp. 166-69. Wilhelm Maurer, "Geschichte von Firmung und Konfirmation bis zum Ausgang der Lutherischen Orthodoxie," in *Confirmatio, Forschungen zur Geschichte und Praxis der Konfirmation* (Munich: Evangelischer Presseverband für Bayern, 1959), pp. 9-38. John Payne shows that Erasmus was not the originator of the idea although Bucer and others may have understood Erasmus in this way, *Erasmus: His Theology of the Sacraments* (Richmond, Va.: John Knox Press, 1970), pp. 179-80.

30. It seems quite unlikely that the document from Strasbourg that Fisher includes in his collection actually reflects any kind of confirmation service held in Strasbourg under the ministry of Bucer. It is hard to agree with Fischer that the document breathes the spirit of Bucer. This document, for instance, speaks of the altar rather than the Lord's table. This should make it clear that the document originated after the beginning of the Interim. Hubert, *Ordnungen,* pp. 174-78.

theory explained why it was that a practice which was not really apostolic had come into existence. In other words, the theory explained why one did not need a rite of confirmation. Confirmation did not appear until Bucer began to realize the full strength of the Anabaptist movement.

Perhaps the following passage from Bucer's *Bericht* best explains what Bucer was really doing when he set up his rite of confirmation for the Church of Cassel.

> . . . it is appropriate that publicly, at least once in one's life, one make a profession and affirmation of faith, that one renounce the devil, and surrender oneself to Christ. This could well be done after children baptized in infancy have grown and have regularly received catechetical instruction and Christian teaching and are prepared to make such an affirmation of faith. One could well revive that ancient practice, out of which confirmation developed, that the bishop laid hands on the baptized and conferred *(mitlesteten)* the Holy Spirit, following the example of the Apostles in Samaria. We read about this same usage in Jerome's *Dialogue against the Luciferians.*[31]

This statement comes from a letter written to the Anabaptists of Münster. In it we find Bucer at his most conciliatory. The Reformer of Strasbourg really hopes to win over the Anabaptists, and so he presents this "evangelical confirmation" as a sort of compromise. Bucer's proposal suggests a way of retaining infant baptism in the Church without completely overlooking the importance of the individual Christian making a personal profession of faith. Not long before this Kaspar Schwenckfeld had proposed something similar to the Church of Strasbourg. Perhaps Bucer saw in this proposal a means of meeting the objections of the more conciliatory Anabaptists.[32] Bucer was an irenic spirit. Not only was he a sincere peacemaker, but he was creative and inventive as well. It is not altogether surprising that Bucer should develop his "evangelical confirmation" out of a desire to win over the Anabaptists. The question is, Has Bucer compromised his principle that worship should be "according to Scripture?"

31. "Und so men meinet, es solte je so vil zur sachen thun, das man auch offentlich einmal in Christlichem thun profess und zusag thate, sagte dem teufel ab, ergebe sich selb an Christum, konde dasselbige doch auch wol hernaher beschehen, so man die getaufften kinder, als sy dazu erwachsen, durch vorgenden catechismum, christliche underweisung, zu solicher verjehung des glaubens bereitet hette und konde man mit inen also den alten brauch widerbringen, daruss die confirmation entstanden, das die Bischoff den geteufften die hand ufflegten und in den H. geyst also mitleysteten nach dem exempel der Apostel in Samaria, Act. 8[17], von welchem brauch wir lesen by dem Hieronymo in Dialogis contra Luciferianos. Hieran wurd nun, das man sy in der kindtheit geteuffet, je nit hinderen, wie es auch by den alten kirchen niehts gehinderet hatt." *Bericht, BDS* 5, 175ff.

32. W. Caspari, *Die evangelische Konfirmation,* pp. 14-17.

A careful reading of Bucer's words shows that Bucer is not at this point, at least, basing his argument on the erroneous theory of the origin of confirmation which was so popular in his day. Bucer is talking about the rite of the laying on of hands. It is the rite of laying on hands which Bucer finds in the eighth chapter of Acts and in Jerome's *Dialogue with the Luciferians,* not the whole rite of confirmation. In biblical times this rite was used on many occasions when particularly solemn prayers for someone were appropriate. The laying on of hands was practiced frequently in New Testament times. It was used for the blessing of children, for the healing of the sick, for the ordination of ministers, and for the imparting of spiritual gifts. In the Bible, the laying on of hands was a gesture which accompanied prayers of intercession. This is what Bucer means when he calls the laying on of hands a sacrament.[33]

Bucer sees the laying on of hands as having a much broader significance than it had at the end of the Middle Ages. The laying on of hands was appropriate to much in the life of the Church other than confirmation and ordination. Unless one realizes that this is what Bucer has in mind, neither the biblical passage nor the patristic passage which he had in mind make any sense at all. The passage in Acts 8 has nothing to do with children baptized in infancy. The passage from Jerome has nothing to do with children baptized in infancy either, but rather with the reconciling of penitents. These passages have to do with two very different usages of the laying on of hands. Confirmation would be still a third usage of this same biblical sign of laying on hands. As Bucer sees it, the medieval sacrament of confirmation developed out of the biblical rite of laying on hands when intercessory prayer was made for someone. Even though Bucer did give fairly respectable scriptural support for his "evangelical confirmation," it is understood much better as an attempt to make a practical compromise with the Anabaptists.

Calvinian Admission to the Lord's Table

While Geneva followed the lead of Strasbourg in many liturgical matters and while Bucer exercised a very important influence on Calvin, when it comes to the "evangelical confirmation" which Bucer developed we find Calvin going a different direction. For Calvin, the making of the baptismal vows is accom-

33. "Mag nun diss segnen Christi diser Kindlinen mit dem sacrament dess hendauflegens. . . ." *BDS* 5, p. 170. It is clear from the context that Bucer has in mind the story of Jesus' blessing of the children in the nineteenth chapter of Matthew.

plished by means of a public reciting of the catechism before one of the four annual communion services. The saying of the baptismal vows is followed by the young people receiving communion for the first time. This is clearly a rite of admission to the Lord's Table or, as some might call it, a rite of First Communion. Unfortunately, we do not have for the Genevan service anything like the complete text which Bucer drew up for the church order of Cassel. Calvin's service of admission to the Lord's Table is not found in the *Genevan Psalter.* The service must be reconstructed from *The Ecclesiastical Ordinances* and the *Genevan Shorter Catechism.*[34]

The reconstruction we would make is for a period considerably after the publication of the *Genevan Psalter* of 1542. The first edition of the *Genevan Shorter Catechism* which has come down to us is from 1553. It received an important addition in 1562. Likewise it is the 1561 edition of *The Ecclesiastical Ordinances* which is most informative in regard to this subject. Some of the practices that Calvin would have liked to have instituted may have taken longer than he wished, and then again some of these practices may go back further than the documentary evidence. The service which we are able to reconstruct, then, is for sometime after 1561, that is, at the very end of Calvin's ministry in Geneva.

The making of the vows took place on the Sunday before one of the communion services, that is, the Sunday before Easter, Pentecost, the first Sunday in October, or Christmas.[35] It was probably done on Sunday afternoon at the usual catechetical service. The catechizing was done publicly.[36] On several occasions Calvin tells us that it is good to do this in public, in order that the parents may be more diligent in seeing that their children demonstrate before the community their mastery of the catechism.[37] This is not a very theological reason, but then the theological ivy which had grown around Calvin's academic tower had in no way impaired his sight. Although one wonders if each child was indeed asked all twenty-eight questions separately, the questions are, in the text, at least addressed to the child separately in the second-person singular, "In whom doest thou believe?" The questions may have been divided up, each child getting a question down the line. On this we can only speculate. The shortness of the catechism leads one to believe that at least the children were expected to know the whole thing by heart.

We have already spoken at some length of the contents of various

34. *Les ordonnances ecclesiastiques, OS* 2, pp. 325-89; *La maniere d'interroguer, CR* 34, cols. 147-60; see above, n. 12.

35. ". . . et que pour ce faire on reserve les quatres dimanches devant la Cene." *Les ordonnances ecclesiastiques, OS* 2, p. 356, n. 10.

36. A letter from Calvin to Ovevianus, *CR* 46, col. 236.

37. *Institutes* 4.19.13.

Reformed catechisms. Let us quickly review the contents of the *Genevan Shorter Catechism.* It is very different from the *Genevan Catechism* of 1542, which is in the nature of a larger catechism rather than a shorter catechism. It begins with a very personal confession of faith, "I believe in God the Father and in Jesus Christ his Son and in the Holy Spirit and look for salvation in none other." It continues with the repeating of the Apostles' Creed because it is the confession of faith "which the Christian Church has always made."[38] The child is asked the meaning of the Creed, and he or she recites an explanatory paraphrase of it. Then the child is asked to recite the Ten Commandments, whereupon the minister asks a few questions on how one is to follow the Law and how one receives salvation by faith in Christ. There are several questions concerning prayer, and the child is asked to recite the Lord's Prayer. Questions on the meaning of the sacraments follow. The catechizing approaches its conclusion with the following words:

> Minister,
> Is it necessary for us, therefore, to have true faith before we are able to rightly participate in this sacrament?
>
> Child,
> Yes.
>
> Minister,
> And how can we have this faith?
>
> Child,
> We have it through the Holy Spirit, who dwells in our hearts and who makes sure to us the promise of God, which we have in the gospel.
>
> Minister,
> Go then in peace, and may the good God increase more and more his graces in you, and to us all his children.
>
> Child,
> So be it, through our Lord Jesus Christ. Amen.[39]

38. See above, n. 12.

39. "Le ministre. Il nous faut donc avoir vraye Foy, avant que nous puissions bien user de ce sainct Sacrement. L'enfant. Ouy. Le ministre. Et comment pouvons nous avoir ceste Foy? L'enfant. Nous l'avons par le sainct Esprit, qui habite en noz cuers, et nous rend certains des promesses de Dieu, qui nous sont faictes en l'Evangile. Le ministre. Or lalex en paix, et que ce bon Dieu augmente de plus en plus ses graces en vous, et à nous tous ses enfans. L'enfant. Ainsi soit-il, par nostre Seigneur Iesus Christ. Amen." *La maniere d'interroguer, CR* 34, col. 160.

Let us observe five things here. The scene is not unlike the scene which occurred at the service of the *Redditio symboli* in the fourth or fifth century.[40] It was the practice then, on the Saturday before Easter, for those to be baptized to come to a special service at the church and there to repeat the Creed. Part of the repetition was in dialogue form. It is surely from this that the Reformers got the idea of making their catechisms in dialogue form.[41] At an earlier service the bishop had recited the Creed to the candidate and given an explanation. This earlier service was called the *Traditio symboli,* that is, the Creed had been handed over to the candidate to be learned. It was the duty of the sponsors, then, to teach the Creed to the candidate in the intervening time, so that at the *Redditio symboli* the candidate could recite the Creed himself. The *Redditio symboli* was held the day before the baptism. At that time the candidate returned to the church and recited the Creed as his confession of faith. Late that night the candidate was baptized, and then at dawn he or she received Communion for the first time.

The situation which Calvin developed in Geneva was not unlike that which had existed in the days of Ambrose and Augustine. Of this Calvin was certainly aware. The picture of the *Traditio symboli* and *Redditio symboli* is easily gained from a number of the writings of the fourth- and fifth-century Fathers. Calvin had made adaptations, of course. In Geneva, it was at the baptism that the *Traditio symboli* had taken place, and the *Redditio symboli*

40. Regarding the service of the *Redditio symboli,* see the introduction by Suzanne Poque, *Augustin d'Hippone, Sermons pour la pâque* (Paris: Les Editions du Cerf), pp. 26-33. See also *Sacramentarium Gelasianum* 42. Cf. further P. de Puniet, "Catéchuménat," *DACL* 2:2, pp. 2579-2621; H. Leclercq, "Scrutin," *DACL* 15:1, pp. 1037-52; André Turck, *Evangelisation et Catéchèse aux deux premiers siécles* (Paris: Editions du Cerf, 1962); Joseph Crehan, *Early Christian Baptism and the Creed,* pp. 118-23. The time of the tradition as well as the time of the reddition of the Creed or the prayer might be quite different from one church to another.

41. Here again there was considerable difference from one church to another over how much was done in dialogue and when it was done. H. Leclercq, "Catéchèse," *DACL* 2:2, pp. 2530-79. On the dialogue form of the sixteenth-century catechisms coming from the ancient *Redditio symboli,* see the remarks of Bucer in the *Censura* (*Scripta Anglicana fere omnia iis etiam, quae hactenus vel non dum, vel sparsim, vel peregrino saltem idiomate edita fuere, adjuntis,* ed. Conrad Hubert [Basel: Petrus Perna, 1577]). There he calls the renunciation of the devil and the confession of faith "catechizing." "De catechismo baptizandorum. . . . Hoc loco iubentur compatres et commatres renunciare Sathanae, prositeri fidem pro infantibus, vt dum infantes rogantes, An renuncient diabolo, & eius operibus, &c. Et. An credant in Deum patreum, & filium, & Spiritum S. ipsi vice infantium respondeant. . . . Optarim igitur omnes illas huius Catechismi, nescio cur ita vocati, interrogatines fieri ad ipsos compatres . . . vt hic infans cum eo adoleuerit, discat religionis nostrae Catechismum, eoque percepto renunciet Sathanae, & credere se profiteamur in Deum patrem & filium, &c.?" pp. 480-81.

was held several years later instead of several days later. Whereas in the patristic age there had been simply a *Redditio symboli* and sometimes a *Redditio orationis dominicae,* the Genevan Reformers had added a *redditio* of the Ten Commandments as well as a certain amount of teaching on the sacraments.[42] Calvin had often claimed, as we have seen, that the ancient Church had used a formula as the basis of catechetical instruction. He had in mind, of course, the Creed, which as Calvin knew differed slightly from Church to Church. Calvin augmented the formula considerably by adding to the Creed and the Lord's Prayer the Ten Commandments and some formulations on sacramental doctrine. Nevertheless one thing is clear, the special service at which the Creed was recited was, as Calvin said, nothing novel. Its prototype was in the service of the *Redditio symboli* as it was celebrated in the fourth and fifth centuries.

The second thing we want to observe is that the catechetical instruction leads from baptism to communion. This is most clear from the *Genevan Shorter Catechism.* In emphasizing this aspect of the service, Calvin has of course gone beyond the suggestion of Erasmus quite considerably. The famous suggestion of Erasmus was meant to be neither a service which took the place of confirmation, nor was it meant to be a service which admitted young people to communion. Luther, on the other hand, quite definitely connected the reciting of the catechism with admission to communion. At this point, it may well be Luther whom Calvin is following. This whole chain of events which begins with baptism, continues with catechetical instruction, followed by a confession of faith on the Sunday before communion, finally culminates in being admitted to the Lord's Supper. With this the ancient progression from baptism to communion is now re-established. It was not that baptism was somehow incomplete without communion, but rather that baptism always leads to communion.[43] The great Paschal baptismal services of the fourth and fifth centuries always led from the baptistry to the church proper. In the church proper the Easter sermon was preached and communion celebrated. This sequence was indeed a very ancient order. It was as in the days of Jesus, when a visitor came from a great distance, or in our Lord's parable about the Prodigal Son who returned home from a far country. First one was bathed, then given a clean robe, and only then was he or she seated at the table for dinner. Washing before a meal was important. The Jews did not have table fellowship with the unclean, nor

42. On the *traditio orationis dominici, Sacramentarium Gelasianum* 34, see S. Poque, *Augustin d'Hippone,* pp. 65-69. In the Gelasian Sacramentary there was also a "tradition" of the four Gospels. *Sacramentarium Gelasianum* 33.

43. *Institutes,* 4.19.8, 1456-57. The Reformers were very careful to object to any insinuation that baptism was incomplete.

did they eat with Gentiles. Baptism was the great washing which enabled true fellowship. It was the washing away of sin which makes the sacred community possible. Baptism is the sacrament of Christian initiation. According to the *Genevan Shorter Catechism,* "For our Lord represents to us here . . . our regeneration or spiritual renewal."[44] One might say that baptism is the sacrament of the beginning, while communion, on the other hand, is the sacrament of the end and consummation of the Christian life. As the *Genevan Shorter Catechism* puts it, the Supper signifies that "our spirits are nourished in the hope of eternal life."[45] It is by faith that we move from baptism to communion. That faith, the catechism tells us, "we have through the Holy Spirit who dwells in our hearts and makes us sure of the promises of God, which are made in the gospel."[46]

This service, which in so many ways resembles the ancient liturgy for the *Redditio symboli,* is strictly speaking a service for admission to the Lord's Table. While the *Redditio symboli* of Christian antiquity was a liturgy for admission to baptism, this Genevan service was for admission to communion. It is a solemn liturgy for the profession of Christian faith. It is not a confirmation of baptismal vows which had already been made by the baptismal sponsors. In Geneva there had been no vicarious confession of faith by the sponsors. What had happened at the baptism was that the catechetical pieces had been read by the minister to the parents as a sort of *Traditio symboli.* The parents and sponsors had promised to teach them to the child, and now the child was confessing his or her own faith for the first time. The child was not confirming the vows taken for him in baptism.

The third thing which needs to be observed is that the Genevan Reformers consider true faith to be essential for admission to the Lord's Table. Having in mind the eleventh chapter of First Corinthians, the Reformers were not going to admit anyone to the Lord's Table who could not discern the Lord's Body. While they did not consider a confession of faith necessary before baptism, they did consider it necessary before communion. This is clear from the *Genevan Shorter Catechism* itself, "Is it necessary for us, therefore, to have true faith before we are able to rightly participate in this sacrament?"[47] If one might make a little play on the traditional liturgical vocabulary, one might call

44. ". . . car nostre Seigneur nous y represente la remission de noz pechez: et puis nostre regeneration ou renouvellement spirituel." *La maniere d'interroguer, CR* 34, col. 159.

45. "Elle nous signifie que par la communication du corps et du sang de nostre Seigneur Iesus Christ, noz ames sont nourries en l'esperance de la vie eternelle." *La maniere d'interroguer, CR* 34, col. 159.

46. Above, n. 39.

47. Above, n. 39.

this service a liturgy not of baptismal scrutinies, but of eucharistic scrutinies. The title of this rite ought to make this abundantly clear, *The Manner of Questioning the Children Whom one Wishes to Receive at the Supper of Our Lord Jesus Christ.*[48]

The fourth thing to be observed is that the service scrupulously avoids any suggestion that at this service the Holy Spirit is conferred. Particularly the service was careful to avoid any suggestion that baptism was now being completed by the giving of the Holy Spirit. Over the years, Reformed theology has meticulously obviated any implication that there be two kinds of Christian life: a first kind in which sins are forgiven, and a second kind in which one receives the Holy Spirit. To use a terminology popular in our day, Reformed theology has never been comfortable with the idea that some Christians are merely saved while others are Spirit-filled. For the Reformed theologian the forgiving of sin and filling with the Spirit are two sides of the same coin. They are inseparable. This is clear in all the Reformed baptismal invocations. The washing away of sins is but one aspect of the sanctifying work of the Holy Spirit. It is by the indwelling of the Holy Spirit that the Christian is washed, purified, illumined, fortified, and consecrated. It is the presence of the Holy Spirit within the Christian which makes him holy by endowing him with the manifold gifts of the Spirit. It is the Holy Spirit who accomplishes inwardly in our spirits what the outward sign of washing with water has signified and promised. For the earliest Reformed theologians, baptism with water was the outward aspect of baptism by the Spirit. The two are but the outward and inward aspects of the same reality. While their opponents accused them of cutting the sacrament of baptism in two by making too great a separation between outward baptism and inward baptism or between *res* and *signum,* they in turn thought that their opponents had split the sacrament of baptism in two by making confirmation a second sacrament and dividing the washing away of sins from the gift of the Holy Spirit.

It should be pointed out that this service does not pass over the subject of the Holy Spirit in silence. The *Genevan Shorter Catechism* gives considerable importance to the doctrine of the Holy Spirit. In Question 8 we learn that whenever the Christian does the will of God it is a work of the Holy Spirit.[49] Again, at the end of the catechism in Questions 25 and 27 we learn that Christians arrive in the heavenly presence of Christ through faith, which

48. *La maniere d'interroguer les enfans qu'on veut recevoir a la cene de nostre Seigneur Iesus Christ. CR* 34, cols. 147-49.

49. "Peus-tu accomplir les commandemens de Dieu de toymesme? Non. Qui est-ce donc qui les accomplit en toy? Le sainct Esprit." *La maniere d'interroguer, CR* 34, cols. 156-57.

is the gift of the Holy Spirit dwelling in their hearts. The Holy Spirit dwelling in the hearts of baptized infants brings these children in more mature years to faith and will continue sanctifying them, producing in their lives ever deeper faith and more abundant good works until at last this earthly life is put off and they enter into the heavenly presence of Christ.[50]

The fifth point to be observed is that the saying of the catechism ends with a benediction. The minister says, "Depart, therefore, in peace and may this good God increase more and more his graces in you, and in all of us his children." To this the child responds, "Let it be so through our Lord Jesus Christ. Amen."[51] One would like to know whether the minister gave this benediction with outstretched arms, with the imposition of hands, or without any gesture at all. Normally in Reformed liturgical practice, the benedictions which ended the services of worship were given with outstretched arms, the palms of the hands turned toward the congregation. The Reformers recognized this as the biblical gesture which normally accompanied a benediction. They also recognized that a benediction could be given by laying hands on the head of the person to receive the benediction particularly when it was an individual, rather than a group, who was to receive the benediction. Calvin's commentaries provide us with several examples.[52]

For Calvin the essential thing about this benediction was the benediction itself, not the laying on of hands which accompanied it. The laying on of hands was *adiaphora:* one of those indifferent things which could be done or could be left undone.[53] In speaking about the service of worship at which one was examined and at which one makes the confession of faith, Calvin says:

> But in order that this act, which ought by itself to have been weighty and holy, might have more reverence and dignity, the ceremony of the laying on of hands was also added. Thus the youth, once his faith was approved, was dismissed with a solemn blessing. . . . Therefore, I warmly approve such laying on of hands, which is simply done as a form of blessing. . . .[54]

What we clearly have at the end of the *Genevan Shorter Catechism* is just such a blessing. Whether or not it was accompanied by the gesture of the

50. See above, n. 39.

51. See above, n. 39.

52. *Commentary on the Harmony of the Gospels* at Matthew 19:15; *Commentary on Acts* at Acts 8:14-18; *Commentary on Genesis* at Genesis 48:12-15.

53. See Calvin's remarks on the laying on of hands in the days of Cyprian. In this case the laying on of hands was to reconcile penitents. Here it is plainly called "adiaphora." *Institutes* 4.19.14, 1461-63.

54. *Institutes* 4.19.4.

laying on of hands was, for Calvin, a secondary consideration. The blessing was there. It was, of course, this postbaptismal blessing which had been so misunderstood by theologians of an earlier age. It was this same blessing from which earlier centuries had developed the sacrament of confirmation. However much this blessing may have been misunderstood in the past, Calvin did include it in the service at which young people made their profession of faith.

Having carefully looked at this service, we need to ask two questions. The first is, Did Calvin consider this service to be confirmation? To this question one can only answer, No! For Calvin the word "confirmation" was to be avoided. The word itself implied too much of the old Scholastic theology. This service was the conclusion of catechetical instruction. The purpose of catechetical instruction was to prepare the child to make an intelligent profession of faith. It was the profession of faith implied, even demanded, by the baptism of the child. Just as the living of the Christian life was demanded by baptism, so was the profession of Christian faith. This solemn profession of faith was the logical working out of the sacrament of baptism. It was not that the sacrament had been incomplete without the confession of faith. The baptism was unto faith. Baptism was initiation, as Zwingli from the very beginning had emphasized. As initiation, baptism was the beginning of a life that would bear the fruit of faith. Leo Jud put it very well: baptism is both a "memorial sign" and a "responsibility sign."[55] Baptism is both *gabe* and *aufgabe,* both gift and assignment. Baptism is both a calling and a sending. This solemn profession of faith is the logical consequence of baptism. There is something more. Not only are the catechumenate and the profession of faith related to baptism, they are related to communion as well. The saying of the catechism was accepted by the Church as evidence that the faith of the child had reached sufficient maturity for him to be admitted to the Lord's Table. This service is also then a service of admission to communion. At its center is the profession of faith, but the service should also be understood to proceed from baptism and to move toward communion.

The second question is, Why does Calvin not follow Bucer in developing an Evangelical or Reformed rite of confirmation?

For Calvin the laying on of hands was a gesture which belonged to prayer. He understood that in Scripture it was used whenever a prayer was made especially asking God's blessing on someone and commending that one to God.[56] "The ancients speak of the laying on of hands, but do they call it a

55. Jud, *Christliche, klare, und einfache Einfuhrung, Katechismen,* p. 220. See above, Chap. 7, n. 41.

56. *Institutes* 4.19.6.

sacrament? Augustine openly affirms that it is nothing but prayer."[57] Calvin points to the fact that it was used frequently in biblical times in praying for the sick, as when Ananias laid hands on Paul so that he might recover his sight; in ordination to the ministry; and in blessing children, as in the case of Jesus blessing the children, or Simeon blessing the baby Jesus, or Jacob blessing the children of Joseph. For Calvin it was appropriate to give a blessing at the time young people finished their catechetical instruction, at a marriage service, at a service of ordination, or at the end of any service of worship. In each case the essential thing was the prayer of blessing.[58] To this prayer the gesture of laying on hands might appropriately be added. The gesture indicated the particularly solemn nature of the prayer. In other words, the laying on of hands had a far wider significance than what later centuries understood as confirmation. Doubtlessly, Calvin would have been quite pleased to see a restoration of the ancient practice of the laying on of hands in all its fullness and in the whole range of its original usage. Calvin did not want the laying on of hands monopolized by the sacrament of confirmation.

Confirmation was an offense to Calvin because it, like penance, sapped the meaning of baptism.[59] In the Scholastic scheme of things, as Calvin understood it, baptism only washed away original sin and, in addition, those sins which had been committed before baptism, thus cutting away the prophetic aspect of baptism as a sign of washing from our sins for the rest of life.[60] In the same way confirmation tended to take away the positive aspects of baptism as a sign of spiritual renewal and the gift of the Holy Spirit. For Calvin baptism was a sign under which the whole of the Christian life was to be lived. It was a prophetic sign. It was a sign of repentance which is a continual aspect of the Christian life. It was a sign of the renewal of the Holy Spirit which is also a continual reality in the Christian life.

Confirmation was in no way a sacrament for Calvin. Here Calvin stands very close to Luther.[61] As Calvin saw it, Jesus did not institute confirmation, nor did he give any word of promise to confirmation. The New Testament Church did not know a sacrament of confirmation. For Calvin this was particularly the case if one defined confirmation in terms of anointing with oil. Neither Jesus nor the apostles, Calvin insisted, ever anointed with oil as a sign

57. *Institutes* 4.19.12.

58. *OS* 2, pp. 53-55. These marriage benedictions are one of the most interesting features of the *Genevan Psalter.* Originally they were the work of William Farel.

59. *Institutes* 4.19.8.

60. *Institutes* 4.19.8.

61. For a concise statement on Luther's position in regard to confirmation, see A. Repp, *Confirmation in the Lutheran Church* (St. Louis, Mo.: Concordia, 1964), pp. 15-20.

of the giving of the Holy Spirit. For both Calvin and Luther, confirmation was a rite which developed at a later period in the history of the Church.

We can probably best understand the situation in the following way. Calvin did not have any desire to establish a Reformed confirmation because he did not believe that one could construct a confirmation which was according to Scripture. What Calvin was concerned to do was to re-establish catechetical instruction adapted to the situation of the Church of his day.

> How I wish that we might have the custom, which as I have said existed among the Christians. . . . Not that it would be a confirmation such as they fancy, which can not be named without doing injustice to baptism; but catechizing, in which children or those near adolescence would give an account of their faith before the church.[62]

Calvin was mistaken if he accepted the theory, as it was often advanced in his day, that in the ancient Church children who had been baptized in infancy were asked to go through catechetical instruction, and when they had finished it they received a prayer of blessing and the laying on of hands. There is some evidence that starting in 1547, when Calvin wrote his antidote to the decrees of the Council of Trent, he began to have some doubts regarding the accuracy of this theory. To go into all that is beside the point. Calvin was right about his basic concern. There was a time when the Church considered it important to teach those who were baptized. There was a time in the Church when it was considered an important part of baptism to make public profession of faith.

For Calvin the primary concern was not to develop a Reformed confirmation, but rather a Reformed catechumenate. Calvin saw that in his day instruction in the basics of the Christian faith was just as necessary for Christian children, baptized in infancy, as it had been for converts coming over from paganism in the fourth and fifth centuries. To be sure, if Calvin was interested in reviving the ancient catechumenate it was because that particular practice of the patristic age was a witness to what Scripture taught. Jesus himself had instructed his apostles to make disciples by baptizing them and teaching them. This teaching should culminate in making a profession of faith.

62. *Institutes* 4.19.13.

CHAPTER IX

The Baptismal Invocation

Let us now turn to the third major element of the baptismal rite, the Baptismal Invocation. The early Reformed Churches produced a number of Baptismal Invocations. We will want to look with particular interest at those of Zurich, Strasbourg, and Geneva, follow the development of this form of prayer, and search out the reasons for its development.

The Baptismal Invocation of Zurich

The first baptismal Invocation used by the early Reformed Church was Leo Jud's adaptation of Luther's famous Great Flood Prayer.

Before we discuss Jud's revisions of Luther's prayer let us look at Luther's Great Flood Prayer and then discuss briefly the probable sources. When we understand Luther's sources, the true nature of Jud's work will become clear.

> Almighty eternal God, who according to thy righteous judgment didst condemn the unbelieving world through the flood and in Thy great mercy didst preserve believing Noah and his family, and who didst drown hardhearted Pharoah with all his host in the Red Sea and didst lead thy people Israel through the same on dry ground, thereby prefiguring this bath of thy baptism, and who through the baptism of thy dear Child, our Lord Jesus Christ, hast consecrated and set apart the Jordan and all water as a salutary flood and a rich and full washing away of sins: We pray through Thy same groundless mercy that thou wilt graciously behold this N. and bless him with true faith in the spirit so that by means of this saving flood all that has been born in him from Adam and which he himself has added thereto may be drowned in him and engulfed, and that he may be sundered from the number of the

unbelieving, preserved dry and secure in the holy ark of Christendom, serve thy name and at all times fervent in spirit and joyful in hope, so that with all believers he may be made worthy to attain eternal life according to thy promise; through Jesus Christ our Lord. Amen.[1]

This discussion of where Luther got this prayer has been long and complicated, but the evidence seems to indicate that Luther is indeed the author of the prayer.[2] If Luther translated an older Latin prayer or used an older German prayer, the original has yet to be produced. As original as the prayer seems to be, it is clear that Luther put into the prayer a great amount of traditional material. One needs to recognize that Luther gathered this traditional material from certain specific sources.

The first and most obvious source is the prayer from the Latin baptismal rite, *Deus patrum nostrorum.* This prayer is very ancient, going back to the fourth or fifth century. Originally it belonged to the rites of enrolling the catechumen for baptism.[3] The prayer followed the rite of giving the catechumen exorcised salt. The passages of the Latin prayer which passed into Luther's prayer will be italicized.

> God of our father, creator of the true universe, we *beseech you to hear our supplications that you deign to regard this your servant with favor,* that having tasted this first food of salt you permit him not long to thirst till at last he be filled with heavenly food. *Grant that he always be fervent in spirit, rejoicing in hope, serving your name,* lead him at last, O Lord, to that new bath of regeneration, *that with your faithful ones he might worthily receive the eternal prize according to your promises, through Jesus Christ Our Lord. Amen.*[4]

1. English translation quoted from *LW* 53, p. 97. For the original German text see *WA* 12, p. 467.

2. Kawerau, *Taufbüchlein,* pp. 423ff.; Paul Drews, *Beiträge zu Luthers liturgischer Reform* (Tübingen: J. C. B. Mohr, 1910), pp. 112-19; Alfred Adam, "Das Sintflutgebet in der Taufliturgie," in *Wort und Dienst, Jahrbuch der theologischen Schule Bethel;* Bruno Jordahn, "Die Taufliturgie bei Luther," in *Leiturgia,* vol. 5, pp. 380ff.; Walter Durig, "Das Sintflutgebet in Luthers Taufbüchlein," in *Warheit und Verkündigung: Festschrift für Michael Schmaus,* vol. 3 (Munich, 1967), pp. 1036-47; and Fritz Schmidt-Clausing, "Die liturgie-theologische Arbeit Zwinglis am Sintflutgebet des Taufformulars," *Zwingliana* 13 (1972), pp. 516-43 and 591-615.

3. The prayer *Deus patrum nostrum* is found in *Sacramentarium Gelasianum* 33, Mohlberg, p. 44.

4. The Latin text as Luther found it in the *Agenda Communis* is as follows:

"Deus patrum nostrorum, deus universe conditor creature, tu supplices exoramus, ut hunc famulum tuum respicere digneris propitius, et hoc primum pabulum salis gustantem non diutius esurire permittas, quominus impleatur cibo celesti, quatenus sit semper spiritu

If Luther used this prayer as a foundation for his Great Flood Prayer, it is obvious that Luther completely changed its liturgical function and filled it with a completely new content. The original Latin prayer was not intended to be used as a baptismal invocation. It was rather a prayer that the catechumen might begin to receive the first graces of conversion. It is a prayer for those who are on the threshold of faith. Luther, who would never speak of different graces, makes this a prayer for grace in all its fullness. It is no longer a prayer for the beginning of the forty days of preparation for baptism but rather for the day of baptism itself.

Of particular interest is the question of where Luther got the very pictorial typological anamnesis with which the prayer begins. It consists first of the two Old Testament types of baptism, the saving of Noah from the Great Flood and the saving of the children of Israel at the Red Sea. To this has been added the New Testament type of Jesus' baptism in the Jordan at the hand of John the Baptist. This threefold anamnesis is not taken directly from any previously existing prayer, although there has been a rather exhaustive search for such a prototype.[5] The general drift of Luther's prayer has led many to imagine that he might have modeled it on an ancient prayer for the consecration of baptismal waters.[6] A careful comparison to these prayers shows as many dissimilarities as similarities. None of the historic prayers for the consecration of the font uses precisely these three types. If these ancient prayers for the consecration of the font inspired Luther, it was in a very general way rather than in a direct way.

Beside the recounting of the types of baptism, Luther's prayer reminds us of the prayer for the consecration of the font in another way. The baptism of Jesus in the Jordan is remembered as having consecrated all water for baptism:

---

fervens, spe gaudens, tuo semper nomini serviens, perdue eum domine ad nove regenerationis lauacrum, ut cum fidelibus tuis promissionum tuarum eterna premia consequi mereatur. Per christum." *Agenda Communis,* p. 18.

5. Suggested sources of the Great Flood Prayer: Augustine, *Contra Faustum Manichaeum, MPL* 42, pp. 263-66; Isidore of Seville, *De ecclesiastibus officiis, MPL* 82, pp. 814-26; Rabanus Maurus, *De clericorum institutione, MPL* 107, p. 313; Rupert of Deutz, *De Trinitate et operibus, MPL* 167, p. 342; Belethus, *Rationale divinorum officiorum, MPL* 202, p. 115; and Hugh of Saint Victor, *De Sacramentis* 2.6.15. English translation by Roy J. Deferrari (Cambridge, Mass.: Medieval Academy of America, 1951), pp. 301-2.

6. Per Lundberg, *La typologie baptismale* (Leipzig: A. Lorentz, 1942); and Hubert Scheidt, *Die Taufwasserweihegebete im Sinne vergleichender Liturgieforschung untersucht* (Münster in Westphalia: Aschendorff, 1935). This work gives a large number of ancient prayers for the consecration of the font. Luther's prayer is not markedly similar to any of these ancient prayers.

> . . . and who through the baptism of thy Child, our Lord Jesus Christ, hast consecrated and set apart the Jordan and all water as a salutary flood and a rich and full washing away of sins. . . .

This idea is very ancient, to be found frequently in the works of the Fathers as well as in the oldest liturgical texts. In the Scriptures, however, the theme is absent. Luther has obviously taken the theme over from the tradition of the Church, but by whom it was mediated is not at all clear.

Luther has used his sources with originality. One phrase which clearly reveals the pen of Luther is:

> . . . who according to thy righteous judgment didst condemn the unbelieving world through the flood and in thy great mercy didst preserve believing Noah and his family. . . .

This is an interesting contrast to the text of 1 Peter 3:20-21 and 2 Peter 2:5. In Luther's prayer Noah is characterized as "believing" and the drowned world as "unbelieving." In this turn of phrase Luther's emphasis on justification by faith comes to clear expression. While the text of 1 Peter might allow one to argue that Noah was saved by his obedience, or perhaps that he was saved "through water," Luther brings out that Noah was saved by faith. Again 2 Peter characterizes Noah as "righteous," while Luther characterizes him as "believing." Luther's emphasis on the faith of Noah in no way does violence to the story of Noah, for it is in just this way that the Epistle to the Hebrews interprets Noah (Heb. 11:7). The point is that it took someone of Luther's originality to penetrate the story to that depth.

Whatever questions there might be about the sources of Luther's prayer, the liturgical function of the prayer is clear. It is a prayer for the salvation of those who are to be baptized. It is a prayer that those baptized be blessed with true faith, washed from their sins, separated from the world, joined to the Church, serve God throughout their lives, and in the end inherit eternal life. As Luther expressed it in his remarks at the end of the *German Baptismal Book,* the grace signified by baptism was given to the child as an answer to the prayers of the Church.[7] It was important, therefore, that the rite of baptism contain prayers calling on God to grant that grace signified by the sacrament.

Just a few months after the appearance of Luther's baptismal rite, Leo Jud published a baptismal rite for the Reformers of Zurich. As we have stressed before, Leo Jud's German baptismal service is a revision of Luther's service suited to the local rite of the Diocese of Constance. Most of the variations

7. *LW* 53, pp. 101ff.; *WA* 12, p. 47.

between Jud's rite and Luther's rite are to be explained by the differences between the local rite of Wittenberg in the archdiocese of Magdeburg and the local rite of the Diocese of Constance.[8] When it comes to the Great Flood Prayer, however, we are dealing with a prayer composed by Luther himself. Jud's revision of this prayer is much more free than his revision of other parts of the rite. Jud evidently feels much more free to revise Luther than to revise the traditional texts. Jud's version of the prayer runs as follows:

> O Almighty, Eternal God, who by the Great Flood in accordance with your righteous judgment condemned the unfaithful world, and out of your great mercy upheld faithful Noah, together with him and his family, and in the same way did drown the hardened Pharaoh, together with all his people in the Red Sea and did nevertheless bring your people Israel, with dry feet to the other side, all of which had signified the baptismal washing. Wherefore we pray that through your free mercy, you graciously regard your servant N. and give to him the light of faith in his heart, that through this saving flood all might be drowned which he inherited from Adam and he be taken out of the number of the unfaithful children of wrath. O heavenly Father, graciously receive him as a child, and join him together in one body with your Son in his cross, daily suffering, and burial together in one grave, to the end that in fervent love, steadfast hope and true faith, he might overcome death without fear and enter eternal life, through the same Lord Jesus Christ, your Son. Amen.[9]

One notices that Jud has made two major revisions.

1. While Jud follows exactly Luther's use of the two Old Testament types, he has completely left out the reference to Christ's baptism in the Jordan. It is probably because Luther had interpreted this to mean that Christ had by his baptism sanctified all water for baptism. To be sure, this is a favorite

8. Cf. Chap. II above.

9. "Allmechtiger, ewiger got, der du hast durch den sündflut nach dinem strengen urteyl die ungleubigen welt verdampt unnd den gleubigen Noe selbacht nach diner grossen erbärmd behalten [cf. 2. Petr. 2.5] und den verstockten Pharao mit allen sinen im Rotem Mör ertrenckt unnd din volck Israel truckens fuss hindurch gefurt hast, in welichem dises had des touffs bezeichnet ist gewesen [cf. 1. Kor. 10.1f.]. Wir bittend durch din grundlose barmhertzigkeit, du wöllest gnädigklichen ansehen disen dinen diener N. und im das liecht des gloubens in sin hertz geben, das durch diese heylsame sündflut an im ertrincke und undergang alles, was im von Adam anerborn ist, damit er uss der ungleubigen und kinderen des zorns von dir, o himelscher vatter, gnädigklich zu einem kind angenommen werd, dinem sun durch das crütz und täglich lyden yngelypt und mit im vergraben [cf. Rom. 6.4], in indrünstiger liebe, styffer hoffnung und warem glouben den tod unerschrockenlich überwinden und zu ewigen leben kummen mögy durch denselben unseren herren Jhesum Christum, dinen sun. Amen." *CR* 91, p. 71.

patristic theme, but it is nowhere even hinted at in the Scriptures. In time the South German Reformers would develop an interpretation of John's baptism which would take a very different line from the Scholastic interpretation. The Schoolmen had seen John's baptism in terms of the Old Testament. Zwingli and the South German Reformers would go more and more in the direction of interpreting John's baptism in light of the apostles' baptism.[10]

2. Luther's supplication for the benefits of baptism, so artfully clothed in an elaboration of the typology of the Flood, is replaced by a more straightforward list of the benefits of the sacrament. Adoption is mentioned with the words, "graciously receive him as a child." Incorporation into the body of Christ is mentioned with the phrase, "join him together in one body with your Son." Jud's prayer asks God to grant to the child the spiritual gifts of faith, hope, and love, "in fervent love, steadfast hope and true faith." Possibly Jud did not recognize Luther's reference to Romans 12:11. Finally, Jud mentions the achieving of eternal life and the overcoming of death. Luther prays, ". . . so that with all believers he might be made worthy to attain eternal life according to thy promise." For this Jud substitutes, "he might overcome death . . . and enter eternal life." Jud's elaboration of the benefits of the sacrament does not imply any particular criticism of Luther's text. It seems to be due rather to a natural tendency to elaborate, to add something more, and to try to make better what was already recognized as being good.

In evaluating Jud's revision, two things stand out. First, the prayer no longer has any trace of the theme of the consecration of water. It is entirely a prayer that through faith those baptized might be joined to Christ. Second, there is a clear acceptance of typology as a way of understanding baptism.

A year and a half after Jud's publication of Zurich's first German baptismal rite, Zwingli published a much simpler rite which was not just a translation of the old Latin rite, but was a thoroughgoing reform of the rite. The Baptismal Invocation in this rite is a further revision of Luther's Great Flood Prayer.

> O Almighty, eternal God, who by the Great Flood destroyed an unfaithful world through your righteous judgment and still out of your great mercy preserved faithful Noah and in the same way drowned the hardened Pharaoh and all his host in the Red Sea and yet your people Israel you brought out dry shod on the other side, all of which signified beforehand this baptismal

10. Cf. David Steinmetz on Zwingli's interpretation of John's baptism. "The Baptism of John and the baptism of Jesus in Huldrych Zwingli, Balthasar Hübmaier and late Medieval Theology," *Continuity and Discontinuity in Church History,* Studies in the History of Christian Thought, vol. 19 (Leiden: E. J. Brill, 1979), pp. 169-81.

> washing. We pray that in your unfathomable mercy you might graciously look upon this your servant N., and give to him the light of faith in his heart, in order that he be made one body with your Son and be buried with him and with him also raised up to a new life and joyfully bear his cross in daily discipleship; grant to him true faith, firm hope and fervent love, that in the end according to your will and unwavering in strength he leave this life, which indeed is no better than death, in accordance with your will and on that last day appear before the judgment seat of your Son without fear. Through the same Lord Jesus Christ, your Son, who with you ever lives and reigns in unity with the Holy Spirit, one God forever. Amen.[11]

By this time the resemblance to Luther's prayer is reserved for the most part to the anamnesis of the Old Testament types of baptism. The references to the Great Flood and to the crossing of the Red Sea are still almost word for word the same as Luther's Baptismal Invocation. The second half of the prayer, however, is by this time distant from Luther. The mention of original sin has disappeared. The enumeration of the benefits of the sacrament, which Jud began, has been further elaborated by Zwingli. Even with these changes, Zwingli's version of the prayer, as Luther's original and as Jud's revision, is still a baptismal epiclesis. To be sure, it prays not for the consecration of the water but for the salvation of the one baptized. One notices this particularly in the way the figure of baptism as burial and resurrection with Christ has been filled out. Zwingli is usually thought of as putting the emphasis on the ecclesiological nature of baptism, with water as the sign of being joined to the visible Church, but here Zwingli prays for incorporation into the body of Christ in its most inward and spiritual aspect.[12] To be joined to Christ in his death and

11. "O allmechtiger, ewiger gott, der du hast durch die sündflut nach dinem strengen urteil die unglöubigen welt verdampt, und den glouben Noe selbacht [cf. 1. Mos. 7.7, 6.10] uss diner grossen erbermd behalten, und den verstockten Pharao mit allen synen imm Roten Meer ertrenckt, und din volck Israel truckens fuss hindurch gefurt hast [cf. 2. Mos. 14.22-30], in welchem dises bad des touffs bezeichnet ist gewesen wir bittend dich durch din grundlose barmhertzigkeit, du wollist gnadicklichen sehen disen dinen diener N. und imm das liecht des gloubens in sin hertz geben, damit er dynem sun yngelybt und mit imm in den tod vergraben werde, in imm ouch uferstande in eim nüwen läben, in dem erssin krutz, imm täglich nachvolgende, frölich trag, imm anhange mit warem glouben, styffer hoffnung und ynbrunstiger liebe, das er diss leben, däs nutz anders ist weder ein tod, umb dinetwillen mannlich verlassen mög, und am jungsten tag, an dem gemeinen gricht dines suns, unerschrockenlich erschinen, durch denselben unseren herren Jesum Christum, dynen sun, der mit dir lebt und rychssnet in einigheit des heiligen geistes, ein gott. Amen!" *CR* 91, pp. 334ff.

12. Johann Martin Usteri, "Darstellung der Tauflehre Zwinglis (mit besonderer Berücksichtigung der wiedertäufischen Streitigkeiten)," *Theologische Studien und Kritiken* 55 (1883); Gottfried Wilhelm Locher, *Die Zwinglische Reformation im Rahmen*

resurrection is far more than incorporation into the visible Church. One recognizes the way the vivid picture of the Flood is balanced by an equally strong presentation of the Last Judgment. Zwingli brings the prayer to a solemn conclusion by adding to it one of the classical trinitarian doxologies: "through the same Lord Jesus Christ, your Son, who with you ever lives and reigns in unity with the Holy Spirit, one God forever. Amen."

The Baptismal Invocation of Strasbourg

The earliest Baptismal Invocation of the Reformed Church of Strasbourg is found in the *Strasbourg Order for the Lord's Supper* (D).

> Almighty eternal God, merciful Father, seeing that the righteous shall live by faith alone and seeing that it is impossible to be pleasing to you except by faith, so we pray you would grant the gift of faith to this child, who is of your creation. Seal and confirm him by the presence of the Holy Spirit in his heart, according to the promise of your Son, in order that there might be that inward renewal and rebirth of the spirit through this our outward baptism of water, seeing that this is indeed its true meaning; and that as he is baptized into the death of Christ Jesus, buried with him, and through him awakened from the dead so grant that he walk in a new life, to the praise of God's glory and to the profit of his neighbor. Amen.[13]

This prayer celebrates the relation of faith and baptism to the salvation of the Christian. As one administers the sign of spiritual cleansing, renewal, and rebirth, one prays that the outward sign might be fulfilled by an inner reality. This prayer makes clear, as do the prayers of Luther, Jud, and Zwingli, that the power belongs to God. This prayer, like its predecessors, is a true Baptismal Invocation or baptismal epiclesis. There is in this prayer, however,

---

der europäischen Kirchengeschichte (Göttingen: Vandenhoeck & Ruprecht, 1979); and Jacques Courvoisier, *Zwingli, A Reformed Theologian* (Richmond, Va.: John Knox Press, 1963), pp. 67ff.

13. "Allmechtiger, ewiger got, barmhertziger vatter, dieweyl der gerecht lebt allein ym glauben und unmöglich ist, das dir etwas on glauben gefall, so bitten wir dich, das du disem kindt, das da ist dein creatur, die gab des glaubens verlühen wellest, in welchem du sein hertz mit dem heylgen geist noch deins suns verheissung versiglen und versicheren wollest, vff das dein innerliche ernewerung vnd widergeburt des geists durch den vnsern tauff warhafftiglich bedeutet werde, vnd das es als in den todt Christi Jesu getaufft mit ym begraben vnd durch yn von den todten vfferweckt sy, zu wandlen in eim newen leben zu lob der herrlicheit gots vnd zu vffbauwung seiner nechsten, amen." Hubert, *Ordnungen*, pp. 40-41.

a deepening of the concept of epiclesis. This prayer begins to make very specific that it is the work of the Holy Spirit in our spirits that brings about the benefits of the sacrament. As we shall see, this theme will continue to gain importance in the baptismal rites of both Strasbourg and Geneva.[14]

One should notice that this prayer asks the Father for the sealing presence of the Holy Spirit in the hearts of those baptized. The word "sealing" is particularly significant. One might say that it is a New Testament term referring to the inward experience of which baptism is the outward sign. In the history of theology the term was often understood as referring to confirmation. Bucer's use of the word here is therefore most striking! It makes clear as nothing else could that the sacrament of baptism is for the forgiveness of sins and the gift of the Holy Spirit. Obviously one of Bucer's major concerns in the reform of the rite of baptism is to make clear that the sacrament is a sign and promise of the giving of the Holy Spirit.

In succeeding years the text of this prayer was augmented. In the *Strasbourg Psalter of 1530* (G) we find the following redaction of the Baptismal Invocation:

> Almighty, eternal God, merciful Father, since your kingdom may be seen only by those who are born anew, and since nothing is pleasing to you except by the presence of your Spirit, so we pray that this child who is your creature might receive the Spirit of sonship and that thereby in his heart there be a dying away of the natural powers, a sealing and a confirming, for the purpose of that inner renewal and spiritual rebirth, which is truly signified by the outward baptism. Grant that as he is baptized in the death of Christ Jesus, buried with him, and through him is awakened from the dead, he might walk in a new life, to the praise of God's glory and the profit of his neighbor. Amen.[15]

The theological content of the prayer has been altered considerably. Where the first prayer asked that the child baptized might receive the gift of

14. On Bucer's doctrine of the Holy Spirit see the work of W. P. Stephens, *The Holy Spirit in the Theology of Martin Bucer* (Cambridge: University Press, 1970). Bucer gave great emphasis to the doctrine of the Holy Spirit. August Lang, *Der Evangelienkommentar Martin Butzer's und die Grundzüge seiner Theologie* (Leipzig: Dietrich, 1900).

15. "Allmechtiger, ewiger gott, barmhertziger vatter, dieweyl dein rych nur die newgebornen sehen mogen vnd dir nichts gfallt, das nit deinen geyst hat, so bitten wir, das du dissem kind, das da ist dein creatur, die gab des glaubens deinen heiligen kindergeist hienoch verlühen wollest, vnd sein hertz mit demselbigen noch abtodtung der naturlichen krafft versiglen und versichern wollest, auff das die innerlichen ernewerung vnd widergeburt des geysts durch den eusseren tauff warhafftigklichen bedeutet werde, und das es als in den todt Christi Jesu getaufft mit jm begraben vnd durch jn von den todten aufferweckt sey werde, zu wandlen in eim newen leben, zu lob der herlikeit gottes vnd zu auffbawung seines nechsten, amen." Hubert, *Ordnungen,* pp. 40-41.

faith, the Baptismal Invocation of 1530 prays that the child might receive the gift of the Holy Spirit, very specifically after the form of Romans 8:15 and Galatians 4:6 where the Holy Spirit is called the Spirit of sonship which cries, "Abba, Father." As the apostle Paul understood it, the prayer which cries out from our hearts, "Abba, Father," is the work of the Holy Spirit himself who cries out from our hearts. It is the saying of this prayer which proves that we are children of God. We know that we are children of God because we pray, "Abba, Father," and we can trust this prayer because it is the work of the Holy Spirit. Bucer has taken the apostles' words to heart. This last touch, the reference to the *heiligen kindergeist,* or Spirit of sonship, is probably to remind the faithful that whether one is a child or an adult before baptism, after baptism one is a child of God. Bucer would remind us that unless one becomes as a little child one cannot enter the Kingdom of Heaven.

The formulation of the Baptismal Invocation was further revised in the *Strasbourg Psalter of 1537* (J). Here the prayer is expanded considerably by new theological insights and accents.

> Almighty, eternal God, merciful Father, since the newborn alone may see your kingdom and since no one can be pleasing to you except that your Spirit live within him, we pray that you grant your Holy Spirit to this child whom indeed you have created after your own image and with that same Spirit establish and seal his heart. Also grant that as we being your servants and the ministers of a new covenant do now administer this holy baptism according to your command and promise, so grant to this child inner renewal of spirit and true regeneration, making him your son. Through your name bestow and bequeath that this child be baptized into the death of Christ Jesus, that he be buried with him, that he die to all sins, and through him be raised up to life, to the service of righteousness and all that is good. Grant also that through him your holy name might evermore be hallowed and magnified, that your kingdom come to us more fully and spread about more widely, and that your will so uniquely good by us and by all about us be eagerly done as it is in heaven. Grant to him bodily health as well. Care for him in regard to all his needs and give to him your Fatherly protection in time of trouble. Through our Lord Jesus Christ. Amen.[16]

16. "Allmechtiger, ewiger gott, barmhertziger vatter, diewil dein reich allein die new gepornen sehen mogen, vnd dir nichts gefallet, das nicht durch deinen geist lebet, bitten wir, das du disem kind, das du doch zu deiner bildnüs erschaffen hast, deinen h. geist verleihen und sein hertz mit demselbigen nach deines suns verheissung versichern vnd versigeln wollest; vnd also geben vnd wurcken, das wir yetzung als deine diener vnd diener des newen testaments mit disem deinem h. tauffe nach deinen beuelch vnd verheissen disem kind die innerlich ernewerung des geists vund ware widergepurt inn deine kindschafft durch deinen namen warlich mittheilen vnd ubergeben, das es inn den todt Christi Jesu, getteuffet mit jm

The most important aspect of the revision is the enlarging of the final lines. The elaboration shows a greater concern for the fruit of baptism, or, in more theological terms, for the benefits of the sacrament. It is in the form of a paraphrase of certain of the petitions of the Lord's Prayer together with a prayer of intercession for the material needs of the child. This expansion is primarily of a pastoral nature, as were many of the revisions found in the *Strasbourg Psalter of 1537.*[17]

One notices with particular interest the reference to mankind's creation in the image of God. Bucer is eager to bring the doctrine of the *imago dei* to bear on the doctrine of baptism. For Bucer, as a former Dominican friar, the doctrine of creation in the image of God was of great importance.[18] It is often claimed that Protestantism in its strong doctrine of redemption has overlooked the doctrine of creation. Here is evidence to the contrary. "We pray that you grant your Holy Spirit to this child whom indeed you have created after your own image and with that same Spirit establish and seal his heart." This is a theological theme which the Strasbourg Reformers have given a significant place in their prayer. They evidently do not wish to come out in favor of a doctrine of grace perfecting nature as opposed to a doctrine of grace replacing nature. They seem to want to recognize both positions. The two themes are found in the prayer in a paradoxical balance. It is with the theme of baptism as death, burial, and resurrection with Christ that the understanding of grace replacing nature is heard.

In addition to this final revision of the original Strasbourg Baptismal Invocation we find an alternate form for the Baptismal Invocation.

> Almighty, merciful God and Father, who has promised us in Abraham, the father of us and all the faithful, that it is your will to be not only our God but the God of our children as well, it was, therefore, that in ancient times you established the children of the Covenant of Grace through circumcision.

---

begraben zum absterben aller sünden vnd durch jn vfferwecket werde zum leben vnd dienst der gerechtigkeit vnd alles guten, das also auch durch es dein heiliger namme jmmer mehr geheilget vnd gros gemachet, dein reich vollinger zu vns komme vnd erweitert werde vnd deinen allein guten willen hei vns und allethalb mit allem lust wie imm himmel gelebet werde, dazu du es auch inn leiblicher gesuntheit bewaren, mit aller notdurff versehen vnd vor allem vnrath vetterlich behüten wollest durch vnsern herren Jesum Christum, amen." Hubert, *Ordnungen,* p. 46.

17. Old, *Patristic Roots,* pp. 80-87.

18. On Bucer's anthropology cf. Friedman Krüger, *Bucer und Erasmus, eine Untersuchung zum Einfluss des Erasmus auf die Theologie Martin Bucers* (Wiesbaden: Franz Steiner Verlag, 1970), pp. 128-47. On the development of this theme in Reformed theology see Ronald S. Wallace, *Calvin's Doctrine of the Christian Life* (Grand Rapids: Wm. B. Eerdmans Publishing Company, 1959), pp. 103-11.

So also your Son, our Lord Jesus, received the children which were presented to him, graciously accepting them, bestowing upon them his blessing and declaring that to such belong the Kingdom of Heaven.

O good God and Father, trusting in this your promise and your example, we presume to appear before the sight of your divine majesty in the name of your Son, Our Lord Jesus, and pray that you forgive us for never having been truly thankful for your grace toward us and the redemption of your Son which you have imparted to us in baptism and that we have never really striven to die to ourselves and to live alone to you our heavenly Father.

O merciful Father, we pray and beseech you, grant to us and increase in us your Holy Spirit that we recognize more and more your unspeakable grace, demonstrated in baptism, whereby you have accepted us as your children, that we be truly thankful and show ourselves to be your people and children. Graciously accept from us this child, born of your own people, whom you have given to them and whom you have created in your image. Grant that this child not suffer for our sins and unrighteousness because he unfortunately is born from us; rather let him be nourished by the death and resurrection of our Lord Jesus and thereby grant that your image be restored in him.

Heavenly Father, since our Lord and Savior wishes to be in the midst of us and calls us to bring our children to him, grant that with true hearts we might desire your grace and the redemption of your Son for this child by true faith without wavering, so we baptize him in your name, as we have him before us by your grace, that you completely forgive all inherited sin through our Lord Jesus Christ and never reckon it to him. Truly impart to him sonship and in all things receive him as an heir and fellow heir of our Lord Jesus Christ.

Heavenly Father, grant in such faith, that as we baptize this child we might be inclined and impelled to receive him as a fellow member of the body of Christ, faithfully pray for him, earnestly educate him, that through him your name might be glorified, your Kingdom increased and your will be done on earth as it is in heaven. And to these spiritual graces grant to this child physical health, minister to all his needs and grant to him your fatherly protection, through Jesus Christ our Lord. Amen.[19]

19. "Allmechtiger, barmhertziger gott vnd vatter, du hast in Abraham vnserm vnd aller gleubigen vater, vns verheissen, du wollest vnser vnd vnsers samens gott sein, darumb du auch den kindern der alten woltest deinen gnadenbund mit der beschneidung zugestellet werden, vnd dein sun, vnser herre Jesus hatt auch die kindlin, die man im zubracht, so gnediglich angenommen vnd jhn seinen segen so gar freuntlich mitgetheilet vnd gesprochen: das himelreich seie solchen. Auff solche deine, o gutiger gott vnd vatter, also genedige zusag vnd handlung vertrostet, erscheinen wir vor den augen deiner gottlichen maiestat imm namen deines suns, vnsers herren Jesu, vnd bitten dich, du wollest vns allen verzeihen, das deiner genaden vnd erlosung deines suns, die du vns hast imm heiligen tauff mit geteilet, nie recht

The prayer divides into five parts, as the arrangement above shows. The first is the memorial or anamnesis. Like the anamnesis of the Baptismal Invocation of Zurich, it is twofold. It remembers the covenant made with Abraham, which was sealed by circumcision, and it remembers Christ's blessing of the children. This doxological anamnesis is followed by a corporate confession of sin by the whole Church and a supplication for pardon. This is a most interesting addition. Prayers of repentance must have been a significant part of the earliest baptismal rites, yet such prayers are conspicuously absent from the Latin baptismal rites of the late Middle Ages. With the institution of the sacrament of penance, the Church had lost sight of baptism as a sign of repentance in much the same way as with the institution of confirmation the Church lost sight of baptism as a sign of the giving of the Holy Spirit. On this subject we will have more to say toward the end of this chapter. The third part of the prayer asks for the granting and increase of the Holy Spirit. Supplications follow asking that God receive the child and that God's image be restored in the child. The fourth part asks for redemptive grace and saving faith, that original sin be forgiven and that the baptized be adopted into the household of faith. The final part of the prayer asks that the Church receive the child as a fellow member of the body of Christ, continue to pray for the child, and educate the child. Finally, God is asked to remember the physical needs of the

---

danckbar gewesen sind vnd vns nie recht geflissen haben, vns selb abzusterben vnd dir als vnserem himmlischen vatter allein zu geleben. Darumb bitten vnd flehen wir, o barmhertzige: gott vnd vatter, gibe vnd mehre inn vns deinen heiligen geist, das wir dein so vnaussprechliche genad, die vns im heiligen tauff vnd sunst bewisen hast, taglich mehr vnd mehr erkennen vnd bedencken vnd uns derselbigen inn allem vnserem leben danckbar beweisen vnd also warlich dein volck vnd kinder seien vnd dises kindlin, die frucht der deinen, die du ihnen gegeben vnd nach deiner bildnüs erschaffen hast, nimme von vns gneddiglich vff, lass es nicht entgelten vnser sünden vnd vngerechtigkeit, inn die es leider von vns geporen ist, sonder lasse es geniessen des todes vnd der vrstende deines suns vnsers herrn Jesu, durch den es zu deiner bildnüs widergeboren werde, vnd wie er, vnser herre vnd einiger heiland, wille mitten vnder vns sein vnd heisset vns jm vnsere kinder zu bringen, gib himmlischer vatter, das wir solliche dein genad vnd erlosung deines suns an disem kind recht von hertzen begeren mit warem glauben fassen vnd nit zweiflen, so wir es teuffen vff deinen namen, wie wir aus deinen genaden jetz vorhaben, du werdest jm durch vnseren herren Jesum die angeborn sünde gantzliche vergeben vnd nimmermehr zurechnen, deine kindschafft warlich mitteilen deinen waren erben vnd miterben vnsers herren Jesu Christi in allen dingen solchem glauben gib himmlisch vatter, das wir dis kindlin teuffen vnd daher auch alle geneigt vnd alweg getriben werden es hinfür inn allem auch zu halten vnser mitglid inn Christo, für es getrewlich biten, ernslich vffziehen vnd inn all weg jm dazu dienen, das auch durch es dein namme geheiliget, dein reich erweiteret vnd deinem allein guten willen bei vns vnd allenthalb mit allem lust, wie imm himmel, gelebet werde. Dazu du es auch inn leiblicher gesuntheit bewaren, mit aller notdurfft versehen vnd vor allem vnraht vatterliche behuten wollest durch vnsern herren Jesum Christum, amen." Hubert, *Ordnungen,* pp. 47-49.

child, asking for him or her good health and protection. This is a long prayer, perhaps too long for practical purposes. One can well imagine how difficult it might be to say the whole of this prayer at a baptismal celebration where, through some unexpected perversity, one of the children decided to shriek through the whole of the rite. However this may be, the prayer is a noble guide to the prayer of the Church at the time of baptism.

Taken as a whole the Strasbourg prayers are impressive. The different revisions of the Baptismal Invocation evidence a continuing reflection on the meaning of baptism. Like the Baptismal Invocation of Zurich they call upon God to bring about in the child what is signified by the outward sign of the sacrament. These prayers make it clear that the simple doing of the rite is not magic. The power to save and sanctify remains with God. The epicletic nature of the baptismal rite is clear. Particularly clear in the Strasbourg prayers is the enormous importance of the doctrine of the Holy Spirit. This prayer that the Father pour out the Holy Spirit in accord with the promise of the Son might well be regarded as the key to the whole rite.

The Baptismal Invocation of Geneva

The *Genevan Psalter* of 1542 contains a Baptismal Invocation based on the *French Evangelical Service Book* of 1533. Calvin's edition of this prayer is as follows:

> Lord God, Eternal and Almighty Father, who by your infinite mercy and good pleasure have promised to be not only our God but the God of our children as well, be pleased then, we pray you, to confirm that grace to this child before us, being born of a mother and father whom you have called into your Church; and as he is presented to you and set apart by us, grant that he be received into your holy protection, declaring yourself to be his God and Savior, remitting in him that original sin of which the whole lineage of Adam is guilty, then sanctifying him by your Spirit to the end that when reaching the age of understanding, he might know and worship you as his only God, glorifying you in all his life, that always he receive from you the remission of his sins. And that he might receive from you all such graces, be pleased to incorporate him into the communion of our Lord Jesus that he share all his goods as one of the members of his body. Hear us, Father of mercy, to the end that the baptism which we administer according to your command might produce its fruit and its virtue as it is declared to us by the Gospel: Our Father. . . .[20]

20. "SEIGNEUR Dieu, Pere eternel et tout puissant, puis qu'il t'a pleu, par ta clemence infinie, nous promttre, que tu seras Dieu de nous et de noz enfans: nos te prions, qu'il te

We have already quoted Farel's Baptismal Invocation in the course of Chapter VI. Calvin's prayer preserves many of the best features of Farel's work. Farel's prayer likewise begins with an anamnesis of the covenant granted to Abraham. It, too, had put the invocation of the Holy Spirit at the center of the prayer. Likewise Farel's prayer had also prayed that when the child should reach the age of understanding he or she might know and worship the one true God. To Farel's prayer, Calvin has added some of the features of Bucer's prayers, such as the idea that in baptism Christian parents present their children to God. Once more we observe, as we have often observed in the past, that Calvin has produced a text which sums up the best insight of the Reformers who preceded him.

At the beginning of Calvin's prayer, we find an anamnesis of the covenant. The prayer begins with an allusion to the seventeenth chapter of Genesis and to the promise made with Abraham to be not only his God but also the God and Father of his children. This anamnesis may well originate with Farel, and it may be to Farel that we should trace the reference to the same passage of Scripture in the Strasbourg prayer. It should be remembered, however, that the doctrine of the covenant was at the very center of the early Reformed defense of the baptism of children. There is no reason why the ministers of Strasbourg could not have come up with the idea themselves. Particularly worthy of note is the fact that the children are specifically said to be the children of Christian parents. A reference to 1 Corinthians 7:14 seems to be intended. There, the apostle Paul tells us that the children of even just one believing parent are holy. The prayer intends to claim the covenant. To pray on the basis of a covenant promise of God is a very biblical method of prayer.

A particularly interesting idea found in this prayer is that baptism is an offering of the child to God on the part of the child's parents, "As he is presented to you and set apart by us." Here again the idea develops from the analogy between baptism and circumcision. Behind this idea is surely the story

---

plaise de confermer ceste grace en l'enfant present, engendré de pere et de mere, lesquelz tu as appellé en ton Eglise; et comme il t'est offert et consacré, de par nous, que tu le vueilles recevior en ta saincte protection, te declarant estre son Dieu et Sauveur, en luy remettant le peché originel, duquel est coupable toute la lignée d'Adam: puis apres le sanctifiant par ton Esprit: afin que quand il viendra en eage de congnoissance, il te recongnoisse et adore, comme son seul Dieu, te glorifiant en toute sa vie, pour obtenir tousiours de toy remission de ses pechez. Et afin qu'il puisse obtenir telles graces, qu'il te plaise l'incorporer en la communion de nostre Seigneur Jesus, pour estre participant de tous ses biens, comme l'un des membres de son corps. Exaulce nous Pere de misericorde: afin que le Baptesme, que nous luy communiquons selon ton ordonnance, produise son fruict et sa vertu, telle qu'elle nous est declarée par ton Evangile." *OS* 2, p. 34.

of Abraham's sacrifice of Isaac on Mount Moriah as well as the story of the presentation of the infant Jesus at the temple in Jerusalem. Luke makes a strong point of the presentation of Jesus (Luke 2:21-33). It seems quite possible that this idea was also found by the Reformers in the baptismal sermons of Gregory of Nazianzus. The great Byzantine theologian suggests Hannah's presentation of the child Samuel in the temple as a type of the baptism of children.[21] In the *Institutes* Calvin expresses the same line of thought when he says that the whole Church should pray over the child and that the prayers should offer the child to God.[22]

Another point which should be emphasized is that at the center of the prayer is the petition that the child might be sanctified by the Holy Spirit to the end that he might know and worship God. Here we find the theme of illumination. Illumination is understood as part of the sanctifying work of the Holy Spirit. That baptism is to be understood as illumination is most assuredly taught in the New Testament. This theme is found in Hebrews, where baptism is called illumination. In many of the ancient baptismal rites the story of Jesus healing the blind man was read as a type of baptism. Illumination was a frequent theme of the prayers for the catechetical rites. One might mention, for example, the prayer *Eternam ac justissimam,* especially the following lines:

> . . . Eternal God, author of light and truth, illumine these your manservants and maidservants with the light of your understanding: cleanse them and sanctify them; give to them true knowledge. . . .[23]

This is certainly very close to "sanctifying him by your Spirit to the end that when reaching the age of understanding, he might know and worship you. . . ." We find then, in the Genevan Baptismal Invocation, a reaching back to the concerns of the prayers of the old catechetical rites. In baptism the child is committed to receiving catechetical instruction. This was repeatedly emphasized by the Reformers. It was the prayer of the Church that the children of the covenant receive the teaching and illumination which belonged to the children of light.

Taken as a whole the Baptismal Invocation of the *Genevan Psalter* follows very closely the pattern which had been developing ever since 1523

21. Gregory of Nazianzus, *Sermon on the Sacrament of Baptism* (Oration 40.25).

22. This particular passage goes back to the *Institutes* of 1536 ". . . in coetum fidelium ipsum repraesentari, et tota ecclesia, velut teste, spectante et orante super eum, Deo offerri. . . ." *OS* 1, p. 160.

23. ". . . aeterne deus luminis et ueritatis, super hos famulos et famulas, ut digneris eos inluminare lumen intellegentiae tuae. Munda eos et sanctifica; de eis scientam ueram. . . ." Mohlberg, *Sacramentarium Gelasianum,* p. 45.

when Luther produced his famous Baptismal Invocation. Calvin has picked up on Luther, but he has also picked up on Bucer's strong emphasis on the Holy Spirit. For Calvin, as for his predecessors, this prayer makes clear the epicletic nature of baptism.

Baptism and the Prayer of Confession

Prayers of repentance and confession of sin were part of the baptism administered by John the Baptist. John's ministry was characterized by a call to repentance. This should be sufficient reason to suggest that in John's baptismal rites prayers of repentance were used; however, the text of Matthew 3:6 very specifically mentions, "He baptized them in the river Jordan, confessing their sins." In Luke 3:21 we read that Jesus was praying after his baptism. Such a profound occasion was bound to have been couched in prayer both before and after. It almost goes without saying. Long confessions of sin such as we find in Daniel 9 were a standard feature of the piety of the Jews in New Testament times.[24] For the baptism of the apostles the same thing can be said. In Acts 2, at the day of Pentecost, Peter urged the people of Jerusalem to repent and be baptized. We can assume that this repentance must have taken place in some form of prayer or was intended to be expressed in prayer.[25]

On this basis we should expect to find a penitential prayer in the Reformed baptismal rite, but what do we find? In the actual baptismal rite of the early Reformed Churches there are no prayers of confession. The Reformed Baptismal Invocation is not a confession of sin. While this prayer usually has a supplication for the forgiveness of sin, the confession of sin and expressions

24. The liturgy of both the temple and the synagogue provided for a silent, individual reciting of prayers of repentance. Prayers such as David's prayer of confession, the Prayer of Azariah, and the Prayer of Manasseh were often recited by the worshipers during the Tachanunim. Some of the penitential psalms, particularly Psalm 25, and the prayer of confession for the Day of Atonement might likewise be recited during the Tachanunim. Eduard Freiherr von der Goltz, *Das Gebet der ältesten Christenheit* (Leipzig: J. C. Hinrichs'sche Buchhandlung, 1901), pp. 147-49 and 246-49; Ismar Elbogen, *Der jüdische Gottesdienst in seiner geschichtliche Entwicklung* (Leipzig: G. Foch, 1913), pp. 73-81; Friedrich Heiler, *Das Gebet, eine religionsgeschichtliche und religions-psychologische Untersuchung,* 4th ed. (Munich: Verlag von Ernst Reinhardt, 1921), pp. 58-99; and A. B. Macdonald, *Christian Worship in the Primitive Church* (Edinburgh: T. & T. Clark, 1934), pp. 98-100.

25. On the subject of baptismal repentance in the early Christian Church cf. O. Michel, "Die Umkehr nach der Verkündigung Jesu," *Evangelische Theologie* 5 (1938): 403-13; H. Pohlman, *Die Metanoia als Zentralbegriff der Christlichen Frömmigkeit* (Leipzig: J. C. Hinrichs, 1938); and J. Behm, *Theologisches Wörterbuch zum Neuen Testament* 4:792ff.

of repentance are not a prominent part of the prayer. The longer prayer of Strasbourg contains a confession of sin for the whole Church, but this is an exception. One is struck by this omission. If indeed baptism is the sacrament of repentance, why are there no prayers of repentance in the actual baptismal rite? The reason for this is simple; the confession of sin is postponed until after baptism. The Reformers understood baptism as being unto repentance. Repentance, turning away from sin and toward God, is a fruit of baptism. It is for this reason that every service of worship in both Strasbourg and Geneva began with a prayer of confession. That prayer of confession is in a most profound sense a baptismal prayer. It is a baptismal prayer even when it is said at the beginning of each service of worship. The Prayer of Confession found in the typical Reformed liturgy might be regarded as a remembrance of our baptism. It stands at the beginning of each service of worship to remind us that baptism is the presupposition of all our worship. It is by virtue of our baptism that we stand before God as a purified and holy priesthood to render to him our spiritual service.

Already at the very beginning of liturgical reform in Strasbourg, Bucer stresses this point in the *Grund und Ursach.* He tells us that the Prayer of Confession with which every service of worship begins has its basis in the prayers of repentance which the first Christians offered before their baptism. In explaining the prayers of confession at the beginning of the worship service he says:

> Our reason and basis in Scripture is this: the beginning of Christian life is in confession that all our actions are sinful. It is for this reason that John the Baptist, Christ and the Apostles began their preaching with the call, "Repent!" In the assembly of God's people the confession of sin has always been first; in the ancient Church it also preceded baptism, for at that time children were not normally baptized but rather only people who were capable of understanding. Therefore, we begin our service with a general confession of sin and supplication for grace.[26]

The point is quite clear. Since almost everyone in the sixteenth century was baptized in infancy, it is necessary that the confession of sin be postponed

26. "Unser grund und ursach auss der schrifft ist diser: Der anfang christlichs lebens bekennen, das alles unser thun sünd ist, darumb Johannes der tauffer, Christus und die Apostlen ire predigen an dem angefangen haben: bessert euch! und in den versamlungen gottes ist je und je die beicht der sünd das erst gewesen, die bey den alten auch dem tauff vorgangen ist, dann man gemeinklich nur die verstendigen, nit kinder geteüfft hat. Darumb fahen wir unser dienst auch an mit gemeiner bekanntniss unser sunden und gnad bitten." *BDS* 1, p. 247.

until later in life. Bucer does not intend us to understand that if baptism were left to more mature years, then prayers of confession would no longer be necessary. Quite to the contrary, he understands that even the earliest Church began each service with prayers of confession.[27] Prayers of confession not only begin the Christian life, they continue to be part of the Christian life, throughout the whole of life.

With the Reformers' attack on the sacrament of penance, the institution of the confessional, and the whole tradition of canon law regarding the disciple of repentance, the Reformers were forced to rethink the relation of baptism to repentance.[28] The medieval Church, at least as far as folk theology was concerned, had tended to separate the discipline of repentance from baptism by making it another sacrament, the sacrament of penance.[29] Of this approach the Reformers were very critical.

If the Reformers were very critical of the way the sacrament of penance had been institutionalized in their day, they were just as critical of the error which had led to the establishing of the sacrament of penance.[30] It was the approach of

27. In the strictest sense of what Bucer says here, one must say that the Reformer of Strasbourg was in error. But in the larger sense Bucer was quite correct. There was no Christian worship without repentance. This is well documented by the study of André Benoît, *Le baptême chrétién au second siècle* (Paris: Presses Universitaires de France, 1953), pp. 49ff., 89ff., 91-93, 108-27, 154-63, 193-97.

28. For the South German Reformers it was particularly John Oecolampadius who was involved with the controversy over the sacrament of penance. Immediately before the beginning of the Reformation Oecolampadius had been confessor general for the bishop of Basel. During this time he published a work on the discipline of penance in the Eastern Church. This work was widely read and received a refutation from Latomus, the famous theologian of the University of Louvain. Cf. Staehelin, *Lebenswerk Oekolampads,* pp. 84-90, 121, and 259-63. Calvin, as were his predecessors, was fully aware that the discipline of penance had changed considerably over the years. The Reformers had learned much about the practice of penance from the Church Fathers. See, for example, Calvin's remarks on the practice of Cyprian, *Institutes* 4.19.14.

29. The definition given the sacrament of penance in the preface to the *Ritual of Constance* reads as follows: "Penitencia, que est secunda tabula post naufragium pro materia habet actus penitentis scilicet: Contricionem, Confessionem et Satisfactionem. Forma est: Ego absoluo te a peccatis in nomine patris et filij et spiritus-sancti. Minister est sacerdos habens auctoritatem absoluendi. Effectus est absolucio a peccatis." *Obsequiale constantiensis,* p. 2. For Calvin's commentary on the well-known saying that penance is "the second plank after shipwreck," see *Institutes* 4.19.17. For the more developed statement of the Scholastic doctrine see Peter Lombard, *Sentences, MPL* 192, pp. 868-99; Gratian, *Decretals, MPL* 187, pp. 1519-1644; Thomas Aquinas, *Summa Theologica* 3.84-89; Hugh of Saint Victor, *De Sacramentis* 2.14; and Heiko Oberman, *The Harvest of Medieval Theology,* pp. 146-84.

30. On the history of the doctrine of penance see Paul Galtier, *L'Église et al remission des péchés aux premiers siècles* (Rome: Beauchesne, 1932); Paul Galtier, *Aux origines du*

certain rigorists of the second and third centuries that repentance was essentially a prebaptismal experience. After baptism there was to be no second repentance according to some thinkers of Christian antiquity.[31] It was in opposition to this rigorism that the Church developed its sacrament of penance. The Reformers were not at all interested in joining ranks with the rigorists. Quite to the contrary, they believed very strongly in postbaptismal repentance.

It was over against both the Scholastic solution and the rigorist position that the Reformers developed a very definite understanding on the relation of baptism to repentance. That the confession of sin and the forgiveness of sin are to be thought of in terms of the baptism which one has already received is a theme found in many of the baptismal prayers of the early Reformed Church. The confession of the daily sins of the already baptized Christian, the forgiveness of these sins, growth in grace, the spiritual gifts of understanding and enlightenment, the daily increase of faith, hope, and love, and the sanctifying of the Christian life are understood as the fruit of baptism. While baptism stands at the beginning of the Christian life, its fruit is born throughout the whole of the Christian life. The earliest Reformed theologians saw in baptism a sign not of a one-time-only repentance and cleansing of sin, but rather as a sign of a continual cleansing of sin.

In Luther's Baptismal Invocation we begin to hear the first stirrings of this theme, when he prays:

> . . . that by means of this saving Flood all that has been born in him from Adam and which he himself has added thereto may be drowned in him and engulfed, and that he may be sundered from the number of the unbelieving, preserved dry and secure in the holy ark of Christendom, . . . so that with all believers he may be made worthy to attain eternal life. . . .

The usual presentation of Luther's theology would explain this prayer to mean that baptism is the sacrament of the forgiveness of all sin, past, present, and future.[32] Luther was much more concerned with the forgiving of sin than with

---

sacrament de penitence (Rome: Gregorian University Press, 1951); R. C. Mortimer, *The Origins of Private Penance in the Western Church* (Oxford: Clarendon Press, 1939); J. A. Jungmann, *Die lateinischen Bussriten in ihrer geschichtlichen Entwicklung* (Innsbruck: F. Rauch, 1932); and A. Michel and E. Amman, "Penitance," in *Dictionnaire de théologie catholique* 12, cols. 722-1138. Notice particularly the sections on Scholastic doctrine and the section on the Reformers.

31. On the Penitential Controversy of the second and third centuries cf. the article "Penitential Controversy" by F. X. Murphy in *New Catholic Encyclopedia* 9: 84-85. See further R. Poschmann, *Paenitentia secunda: Die kirchliche Busse im ältesten Christentum bis Cyprian und Origines* (Bonn: P. Hanstein, 1940).

32. On Luther's theology of penance: Paul Althaus, *The Theology of Martin Luther,* trans. R. C. Schultz (Philadelphia: Fortress Press, 1156), pp. 251-73 and particularly p. 354; and Werner Elert, *The Structure of Lutheranism,* trans. W. A. Hansen, vol. 1 (St. Louis:

the forgiving of sins. Luther departs from the usual Scholastic interpretation of baptism being the sacrament of the forgiveness of original sin and all those actual sins committed before baptism, while the sacrament of penance had to do with the forgiveness of postbaptismal sins. The figure of the ark implies that the grace of continuing in the Christian life is a fruit of baptism. It is to this end that God grants the spiritual gifts of being fervent in Spirit and joyful in hope. The theology of the Anabaptists had a tendency to regard repentance as a pre-Christian state. We have already seen this with particular clarity in the thought of Balthasar Hübmaier. As Hübmaier explained it, the ministry of John the Baptist was to bring one into a loathing of sin which produced the conversion experience. The whole theory of salvation by conversion experience would tend to encourage the idea that repentance was something which one went through once and would never go through again. Prayers of repentance after baptism hardly made sense to those who stressed the conversion experience. For those who had had the real experience of conversion, sin had already been left behind.

The Reformers of Zurich, Jud and Zwingli, were, like their colleagues elsewhere, very much concerned to find their way out of the very legalistic discipline of penance as they experienced it in their day. The Zurich revisions of the Great Flood Prayer give evidence of their attempts to reconsider the relation of baptism and repentance. For example, in 1525 Zwingli drops any reference to a distinction between original and actual sin. It is replaced by two images, the image of Christians daily bearing the cross of Christ, and the Pauline image of burial with Christ in baptism.

> . . . that he be made one body with your Son and be buried with him also raised up to a new life, and joyfully bear the cross in daily discipleship, grant to him true faith, firm hope and fervent love, that in the end, according to your will and unwavering in strength, he leave this life, which indeed is no better than death, in accordance with your will, and on that last day appear before the judgment seat of your Son without fear.

We leave aside the question whether Zwingli believed in original sin.[33] The point is much more that Zwingli had clear insight into the fact that baptism

---

Concordia Publishing House, 1962), pp. 291-300. On the relation of baptism to repentance see particularly p. 299.

33. Zwingli's writing on the subject of original sin, *De peccato originali declaratio ad Urbanum Rhegium,* tells us that indeed one needs to make a distinction between sinful acts and the human sickness *(contagio)* which produces these sins. Cf. Rudolf Pfister, *Das Problem der Erbsunde bei Zwingli,* eds. Oskar Farner and Leonhard von Muralt, vol. 9 (Leipzig: Verlag von M. Heinsius Nachfolger, 1939); Christof Gestrich, *Zwingli als Theologe, Glaube und Geist beim Zürcher Reformator* (Zurich: Zwingli Verlag, 1967), pp. 161ff.; and G. R. Potter, *Zwingli* (Cambridge: University Press, 1976), p. 186.

had to do with full and complete forgiveness of all sin. From this prayer it is clear that the Zurich Reformers understood that it was in baptism that a child is joined to the people of God which is moving from death to life, from a sinful life to a new life.

In the same way the Strasbourg Reformers are concerned to overcome the breach which had developed between the sacraments of baptism and penance. They were indeed concerned to show baptism to be the sign of the washing away of sin.[34]

Bucer's first Baptismal Invocation is not so much concerned with the forgiveness of sin as it is with the gift of faith, the inner renewal and spiritual rebirth which comes about through the indwelling of the Holy Spirit. He is concerned with the fruit of baptism which is promised in the outward sign of baptism. Through the work of the Holy Spirit the Christian bears this fruit. Nevertheless the outward baptismal washing is a sign of the purifying of the Christian through the whole of life. It is a prophetic sign. It proclaims the forgiveness of sin.[35]

In Calvin's Baptismal Invocation we find the same concern expressed. Baptism is the sign which God gives to us of the forgiveness both of original sin and actual sins.[36] God is asked to take the child to himself,

> . . . remitting in him that original sin of which the whole lineage of Adam is guilty . . . that always he receive from you the remission of his sins. . . . Hear us, Father of mercy; to the end that the baptism which we administer according to your command might produce its fruit and its virtue as it is declared to us by the Gospel. . . .[37]

All these prayers have a common theme. Baptism stands at the beginning of Christian life as the visible Word of God, the promise of the gospel, that in Christ all sins have been washed away, are being washed away, and will be washed away. Baptism is the sealing of the divine promise on which are grounded all the prayers for growth in grace which every Christian pours out in the course of his or her pilgrimage. The waters of baptism flow from the beginning of the Christian life all the way to paradise.

34. *BDS* 1, pp. 254ff.

35. On Bucer's understanding of this relation of baptism and repentance see Usteri, "Die Stellung," pp. 456-525.

36. On Calvin's theology of repentance see *Institutes* 3.4.1-37 and *Institutes* 4.19.14-17. Calvin makes himself particularly clear with the striking play on words that baptism is the sacrament of penance. *Institutes* 4.19.17. Cf. further Ronald S. Wallace, *Calvin's Doctrine of the Christian Life* (Grand Rapids: William B. Eerdmans, 1959), pp. 94ff., and H. Strathman, "Die Entstehung der Lehre Calvins von der Busse," *Calvin Studien* (Leipzig, 1909).

37. For the original see above, n. 20.

CHAPTER X

The Washing and the Word

It is to the core of the baptismal rite that we now turn our attention. Two parts make up this core, washing with water and the repetition of the words of Jesus. Even in New Testament times baptism was understood to be "washing of water with the word" (Eph. 5:26).[1] In this chapter we will look at how the earliest Reformed Churches actually celebrated this central core of the rite. Particularly we will look at the rubrics of the early Reformed baptismal rites to see how the washing was actually done. Why did the Reformers finally settle on sprinkling rather than immersion? We will look at the precise words which accompanied the washing. Going further, we will ask what the Reformers understood the sign itself to be, and how they worked out some of the secondary liturgical questions in the light of this.

That there was an essential core to the rite was agreed on by the High Rhenish Reformers from the outset. Capito repeated the axiom that the essential thing in baptism is that it be with water and in the name of the Father and of the Son and of the Holy Spirit.

> To baptism belongs only water and these words, "I baptize you in the name of the Father and of the Son, etc." All the rest is supplementary which long ago was brought in as decoration of baptism. We (here at Strasbourg) leave aside the chrism and the oil whenever those coming to us will allow us. For such things get too much attention . . . and tend to obscure the grace of baptism.[2]

1. T. K. Abbott calls attention to the fact that the Greek commentators understand the phrase to mean the baptismal washing and formula. After discussing the various arguments against this interpretation, he decides in its favor, "Surely baptism could not fail to be suggested by these words to the original readers." *Epistles to the Ephesians and to the Colossians* (Edinburgh: T. & T. Clark, 1979), p. 169.

2. Capito, *Was man halten soll,* fol. B iiij r. The German text is found in Chap. III, n. 5.

The point of the liturgical reform, then, was to make clear the basic, divinely given sign of washing with water and the Word. This was not so much a fresh assessment of the words of Jesus at the end of the Gospel of Matthew as it was the repeating of a common Scholastic maxim.

The Rubrics

The manner in which the actual baptism took place is supposed to be found in the rubrics. Unfortunately for the liturgical historian the virtue of rubrics is brevity. The rubrics of a liturgical text do not always tell the liturgical historian what he or she would like to know. The rubrics of a given text could easily have been quite sufficient for the community which used the rite in question. For that community many things could be assumed. The force of local custom was so strong that it was not necessary to explain. For example, today no one would think of adding a rubric to an American Methodist, Baptist, or Presbyterian service book that the whole of the service was to be conducted in the common tongue. Such a rubric would be quite superfluous. It was another matter in 1533, when William Farel published the *French Evangelical Service Book.* In that document it was quite appropriate to specify that the rite was to be in the common tongue. We might wish that some of these rubrics in the documents before us were more detailed, but we will simply have to read them as best we can. This we will do while making allowances for the principle that what would be obvious to the intended celebrant would not have to be written in the rubrics.

We will start with the Zurich German baptismal rite published by Leo Jud in 1523. There the rubrics regarding the actual baptism are as follows:

> Therefore name the child, *then the priest takes the child and dips him in the water saying:* N. I baptize you in the name of the Father, of the Son and of the Holy Spirit.[3]

To put this in perspective we should compare it both to Luther's rite and to the ritual of the Diocese of Constance. Luther's German Baptismal Rite of 1523 directs the following:

> *Then he takes the child and dips him in the baptism and says:* And I baptize you in the name of the Father, and of the Son and of the Holy Spirit.[4]

3. "So nemmend das kind. *Denn so nem der priester das kind und duncke es in das wasser, sprechende:* N., ich touff dich in dem namen des vatters, des suns und des heyligen geists." *CR* 91, p. 713.

4. "*Da neme er das kind und tauche es ynn die tauffe, und sprech:* Und ich teuffe dich ym namen des vatters und des sons und des hyeligen geysts." *WA* 12, p. 45.

While the differences are considerable, one thing is the same in both rites — immersion is very specifically indicated. Otherwise we notice that Jud's rite repeats the name of the child in the course of reciting the baptismal formula while Luther's rite does not. When we compare the rite of Leo Jud to that of the Diocese of Constance, we find still other differences. The rite of Constance reads as follows:

> *Then the priest with his hand touches the baptismal font. And three times pours water on the head of the child in such a manner that the water touches the head and the shoulders. . . .* Name the child. I baptize you: In the name of the Father; *and he pours with his hand in the manner we have just mentioned.* And of the Son; *he pours a second time.* And of the Holy Spirit; *he pours a third time.*[5]

The rite of Constance specifies trine pouring. The priest asks the name of the child, but it is not clear that the name of the child is repeated by the priest in pronouncing the formula.

In Zwingli's rite of 1525, we find no rubric at all on whether the baptism is to be by a single immersion or by trine pouring:

> N. I baptize you into the name of the Father, of the Son and of the Holy Spirit.[6]

The most noteworthy feature of this text is the grammatical change in the formula from "in the name" to "into the name." The name of the child is repeated by the celebrant. Nothing is said about immersion, pouring, or sprinkling.[7] Bullinger's version of the baptismal rite of Zurich in 1532 gives the following rubric:

> If then it is your desire that this child be baptized in the baptism of our Lord Jesus Christ, then name the child. *Here the minister takes the child and*

5. "*Tunc sacerdos manu sua fontem attingat baptismatis. Et trina vice fundat super caput pueri: Ita tamen quod aqua tangat caput et scapulas* . . . nemet das kind. Ego te baptizo: In nomine patris *Et fundat manu semel secundum modum predictum.* Et filij *Fundat secundo.* Et spiritussancti *Fundat tercio." Obsequiale constantiensis,* pp. 12ff.

6. "N. Ich touff dich in den namen des vatters und des suns und des heiligen geistes." *CR* 91, p. 336. Possibly the Zurich Reformers had reverted to trine pouring. See the critical notes to the text of *Ordnung der christlichen Kirche zu Zurich.* The critical apparatus tells us that B has the rubric, *"Daruff der diener dem kind dry malen das wasser angusst und spricht," CR* 91, p. 682.

7. According to Schmidt-Clausing's footnote, immersion was the practice in much of Germany at the time. *Zwingli als Liturgiker,* p. 163. As we shall see, immersion was close to disappearlng in Germany by 1523. In a later book Schmidt-Clausing claims that Luther, followed by Jud and Zwingli, tried to reintroduce immersion because of the classical meaning of the Greek word. *Zwingli's Formulare,* n. 66, p. 83.

pours water upon him and says: N. I baptize you in the name of the Father, the Son and the Holy Spirit.[8]

Here a single pouring is apparently intended.

In Strasbourg we find a very different development. The *Agenda Argentinensis* of 1513 reads as follows:

Then the priest either washes with water or immerses the infant with a simultaneous invocation of the Holy Trinity, saying, N. I baptize you in the name of the Father and of the Son and of the Holy Spirit. Amen.[9]

This rubric gives an option of either pouring or immersion; nothing is said about how many times it is to be done. The *Strasbourg German Baptismal Rite* of 1524 has opted for trine pouring:

Then the priest takes the child and pours water over the child three times in the form of a cross, and says, I baptize you in the name of the Father and of the Son and of the Holy Spirit.[10]

The *Strasbourg Church Order of 1525* (D) has the following rubrics and formula:

Name the child, *answer,* N. *The minister says while pouring out water:* I baptize you in the name of the Father, and of the Son and of the Holy Spirit. Amen.[11]

While trine pouring is not specifically indicated, we can assume that it was nevertheless the practice. It is not specifically said that the minister repeats the name of the child, but again it is probably the case that he did repeat it. In the immediately following editions of the *Strasbourg Psalter* (F and G) it is indicated that the child's name is included in the formula. The final form found in the *Strasbourg Psalter of 1539* (K) makes everything quite explicit.

8. "Wöllend ir nun, dass das kind getouft werde in den touf unsers Herrn Jesu Christi, so nemend das kind. Hie nimpt der diener das kind und übergüsst es mit dem wasser und spricht: N., ich touf dich in dem namen des Vaters, Sons und heyligen geystes." The text is taken from the edition prepared by Leo Weisz, "Heinrich Bullingers Agenda," *Zwingliana* 10 (1954): 17.

9. "Tunc sacerdos vel abluat cum aqua vel immergat infantum simul cum invocatione sanctae trinitatis dicendo . . . amen." Hubert, *Ordnungen,* pp. 35ff.

10. "*Da nem der priester das kind, vnd gyess dreymal creutzweyss wasser über das kind vnd sprech:* N., ich tauff dich in dem namen vaters vnd suns vnd heyligen geists." Hubert, *Ordnungen,* pp. 35ff.

11. "Nennen das kindt! *Antwort:* N. *Spricht der diener mitt vffgiessung des wassers:* Ich tauff dich ym namen des vatters vnd des suns vnd des heyligen geists, amen." Hubert, *Ordnungen,* p. 43.

> *After this the minister, in proper order, requests the child be given to him; he takes him in his hand and removes his cap as he asks what the child is to be called and calls the child by name; he pours water over him three times and says:* N., I baptize you in the name of the Father, and of the Son and of the Holy Spirit. Amen.[12]

We are inclined to think that the actual practice of the Church of Strasbourg remained much the same from 1513 to the Interim in spite of the fact that the rubrics differ considerably. Trine pouring, for example, we believe to have been the continual practice in Strasbourg. We can in the same way assume that it was the continual practice to repeat the name of the child in the course of reciting the formula even if it is not specifically mentioned in the *Strasbourg German Church Service* (D).

The *Basel Service Book* of 1526 has no rubric at all, only the baptismal formula:

> N., I baptize you in the name of the Father, and of the Son, and of the Holy Spirit.[13]

Nevertheless it is clear that the name of the child is repeated in the saying of the formula. The baptismal rite of Bern tells us little more:

> *After this the minister takes the child in his hand and says,* Do you wish the child to be baptized? *They answer,* Yes. *Then name the child.* N. *Then the minister says,* I baptize you in the name of the Father, of the Son, and of the Holy Spirit.[14]

Here again we have no hint as to the method of the baptismal washing.

Finally, let us look at the rite of Geneva. Farel's *French Evangelical Service Book* of 1533 tells us that after the minister asks the name of the child he says, "I baptize you in the name of the Father, and of the Son, and of the Holy Spirit. Amen." This is followed by the rubric, "then he puts water on the head of the child with his hand." The water, it is noted, is to be "pure

12. "*Vff dises begeret der diener, imm das kindlin nach ordnung darzugeben; das nimmet er dann inn seine hend, entplosset es vnd, als er gefraget, wie es heissen solle, nennet er es mit seinen nammen, begeusset es dreystet mit wasser vnd sagt:* N., ich teuffe dich imm namen des vatters vnd des suns vnd des heiligen geists, amen." Hubert, *Ordnungen,* p. 51.

13. "N. Ich Tauff dich in dem namen des vatters, vnd des suns, vnd des heiligen geysts." *Form vnd Gstalt,* fol. A vi r.

14. "Demnach nimpt der diener das kind in sin hand, vnd spricht: Wellend jr dass das kind getouft werde? Sy sprechend: Ja. So nennend es. N. Als dann spricht der Diener: Ich touffen dich in den nammen des Vatters, des Suns, vnd des Heyligen geysts." A. Fluri, *Das Berner Taufbüchlein von 1528* (Bern: E. Baumgart, 1904), p. 18.

and plain, without salt or oil."[15] The *Genevan Psalter* of 1542 gives us the following:

> *The name is given to the child while the minister baptizes him.* In the name of the Father, and of the Son, and of the Holy Spirit. *The whole thing is to be said in a loud voice and in the common language. . . .*[16]

Several things can be deduced from this. Sprinkling was used in Geneva from the beginning. This was the practice in French-speaking lands at the time of the Reformation, and it had been the practice since the High Middle Ages. It is specified that the water is "pure et nette," which meant that it was not to be consecrated.[17] The consecration involved putting oil and sometimes salt into it. A baptismal shell was not to be used, but rather the hand alone. Nothing is said about trine baptism.

Having examined the rubrics and the formula used in the earliest Reformed baptismal rites, let us now turn to a systematic examination of the different features.

The Formula

The baptismal formula itself comes first into consideration. While the Scholastic tradition had given great weight to the exact recitation of the baptismal formula there existed at the eve of the Reformation considerable diversity in the manner in which it was recited. The variations we have just noticed in the formulas used in various Reformed Churches reflect the local variations of the different diocesan ritual books of the late Middle Ages.[18] The diversity touches several minor points, such as the fact that some rites such as the rite of Bamberg begin the formula with the conjunction, "Et ego te baptiso. . . ." Certain rites conclude the formula with an "amen." Of the Reformed liturgies only those of Strasbourg specify the use of an "amen."

15. Le servitur: Nommez le. N. Je te baptise au nom du pere, et du filz et du sainct esprit. Amen. *Puis luy auoir mis sur la teste avec la main deaue pure et nette, sans sel ne nuyle, ne crachatz. . . . La Manière et Fasson,* ed. Baum, p. 25. The critical apparatus in the *Opera selecta* indicates that Farel's text was simply "Au Nom du Pere, et du Filz, et du sainct Esprit." *OS* 2, p. 38.

16. ". . . *on impose le nom à l'enfant: et lors le Ministre le baptise.* Au Nom du Pere, et du Filz, et du sainct Esprit." *Le tout se dit à hault voix, en language vulgaire. . . ." OS* 2, pp. 37ff. Cf. the photolithographic facsimile edition of *La Forme de Prières* (Cassel and Basel: Pierre Pidoux [Edition Barenreiter], 1959).

17. "En apres le ministre le baptizera luy mettant de l'eaue pure et nette sur la teste. *OS* 2, p. 37.

18. Spital, *Der Taufritus,* p. 116.

There is considerable variation as to whether the name of the child is to be included in the formula. The 1510 edition of the rite of Constance does not specify that the child is to be addressed by name, although the priest asks the name of the child immediately before pronouncing the formula. This may surely be taken to imply that the name was then spoken by the celebrant in the course of reciting the formula. The whole point of asking the name of the child is that the priest may be sure of having the right name. Any minister who has been faced with baptizing half a dozen children at one time can appreciate immediately why the priest made a ceremony of asking the name. What parent would forgive a last-minute lapse of memory which called little John "Jonathan," or George "Gregory." If the child is not addressed by name in the course of repeating the formula, then there is no need to ask the child's name. Some of the liturgical books neither ask the name of the child at this point nor indicate that the child is addressed by name when the formula is repeated. This is the case with Luther's *Taufbüchlein.* In such cases it may well be that the name of the child was not used in the formula. The Reformed rites of Strasbourg first ask the name of the child and then specify the use of the child's name in the formula. In this they are following the *Agenda Argentinensis* of 1513. In Basel the name is used in the formula, although, as we have seen, there is no rubric directing the minister to ask the child's name. Perhaps the celebrant asked the name even if there was no rubric directing him to do so. As for the rite of Zurich, we find that the name of the child is included in the reciting of the formula. This is the case in the editions of Jud, Zwingli, and Bullinger. Here the Reformers are undoubtedly following the practice of the Latin rite of Constance even if this is not expressly stated in the text of the Latin rite. In Geneva we again have the requesting of the name, although its use in the formula is not indicated.[19] In the *Genevan Psalter* of 1542, the rubric "on impose le nom a l'enfant" is given. We take this to mean that the minister pronounces the child's name, although perhaps this indefinite pronoun refers to the parents or godparents.[20]

Calvin understood that at baptism Christians gave names to their children. This is implied in the phrase "on impose le nom a l'enfant." The idea that with this pronouncing of the child's name the child actually is given his or her name is certainly implied by the Genevan rite.[21] This idea might be

19. According to Fisher, *Christian Initiation* pp. 150-51, the taking of the name into the baptismal formula first appears in the Gallican rites before the time of Charlemagne. Is this another French custom?

20. The two phrases "nommez le" and "on impose le nom" make clear that the intention is to give the child his name. It is also clear that the giving of names is considered part of baptism from the Genevan *Ordonnances ecclesiastiques, OS* 2, pp. 343ff.

21. On the history of giving names at baptism see Jules Corblet, *Histoire dogmatique,*

gathered from both Zurich and Strasbourg as well, but it is by no means as clear.[22] The idea would come naturally to the Reformers as they began to work out the relation of baptism to circumcision. In Genesis 17, Abram is given the name Abraham at the time of his circumcision. It is in connection with their circumcision that both John the Baptist and Jesus are given their names (Luke 1:59 and 2:21). As the Reformers saw it, giving the child his or her name was surely one of those ancient Christian customs which was quite clearly according to Scripture. For Calvin, it was not only a matter of giving a name to a child at baptism, but also a matter of giving a Christian name to the child.[23] The choosing of a name had religious significance. Certain names were appropriate and certain names were not appropriate. This concern to give an appropriate Christian name at baptism has had a lasting effect on Reformed Protestantism. In France, even today, there is a marked difference between the names of Protestants and Catholics. In the same way the Puritans of New England were inclined to choose biblical names for their children. This concern can quite legitimately be traced back to Geneva.

Zwingli introduced a variation into the baptismal formula which is of considerable theological interest. Student of the Christian Humanists that he was, Zwingli pointed to the fact that what the Greek text of the Gospel of Matthew actually said was "baptizing them *into* the name" rather than "baptizing them *in* the name." Zwingli treats this in his first work against the Anabaptists in order to emphasize that baptism is initiation into the Church.

---

liturgique et archeologique du sacrement du baptême, vol. 2 (Paris: Société générale de librairie catholique, 1881-82), pp. 223-96. *DACL* 2, pp. 1518ff. and 7, pp. 635- 37. Eusebius, *Ecclesiastical History* 7.14.

22. Henry Bullinger, *The Decades of Henry Bullinger,* ed. Thomas Harding, Parker Society edition, Part 5 (Cambridge: The University Press, 1968), p. 7. To be abbreviated *Decades* 5.

23. The *Corpus Reformatorum* contains a proposal drawn up by Calvin on the subject of appropriate and inappropriate names given children at baptism. For example, the names Claude, Suaire, and Mama should not be given because of their connection with idolatry. The names of the three kings Caspar, Balthazar, and Melchior are to he avoided because they are legendary and connected with superstition. The names of offices Baptiste, Evangeliste, or Ange (Angel) are proscribed because they belong only to those whom God has called to these offices or ministries. Likewise, names which are titles of our Lord — for example, Emanuel or Jesus — are inappropriate. Calvin thought it inappropriate to name children for the feast days on which they had been born. Children should not be named Noel, Typhaine (Epiphany), Pasques, Pentecoste, Toussainctz, or Dimenche. Furthermore, Calvin tells us, corrupted forms of Christian names should not be used, for example, Tyvan or Tevenot in place of Estienne or Monet in place of Simon. The giving of Old Testament names became popular in Geneva at the time of Calvin's pastorate. *Corpus Reformatorum, Calvini opera* 10, p. 49.

The baptismal rite which comes at the end of his work *Of Baptism* actually revises the text of the formula to translate the Greek more precisely. The question is still discussed today.[24] Is the point of the text of Matthew 28:17 that the one baptized is put into Christ, or is it that the apostles are to go out into all the world and baptize as the agents or ministers of Christ? Zwingli has taken the former alternative. Interestingly enough, the manner in which the Genevan rite is printed emphasizes just the opposite understanding of the text. "The name is given to the child while the minister baptizes him, 'In the name of the Father, and of the Son, and of the Holy Spirit.' " This apparently means that the minister actually said, "John, I baptize you in the name of the Father, and of the Son, and of the Holy Spirit." What is clear, however, is that in Geneva baptism was regarded as an act of God performed by a servant of God, acting in God's name.

Another question brought up by Zwingli in his *Of Baptism* is whether the words of Jesus by which he sends out his disciples are properly understood as a formula. Here Zwingli is struggling with the thought forms of Scholasticism.

> I do not mean that when we give baptism we are not to baptize "in the name of the Father, the Son and the Holy Ghost." But we must speak the truth, and the truth is that when he uttered these words Christ was not instituting the form of baptism, as the theologians maintain. . . . The disciples did not use this form, but baptized in the name of Jesus (Acts 10 and 19). This has so confounded the theologians that they do not know where to turn to avoid the force of it. . . . Christ does not say: when you baptize pronounce these three names. And that was not what he intended. Certainly I commend them, but what we understand by the words, "I baptize thee in the name" is this, I dedicate thee to the name, that is, the power, the majesty, the grace of the Father, the Son and the Holy Ghost . . . and does that not mean that water-baptism is an initiatory sign dedicating and pledging us to God.[25]

Here Zwingli is addressing the Scholastic discussion of sacramental theology which tried to explain the sacraments in terms of form and matter. The form of the sacrament was understood to be the so-called baptismal formula. From a Scholastic point of view, if these words were to be regarded as the form of the sacrament, their exact repetition was essential.[26] Zwingli, however, was

24. Ernst Lohmeyer, *Das Evangelium des Matthaus,* ed. Werner Schmauch, 3rd edn. (Göttingen: Vandenhoeck und Ruprecht, 1962), p. 400. Cf. bibliography in the footnote. Alfred Plummer, *An Exegetical Commentary on the Gospel according to S. Matthew* (Grand Rapids, Mich.: Eerdmans, 1957), pp. 433ff. H. Bietenhard, *TWNT* 5: 274ff.

25. *LCC* 24, pp. 144-45.

26. On the question of form and matter in the sacraments see Bernard Leeming,

trying to understand baptism from the point of view of its being a covenant sign. He was trying to understand baptism not from Platonic or Aristotelian thought forms, but rather from the Hebrew thought forms of both the Old and New Testaments.

For Bucer the naming of the child and the baptismal formula are closely connected because he understands the baptismal formula to be an invocation of the divine name. The aspects of the initiation and adoption are closely connected as he explains that through this invocation we are made fellow members of the household of God, that we are given the family name of the people of God. By baptism the promise is given to us

> . . . now we are among the members of the household of God. That is what is meant by being baptized into the name of Christ, or rather of the Father, and of the Son, and of the Holy Spirit. What else does this mean other than that we be consecrated to God, that his name be invoked above us, that we also bear the family name of the sons of God, and so indeed we are.[27]

Once again we see the epicletic aspect of the sacrament of baptism being emphasized by Bucer. Once again it seems that Bucer moves from the traditionally Western emphasis on the reciting of the Word of baptism to the Eastern emphasis on calling on the name of the Lord. It is because of this insight that Bucer was so fond of the text from Acts 22:16, "Rise and be baptized, and wash away your sins, calling on his name." For Bucer, of course, there was never any doubt but that the words from the end of the Gospel of Matthew were to be used. It is just that he understood them not as a formula but as an invocation.[28]

For Calvin the matter takes an entirely different turn. Calvin follows the typically Western approach that when the word is added to the element it becomes a sacrament, but he seeks a wider understanding of "word" than the Scholastic theologians, who understood it simply as the baptismal formula. Calvin has come to this insight through his study of St. Augustine, as the following quotation shows:

Principles of Sacramental Theology (London, New York, and Toronto: Longmans, Green and Company, 1956), pp. 403-7. Leeming quotes, p. 406, a passage from Thomas indicating that changes in the words of the form which leave the meaning intact, leave the sacrament intact.

27. ". . . deum jam nos inter suos habiturum. Id eum sibi vult, quod baptizamur in nomen Christi, vel patris, et filij, et spiritus sancti. Hoc siquidem quid sit aliud? quod nos consecrari Deo, ut eius super nos nomen invocetur, ut Dei filij cognominemur, et simus?" *Quid de baptismato,* fol. A vii r-v. See also fol. D v; also *Bericht,* fol. F iii r-f, iv r.

28. On the similar position of Bullinger see *Decades* 5, p. 7.

> For we ought to understand the word not as one whispered without meaning and without faith, a mere noise like a magical incantation, which has the force to consecrate the element. Rather it should, when preached, make us understand what the visible sign means. . . .
>
> Far different is the teaching of Augustine concerning the sacramental word: "Let the word be added to the element and it will become a sacrament, from whence comes this great power of water, that in touching the body it should cleanse the heart, unless the word makes it? Not because it is said but because it is believed. In the word itself the fleeting sound is one thing; the power remaining, another. . . ."
>
> You see how the sacrament requires preaching to beget faith. And we need not labor to prove this when it is perfectly clear what Christ did, what he commanded us to do, what the apostles followed, and what the purer Church observed.[29]

It is for this reason that the Reformed Church has always had either a sermon on baptism before celebrating baptism, or else an exhortation explaining the promises of the New Covenant in the course of the rite. This Calvin believed to be the practice of the ancient and purer Church, as he puts it. For him it was one of the essential reforms of the baptismal rite. The baptismal formula itself was a sort of quintessence of the promises of the New Covenant, particularly when read to the end, ". . . and lo I am with you always." It became more and more the case that such texts, setting forth the baptismal promises, were drawn into the Reformed baptismal rites. In the course of time it became the usual practice in Reformed baptismal rites to read the "Words of Institution," that is, the whole passage of Matthew 28:18-20, in the baptismal service itself. Another text which might be used is Acts 2:38-39:

> Repent, and be baptized every one of you in the name of Jesus Christ for the forgiveness of your sins; and you shall receive the gift of the Holy Spirit. For the promise is to you and to your children and to all that are far off.

Because this text is so explicit about the baptismal promise, it is particularly appropriate to be read or expounded in connection with the baptismal rite.

For Calvin this in no wise compromised the use of the baptismal formula as part of the rite, for as we have said, Calvin regarded these words as having all these promises in concentrated form. Calvin interprets quite differently from Zwingli the passages of Acts which tell that the apostles baptized "in the name of Jesus." In his sermon at Pentecost, Peter tells the people to be baptized in the name of Jesus Christ (Acts 2:38) and again directs that Cornelius and his

29. *LCC* 12, p. 1279, *Institutes* 4.11-12.4.

family are to be baptized in the name of Jesus Christ (Acts 10:48). Calvin understands that even in these instances the apostles did in fact baptize with the so-called Trinitarian formula just as Jesus had commanded them.[30] It was understandable, as Calvin saw it, that they mention only baptizing in the name of Jesus, because all the benefits of baptism are to be had in Christ. "Yet this cannot take place unless he who baptizes in Christ invokes also the names of the Father and the Spirit."[31]

Taken all together the Reformers had a very full and many-faceted understanding of the use of the baptismal formula.

The Water of Baptism

When the *Genevan Psalter* of 1542 specifies that the water is to be "pure and simple," the obvious implication is that it is not to be consecrated water. Traditionally the water used at baptism was consecrated by the bishop once a year at the Easter Vigil. This tradition caused no practical problems back in the fourth century when most baptisms were performed at the annual Easter Vigil. As time went on problems began to arise. For example, what happened to the rite of the consecration of the font when a child in Zurich was to be baptized in November? For the bishop of a large diocese like Constance to consecrate enough water for a year's worth of baptisms over a good part of what is today Southern Germany and Northern Switzerland must have been a practical problem of some magnitude. This venerable tradition struggled under the weight of several casuistic arrangements which in the early sixteenth century, we can well imagine, seemed more than ridiculous. Most of the High Rhenish bishops of the time had one or more suffragan bishops, or, as they were popularly called, *Weihbishöfe,* who traveled around the country consecrating whatever needed to be consecrated. In practice, however, another solution was more popular. Normally, the ritual books of the day contained the text of an exorcism with which the parish priest might exorcise water for use in baptism if no properly consecrated water were available.[32]

It is easy to understand that many of the Reformers were contemptuous of the consecration of the baptismal waters. More than one of the Reformers called it *"gezaubertes wasser,"* bewitched water. It appeared to be among the

30. Cf. Calvin's commentary on Acts 2:38.

31. *LCC* 21, p. 1308; *Institutes* 4.15.6.

32. *Obsequiale constantiensis,* pp. 4ff., gives an exorcism followed by a short collect. Other aspects of the consecration of the font have been treated in Chap. I.

most magical elements of popular religion. It was among those rites which beclouded the true nature of the sacrament, as Wolfgang Capito put it.[33] The simple, pure water which God by his Word had appointed to be a sign was the best possible sign. The consecration of the water only confused the basic sign. For Capito, pouring oil into the water, dipping the paschal candle into it, and tracing crosses over it only detracted from the basic sign. A few months later Bucer makes much the same point in his *Grund und Ursach;* the use of exorcised salt, the rites of anointing with oil and chrism, and the use of consecrated water tended to hide the basic sign of baptism.[34] The introduction to the baptismal rite in the *Strasbourg Psalter of 1526* (F) starts out by saying, "Oil, chrism, and bewitched water are no longer used in the celebration of baptism"; however, by 1530 the word "bewitched" had been changed to the less polemic "blessed."[35] Perhaps the reason for this change is that certain Anabaptists had argued that baptism by "bewitched" water was invalid. Oecolampadius found himself faced with this argument, and he gave as his response that the important thing is that the baptism which had been administered before the beginning of the Reformation was in the name of Christ, and that was sufficient.[36] The Reformers had no intention of denying the validity of baptisms performed by their pre-Reformation predecessors. Oecolampadius was well enough aware that the Scholastic theologians had not in fact taught that the consecrated water contained grace, or that there was any sort of transubstantiation of the water.[37] In arguing against consecration of the water, the Reformers were arguing against folk religion, not Scholasticism.[38] Calvin, while he had no intention of denying the validity of the baptisms performed with the old rites, finds in the rite of the consecration of the baptismal waters a most irreverent practice. "For as though to be baptized with water according to Christ's precept were a contemptible thing, a benediction, or rather incantation, was devised to defile the true consecration of water. Afterward, a candle was added, with the chrism. . . . How much better it would be to omit from baptism all theatrical pomp, which dazzles the eyes of the simple and deadens their minds. . . ."[39] For Calvin the consecration of the font was one of those ceremo-

33. *Was man halten, und antworten soll.* . . . B iiij r.

34. Bucer, *BDS* 1, p. 254.

35. "Das öl, chrisam vnd das verzaubert wasser geprauchen sye nit mer zum tauff." Hubert, *Ordnungen,* p. 37.

36. Oecolampadius, *Wiederichtung . . . auf Carlin,* fol. c iiij r.

37. *Ibid.,* fol. D i v.

38. Hughes Oliphant Old, "Bullinger and the Scholastic Works on Baptism," *Heinrich Bullinger, 1504-1575,* ed. Ulrich Gäbler, vol. 1 (Zurich: Theologischer Verlag, 1975), pp. 191-207. Vol. 1, pp. 196ff.

39. *Institutes* 4.15.19.

nies which obscured the central meaning of the sacrament. Calvin would no doubt have very much agreed with the patristic maxim that the baptism of Jesus in the Jordan, by which he instituted baptism as a sacrament, and by which he demonstrated that water was to be used for baptism, consecrated all water for baptism.[40]

But if the secondary symbols and rites obscured the primary rites and signs, what then was the true sign found in baptism? Two things are involved here, first the water itself, and second, what is done with it.

The pre-Reformation tradition had put considerable emphasis on the relation between the water of baptism and the waters of creation as well as the relation to the prenatal waters of the womb. The baptismal font was commonly called the womb of the Church. This was given special emphasis in the old Latin prayer for the consecration of the font which speaks of the waters of creation in Genesis and how the Spirit of God moved upon the waters. The prayer even remembered the four rivers of Paradise. The ceremonial which accompanied the rite went so far as to plunge the paschal candle into the font in order that the font might be impregnated. To contemporary sensitivities this may be more laughable than venerable. To the Reformers it was objectionable because it went so far afield from what Scripture specifically teaches about baptism. To be sure, many of these ideas have sound roots even if they have branched out into some rather lush and exotic foliage. It is because of the role water plays in the first creation that the waters of baptism speak of the second creation. It is from such a passage as John 3:5, "unless one is born of water and the Spirit, he cannot enter the kingdom of God," that the connection between birth and water arises. The same connection between water and birth is also found in Paul's phrase "the bath of regeneration" (Titus 3:5). The Reformers, however, are extremely chaste in working out such an image. They simply say that water is a sign of regeneration. They do not elaborate the image further.[41]

While the Reformers spoke of water as a sign of regeneration, they spoke more frequently of water as a sign of purification. Farel and later the *Genevan Psalter* make the point that baptism should be administered with pure water.[42]

40. Cf. the explanation of this tradition in Georg Kretschmar, *Leiturgia* 5, p. 92. Among the many patristic passages which allude to this tradition are the following: Tertullian, *Adversus Judaeos* 8; Clement of Alexandria, *Eclogae propheticae* 7:1; and Cyril of Jerusalem, *Mystagogical Catechism* 3. Further, see Burkhard Neunheuser, *Baptism and Confirmation,* pp. 143, 152, 157, 160, 165, 180.

41. Cf. Calvin's *Commentary on the Gospel of John* (John 3:5) and Henry Bullinger's *Decades* 5, sermon 7, pp. 306-7.

42. *OS* 2, pp. 37-38.

One can certainly understand why they thought that the purity of the water contributed to the sign. Texts such as Ezekiel 36:25, "I will sprinkle clean water upon you, and you shall be clean," and Hebrews 10:22, which speaks of our bodies being "washed with pure water," would encourage the Reformers to make a point of the purity of the water. In regard to Calvin one has to admit, however, that relatively little is made of the significance of water as a nature symbol. Henry Bullinger, who was as sensitive to the Scholastic discussion concerning *materia sacramenti* as any of the Reformers, tells us quite simply that water is used in baptism because we humans use water for cleansing, for washing our bodies and renewing ourselves.[43] The nature symbolism found in water is not ignored by the Reformers, but it is certainly not primary. Much more important to the Reformers is the meaning given to the water of baptism by Scripture. The Reformers were, of course, aware that this was a particularly biblical way of thinking. Both the rites and feasts of ancient Israel had at one time been nature rites and nature festivals. The time came, however, when they were reinterpreted in terms of holy history. Passover had at one time, no doubt, been a lambing festival, but there came a time when it was reinterpreted in terms of the Exodus from Egypt. The nature symbol became secondary, while the reinterpretation made in the light of holy history became primary.

It is Calvin who makes a special point of showing that in Scripture water is a sign of the Holy Spirit. Commenting on the passage from John 3:5, ". . . unless one is born of water and the Spirit, he cannot enter the kingdom of God," he tells us that this does not refer to two kinds of baptism, but rather by the two terms the text is speaking of the same thing. Water is a sign of the Holy Spirit.[44] Calvin goes on to say that Scripture often speaks of the Holy Spirit as both water and fire, but when the Holy Spirit is spoken of as water, then the intention is to emphasize the purifying work of the Holy Spirit. We find the same thing said in Calvin's chapter on the Holy Spirit in the *Institutes* where the Reformer discusses the names of the Holy Spirit. Sometimes he tells us that the Holy Spirit is called water because of his power to cleanse and purify. The Reformer cites the text from Ezekiel 36:25, "I will sprinkle clean water upon you and you shall be clean. . . . A new heart I will give you, and a new spirit I will put within you."[45]

The water of baptism has been given other meanings by Holy Scripture. The Reformers explored at some depth the meaning of water as it is defined by biblical typology. Again in the *Decades* Bullinger tells us that Jesus told

43. *Decades* 5, sermon 7, p. 329.
44. Cf. Calvin's *Commentary on the Gospel of John* (John 3:5).
45. *Institutes* 3.1.3.

his disciples to use water in baptism for a number of reasons. There had been many types and figures which had gone before baptism in water, such as the Flood, the Red Sea through which the children of Israel passed, and the ablutions and washings mentioned in the Old Testament law. In fact, for Bullinger it was a principle of sacramental theology that the New Testament sacraments summed up a whole host of Old Testament sacraments and signs. The apostles, Bullinger tells us, were aware that these things were types of baptism.[46] It is the common element of water which unites baptism to the type of Noah and the Great Flood. The sacramental action of baptism is in no way prefigured by the Great Flood. Those who got wet were drowned in the Flood. The text of 1 Peter 3:20 actually says that Noah and his family were saved by water. The same is the case with the crossing of the Red Sea. The children of Israel passed through the sea dry shod. These types, as Bullinger saw it, demonstrate how water can be a sign of both mortification and vivification. Both Noah and his family and the children of Israel were saved by water, and both Pharaoh and his armies and the wicked of Noah's day were drowned by the water. We shall have occasion to speak of this again, but at this point all we want to get across is the way biblical history has given meaning to water.

Now we must turn to the question of what is signified by the sacramental action.

Immersion, Pouring, and Sprinkling

Is baptism to be done by immersion or by some form of sprinkling or pouring?[47] Since this question is of such great interest to several very important groups of American Protestants who have strong roots in the Reformed tradition, we will follow it out in a bit more detail than we might otherwise. We want to make the point that the Reformers considered the matter more fully than one might imagine.

At the threshold of this discussion one thing should be made clear. The Reformers, as the Schoolmen before them, were agreed that immersion, pouring, and sprinkling were all acceptable modes of baptism. Calvin, typical of his colleagues, says that it matters not which form is used as long as the usage

46. *Decades* 5, sermon 8, p. 364.

47. Spital observes that in the fifteenth and early sixteenth centuries one probably thought in terms of two forms of baptism — immersion on the one hand, and some form of pouring or sprinkling on the other — rather than in terms of three forms — immersion, pouring, and sprinkling. *Der Taufritus,* pp. 112ff.

of the local Church is followed.[48] As we have seen, a good number of the early Reformed liturgical books do not specify which is to be used. This may well be the case, at Berne and Basel, for example, because the custom of sprinkling or pouring was already so well established as to be self- evident. We have observed, on the other hand, that in some of the early Reformed rites a very specific usage is indicated. In 1523 Leo Jud's *German Baptismal Book,* following the lead of Luther, specifies immersion. The baptismal rites of Strasbourg direct that water is to be poured over the child three times. The rubrics of Geneva tell us that the minister is to put water on the head of the child with his hand. That we take to mean that Geneva practiced sprinkling. There was then, as we have seen, quite a variety in the mode of baptism in the early Reformed Churches. This is not at all surprising because the Reformers generally regarded the mode of baptism as *adiaphora,* that is, they regarded it as theologically indifferent.

A. Variety of Modes in the Latin Rituals

The variety in the mode of baptism among the Reformers reflects the Latin ritual books of the early sixteenth century.[49] In some of these books only immersion is mentioned, but most of the rituals of the German dioceses allow for either immersion, pouring, or sprinkling.[50] By the time the Reformation began, even if the ritual books allowed for, or even prescribed, immersion, sprinkling was in practice almost universal. Immersion was practiced only in very conservative circles. The rubrics of the Latin ritual books seem to have been written at a time when the transition between immersion and sprinkling was taking place. This does not mean, to be sure, that the rubrics were being composed at the time the rituals were first being printed. The rituals had been taking shape for a couple of centuries. We can not always be sure how old some of these rubrics actually are. The rubrics in question may well go back fairly far into the Middle Ages. As late as 1100, full immersion was used by Otto of Bamberg in converting the Pomeranians. Thomas Aquinas, who lived in the middle of the thirteenth century, reports that sprinkling was widespread, but that immersion was the more usual practice.[51] Surely he was correct for the area south of the Alps. It seems to have been in northern France that sprinkling first became the usual practice.

48. *Institutes* 4.15.19.

49. Spital, *Der Taufritus,* pp. 112ff.

50. The Latin words used are *immersio, infusio, superfusio,* and *aspersio.* Apparently the last three of these terms should be regarded as synonyms. Spital, *Der Taufritus,* p. 112.

51. Thomas Aquinas, *Summa theologica* 3, 66, 7.

Bonaventure indicates that sprinkling was a custom found in French-speaking countries.[52] Johann Ulrich Surgant, writing in Basel in 1502, still calls it a French custom.[53] It must have been more noticeably the method used in France than in Germany in order to elicit Surgant's comment. Besides that, the comment implies that immersion was still fairly common in Germany. On the other hand, in the German-speaking diocese of Constance the 1502 edition of the ritual shows that pouring was already the usual practice in that large and important diocese. When the Reformers began their work, sprinkling was not by any means the self-evident mode of baptism. If sprinkling was the more popular method in the Upper Rhineland, one was aware that it had not always been the practice. One was aware that it was a transition which had only recently taken place.

B. The Transition from Immersion to Sprinkling

The following rubric from the ritual of Constance gives us an interesting insight into the nature of the transition from immersion to sprinkling or pouring.

> As to the question of whether the act of baptising ought to be done by trine immersion, or through pouring water over the person, let it be observed that the Church accepts both practices.
>
> Whether one should be immersed one time or three times does not vary the essence of baptism. The same is true if water is poured three times by the hand of the priest.
>
> It is more important, however, to beware of certain dangers:
>
> First, if the priest is elderly or has shaky hands, if the infant is weak, if it is very cold in winter time, or if it appears that the person has lived to a great age, in such cases it is not suitable that persons be immersed.
>
> Besides this we are able to draw examples from the Holy Apostles, Saint Laurence, Remigius, and others who baptized by sprinkling or pouring the water. Concerning the Apostles, it can be read in the second and third chapters of Acts that five thousand and again three thousand were converted and baptized. Concerning Saint Laurence, we learn that carrying a pitcher of water he baptized a Roman. Concerning Remigius we know that he baptised the king of the Franks by pouring and so forth. . . .[54]

52. Bonaventure, *Commentaria* 4.3/2.2/2.

53. For an extensive list of documents showing the progress of the transition from immersion to some form of sprinkling or pouring, see Jules Corblet, *Histoire dogmatique, liturgique et archéologique du sacrament dè baptême,* 2 vols. (Brussels, Paris, and Geneva, 1881-82), vol. 1, pp. 235ff.

54. Dold, *Die Konstanzer Ritualientexte,* pp. 12-13. "Utrum autem actus baptizandi

This text is most suggestive. In the first place, the very fact that the rubrics of the ritual of Constance give this rather long defense of the practice of sprinkling suggests that the practice had only recently become the normal procedure. Obviously there were those who had questioned the generalized use of sprinkling for baptism. In the second place, this text suggests the reason why the Western Church gave up immersion. While the age of the priest was doubtless only a minor consideration, the cold of winter was another matter. The stone churches north of the Alps can be rather chilly for a good half of the year. Even today they are often poorly heated in winter. To immerse a child, even the healthiest child, in a chilly church would hardly have been the wisest procedure. In the third place, the text suggests that it had been recognized from earliest times that pouring or sprinkling was an acceptable practice when practical considerations suggested it. The rubrics found in the rite of Constance give three examples from the ancient Church which showed that baptism could be administered by pouring.[55] One of these is a reference to the practice of the New Testament Church; the other two are references to early Christian history. The references are intended to show that from the day of Pentecost on the church has accepted some form of pouring or sprinkling as an alternate form of baptism. It follows these three with an *et cetera,* indicating that the author knew of other examples. Indeed, there are plenty of other evidences that the Church had always allowed pouring or sprinkling. The two historical examples advanced by our document, the examples of St. Lawrence and Remigius, are not as solid from the standpoint of modern historical criticism as they might be, but there were plenty of other solid witnesses to the practice which we shall take up in a moment. The historical examples found in the rubrics of Constance are not, as some have claimed, misleading. The Church had allowed for more than one mode of baptism for some time. Furthermore, the fact that this was the case was well known at the beginning of the sixteenth century.

---

debeat fieri per trinam immersionem, aut per ipsius aque supereffusionem: utrumque ritum et modum ecclesia recipit.

"Utrum autem semel aut ter inmergatur, non uariat baptismi essentiam, aut si agua supereffundatur manu sacerdotis tercio.

"Magis sustinendum tamen multaque ex eo cauentur pericula:

"Primo si sacerdos sit senex aut habens manus tremulas, si infans debilis, si uehemens frigus tempore hyemis, si advultus aut perfectioris etatis debilis, qui commode inmergi non possunt.

"Et quia exemplum trahimus a sanctis apostolis, Sancto laurencio, Remigio ceterisque pluribus, qui aspergendo et super effundendo aquam baptisabant. De apostolis legitur actuum secundo et tercio quod uno die conversi sunt quinque milia et alia tria milia et baptizati et cetera. De sancto Laurentio, qui afferens urceum cum aqua baptisauit romanum. De remigio regem francie et cetera. *Obsequiale Constantiensis,* pp. 12-13.

55. The exact references implied by these examples have been searched out by Spital, *Die Taufritus,* p. 181, n. 1018.

C. The Antiquity of Immersion and of Sprinkling

Let us take a moment to put into proper perspective this transition from immersion to some form of sprinkling or pouring. It would be a mistake to imagine that until the High Middle Ages immersion had been the universal practice of the Church. The Church has often in her history practiced more than one mode of baptism. Jewish proselyte baptism, from which Christian baptism developed, was administered by immersion.[56] The immersion was probably intended to symbolize the completeness of the washing. Obviously Jewish proselyte baptism was not interested in symbolizing death and resurrection. For the Jewish rite the concern was to purify the proselyte from the impurities of paganism. There were, however, other Jewish baptisms besides proselyte baptism. As the Gospel of Mark puts it, the Jews had many traditions about baptisms, religious washings, and ablutions (Mark 7:4). The religious community at Qumran also baptized by immersion.[57] Here, too, the immersion signified washing. While Jewish proselyte baptism and the religious washings of Qumran were undoubtedly done by immersion, there may well have been considerable diversity in the mode of baptism as it was practiced in the New Testament Church.[58] We imagine that immersion was used normally, but on the basis of the New Testament it is hard to insist that immersion was the only form used. It is often claimed that the Greek word for baptism implies exclusive immersion. While in classical Greek the verb "to baptize" does mean to submerge, dunk, or immerse, the word had picked up other meanings in the popular Greek spoken by the Jews of New Testament times. In its New Testament context the word "baptism" can mean washing or religious ablution

56. On Jewish proselyte baptism, see Hermann Strack and Paul Billerbeck, *Kommentar zum Neuen Testament aus Talmud und Midrasch,* 4th edn., vol. 1 (Munich: C. H. Beck, 1965), pp. 102-13.

I. Abrahams, "How did the Jews baptize?" *Journal of Theological Studies* 12 (1910-12): 609-12.

W. Michaelis, "Zum judischen Hintergrund der Johannes taufe," *Judaica* 7 (1951): 81-120.

The most important sources involved are the tractate *Yebamoth* of the *Babylonian Talmud* 46b and the *Sibylline Oracles* 4:162-67.

57. O. Betz, "Die Proselytentaufe der Qumransekte und die Taufe in Neuen Testament," *Revue de Qumran* 1 (1958-59): 213-34.

J. Gnilka, "Die essenischen Tauchbäder und die Johannestaufe," *Revue de Qumran* 3 (1961-62): 185ff.

58. That the New Testament practiced a variety of modes of baptism depending on the circumstances seems to be recognized by a growing number of scholars: M. Barth, *Interpreter's Dictionary of the Bible, Supplementary Volume,* p. 87; H. Mueller, *New Catholic Encyclopedia* 2: 57; H. Leclercq, *DACL* 7/1: 305-8.

just as well as immersion. Baptism was the word used by Greek-speaking Jews to speak of various Jewish rites of purification which involved washing. These rites did not necessarily involve immersion; sometimes these rites involved only rinsing or sprinkling.[59]

When we turn to the Acts of the Apostles, several of the baptisms we find there suggest other modes of baptism. In fact, it has often been pointed out, just as the ritual of Constance pointed out, that immersing three thousand converts on the day of Pentecost would have posed a considerable logistical problem. One would not want to say that it would have been impossible, but it does lead one to ask if perhaps on occasion other modes might not have been used. Again one wonders whether Paul baptized the Philippian jailor by immersion or by some more convenient method which the rather difficult circumstances might have presented (Acts 16:33).

The most remarkable evidence that sprinkling was considered an acceptable form of baptism from earliest times is found in the *Didache*. The *Didache* allows that baptism may be performed by putting a little water on the top of the head.[60] In the *Didache* the primary consideration is whether one has a

59. More recently an increasing number of scholars have recognized that immersion is not implied by the Greek word itself. It is the Hebrew concept behind the Greek word which is decisive. By New Testament times the Greek word βαπτίζειν had become the common translation of the Hebrew טָבַל which was the Hebrew word most often used for the Jewish ceremonial washings. In Luke 11:38 βαπτίζειν can be used to speak of the ceremonial washing of the hands before meals. In Mark 7:4 βαπτισμός can refer to the ceremonial washings of eating vessels which Jewish law required. It is the same way with Hebrews 6:2 and 9:10, which the RSV quite correctly translates "ablutions." The writer to the Hebrews is speaking of the ceremonial washings of the Law. It was no doubt because βαπτίζειν was already used to refer to these Jewish ceremonial washings that the word was used by the writers of the New Testament to refer to the Christian sacrament. It should also be noted that words for washing are found in the New Testament as synonyms of baptism. For example, in Acts 22:16 we read, "Rise and be baptized, and wash away your sins." The verb used here is ἀπολούειν, which means "to wash off" or "wash away." The same verb is used in 1 Corinthians 6:11 as a synonym for baptism, "But you were washed, you were sanctified, you were justified in the name of the Lord Jesus Christ and in the Spirit of our God." Another extremely interesting text in terms of synonyms for baptism is Hebrews 10:22, "Let us draw near with a true heart in full assurance of faith, with our hearts sprinkled clean from an evil conscience and our bodies washed with pure water." The first of these two, ῥαντίζειν, "to sprinkle," is particularly remarkable because it understands baptism as the fulfillment of so many of the rites of the Law which involved purifications through sprinkling. The second synonym, λούειν, means "to wash."

On the use of the Greek word βαπτίζειν to speak of the Jewish ceremonial washings see the article by Albrecht Oepke in *TWNT* 1: 532ff.

60. The text given in the *Didache* 7 runs as follows, "Concerning baptism, baptize thus: Having first rehearsed all these things, baptize in the Name of the Father and of the Son and of the Holy Spirit, in running water; but if thou hast no running water, baptize in

sufficient supply of water. If one does not have a sufficient supply, then sprinkling is sufficient. This evidence from the *Didache* is particularly strong because it provides an historical context which helps us interpret the New Testament text.

About the year 200, Tertullian gives us several indications that pouring or sprinkling could be used as well as immersion for the administration of baptism.[61] Cyprian a few years later tells us that sprinkling was used rather than immersion if those to be baptized were of advanced age or delicate health.[62]

---

other, and if thou canst not in cold, then in warm. But if thou hast neither, pour water three times on the head in the name of the Father, Son and Holy Spirit." *The Apostolic Fathers,* trans. Kirsopp Lake, vol. 1 (London: William Heinemann; Cambridge, Mass.: Harvard University Press, 1965), pp. 319ff. This passage we can regard as throwing a particularly strong light on the practice of the New Testament Church because both in time and geography the *Didache* is very close to the New Testament writings. It was probably written about the same time and place as the Gospel of Matthew. It is also the case that there is marked similarity between what is said of Christian baptism here and what we find in the oldest rabbinical documents about proselyte baptism. Clearly in this text the word "baptism" is not regarded as being violated by a sort of minimal pouring. What seems to be at stake is whether the water is available.

61. Tertullian, who was the first major Christian writer to use the Latin language, is responsible for coining a great part of the Latin Christian vocabulary. Tertullian was an ingenious writer with a flair for using words in an inventive and imaginative way. One finds a great number of synonyms for baptism in the works of Tertullian. These synonyms give us an idea of what was understood as the essence of the central act of baptism. *Abluere:* to wash or cleanse; *tingere:* to wet, moisten, or bathe by applying water; *lavare:* to wash away, to bathe, or to cleanse by pouring water over something; *diluere:* to wash away, loosen, or dissolve; *mergere:* to plunge or push into, to cover or overwhelm; *aspergere:* to sprinkle. A rather amusing indication that in his day sprinkling was acceptable is the argument that the disciples were baptized when they were in the boat with Jesus and were sprinkled by the waves. There were those in Tertullian's day who were embarrassed by the silence of the Gospels on the subject of when and where the disciples were baptized. They grabbed on to this argument, which evidently Tertullian did not find too convincing. Nevertheless, the fact that such an argument could be advanced would indicate that sprinkling was recognized as an acceptable form of baptism in the African Church in Tertullian's day. Cf. *De baptismo* 12.6. The Reformers, being excellent philologists, greatly appreciated Tertullian and were particularly sensitive to his use of words. Cf. Old, *Patristic Roots,* p. 179.

62. Cyprian, *Epistula* 69.12.1ff. *Ad Magnum* (This appears as *Epistula* 75 in some editions.) One of the questions which this letter attempts to answer is what Cyprian thinks of sprinkling rather than immersion being used in the baptism of those who are in poor health. Cyprian answers that true faith is the essential thing, not the amount of water. The manner in which the ceremony is performed cannot lessen the grace of God. Alluding to 1 Peter 3:21, the bishop of Carthage says that the sacrament of washing is quite different from the carnal bathing in which everything depends on soap and other bathing lotions and on basins and pools. What makes the difference is faith. If the quantity of water used were the issue, then one could hardly expect the heart to be cleansed or the mind to be

That immersion was not the only method of baptism used in the early Church is indicated by another piece of evidence. All the early pictures of baptism show pouring. These pictorial representations of the sacrament invariably show the one being baptized standing naked in water about waist deep. The one performing the baptism is pouring water over the head of the one being baptized. The pouring is done simply with the hand. In most cases over this hand of the one baptizing there is a representation of the Holy Spirit in the form of a dove. Anyone familiar with the art of the classical world and particularly with the beginnings of Christian art is aware of the way the pictures of this period evolved into stylized representations and the way, once these representations were established, they remained fixed for a long time. This belongs to the philosophy of art. In those days the artist strove not for originality but for fidelity. It was the job of the artist faithfully to reproduce the pattern of reality. To be sure, the ideas of Plato are behind this philosophy of art. Once a tradition had been established as to how a particular subject should be presented, it never changed.

What seems to be the earliest pictorial representation of baptism which has come down to us is the picture of the baptism of Jesus found in the cemetery of Calixtos.[63] The picture, which comes from the end of the second century, indicates pouring.[64] There are a number of representations of baptism in the Catacombs from the third and fourth centuries.[65] None of these shows baptism by immersion.

Perhaps the most remarkable picture of a baptism is in the ceiling of the

---

purified. Cyprian defends the use of sprinkling with a quotation from Ezekiel 36:25-26, "And I will sprinkle clean water upon you. . . ." Even more interesting is the way Cyprian defends the practice by appealing to the purifying of the Levites by sprinkling them with the water of expiation (Num. 8:5-7 and 19:8-13). Obviously, Cyprian sees these ablutions as types of baptism. He goes on, then, taking up the subject of how the types of the Old Testament should be used in the shaping of Christian liturgical practice. One can easily understand how Cyprian's argument would appeal to the Reformers. On the Reformers' knowledge and appreciation of Cyprian, cf. Old, *Patristic Roots,* pp. 164ff.

63. Jungmann, in his article for the *New Catholic Encyclopedia,* gives a reproduction of this picture. *NCE* 2: 59.

64. The house church at Dura-Europa is the oldest example we have of a baptistry painted with the baptismal iconography. The baptismal iconography is only just beginning to evolve. Strictly speaking, the pictures of baptism are pictures of Old Testament types which intimated baptism. Nothing in these pictures gives us any clue as to the mode of baptism. On the other hand, there is evidence that this church used some form of sprinkling or pouring. The baptismal font found in this church would be too small for total immersion. Cf. F. van der Meer and Christine Mohrmann, *Atlas of the Early Christian World,* trans. and eds. Mary F. Hedlund and H. H. Rowley (New York: Thomas Nelson, 1958), p. 46, fig. 71.

65. For pictures of baptism in the Catacombs, see van der Meer and Mohrman, *Atlas,* p. 42, fig. 48 and p. 126, fig. 396. See also H. Leclercq, *DACL* 2/1: 346-80.

Baptistry of the Orthodox at Ravenna.[66] In this case the picture of John baptizing Jesus in the dome of the baptistry had by this time become a convention. By A.D. 450, when this mosaic was put into place, the philosophy of the icon was developing rapidly. Everything in the baptistry was built as the setting for the baptismal mysteries of the Christian Passover. Clearly the baptisms performed in this baptistry were immersions. In the center of the room was a large pool obviously built for immersions. How is it, then, that the picture of the baptism of Christ in the ceiling, put there to be seen by those being baptized as they were laid into the water, is a baptism not by immersion but by pouring? The answer is simple. The traditional picture of baptism had evolved at a time when pouring was the normal way to baptize. The traditional icon must have evolved in the second century; by the third century we find traces of it all over the Empire.[67] Here we have clear evidence that in the second century baptism was most often performed by pouring.[68]

If baptism by pouring was normal in the second century, how are we to explain that by the third and surely the fourth century immersion became the preferred mode? Once again, we would want to call to mind what was said about the desire in the late Classical Period to develop impressive Christian mysteries. When Christians began to see in baptism a dramatization of the death and resurrection of Christ, and began more and more to celebrate baptism at Easter, then the symbolic representation of the burial and resurrection became increasingly important. In this setting the dramatization of the burial and resurrection came to overshadow the sign of washing. It was the desire of the Church to make baptism a splendid Christian mystery which made immersion the general mode of baptism by the end of the fourth century. Immersion held sway for the next six to eight centuries.

The history of the rite of baptism shows a number of features which have waxed and waned. We have already spoken of this in Chapter I. There we pointed out how the tradition of baptism at Easter became very popular and then disappeared. The prolonged catechumenate was another thing which waxed and waned. It appears to have been the same way with immersion. Having made this little excursus on the history of the mode of baptism, let us return to the sixteenth century.

66. van der Meer and Mohrmann, *Atlas,* p. 130, fig. 412. The same subject is depicted in the dome of the Arian baptistry in Ravenna.

67. P. de Puniet, *DACL* 2/1: cols. 251-346.

68. The iconographic and archaeological evidence for the predominance of pouring is very strong, and we cannot go into it at the length it deserves here. See the articles in *RGG, DACL,* and *NCE* for the current literature.

D. The Reformers Attempt to Re-establish Immersion

While at the beginning of the sixteenth century the ritual books published in Germany reflect a transition from immersion to some form of pouring or sprinkling, Luther, followed by Jud and Zwingli, began to advocate a revival of immersion. Their interest in a revival of immersion was short- lived, but we need to look at it just the same. What was their reason for wanting to restore immersion? Evidently they wanted to re-establish what they regarded as the main force of the sign of baptism. They figured, at least at the outset, that the essential force of the sign was a reenactment or visual presentation of the death and resurrection of Christ. This was the way the matter had been presented for centuries. One cited the sixth chapter of Romans to show that baptism was supposed to be a dramatization of Christ's death and resurrection. This interpretation they found in many of the writings of the Church Fathers of the fourth century. This interpretation had become traditional from that time down through the Middle Ages.[69]

Their original preference for immersion was also supported by their understanding of the Greek word for baptism. The Reformers used lexicons based on classical Greek.[70] These lexicons told them that the Greek word *baptizein* meant to immerse or dip. If the Reformers were misled by the lexicons of their day, they were not the first nor the last to have made this mistake. As time went on, they looked into it more deeply. Many of the Reformers were good biblical philologists, and in time they realized that the biblical use of the word was not the same as the classical usage.

69. André Benoît has pointed out that in the second century we find no trace of the idea that baptism is a dramatization of the burial and resurrection of Christ. The idea seems to have first appeared as an interpretation of the sixth chapter of Romans influenced by the acquaintance of early Christians with the mystery religions. Benoît's study makes very unlikely the theory that New Testament baptism originated from Hellenistic mystery religions. It also shows how late the idea developed that the sacraments were to be understood as Christian mysteries. The importance of Benoît's study both to the theology and the liturgy of baptism is enormous! A. Benoît, *Le baptême chrétien au second siècle* (Paris: Presses Universitaires de France, 1953).

70. The lexicon most likely used by the High Rhenish Reformers was the lexicon of Suidas. This work of the tenth-century Byzantine lexicographer was a dictionary-encyclopedia greatly prized by Westerners who wanted to learn both classical and ecclesiastical Greek. This lexicon, of course, reflected the theology and liturgy of baptism of the Eastern Church which had taken shape in the fourth century. The Reformers no doubt used the edition of D. Chalcondylas first published in Milan in 1499 and subsequently by Aldus, the famous Venetian publisher, in 1514. The appreciation of the Reformers for this work is indicated by the fact that the work was published in Basel in 1544 and in Geneva in 1619.

E. The Reformers Abandon the Attempt

If early in the Reformation the Reformers had attempted to revive immersion, they soon gave up their attempt. To understand just why they gave up the attempt we will need to look at some statements about what the Reformers understood was signified by the act of baptism. What was the sacramental action supposed to mean? If baptism was a sign, what did it really signify?

Let us look at some passages of the Reformers to see what they had to say about immersion. Zwingli in his first work on baptism understands the sacramental action to be a sign of the death and resurrection of Christ.

> Do you not see that when we are plunged into water, it is as though we were buried in Christ, that is, in his death, signifying thereby that we are dead to the world. And as Christ was raised from the dead and dies no more, so we who have been raised up from the water of baptism must walk in newness of life. For as we are made like unto him in his death when we are plunged into the waters of baptism, so we are made like unto him in his resurrection.[71]

For Zwingli, in the early stage of the discussion at least, the sacramental action was understood to signify death and burial with Christ quite simply and unambiguously. Zwingli is obviously basing his thoughts on the sixth chapter of Romans as it was understood from the fourth century onward.[72] We have had occasion before to remark that Zwingli's first work on baptism is best regarded as a preliminary study of the subject. It was written in haste at a time when Zwingli was preoccupied with other concerns. As we shall see, Zwingli's successor Bullinger will develop a very different understanding.

F. Washing as the Primary Sign

Bucer's thoughts are much more complex. Bucer speaks of the sign of baptism most often as a sign of washing, but he also speaks of it as a sign of burial. This is particularly clear from the actual liturgical texts themselves. In the *Strasbourg Church Service of 1525* (D), the congregation is admonished, "Let us pray that the Lord baptize in water and in the Holy Spirit, that the outward

71. *Of Baptism, LCC* 24, pp. 150-51.

72. It is, of course, this passage which in the Hellenistic world gave rise to understanding baptism as a mystery. From Romans 6 the Church of the fourth century began to develop rites which made of baptism a dramatization of the death and resurrection of Christ. Cf. Rudolf Schnackenburg, *Baptism in the Thought of St. Paul,* trans. G. R. Beasley-Murray (Oxford: Blackwell, 1964); G. W. H. Lampe, *The Seal of the Spirit,* 2nd edn. (London: S.P.C.K., 1967).

washing performed by me may be inwardly accomplished by the Holy Spirit."[73] Then in the Baptismal Invocation which follows, the minister prays, ". . . for inner renewal and spiritual rebirth, which is truly signified by the outward baptism. Grant that as he is baptized in the death of Christ Jesus, buried with him, and through him is awakened from the dead, he might walk in a new life. . . ."[74] Possibly the phrase "buried with him" in this prayer implies that he understands the rite to represent a burial. Unfortunately, Bucer's writing lacks precision and clarity at this point; however, one can get the point of what he is trying to say. For Bucer the outward sign or sacramental action is primarily washing which signifies a spiritual purification; furthermore, this outward washing signifies a purification which is actually accomplished by a new birth. That the act of baptism should visually represent birth is not suggested by Bucer. For him the new birth, signified by baptism, and the renewing of the mind which the apostle Paul speaks about in both the sixth and twelfth chapters of Romans are brought about by being joined to Christ in his death and resurrection. To put it simply, for Bucer the outward sign of washing quite naturally signifies purification, but it means more than it visibly signifies. It means new birth through union with Christ in his death and resurrection. The outward sign, nevertheless, remains the sign of washing.

In other places he is more clear. In his *Grund und Ursach* we read, "From this then it should be clear that outward water baptism is nothing other than a sign of inner, spiritual baptism, that is, cleansing from all sins. . . . It is, therefore, that the apostle Paul in the fifth chapter of Ephesians tells us that Christ has cleansed his Church through the washing of water. . . . In the same way he writes to Titus, 'he makes us blessed through the bath of regeneration and renewal of spirit. . . .' "[75] It is this sign of washing which is the primary visible sign of the sacrament. In Bucer's *Bericht* we read, "In baptism one is baptized in the name of the Father, Son and Holy Spirit and immersed into water. What is that supposed to be? Saint Paul calls it a bath of regeneration

73. "Wollen also bitten, das es der herr teuff ym wasser vnd ym heyligen geist, vff das eusserliche weshung, so er durch mich volenden wirt, inwendig durch den heyligen geist eygentlich vnd in warheit volbracht werde." Hubert, *Ordnungen,* p. 39.

74. ". . . vff das dein innerliche ernewerung vnd weidergeburt des geists durch den vnsern tauff warhafftiglich bedeutet werde, vnd das es als in den todt Christi Jesu getaufft mit ym begraben vnd durch yn von den todten vfferweckt sy, zu wandlen in eim newen leben. . . ." Hubert, *Ordnungen,* p. 41.

75. "Also is auss disem allen clar, das der eüsserlich wassertauff nichts dann ein zeichen ist, des innerlichen, geystlichen tauffs, das ist der reinigung von allen sunden. . . . Also auch Paulus Ephe. 5, do er sagt, Christus hab sein gemein gereinigt durchs wasser bad, . . . gleicher weyss schreibt er Tit. 3: Er machet uns selig durch das bad der widergeburt und ernewerung des geists. . . ." *Grund und Ursach, BDS* 1, pp. 256-57.

and renewal of the Spirit." From this it is clear that, for Bucer, even when immersion is used, the immersion in water is not primarily a sign of death and resurrection, but rather, it is understood as a bath; it is understood as washing.[76]

Calvin, while he sees in baptism both the sign of washing and the sign of burial, gives a definite priority to the sign of washing. "We ought to deem it certain and proved that it is he who speaks to us through the sign; that it is he who purifies and washes away sins, and wipes out the remembrance of them; that it is he who makes us sharers in his death. . . . These things, I say, he performs for our soul within as truly and surely as we see our body outwardly cleansed, submerged, and surrounded with water."[77] Then a bit further on Calvin assures us, "But whether the person being baptized should be wholly immersed, and whether thrice or once, whether he should only be sprinkled with poured water — these details are of no importance, but ought to be optional. . . ."[78] Here it is clear that for Calvin baptism is primarily a sign of washing. Whether immersion, pouring, or sprinkling be used, it is washing which is signified. The way Calvin looked at it after the Reformation was well underway was quite different from the way Zwingli looked at it in the early years of the Reformation.

G. Theological Reasons for Regarding Sprinkling as Appropriate

Now we can turn to the question why the Reformers at first tried to reintroduce immersion but then gave up the attempt. In the *German Baptismal Book* published by Leo Jud, the rubric specifies immersion. Zwingli, a year and a half later, omits the rubric in the first baptismal service which he himself published. Why is this omission made?

The answer, it would seem, is that the Zurich Reformers had tried to reintroduce immersion but had failed. That was one aspect of their liturgical reform the burghers of Zurich simply would not accept. The reason they could not accept it was probably the same reason which had brought about the lapse of immersion in favor of sprinkling in the preceding couple of centuries. Such a change would only have come about in the preceding centuries if the faithful had been convinced that the mode of baptism was not an essential aspect of the rite. Popular opinion did not see it as an important issue in the early sixteenth century. How could the Reformers now reverse the process and

76. *Bericht,* g iiij v and h i v, and *Quid de baptismate,* D iiij. "Im tauff wurt der mensch vff den namen des vatters, sons vnd heyligen geists ins wasser getuncket, was solle nun dz sin? S. Paul nents ein bad der widergeburt, vnd ernewerung des geysts. Tit. 3."

77. *Institutes* 4.15.14.

78. *Institutes* 4.15.19.

convince them that whether one sprinkled or immersed was important? How could they now say that such an unpopular and cumbersome rite as undressing the child, dipping the child into the font, drying the child off, and redressing him or her was so very important? If the Reformers had been convinced that immersion was of the essence of the sign, they probably could have pulled it off, but they were not convinced that immersion was of the essence of the sign. They wanted their reform to be based on Scripture, and they began to realize that Scripture itself suggested reasons for using other modes of baptism. Scripture itself put the emphasis on washing, and surely immersion was not the only way of signifying washing. Besides that the historical evidence provided by early Christian documents indicated that the Church had always allowed some form of sprinkling. The Reformers did not have all the evidence which we have today, but they had enough to piece together the picture. As time went on, they began to realize that on the basis of Scripture they could not insist on immersion. Within a short time they gave up the project. It is only in Luther's *Taufbüchlein* and in Leo Jud's editions of the baptismal rite of Zurich that the reference to immersion appears. In Zwingli's own editions of the Zurich baptismal rite, that is, those from 1525 on, there was never any rubric on the mode of baptism. Then with Bullinger's first service book a rubric specifying pouring appears.[79]

The Reformers of Zurich were practical pastors as well as theologians. What evidently happened was that they discovered that while there were some very enthusiastic supporters of reform who were willing to go through the fuss of immersing children, for the majority of the citizens of Zurich the choice between sprinkling in Latin and immersion in German weighed out in favor of the old Latin rites. In Zurich at the time Leo Jud published the first German baptismal rites their use was optional. It was up to the parents to decide whether they wanted to have their children baptized by the old Latin rites or by the new German rites. The reform-minded priests of Zurich soon discovered that their change to immersion was undermining their introduction of the use of German for the celebration. Seeing that was the case, the Reformers lost no time in discarding immersion. For the Reformers of Zurich, there was no question as to which was the more important reform. The use of the common language was one of their cardinal concerns.

It would be a mistake to imagine that the question of reviving immersion was simply settled because of Zwingli's appreciation for the practical politics of reform. We can be sure that his willingness to let this matter drop was

79. "Hie nimpt der diener das kind und übergusst es mit dem wasser. . . ." "Bullingers Agenda," *Zwingliana* 10 (1954): 17.

theologically well considered. In regard to the Lord's Supper, the Reformers had insisted on a number of reforms which aimed at restoring the clarity of the sign. They insisted that the meal was to be served from a table rather than an altar and that the congregation sit at or gather around the table. They insisted on making the Lord's Supper look like a meal. Why then should the Reformers not be consistent and insist on the revival of immersion? The reason is simply this: when they began to study the matter more thoroughly, the Reformers came to the conclusion that the central sacramental action was washing, not a dramatization of the death and resurrection of Jesus in and out of a grave of water. Jud and Zwingli had at first believed that the sacramental action should symbolize death and resurrection, but they changed their minds as they got deeper into the subject. Bucer, Bullinger, Oecolampadius, and Calvin all put the primary emphasis on baptism being a sign of washing.

H. The Sign of Being Washed in Christ's Blood

There was another consideration. If the Reformers recognized that washing is the primary signification of baptism and if they recognized burial and resurrection as a secondary signification, they also recognized there were other secondary significations. Besides burial and resurrection, being washed in Christ's blood is another secondary signification in baptism. If the sacramental action of immersion was particularly suited to signifying death and resurrection with Christ, sprinkling is particularly suited to evoking the image of being washed with the blood of Christ. This is also an important New Testament image for baptism. Bullinger makes the following point.

> The primary attention should be given much more to the meaning of the whole action of baptism and particularly to the action of pouring water rather than to the water alone. Through the outpouring of water is meant that the one on whom the water is sprinkled belongs to the Church and the people of God, that just as water washes away the smudges and stains of our bodies, so also the one upon whom there is this outpouring, being received by grace, is washed with the blood of Jesus and pledged to a new life. This then is . . . the mystery and value of this sacrament.[80]

80. "Darumm werdend die hohen grossen ding, vil me dem gantzen handel des taufs ggeben, vnd fürnamlich dem, dz durch das wasser angiessen bedutet wirt, dann dem wasser allein. Es wirt aber durch das wasser angiessen bedutet, dass der begossen der Kilchen vnd des volcks gottes sye, das wie dz wasser alle mosen des lybs, befleckung, vnd vnreinikeyt abwashct: also werde ouch der begossen, vss gnaden vf genommen, vnd mit dem Blut Jesu gewaschen, vnd gepflichtet zu einem nüwen laben. Das ist nun die reynigung, dz verzyhen der sünden, vnd die widergeburt, die gheimnuss vnd wirde dises sacraments." Bullinger, *Fräfel,* J iii v-iiij r.

From this passage it should be clear that Bullinger understood quite well that in the New Testament *baptizein* meant more than immerse. It meant to perform a religious rite of washing or even sprinkling. His understanding of baptism has obviously taken into account the fact that *baptizein* is used in the New Testament to speak of Jewish rites of purification by means of washing and sprinkling. With his covenantal theology it is important that baptism is a sign that, being washed in the blood of Jesus, we are pledged to a new life. The idea of being washed in the blood of Jesus is a very sophisticated literary figure. It is rich in typological allusions.

Let us look for a moment at some of the key passages of Scripture in which this image is found. In an ascription of praise found in the first chapter of Revelation we read, "To him that loved us and washed us from our sins in his own blood, and hath made us kings and priests unto God . . ." (Rev. 1:15, KJV). In this passage we have a clear reference to the baptismal washing which has cleansed us from our sins and given us a place in the royal priesthood of God's people. Basic to this magnificent imagery is the affirmation that just as under the Law the blood of sacrificed animals cleansed the people of Israel from ceremonial impurity, so for Christians the blood of Christ cleanses from all sin. In its simplest form we find this idea in 1 John 1:7, "The blood of Jesus . . . cleanses us from all sin." In Revelation 1:5 another image is added to this. We are told that through this washing in the blood of Christ we are made kings and priests unto God. The reference to being made "kings and priests unto God" evokes the sacerdotal ordination described in Exodus 29:21. There we learn how Aaron and his sons are to be sprinkled with sacrificial blood. The use of sprinkling in baptism brings out this important facet of the baptismal imagery.

There is another important passage which we should consider. In the ninth and tenth chapters of Hebrews we find the same imagery developed in a different way. There we are told that if under the Old Covenant the sprinkling of the blood of sacrificed animals purified God's people, then how much more under the New Covenant those who are sprinkled with the blood of Christ will be purified. In Hebrews, where covenantal theology is so elaborately developed, the covenantal signs are taken up and developed very carefully. We are reminded of the story of how Moses initiated Israel into the covenant by sprinkling the people with the blood of the covenant. The principle is made very clear, "Indeed, under the law almost everything is purified with blood" (Heb. 9:22). It should be noted that it is precisely these kinds of ceremonies that the writer has in mind when in Hebrews 6:2 he speaks of the baptisms of the Old Testament. The Revised Standard Version quite correctly reads "ablutions" at this point, but the Greek quite literally says baptisms. Sprinkling with blood was both a rite of purification and a rite of initiation into the covenant. This is very clear in the Epistle to the Hebrews. A bit further on in Hebrews 10:22 all this is very clearly related to baptism. "Let us draw near with a true heart . . . sprinkled clean from an evil conscience and our bodies washed with pure water." It is obviously such passages which Bullinger has in mind when he tells us, "so also the one upon whom there is this outpouring . . . is washed with the blood of Jesus and pledged to a new life." By the sacramental action of sprinkling water the sprinkling of Christ's blood is signified with all its rich typological associations. Not the least of these is the type of the sprinkling of the blood of the covenant which pledges the Christian to a new life. When baptism is performed by sprinkling, a whole host of Old Testament rites of purification by the sprinkling of blood is evoked which the New Testament itself clearly understands as types of baptism. Here we have a theological reason for accepting sprinkling as an appropriate mode of baptism.

I. The Sign of Mortification and Vivification

Now let us look at Calvin. The catechism of Geneva takes up the question of the baptismal sign.

> Q. 324. . . . What is the significance of Baptism? It has two parts. For the Lord represents to us the remission of our sins (Eph. 5:26 and 27), and then our regeneration or spiritual renewal (Rom. 6:4).
>
> Q. 325. What similarity does water have with these things that it can represent them? It is because the remission of sins is a kind of washing by which our souls are freed from their imperfections in the same way that by water the body is purified from its odors.
>
> Q. 326. What about the other part? It is because the beginning of our regeneration is that our old nature be mortified and the end that we be new creatures by the Spirit of God, that the water therefore is put on our head as a sign of death, in such a manner, however, that the resurrection is in a similar way represented. And that is done for a brief moment of time, not so much as to drown us in the water.[81]

81. 324 . . . quelle est la signification du Baptesme? Elle a deuz parties. Car le Seigneur nous y represente la remission de noz pechez (Eph. 5,26 et 27), et puis nostre regeneration, ou renouvellement spirituel (Rom. 6,4). 325 Quelle similitude a l'eaue avec ces choses, pour les representer? Pource que la remission des pechez est une espece de lavement, par lequel noz ames sont purgées de leurs macules: ainsi que les ordures du corps sont nettoyées par l'eaue. 326 Touchant l'autre partie? Pource que le commancement de

That the primary sacramental sign is washing comes out clearly enough in this passage. ". . . The remission of sins is a kind of washing . . . in the same way that by water the body is purified." When one thinks about baptism, even briefly, it is quite clear how it is that the washing away of sin may be signified in a baptism performed by either immersion, sprinkling, or pouring. How mortification and vivification are signified in a baptism done by sprinkling is not as clear, and yet the catechism expressly says that sprinkling is sufficient to signify both mortification and vivification. How is that possible? It becomes clear when one reads what Calvin has to say in the *Institutes* about the crossing of the Red Sea, one of the Old Testament types of baptism.

> These things which we have said both of mortification and of washing were foreshadowed in the people of Israel, who were on this account said by the apostle to have been "baptized in the cloud and in the sea" (1 Cor. 10:2). Mortification was symbolized when the Lord, rescuing his people from domination and cruel bondage of Pharoah, made a way through the Red Sea (Ex. 14:21) and drowned Pharaoh himself and the Egyptian army. . . .[82]

Presumably, the same thing could be said even more clearly of the type of Noah and the Flood. The sign of mortification and vivification is, for Calvin, not to be found in a dramatic representation of the death and resurrection of Christ in baptismal immersion, but rather in the associations which water has come to have in the history of God's mighty acts. The water of the Flood and the water of the Red Sea had given to water the meaning of mortification and vivification.

There is more, of course. Calvin, as Bullinger, saw in baptismal sprinkling a reference to several Old Testament types of baptism. In his chapter on the nature of the sacraments Calvin gives considerable attention to the sacraments of the Old Testament and their relation to those of the New Testament.[83] There we read that the rites of purification found in the Old Testament testified

---

nostre regeneration est, que nostre nature soit mortifee: l'issue, que nous soyons nouvelles creatures par l'Esprit de Dieu. L'eaue donc nous est mise sur la teste, en signe de mort: toutesfois en telle sorte, que la resurrection nous est semblablement figurée: en ce que cela se fait seulement pour une minute de temps, et non pas pour nous noyer en l'eaue." Niesel, *Bekenntnis Schriften,* pp. 36ff.

82. *Institutes* 4.15.9.

83. Ford Lewis Battles in his subtitles to Calvin's chapter on the sacraments, *Institutes* 4.14, pointed out that the last paragraphs, 21-26, are devoted to a discussion of the typological relation of the Old Testament sacraments and the New. This should make it clear that Calvin's interest in the subject is not merely a holdover from the past. With the recovery of biblical Hebrew in the early sixteenth century, about which we have already spoken so frequently, the High Rhenish Reformers had taken a fresh interest in such subjects. The typological relation of the two covenants was an important aspect of covenant theology.

to the need of human beings to be pure.[84] They were prophetic signs of the purifying power of Christ. Calvin finds this typological relation between the Old Testament rites of purification and the New Testament in 1 John 1:7, in Revelation 1:5, and in the ninth and tenth chapters of Hebrews.[85] The fact that Calvin appeals to these passages of Scripture makes it evident that he clearly perceives in baptism a sign that we are sprinkled with the blood of Christ, and thereby made participants in his sacrifice. When this facet of the meaning of baptism is pointed out, then we understand even more clearly how baptism by sprinkling can be a sign of both mortification and vivification.

We see here, once again, how important the Old Testament types were to the early Reformed theology of the sacraments. For Calvin they are not Neoplatonic shadows but biblical signs. The New Testament sacraments were for Calvin, as they were for Bullinger, the summing up and recapitulation of a rich history of biblical signs and sacraments. Calvin and Bullinger understood very well what Tertullian and Ambrose had understood before them: the Christian sacraments grew quite naturally from sound biblical roots and those roots were the types of the Old Testament.

If the Reformers were content to administer baptism by means of pouring or sprinkling, it was because they regarded the sacramental action to be washing, which could be accomplished by pouring or sprinkling as well as by immersion. While at the very beginning of their attempts to reform the rite of baptism they thought of baptism primarily as a sign of burial and resurrection and therefore advocated immersion, they began to change their minds as they delved more deeply into their study. The Anabaptist controversy forced them to study baptism more carefully from 1525 on, and indeed from that point on we see the Reformers increasingly willing to settle for some form of sprinkling or pouring. The mode of baptism they considered *adiaphora* because both sprinkling and immersion could be understood as a sign of washing.

At the very heart of the sacrament of baptism is the act of washing with water and the proclamation of the Word. Together they are a sign and a promise of God's purifying activity in our lives. When we are marked by the sign of baptism we are to receive it as a promise of the gift of God's Spirit, who not only claims us for his own but will in time make us his own. A celebration of baptism which is reformed according to Scripture should be conducted in such a way that this sign is clearly seen and this promise distinctly heard.

84. Calvin's Latin text is particularly interesting at this point. He refers to the Old Testament rites of purification as *"Baptismata et purificationes."* This, as we noticed above, is quite consistent with the practice of the first century, which used the Greek word βαπτισμός to speak of the ceremonial washings of the Old Testament as well as the Christian sacrament.

85. Cf. *OS* 5, p. 279. The editor suggests there is a typographical error and that the reference should read Hebrews 9 and 10.

Conclusions

Perhaps the best way to draw this work together and arrive at some clear-cut conclusions is to identify the major goals and intentions of the Reformers in developing their baptismal rite.

The first intention of the Reformers was that their worship should be according to Scripture. As the discussion developed it became clear that they had much more in mind than a simplistic biblicism. They understood worship as the work of God among his people. It was in understanding worship as *opus dei* that they passed beyond the *opus operandi* of medieval liturgical theology. For the Reformers liturgy is far more than "the people's work," as the cliché so often heard today would put it. Although God calls his people to serve him in worship, and although God calls ministers to order and lead the worship of the congregation, worship is essentially God's work. Baptism in particular is understood as a divinely given sign, and therefore the Reformers believed it should be administered according to God's Word.

It was for this reason that the Reformers were so concerned to maintain the simplicity and clarity of the primary sign of washing which God has given us in the sacrament. However appropriate or inappropriate the auxiliary signs of signation, exorcism, and anointing might be, they were understood by the Reformers to obscure the divinely given sign and therefore needed to be removed from the rite. The Reformers had learned from early Christian writers such as Tertullian that early in the history of the Church baptism had been celebrated in a very simple and straightforward manner. The Reformers' desire to recover that simplicity was based on a profound confidence that God used the sign of baptism.

The Reformers did not intend to make a choice between "what is not forbidden is allowed" and "what is not commanded is not allowed." Neither did the High Rhenish Reformers apply the principle of *adiaphora* the way Luther did. They appreciated Luther's point but they saw the problem in a different way. As

Oecolampadius formulated it in his defense of infant baptism, those questions about which Scripture does not specifically speak should be answered in a way consistent with the fundamental teachings of Scripture. If Scripture does not specifically teach that the children of Christian parents are to be baptized, the Church should baptize such children because of what Scripture teaches about the prevenience of grace and the place of children in the covenant community, because of the analogy between circumcision and baptism, and because of what Scripture teaches about baptism being a sign of our entrance into the Kingdom of God. It is in this way that the Reformers understood the baptism of children to be in accordance with Scripture.

The second goal of this reform was to maintain the unity of word and sacrament. Early in the Reformation Luther had explained baptism in terms of giving the promise which faith believes. It was therefore important to state the promise carefully in the actual celebration of baptism. The High Rhenish Reformers picked up on this and saw to it that there was a Baptismal Exhortation in the rite itself. This became one of the major elements of the Reformed baptismal rite. Even more significantly they gave great attention to the reviving of catechetical teaching.

As early as 1522, catechetical instruction began to appear in both Wittenberg and Zurich, and it soon became one of the most carefully cultivated reforms of Reformed Churches generally. Most of the Reformers tried their hand at writing catechisms. Catechetical preaching was revived in conscious emulation of the great catechetical sermons of the fourth-century Fathers.

A third major principle of this reform was to make clear the unity of water and Spirit. The Reformers insisted that according to Scripture there was one baptism. To divide the sacrament into a baptism of water and a baptism of the Spirit, or to make confirmation a second sacrament, or to wash with water as a sign of the forgiveness of sins and then anoint with oil or lay on hands as a sign of the giving of the Spirit was misleading. The Reformers for the same reason carefully avoided any kind of prayer after the baptismal washing which might imply that those who had been washed should then receive the gift of the Holy Spirit. The prayer for the Holy Spirit was intentionally put before the baptismal washing to make clear that unity of water and Spirit. Baptism with water is a sign of both the washing away of sins and the pouring out of the Holy Spirit.

At the beginning of the Reformation Luther put great emphasis on the Church's prayers for those whom she baptized. At Strasbourg Bucer developed the classic Reformed Baptismal Invocation which prayed that the Holy Spirit accomplish inwardly what outwardly the sacramental action signified. This prayer was a baptismal epiclesis, making it clear that the sacrament of baptism is not magic. For the Reformers the Baptismal Invocation made clear that the cleansing of hearts was in the last analysis the work of the Holy Spirit. Calvin in particular liked to point out that in Scripture water is a sign of the Holy Spirit and the sprinkling and washing with water the sign of the renewing of the heart.

It is at this point that Reformed Churches find themselves taking issue with the Pentecostal Churches as well as with Scholastic theology of the Middle Ages. It is not as though baptism with water were merely for salvation, while baptism with the Holy Spirit were for a full empowering with the gifts of the Spirit. Reformed Churches should not in their liturgical practice give ground to a separation of the baptism with water and the baptism of the Spirit.

A fourth goal of this reform was to deal with the pastoral realities of baptizing children. This was in part done by postponing certain elements of the rite. Catechetical instruction and the making of vows were postponed until the child was old enough to understand the instruction, and to make vows on the basis of that instruction. The vows made by the parents at the baptismal service were not understood as a vicarious confession of faith whereby parents made the vows for the child, but rather as an expression of the faith of the parents. The proper baptismal confession of faith was made by the child, in later years, when the catechism was recited in front of the congregation. The Reformers did not mean by this that the baptism of infants was incomplete until "finished" by catechetical instruction and the vows of faith. It was rather that with the washing of water in the name of Christ the baptismal sign in all its fullness had been given, but the giving of that sign entailed catechetical instruction and the making of vows.

It was the same way with the baptismal prayers which confessed sin and asked for forgiveness and growth in grace. Baptism entails these prayers, which should be part of the daily prayer of the Christian. Bucer understood the prayer of confession which began every service of worship as baptismal prayer. It is at this point particularly that we see the Reformers regarding baptism as the sign under which the Christian lives out the whole of life. Faithful to the sign of baptism, God daily purifies us and renews us through his Spirit as we more and more die to sin and live to him. The sign of baptism, although administered but once, is a continuing reality in the Christian life.

Since the great majority of baptisms were administered to the children of Christians, the Reformers felt it was inappropriate to exorcise them or to ask them to renounce the devil. They did not believe that their children were demon-possessed, but as children of the covenant they understood them to be, by the grace of God, holy. They perceived the exorcism of children to be a contradiction of their rationale for baptizing their children.

A fifth goal or intention of the early Reformed theologians was to explain baptism as a sign of the covenant. In the biblical doctrine of the covenant the Reformers found a way to understand the sacraments which they believed to be more true to Scripture than the explanations offered by the Scholasticism of the Middle Ages. Covenant theology is in fact the sacramental theology of the Reformed Churches.

Covenant theology developed as a direct result of the rediscovery of biblical Hebrew by the High Rhenish Christian Humanists at the beginning of the sixteenth century. Pellikan, Capito, and Oecolampadius had been pioneers in this recovery. Both Oecolampadius and Zwingli saw the relevance of the doctrine of the covenant to the question of infant baptism fairly early, but Calvin and, above all, Bullinger then developed covenant theology into a comprehensive sacramental theology.

Essential to this recovery of covenant theology is a deep appreciation of the biblical concept of sign. As the Reformers studied Scripture they discovered what an important role divinely given signs had in inspiring, increasing, and strengthening the faith of God's people. It was because the Reformers prized so highly the divinely given signs that they had such disdain for those signs of merely human invention which obscured them. If the Reformers discontinued much of the ceremonial of the day, it was not because they disapproved of physical signs or were only interested in words but because they had come to a profound appreciation for the true biblical signs, that is, those signs which God himself had given and therefore belonged to God's self-revelation.

The final, and perhaps the paramount, goal of this reshaping of the rite of baptism was the concern that this sacrament should be clearly a sacrament of grace. The Reformation was an Augustinian revival and a reaction against the Pelagianism of late medieval Nominalism. It is against this background that *sola fides, sola gratia,* and *sola scriptura* are all to be explained. It was because of this concern to understand baptism as a sacrament of grace that the Reformers were not too impressed by what they read about many aspects of the baptismal mysteries of the fourth century. The baptismal rites which became so popular in the fourth century were clearly on the road to Pelagianism. One had to prove at repeated scrutinies that one already was a Christian before one was baptized in those days. In the sixteenth century that idea would have appealed to the Anabaptists much more readily than to Luther or Calvin.

When the earliest Anabaptists first advanced their approach to the reform of baptism, some of the Reformers showed interest in their suggestions, but as the discussion advanced they realized that the Anabaptist approach was inconsistent with their understanding of what the Scriptures taught about grace. The Reformers continued to baptize the children of Christians because the practice was consistent with the revelation of God's grace in Jesus Christ.

The reshaping of the rite of baptism which took place in the Reformed Churches of the Upper Rhineland, Alsace, and Switzerland was a well-thought-out and balanced liturgical reform. It was the fruit of careful study of the Scriptures, long theological discussion, and deep reflection. A careful study of these reforms does much to inform those who would faithfully celebrate the sacrament in our generation.

Bibliography

I. Early Sixteenth-Century Baptismal Rites

Augsburg Latin Ritual of 1499.
Obsequiale sive Benedictionale secundum ecclesiam Augustensem. Augsburg: Eberhard Ratdolt *(sic)*, 1499.

Augsburg Service Book of 1537.
Forma, wie von dem hailigen Tauf, und dem hailigen Sacrament des liebs und bluts Christ, und demnach vom Elichen Stand bey dem Einsegen der Eeleut, zu reden sey, Gestellt in die Kirch und Gemaind Christi der Statt Augspurg. Augsburg: P. Ulhart, 1537.

Basel Latin Ritual of 1488.
Informatorium sacerdotum de agendis circa . . . dispensationem sacramentorum et sacramentalium. . . . Basel: M. Wenssler and J. Kilchen, 1488.

Basel Service Book of 1526.
Form und Gstalt wie das Herren Nachtmahl, Der Kinder Tauff, Der Krancken haymsuochung zuo Basel gebraucht und gehalten werden. Augsburg: P. Ulhart, 1526.

Basel Service Book of 1526.
Form und gstalt wie der kinder tauff, Des berren nachtmal, und der krancken heymsuchung jetz zu Basel von etlichen Predicanten gehalten werden. Basel: Thomas Wolff, 1526.

Basel Service Book of 1537.
Form der Sacramenten bruch wie sy zuo Basel gebrucht werden mit sampt eynem Kurtzen Kinder bericht. Basel: L. Schouber, 1537.

Bern Service Book of 1528.

Ein kurtze gmeine form, kinder zetouffen, Die Ee zebestäten. Die Predig anzefahen und zuo enden, wie es zü Bernn gebrucht wird. Zurich: C. Froschauer, 1528.

Bern Service Book of 1529.

Ordnung und satzung des Eegrichts, straff des Eebruchs und Hury ze Bern. Ouch form und gestalt der Eelüten ynfürung, des Touffs und Herrn Nachtmal, wie es ze Bernn gebrucht wirdt. Zurich: C. Froschauer, 1529.

Bern Service Book of 1541.

Cancell und Agendbuchly der killchen zu Bärn. Bern: M. Apiarius, 1541.

Castellani's Latin Baptismal Rite of 1523.

Sacerdotale iuxta s. Romane ecclesie et aliarum ecclessiarum, ex apostolice bibliotece, ac sanctorum patrum iurium sanctionibus, et ecclesiastiorum doctorum scriptis ad optatum commodum quorumcumque sacerdotum collectus, et omni nuper diligentia castigatus ac summorum Pontificum auctoritate multoties approbatum. . . . Venice, 1523. (This went through sixteen editions.)

Common Latin Ritual of 1510.

Agenda sive benedictionale commune agendorum cuilibet pastori ecclesie necessarium. Leipzig: M. Lotter, 1510.

Common Latin Ritual of 1520.

Agenda siue Benedictionale commune agendorum: cuilibet pastori ecclesiae necessarium. Basel: Thomas Wolff, 1520.

Constance Latin Ritual of 1510.

Obsequiale siue benedictionale secundum ecclesiam Constantiensem. Augsburg: Erhard Radolt *(sic)*, 1510.

Constance Service Book of 1526.

Form und Ordnung wie von dem Pfarrer zu sant Steffan in Constantz und sinen Curaten, mit Touffe, Richten Infueren von den abgestorben gehalten wurt. S.l.: s.n., 1526.

French Evangelical Psalter of 1542.

La Manyere de faire prieres aux eglises Francoyses tant devant la predication comme apres, ensamble pseaulmes cantiques francoys . . . le tout selon la parolle de nren seigneur. Rome: T. Bruess, 1542. (This service book, being intended for French Protestant churches, was actually published in Strasbourg, but to get it past the censors it claimed that it was published in Rome.)

Genevan Service Book of 1538.

Lordre et maniere quon tient en administrant les sainctz sacemens: assauoir, le Baptesme, et le Cene de nosttre Seigneur. Item, en la celebration du Mariage & en la Visitation des malades. Avec la form quon observe es predictions, principallement quant aux exhortations and prieres quon y faict. Es lieux lesquelz Dieu de sa grace a visite, faisant que selon sa saincte parolle ce quil a deffendu en son Eglise soit reiette; & ce quil a conmande soit tenu. Geneva: J. Michel, 1538.

Genevan Psalter of 1542.
La forme des prieres et chantz ecclesiastiques, avec la maniere d'administrer les Sacraments, & consacrer le Mariage: selon la coustume de l'Eglise ancienne. Geneva: J. Gerard, 1542.

Loener's German Baptismal Service of 1524.
Ordnung der Tauff nach Bambergischer Rubricken von wort zu wort Verteutscht. Bamberg: G. Erlinger, 1524.

Luther's German Baptismal Book of 1523.
Das tauff büchlin verdeutscht durch Mart. Luther. Wittenberg: N. Schirlentz, 1523.

Luther's German Baptismal Book of 1526.
Das tauffbüchlin verdeutdscht, auffs new zu gericht, durch Mart. Luth. Wittenberg: H. Weiss, 1526.

Mainz Latin Ritual of 1513.
Agenda Maguntinensis cum utilissimis scituque dignissimis (prioribus tamen non insertis) quisbusdam notabilibus: iam noviter ac diligenter impresse. Mainz: J. Schoeffer, 1513.

Neuchâtel Service Book of 1533 (French Evangelical).
La maniere et fasson quon tient en baillant le sainct baptesme en la saincte congregation de dieu: et en espousant celux qui viennent au sainct mariage, et a la saincte Cene de nostre seignr, es lieux dieu de sa grace a visite, faisant q. selon sa saincte parolle ce quil a deffendu en son eglisse soit reiecte et ce quil a commande soit tenu. Aussi la maniere comment la predication commence, moyenne et finit, avec les prieres et exhortations quon faict a tous et pour tous, et de la visitation des malades. Neuchâtel: P. de Vingle, 1533.

Osiander's German Baptismal Service of 1524.
Ordnung wie man Tauffet, bissher im Latein Gehalten, vertaeütscht, hierin ist, auss ettlichen ursachen, was die andern, als uberflussig, veracht haben, nicht aussgelassen. Nuremberg: J. Guttknecht, 1524.

Strasbourg German Mass (A).
Teütsch Messz und Tauff wie sye yetzund zuo Straszburg gehalten werden. Strasbourg: W. Köpphel, 1524.

Strasbourg German Baptismal Service of 1524 (A5).
Das Taufbüchlin, nach rechter Form uff Teütsch zu Tauffen. Strasbourg: (W. Köpphel), 1524.

Strasbourg German Church Service of 1524 (C).

Teutsch Kirchen ampt mit lobgesengen und goetlichen psalmen wie es die gemein zuo Straszburg singt und haltt gantz Christlich. Strasbourg: W. Köpphel, 1524. (Three editions are listed by Hubert, *Liturgischen Ordnungen,* xiii-xv.)

Strasbourg Latin Ritual of 1513.

Agenda siue Exequiale sacramentorum, et eorum in ecclesijs aguntur. Strasbourg: Renatus Beck, 1513.

Strasbourg Church Order of 1525 (D).

Ordnung des herren Nachmahl: so man die mesz nennet sampt der Tauff und Insegung der Ee, Wie yetzt die diener des Wort gots zuo Strassburg Erneüwert und nach götlicher gschrifft gebessert habenuss ursach in nachgender Epistel gemeldet. Strasbourg: J. Schwann, 1515. Two editions are listed by Hubert, *Liturgischen Ordnungen,* xv-xvi.

Strasbourg Church Service of 1525 (E).

Straszburger Kirchen ampt, nemlich von Insegung d'Eeleüt, vom Tauf und von des herren nachtmal, mit etlichen Psalmen die am end des büchlins, ordenlich verseychnet sein. Strasbourg: W. Köpphel, 1525.

Strasbourg Psalter of 1526 (F).

Psalmen gebett und Kirchen ubung wie sie zum Straszburg gehalten werden. Strasbourg: W. Köpphel, 1526. (Three editions are listed by Hubert, *Liturgischen Ordnungen,* xvi-xvii.)

Strasbourg Psalter of 1530 (G),

Psalmen gebett und kirchen uebung wie sie zuo Straszburg gehalten werden. Strasbourg: W. Köpphel, 1530.

Strasbourg Psalter of 1533 (H).

Psalmen gebett und kirchen uebung wie sie zuo Straszburg gehalten werden. Strasbourg: W. Köpphel, 1533.

Strasbourg Psalter of 1537 (J).

Psalmen und Geysttliche lieder, die man zu Straszburg und auch die man inn anderen Kirchen pflagt zu singen. Form und gebett zum einsegen der Ee dem heiligen Tauff, Abentmal, besuchung der Krancken und begrebnüs der abgestorbnen. Alles gemert und bebessert. Strasbourg: W. Köpphel, n.d. (This evidently went through several editions; cf. Hubert, *Liturgischen Ordnungen,* xxii-xxvii.)

Strasbourg Psalter of 1539 (K).

Psalter mit aller Kirchenubüng die man bey der Christlichen Gemein zum Straszburg und anders wa pflaegt zum singen. Strasbourg: W. Köpphel, 1539.

Ulm Service Book of 1531.

Handtbüchlin darinn begriffen ist die Ordnung un weiss, wie die Sacrament und Ceremonien der Kirchen zu Ulm gebraucht und gehalten werden. S.l.: s.n., 1531.

Leo Jud's Service Book (Zurich).

Ein kurtze und gemeine form für die schwach gleubigen: Kinder zuo touffen auch andere ermanungen zuo got: so da gmeinlich geschehen in Christenlichen versamlung. Zurich: C. Froschauer, 1523. (Three editions are given in the *Corpus Reformatorum.*)

Zurich Service Book of c. 1525-26 (Third).

Ordnung der Christlichen Kilchen zuo Zürich. Kinder ze touffen. Die Ee zebestäten. Die Predig anzefahen und zuo enden. Gedächtnus der abgestorbenen. Das Nachtmal Christi zuo begon. Zurich: C. Froschauer, n.d.

Zurich Service Book of 1528.

Eine kurtz allgemeine Form, kiner zu taufen, die Ehe zubestautigen, die Predigt anzufangen und zu unden, wie es zu Zürich gebraucht wird. Zurich: C. Froschauer, 1528.

Zurich Service Book of 1535.

Christlich Ordnung und bruch der Kilchen Zürich. Zurich: C. Froschauer, 1535.

II. Early Sixteenth-Century Catechisms

Basel Catechism of c. 1525-29.

(No copy of this document has come down to us. Presumably the edition of 1537 is a copy of this earlier edition.)

Basel Catechism of 1537.

Form der Sacramenten bruch, wie sy zu Basel gebrucht weren, mit sampt eynem kurtzen Kinderbericht. Basel: L. Schouber, 1537.

Constance Catechism of 1526.

Das Vatter unser in frag vnd betswyss für die jungenn Kind ussgelegt ouch den alten nit undienstlich. Constance: G. Mangolt, 1526-28.

Constance Catechism of 1530.

Bekantnus der zwölff artickel, des Gloubens von Jesu Christo, zuo dem Allmächtigen Gott in himel. Constance: J. Spitzenborg, 1530.

Constance Catechism of 1535.

Das Vatter unser in frag und gebätts wyss, für jung vnnd einfaltig lüt. Zurich: C. Froschauer, 1535.

French Evangelical Catechism of 1542.
Institution purile de la doctrine chrestienne faicte par maniere du dyalogue. Rome (in reality, not Rome at all but rather Strasbourg): T. Bruess, 1542.

Genevan Catechism of 1542.
(No copy of this document has come down to us. Presumably the edition of 1545 is a copy of this earlier edition.)

Genevan Catechism of 1545.
Le catechisme de l'Eglise de Geneve, c'est à dire, le Formulaire d'instruire les enfans en la Chrestienté. (Geneva: I. Girard), 1545.

Genevan Catechism of 1545.
Catechismus ecclesiae Genevensis, hoc est formula erudiendi pueros in doctrina Christi. Strasbourg: W. Rihel, 1545.

Genevan Shorter Catechism of 1553.
La maniere d'interroguer les enfans qu'on veut recevoir a la cene nostre Seigneur Jesus Christ. (For bibliographical information see *CR* VI, p. ix and p. 148.)

Luther's Larger Catechism of 1529.
Deudsch Catechismus Mart. Luther. Wittenberg: G. Rhau, 1529.

Luther's Shorter Catechism of 1529.
Der Kleine Catechismus, für die gemeyne Pfarherr vnd Prediger. Marberg: F. Rhode, 1529.

Luther's Second Shorter Catechism of 1529.
Enchiridion. Der Kleine Catechismus für die gemeine Pfarherr vnd Prediger, gemhreet vnd gebessert, durch Mart. Luther. Wittenberg: N. Schirlentz, 1529.

St. Gall Catechism of 1528.
Ein Christliche underwisung der Jugend, im glouben gegrundt in der heiligen geschrifft, fragens wyss. Zurich: C. Froschauer, 1528.

Strasbourg Catechism of 1527 (Capito's Catechism).
Kinderbericht und Fragstuck von gemeynen puncten Christlichs glaubens. Strasbourg: W. Köpphel, 1527.

Strasbourg Catechism of 1534. (Bucer's Catechism)
Kurtze schrifftliche Erklärung für die Kindere und angehnden. Der gemeinen Artickeln unsers christlichen Glaubens. Der zehn Gebott. Des Vater Unsers. . . . Strasbourg: M. Apiarius, 1534.

Strasbourg Catechism of 1536. (Zell's Catechism)
Frag vnnd Antowrt vff die artkel des christlichen glaubens wie die gemeynklich inn einner summ vnd von menglich zum heyl bekent werden

sollen zu einer erklorung der selbigen für die kinder, durch Matteum Zell Pfarrherr im Munster zu Strassburg. Strasbourg: J. Frolich, 1536.

Strasbourg Catechism of 1537.

Der kürtzer Catechismus und erklärung der XII stücken Christlichs glaubens, des Vaters unsers, und der zehen gebotten. Für die Schüler und andere kinder zu Straszburg. Burch die Prediger daselbst gestellet. Strasbourg: W. Rihel, 1537.

Ulm Catechism of 1528.

Christenliche underweysung der Jungen in fragszweis von dem Glauben, Vatter unser, und zehen Gebotten. Ulm: H. Gruner, 1528.

Zurich Catechism of 1541. (Jud's Shorter Catechism).

Eine kurtze christliche Unterweisung der Jungend in der Erkenntnis in den Geboten Gottes, im Glauben, im Gebet und anderen notwendigen Dingen, durch die Diener des Wortes zu Zürich in Fragen erteilt. Zurich: s.n., 1541.

Zurich Catechism of 1534. (Jud's Larger Catechism).

Christliche, klare und einfache Einführung in den Willen und in die Gnade Gottes, womit nicht nur die Jugend, sondern auch die Eltern unterrichtet werden, wie sie ihre Kinder in den Geboten Gottes, im christlichen glauben und im rechten gebet unterweisen können. Zurich: s.n., 1534.

III. Collections of Source Literature

Andrieu, Michel. *Les ordines romani du haut moyen-âge.* Louvain: "Spicilegium sacrum lovaniense" bureaux, 1931-61. 5 vols.

Andrieu, Michel. *Le pontifical romain au moyen-âge.* Città del Vaticano: Biblioteca apostolica vaticana, 1938-41. 4 vols. (*Studi e teste,* 86-88, 99).

Baillie, J., J. T. McNeill, and H. P. van Dusen, eds. *Library of Christian Classics.* Philadelphia: Westminster Press, 1953-66, 26 vols.

Bromiley, G. W., ed. *Zwingli and Bullinger: Selected Translations.* Philadelphia: Westminster Press, 1952. (*The Library of Christian Classics,* 24).

Bucer, Martin. *Martin Bucers deutsche Schriften.* R. Stupperich, ed. Gütersloh: Mohn, 1960.

Calvin, John. *Ioannis Calvini, opera quae supersunt omnia,* G. Baum, E. Cunitz, and E. Reuss, eds. Brunswick, 1863-1900. (*Corpus Reformatorum,* 29-87).

Calvin, John. *Opera Selecta.* P. Barth and W. Niesel, eds. Munich: C. Kaiser, 1926-62.

Cohrs, Ferdinand, ed. *Die evangelische Katechismusversuche vor Luthers Enchiridion.* Berlin: A. Hofmann, 1900-07. 5 vols. (*Monumenta Germaniae paedagogica,* 20-23, 39).

Corpus Christianorum, series latina. Turnhout: Typographi Brepols, 1953-.

Corpus iuris canonici. Aemilius Friedberg, ed. Leipzig: B. Tauchnitz, 1879-81. 2 vols.

Corpus Reformatorum. Zurich: Berichthaus, 1961.

Corpus scriptorum ecclesiasticorum latinorum. Vienna: Osterreichische Akademie der Wissenschaften, 1866-.

Daniel, Hermann Adalbert. *Codex Liturgicus ecclesiae universae in epitomen redactus.* Vol. 1: "Ecclesiae romano-catholicae." Vol. 2: "Ecclesiae lutheraneae." Lipsiae: T. O. Weigel, 1847-48.

Denck, Johannes. *Schriften.* Eds. G. Baring and W. Fellmann. Gütersloh: C. Bertelsmann, 1955-60. 3 vols. (*Quellen und Forschungen zur Reformationsgeschichte,* 24.) (*Quellen zur Geschichte der Täufer,* 6).

Durr, Emil and Paul Roth, eds. *Aktensammlung geschichte der Baser Reformation in den Jahren 1519 bis unfang 1534.* Basel: Karl Werner, 1933.

Hubert, Friedrich. *Die Strassburger liturgischen Ordnungen im Zeitalter der Reformation.* Göttingen: Vandenhoeck & Ruprecht, 1900.

Hübmaier, Balthasar. *Schriften.* Hrsg. von Gunnar Westin u. Torsten Bergsten. Gütersloh: G. Mohr, 1962. (*Quellen zur Geschichte der Täufer,* 9.) (*Quellen und Forschungen zur Reformationsgeschichte,* 29).

Lake, Kirsopp, ed. *The Apostolic Fathers.* London: Heinemann, 1965. 2 vols. *(Loeb Classical Library)*.

Loeb Classical Library: Greek and Latin Authors. Cambridge, Mass.: Harvard University Press, 1912-.

Lubac, H. de and J. Danièlou, eds. *Sources chrétiennes.* Paris, 1941-.

Luther, Martin. *D. Martin Luthers Werke, kritische Gesamtausgabe.* Weimar: H. Bohlau, 1883-.

Mansi, Joannes Dominicus. *Sacrorum conciliorum nova, et amplissima collectio.* Florence: Expensis Antonii Zatta Veneti, 1759-.

Marténe, Edmond. *De antiquis ecclesiae ritibus.* Rouen: G. Berhourt, 1700, 3 vols.

Migne, J. P., ed. *Patrologiae cursus completus, series graeca.* Paris: Gernier, 1857-91. 161 vols. in 166.

Migne, J. P., ed. *Patrologiae cursus completus, series latina.* Paris: Gernier, 1844-91? 221 vols. in 223.

Monumenta Germaniae Paedagogica. Berlin: A. Hofmann, 1886-.

Müller, E. F. Karl. *Die Bekenntnisschriften und Kirchenordnungen der nach Gottes Wortt reformierten Kirche.* Munich: A. Deichert, 1938.

Münzer, Thomas. *Schriften und Briefe: kritische gesamtausgabe.* Eds. Paul Kirn and Gunter Franz. Gütersloh: G. Mohn, 1968.

Niesel, Wilhelm, ed. *Bekenntnisschriften und Kirchenordnungen der nach Gottes Wortt reformierten Kirche.* 2nd ed. Munich: A. G. Zollikon, 1938.

Oecolampadius, J. *Briefe und Akten zum Leben Oekolampads.* Ernst Staehelin, ed. Leipzig: M. Heinsius, 1927-34. 2 vols.

Osiander, Andreas (der Altere). *Gesamtausgabe.* Hrsg. von Gerhard Müller und Gottfried Seebass. Gütersloh: G. Mohn, 1975-79. 3 vols.

Le Pontifical Romano-Germanique du dixieme siècle. Cyrille Vogel and Reinhard Elze, eds. Città del Vaticano: Biblioteca apostolica vaticana, 1963. 3 vols. (*Studi e Testi,* 226-27, 269).

Quellen zur Geschichte der Täufer. Manfred Krebs and Jans Georg Rott, eds. Vol. 1. Gütersloh: G. Mohn, 1934-.

Reformed Confessions of the 16th Century. Arthur C. Cochrane, trans. Philadelphia: Westminster Press, 1966.

Reu, Johann Michael, ed. *Quellen zur Geschichte des kirchlichen Unterrichts in der evangelischen Kirche Deutschlands zwischen 1530 und 1600.* Gütersloh: C. Bertelsmann, 1904. 4 vols. in 9.

Richter, Aemilius Ludwig, ed. *Die evangelischen Kirchenordnungen des sechzehnten Jahrhunderts.* Weimar: Verlag des Landes-Industrie-Comptoirs, 1846. 2 vols.

Roberts, A. and J. Donaldson, eds. *The Ante-Nicene Fathers.* Reprint. Grand Rapids, Mich.: Eerdmans, 1956.

Schaff, Philip and Henry Wace, eds. *A Select Library of Nicene and Post-Nicene Fathers of the Christian Church.* Reprint. Grand Rapids, Mich., Eerdmans, 1954-71. 14 vols.

Sehling, Emil, ed. *Die evangelischen Kirchenordnungen des XVI. Jahrhunderts.* Tübingen: J. C. B. Mohr, 1905-.

Smend, Julius, ed. *Die evangelischen deutschen Messen bis zu Luthers Deutscher Messe.* Göttingen: Vandenhoeck und Ruprecht, 1896.

Staehelin, Ernst, ed. *Das Buch der Basler Reformation.* Basel: Helbing und Lichtenhahn, 1929.

Thompson, Bard, ed. *Liturgies of the Western Church.* Cleveland: Meridian, 1961.

Wackernagel, Philipp. *Das deutsche Kirchenlied von der ältesten Zeit bis zur Anfang des XVIII. Jahrhunderts.* Leipzig: B. G. Teubner, 1866-77. 5 vols.

Williams, George Huntston. *Spiritual and Anabaptist Writers. Documents Il-*

lustrative of the Radical Reformation. Angel M. Mergal. *Evangelical Catholicism.* Philadelphia: Westminster Press, 1957. 1 vol. (*Library of Christian Classics,* 25).

Zwingli, Huldreich. *Huldreich Zwinglis sämtliche Werke.* E. Egli, G. Finsler, W. Kohler, O. Farner, F. Blanke, and L. von Muralt, eds. Leipzig: M. Heinsius Nachfolger, 1927.

Zwingli, Ulrich. *Selected Works.* Ed. Samuel Macauley Jackson. Philadelphia: University of Pennsylvania Press, 1972.

IV. Dictionaries and Encyclopedias

Allgemeine deutsche Biographie. Leipzig: Duncker & Humblot, 1875-1912.

Altaner, Bertold. *Patrology.* Trans. H. C. Graef. New York: Herder & Herder, 1961.

Bardenhewer, Otto. *Geschichte der altkirchlichen Literatur.* Freiburg in Breisgau: Herder, 1902-32. 5 vols.

Bibliographie zur deutschen Geschichte im Zeitalter der Glaubensspaltung. Karl Schottenloher, ed. Leipzig: K. W. Hiersemann, 1933-62.

British Museum. *General Catalogue of Printed Books.* London: Trustees of the British Museum, 1963-.

Dictionnaire d'archéologie chrétienne et de liturgie. Ferdinand Cabrol and Henri Leclercq, eds. Paris: Letouzey et Ané, 1935-65. 7 vols.

Dictionnaire de droit canonique. R. Naz, ed. Paris: Letouzey et Ané, 1935-65. 7 vols.

Dictionnaire de théologie catholique. A. Vacant, E. Mangenot, and E. Amann, eds. Paris: Letouzey et Ané, 1923-72. 15 vols. in 30.

The Encylopaedia Britannica. New York: Encyclopaedia Britannica Co., 1910-11. 19 vols.

Encyclopaedia of Religion and Ethics. James Hastings, ed. Edinburgh: T. & T. Clark, 1908-26.

Kommentar zum Neuen Testament aus Talmud und Midrasch. Hermann L. Strack and Paul Billerbeck, eds. Munich: Beck, 1922-61.

Lexicon für Theologie und Kirche. 2nd ed. Freiburg im Breisgau: Herder, 1957-65. 10 vols.

The Mennonite Encyclopedia. Hillsboro, Kans.: Mennonite Brethren Pub. House, 1955-59. 4 vols.

New Catholic Encyclopedia. New York: McGraw-Hill, 1967.

The Oxford Dictionary of the Christian Church. F. L. Cross, ed. London: Oxford University Press, 1957.

Quasten, Johannes. *Patrology.* Utrecht: Spectrum, 1966.

Reallexikon für Antike und Christentum. Theodor Klausner, ed. Stuttgart: Hiersemann, 1950-.

Realencyklopädie für protestantische Theologie und Kirche. J. J. Herzog, ed. Leipzig: J. C. Hinrichs, 1896-1913. 24 vols.

Die Religion in Geschichte und Gegenwart. 3rd ed. Tübingen: Mohr, 1957-65. 7 vols.

Theologisches Wörterbuch zum Neuen Testament. Gerhard Kittel, ed. Stuttgart: W. Kohlhammer, 1932-79. 10 vols. in 12.

V. General

Abbott, T. K. *Epistles to the Ephesians and to the Colossians.* Edinburgh: T. & T. Clark, 1979.

Abrahams, I. "How Did the Jews Baptize?" *Journal of Theological Studies* 12 (1910-12): 609-12.

Adam, Alfred. "Das Sintflutbeget in der Taufliturgie." *Wort und Dienst, Jahrbuch der theologischen Schule Bethel.*

Allmen, J. J. von. *Worship, its Theology and Practice.* London: Oxford University Press, 1965.

Althaus, Paul. *The Theology of Martin Luther.* Trans. Robert C. Schultz. Philadelphia: Fortress Press, 1966.

Alting von Geusau, L. G. M. *Die Lehre von der Kindertaufe bei Calvin.* Bilthoven: H. Neilssen, 1963.

Ambrose of Milan. *Des sacrements, des mystéres.* Ed. Dom Bernard Botte. Paris: Les Editions du Cerf, 1959.

Augustine. *Sermons pour la Pâque.* Ed. Suzanne Poque. Paris: Les Editions du Cerf, 1966.

Balke, Willem. *Calvin and the Anabaptist Radicals.* Trans. William Heynen. Grand Rapids, Mich.: Eerdmans, 1981.

Barge, Hermann. *Andreas Bodenstein von Karlstadt.* Leipzig: F. Brandstetter, 1905. 2 vols.

Baring, G. "Hans Denck und Thomas Müntzer in Nürnberg 1524," *Archiv für Reformationsgeschichte* 50 (1959): 145-81.

Baur, Johannes. *Die Spendung der Taufe in der Brixner Diözese in der Zeit vor dem Tridentinum.* Innsbruck: Universitätsverlag Wagner, 1938. (*Schlern-Schriften,* 42).

Beasley-Murray, G. R. *Baptism in the New Testament.* London: Macmillan, 1962.

Bedouelle, Guy. *Lefèvre d'Etaples et l'intelligence des écritures.* Geneve: Librairie Droz, 1976.

Behm, J. "μετανοέω," *Theologisches Wörterbuch zum Neuen Testament,* 4: 972ff.

Beleth, Johannes. *Summa de ecclesiasticis officiis.* Ed. Heriberto Douteil. Turnholt: Brepols, 1976. 2 vols. (*Corpus Christianorum: continuatio mediaevalis,* 41-41a).

Bender, Harold Stauffer. "The Anabaptist Vision," *Church History* 13 (1944): 3-24.

Bender, Harold Stauffer. "The Zwickau Prophets, Thomas Müntzer and the Anabaptists," *The Mennonite Quarterly Review* 27 (1953): 3-16.

Benoît, André. *Le baptême chrétien au second siècle.* Paris: Presses Universitaires de France, 1953. (Etudes d'histoire et de philosophie religieuses, 43).

Benz, S. "Zur Vorgeschichte des Textes der römischen Taufwasserwiehe," *Revue bénédictine* 66 (1966): 218-55.

Bergsten, Torssten. *Balthasar Hübmaier, seine stellung zu Reformation und Taufertum, 1521-1582.* Kassel: J. G. Oncken, 1961. (*Acta Universitatis Upsaliensis: Studia historico-ecclesiastica Upsaliensia,* 3).

"Berner Disputation." *Realencyklopädie für protestantische Theologie und Kirche,* vol. II. Leipzig: J. C. Hinrich, 1896-1913.

Bertholet, Alfred and Adolf Jülicher. "Exorzismus," *Die Religion in Geschichte und Gegenwart,* vol. II. 2nd ed. Pp. 474-77.

Betz, O. "Die Proselytentaufe der Qumransekte und die Taufe im Neuen Testament," *Revue de Qumran* 1 (1958-59): 213-34.

Bieder, Werner. *Die Verheissung der Taufe im Neuen Testament.* Zurich: EVZ-Verlag, 1966.

Bishop, Edmond. "The Liturgical Reforms of Charlemagne: Their Meaning and Value," *Downside Review* 38 (1919): 1-16.

Blanke, Fritz. *Brüder in Christo.* Zurich: Zwingli-Verlag, 1955.

Böcher, Otto. *Christus Exorcista, Dämonismus und Taufe im Neuen Testament.* Stuttgart: W. Kohlhammer, 1972.

Boegner, Marc. *Les catéchismes de Calvin, étude d'histoire et de catéchétique.* Pamiers: L. Labrunie, 1905.

Bornert, René. *La réforme protestante du culte à Strasbourg au XVIe siécle (1523-1598).* Leiden: E. J. Brill, 1981. (*Studies in Medieval and Reformation Thought,* 28).

Brandt, Otto H. *Thomas Müntzer: sein Leben und seine Schriften.* Jena: E. Diederichs, 1933.

Bromiley, Geoffrey William. *Baptism and the Anglican Reformers.* London: Lutterworth Press, 1953.

Bucer, Martin. *Bericht auss der heyligen geschrift von der recht gottseligen anstellung und hausshaltung Christlichen gemeyn, Eynsattzung der diener des worts, Haltung und brauch der heyligen Sacramenten.* Strasbourg: M. Apiarius, 1534.

Bucer, Martin. *Quid de baptismate infantium ivxta Scripturas Dei Sentiendum.* Strasbourg: M. Apiarius, 1533.

Bucer, Martin. *Scripta Anglicana fere omnia ius etiam, quae hactenus vel non dum, vel sparsim, vel peregrino saltem idiomate edita fuere, adjuntis.* Ed. Conrad Hubert. Basel: P. Perna, 1577.

Bucer und seine Zeit: Forschungsbeitr. u. Bibliographie. Hrsg. von Marijn de Kroon u. Friedhelm Krüger. Wiesbaden: Steiner, 1976.

Bullinger, Heinrich. *The Decades of Henry Bullinger.* Ed. Thomas Harding. Cambridge: The University Press, 1968.

Bullinger, Heinrich. "How to Deal with Anabaptists." Eds. H. Fast and J. H. Yoder. *Mennonite Quarterly Review* 33/2 (1959): 83- 95.

Bullinger, Heinrich. *Von dem vnuerschampten fräfel, ergerlichem verwyrren, vnnd vnwarhfftem leern der selbsgesandten Widertöuften, vier gespräch Bücher.* Zurich: C. Froschauer, 1531.

Burckhardt, Paul. *Die Basler Täufer: Ein Beitrag zur schweizerischen Reformationsgeschichte.* Basel, 1898.

Cabrol, Ferdinand. "Alcuin," *Dictionnaire d'archéologie chrétienne et de liturgie,* 1/I: 1072-92.

Calvin, John. *Institutes of the Christian Religion.* Ed. John T. McNeill; trans. Ford Lewis Battles. Philadelphia: Westminster Press, 1960. (*The Library of Christian Classics,* 20-21).

Calvin, John. *La forme de prières.* Bärenreiter edn. Cassel and Basel: Pierre Pidoux, 1959.

Capelle, Bernard. "L'introduction au catechumenat à Rome," *Recherches de théologie ancienne et médiévale* (1933): 129-54.

Capito, Wolfgang. *Was man halten unnd antworden soll von der spaltung zwischen Martin Luther und Andres Carolstadtt.* Strasbourg: W. Köpphel, 1524.

Caspari, Walter, *Die evangelische Konfirmation, vornämlich in der lutherischen Kirche.* Leipzig: A. Deichert, 1890.

Chavasse, Antoine. *Le Sacramentaire Gélasien.* Tournai: Desclée, 1958.

Chrysostom, Jean. *Huit catéchèses baptismales inédites.* Trans. Antoine Wenger. Paris: Les Editions du Cerf, 1958.

Cohn, Norman. *The Pursuit of the Millennium.* New York: Oxford University Press, 1970. Rev. and exp. edn.

Coppens, J. and A. D'Ales. "Baptême," *Dictionnaire de la Bible, Supplément.* (Supplement to Vigouroux's *Dictionnaire de la Bible.*) Paris: Letouzey et Ané, 1928. Vol. 1, pp. 852-942.

Corblet, Jules. *Histoire dogmatique, liturgique et archéologique du sacrament de baptême.* Paris: Société Générale de Librairie Catholique, 1881-82. 2 vols.

Courvoisier, Jacques. "Bucer et l'oeuvre de Calvin," *Revue de theologie de Lausanne* 86 (1933): 66-77.

Courvoisier, Jacques. "Les cátechismes de Geneve et de Strasbourg," *Bulletin de la Société de l'histoire du protestantisme Français* (1935): 105-21.

Courvoisier, Jacques. *Zwingli, A Reformed Theologian.* Richmond, Va.: John Knox Press, 1963.

Crehan, Joseph. *Early Christian Baptism and the Creed.* London: Burns, Oates & Washbourne, 1950. (*The Bellarmine Series,* 13).

Crehan, Joseph. "Ten Years' Work on Baptism and Confirmation, 1945-1955," *Theological Studies* 17 (1956): 494-515.

Cullmann, O. *Baptism in the New Testament.* London: SCM Press, 1950. Trans. J. K. S. Reid.

Cyprian of Carthage. *Correspondance.* Ed. and trans. Louis Bayard. Paris: Société d'édition "Les belles lettres," 1925. 2 vols.

Cyril of Jerusalem. *Catéchèses mystagogiques.* Ed. Auguste Piedagnel; trans. Pierre Paris. Paris: Editions du Cerf, 1966.

Daniélou, Jean. "Exorcism," *Dictionnaire de Spiritualité* 4: cols. 1995-2004.

Daniélou, Jean. *Le figures du Christ dans l'ancient Testament "sacramentum futuri."* Paris: Beauchesne, 1955.

Debongnie, Pierre. "Dévotion moderne," *Dictionnaire de la Spiritualité* 3, pp. 727-47.

Delaye, E. "Baptême," *Dictionnaire de la Spiritualité.*

Delling, Gerhard. *Die Taufe im Neuen Testament.* Stuttgart: W. Kohlhammer, 1952.

Dhotel, Jean Claude. *Les origines du catéchisme moderne, d'apres les premiers manuels imprimés en France.* Paris: Aubier, 1967.

Dölger, Franz Josef. "Beiträge zur Geschichte des Kreuzzeichens," *Jahrbuch für Antike und Christentums* 10 (1962).

Dölger, Franz Josef. *Der Exorzismus im altchristlichen Taufritual.* Paderborn:

F. Schöningh, 1909. (*Studien zur Geschichte und Kultur des Altertums,* 3 Bd., 1./2. Heft).

Dölger, Franz Josef. *Die Sonne der Gerechtigkeit und der Schwarze.* Münster/Westfalen: Aschendorff, 1918. (*Liturgiegeschichtliche Forschungen,* 2).

Douen, Orentin. *Clément Marot et le Psautier huguenot, étude historique littéraire, musicale et bibliographique* . . . Paris: Imprimerie nationale, 1878-99. 2 vols.

Douglass, E. Jane Dempsey. *Justification in Late Medieval Preaching: A Study of John Geiler of Keisersberg.* Leiden: E. J. Brill, 1966. (*Studies in Medieval and Reformation Thought,* 1).

Doumergue, Emile. *Jean Calvin: les hommes et les choses de son temps.* Lausanne: G. Bridel, 1899-1927. 7 vols.

Drews, Paul. *Beiträge zu Luthers liturgischen Reformen.* Tübingen: J. C. B. Mohr, 1910.

du Charlat, Regine. *La catéchèse aux premiers siècles.* Paris: Fayard-Mame, 1968.

Dujarier, Michel. *Le parrainage des adultes aux trois premiers siècles de l'Église.* Paris: Éditions du Cerf, 1962.

Durig, Walter. "Das Sintflutgebet in Luthers Taufbuchlein," *Warheit und Verkundigung.* Munich: Schöningh, 1967. 2 vols. (Festschrift for Michael Schmaus).

Early Protestant Educators: The Educational Writings of Martin Luther, John Calvin, and Other Leaders of Protestant Thought. Ed. Frederick Eby. New York: McGraw-Hill, 1931.

Edwards, Mark U. *Luther and the False Brethren.* Stanford, Cal.: Stanford University Press, 1975.

Eells, Hastings. *Martin Bucer.* New Haven, Conn.: Yale University Press, 1931.

Egli, Emil. "Leo Jud," *The New Schaff-Herzog Encyclopedia of Religious Knowledge* 6: pp. 242ff.

Elbogen, Ismar. *Der jüdische Gottesdienst in seiner geschichtlichen Entwicklung.* Leipzig: G. Foch, 1913.

Elert, Werner. *The Structure of Lutheranism.* St. Louis: Concordia, 1962. Trans. W. A. Hansen.

Ellard, Gerald. *Master Alcuin, Liturgist.* Chicago: Loyola University Press, 1956. (Jesuit Studies).

Ernst, August and Johann Adam. *Katechetische Geschichte des Elsasses bis zur Revolution.* Strasbourg: F. Bull, 1897.

Falk, Franz. *Die deutschen Mess-Auslegungen von der Mitte des fünfzehnten*

Jahrhunderts bis zum Jahre 1525. Köln: Vereinsschrift der Gorresgesellschaft, 1889.

Farel, William. *La maniere et fasson quon tient es lieux que Dieu de sa grace a visites.* Ed. J. G. Bauer. Strasbourg: Treuttel et Wurtz, 1859.

Fast, Heinold. *Heinrich Bullinger und die Täufer: ein Beitrag zur Historiographie un Theologie im 16. Jahrhundert.* Weierhof: Pfalz, 1959. (*Schriftenreihe des Mennonitischen Geschichtesvereins,* 7).

Feller, Richard. *Geschichte Berns.* Vol. 2: *Von der Reformation bis zum Bauernkrieg, 1516 bis 1653.* Bern: H. Lang, 1953.

Fisher, J. D. C. *Christian Initiation: Baptism in the Medieval West.* London: S.P.C.K., 1965.

Fisher, J. D. C. *Christian Initiation: The Reformation Period.* London: S.P.C.K., 1970.

Flemington, W. F. *The New Testament Doctrine of Baptism.* London: S.P.C.K., 1948.

Fluri, Adolf. *Das Berner Taufbüchlein von 1528.* Bern: E. Baumgart, 1904.

Frör, K. "Zur Interpretation der Kasseler Kirchenordnung von 1539," *Reformatio und Confirmatio: Festschrift für Wilhelm Maurer.* Berlin: Lutherische Verlagshaus, 1965.

Galtier, Paul. *Aux origines du sacrament de penitence.* Rome: Gregorian University Press, 1951.

Galtier, Paul. *L'Église et la remission des péchés aux premiers siècles.* Paris: Beauchesne, 1932.

Ganoczy, Alexandre. *Le jeune Calvin: genèse et évolution de sa vocation réformatrice.* Weisbaden: F. Steiner, 1966.

Garside, Charles. *The Origins of Calvin's Theology of Music 1536-1543.* Philadelphia: The American Philosophical Society, 1979.

Gestrich, Christof. *Zwingli als Theologe: Glaube und Geist beim Zürcher Reformator.* Zurich: Zwingli Verlag, 1967.

Gilbert, Allan H. "Martin Bucer on Education," *The Journal of English and Germanic Philology* 18 (1919).

Glade, Winfried. *Die Taufe in den Vorcanisianischen Katholischen Katechismen des 16. Jahrhunderts im deutschen Sprachgebiet.* Nieuwkoop: B. de Graaf, 1979.

Gnilka, J. "Die essenischen Tauchbäder und die Johannestaufe," *Revue de Qumran* 3 (1961-62): 185ff.

Goertz, Hans-Jürgen. *Innere und äussere ordnung in der Theologie Thomas Müntzers.* Leiden: E. J. Brill, 1967. (*Studies in the History of Christian Thought,* 2).

Goeters, J. F. Gerhard. *Ludwig Hätzer (ca. 1500 bis 1529), Spiritualist und*

Antitrinitarier. Gütersloh: C. Bertelsmann, 1957. (*Quellen und Forschungen zur Reformationsgeschichte,* 25).

Goltz, Eduard, Freiherr von der. *Das Gebet in der ältesten Christenheit.* Leipzig: J. C. Hinrichs, 1901.

Gritsch, Eric W. *Reformer Without a Church: The Life and Thought of Thomas Muentzer, 1488?-1525.* Philadelphia: Fortress Press, 1967.

Grönvik, Lorenz. *Die Taufe in der Theologie Martin Luthers.* Abo: Abo Akademi; Göttingen: Vandenhoeck & Ruprecht, 1968. (*Acta Academiae aboensis, Series A: Humaniora,* vol. 36, nr. 1).

Gülden, Josef. *Johann Leisentrits pastoralliturgische Schriften.* Leipzig: St. Benno-Verlag, 1963. (*Studien zur katholischen Bistums- und Klostergeschichte,* 4).

Hagenbach, Karl Rudolf. *Johann Oekolampad und Oswald Myconius, die Reformatoren Basels.* Elberfeld: R. R. Friderichs, 1859.

Hareide, Bjarne. *Die Konfirmation in der Reformationszeit.* Trans. Karin Kvideland. Göttingen: Vandenhoeck & Ruprecht, 1971. (*Arbeiten zur Pastoral theologie,* 8).

Haring, N. M. "One Baptism," *Medieval Studies* 10 (1948): 217-19.

Heer, Joseph Michael. *Ein karolingischer Missions-Katechismus.* Freiburg: Herder, 1911.

Heiler, Friedrich. *Das Gebet: eine religionsgeschichtliche und religionspsychologische Untersuchung.* 4. Aufl. Munich: E. Reinhardt, 1921.

Hillerbrand, Hans-Joachim. "Die gegenwärtige Täuferforschung: Fortschritt oder Dilemma?" *Lebendiger Geist.* Festschrift für H. J. Schoeps. Leiden: Brill, 1959: 64-65.

Hillerbrand, Hans-Joachim. "The Origin of Sixteenth Century Anabaptism: Another Look," *Archiv für Reformationsgeschichte* 53 (1962): 152-80.

Hilpisch, Stephan. "Die Taufspendung nach der Mainzer Agende von 1551; Leben aus der Taufe," *Liturgie und Monchtum* 33/34 (1963/64): 88-93.

Hippolytus. *La tradition apostolique.* Trans. Bernard Botte. Münster/Westfalen: Aschendorff, 1963.

Hoeynck, F. A. *Geschichte der Kirchlichen Liturgie des Bistums Augsburg.* Augsburg: Literar. Institut von M. Huttler, 1889.

Holl, Karl. "Luther und die Schwärmer," *Gesammelte Aufsätze zur Kirchengeschichte I.* 4th and 5th edn. Tübingen: J. C. B. Mohr, 1927.

Hopf, Constantin. *Martin Bucer and the English Reformation.* Oxford: Basil Blackwell, 1946.

Hugh of Saint Victor. *On the Sacraments of Christian Faith (de Sacramentis).*

English version by Roy J. Deferrari. Cambridge, Mass.: Mediaeval Academy of America, 1951.

Huizinga, Johan. *Erasmus.* New York: Charles Scribner's Sons, 1924.

Huizinga, Johan. *Herbst des Mittelalters: Studien über lebens- und geistesformen des 14. und 15. Jahrhunderts in Frankreich und in den Niederlanden.* München: Drei Masken, 1924.

Hyma, Albert. *The Christian Renaissance: A History of the "Devotio Moderna."* 2nd ed. Hamden, Conn.: Archon Books, 1965.

Jacobs, Elfriede. *Die Sakramentslehre Wilhelm Farels.* Zurich: Theologischer Verlag, 1979. (*Zürcher Beiträge zur Reformationsgeschichte,* 10).

Jacoby, Hermann. *Die Liturgik der Reformatoren.* Gotha: F. A. Perthes, 1871-76. 2 vols.

Jeremias, Joachim. *Die Kindertaufe in den ersten vier Jahrhunderten.* Göttingen: Vandenhoeck und Ruprecht, 1958.

Jetter, Werner. *Die Taufe beim jungen Luther.* Tübingen: J. C. B. Mohr, 1954. (*Beiträge zur historischen Theologie,* 18).

Jordahn, Bruno. "Der Taufgottesdienst im Mittelalter bis zum Gegenwart," *Leiturgia: Handbuch des evangelischen Gottesdienstes.* Vol. 5: *Taufgottesdienstes.* Eds. Karl Ferdinand Müller and Walter Blankenburg. Kassel: Johannes Stauda-Verlag, 1970.

Jud, Leo. *Katechismen.* Bearb. von Oskar Farner. Zurich: Max Niehaus, 1955.

Jungmann, Josef Andreas. "Aufbauelemente im römischen Taufritus," *Liturgisches Jahrbuch* 9 (1959): 1-15.

Jungmann, Josef Andreas. *Handing on the Faith: A Manual of Catechetics.* Trans. and rev. A. N. Fuerst. New York: Herder and Herder, 1959.

Jungmann, Josef Andreas. *Die lateinischen Bussriten in ihrer geschichtlichen Entwicklung.* Innsbruck: F. Rauch, 1932.

Karlstadt, Andreas Rudolf. *Schriften aus den Jahren 1523-25.* Hrsg. von Erich Hertzsch. Halle: Niemeyer Verlag, 1956-57. (*Neudrucke deutscher Literaturwerke des 16. und 17. Jahrhunderts,* 325).

Karlstadt, Andreas Rudolf. *Von abtuhung der Bilder, und das Keyn bedtler unther den Christen seyn sollen.* Hrsg. von Hans Leitzmann. Bonn: Marcus und Weber, 1911.

Kawerau, Gustav. "Exorzismus," *Realencyklopädie für protestantische Theologie und Kirche* 5: pp. 695-700.

Kawerau, Gustav. "Liturgische Studien zu Luthers Taufbüchlein von 1523," *Zeitschrift für kirchliche Wissenschaft und kirchliches Leben* 10 (1898): 407-31, 466-77, 519-74, 578-99, 625-43.

Kidd, B. J. *Documents Illustrative of the Continental Reformation.* Oxford: Clarendon, 1911.

Kilger, L. "Taufvorbereitung in der frühmittelalterlichen Benediktinermission," *Benedictus: der Vater des Abendlandes 547-1947.* Hrsg. von Heinrich Suso Brechter. München: Schnell & Steiner, 1947.

Kiwiet, Jan J. *Pilgram Marbeck: ein Führer in der Täuferbewegung der Reformationszeit.* 2. Aufl. Kassel: J. G. Oncken, 1958.

Kirsten, Hans. *Die Taufabsage: eine Untersuchung zu Gestalt und Geschichte der Taufe nach den altkirchlichen Taufliturgien.* Berlin: Evangelische Verlagsanstalt, 1960.

Klassen, Walter. *Anabaptism: Neither Catholic nor Protestant.* Waterloo, Ontario: Conrad Press, 1973.

Kohls, Ernst-Wilhelm. *Die Schule bei Martin Bucer in ihrem Verhältnis zu Kirche und Obrigkeit.* Heidelberg: Quelle & Meyer, 1963.

Kohlberg, A. *Die älteste Agende in der Diözese Ermland und im Deutschordensstaate Preussen nach den ersten Druckausgaben von 1512 und 1520.* Braunsberg: R. Rudiowski, 1903.

Die Konstanzer Ritualientexte in ihrer Entwicklung von 1482-1721. Hrsg. von Alban Dold. Münster / Westfalen: Aschendorff, 1923. (*Liturgiegeschichtliche Quellen* 5/6).

Kretschmar, Georg. "Die Geschichte des Taufgottesdienstes in der alten Kirche," *Leiturgia: Handbuch des Evangelischen Gottesdienstes.* Kassel: Johannes Stauda-Verlag, 1970. 5 vols.

Krüger, Friedman. *Bucer und Erasmus, eine Untersuchung zum Einfluss des Erasmus auf die Theologie Martin Bucers.* Wiesbaden: Steiner, 1970.

Lampe, G. W. H. *The Seal of the Spirit: A Study in the Doctrine of Baptism and Confirmation in the New Testament and the Fathers.* London: S.P.C.K., 1951.

Lang, August. *Der Evangelienkommentar Martin Butzers und die Grundzüge seiner Theologie.* Leipzig: Dietrick, 1900.

Leclercq, H. "Scrutin," *Dictionnaire d'archéologie chrétienne et de liturgie* 15/1: pp. 1037-52.

Le Coultre, Jules. *Maturin Cordier et les origines de la pédogogie protestante dans les pays de langue française (1530-1564).* Neuchâtel: Secretariat de l'université, 1926.

Leeming, Bernard. *Principles of Sacramental Theology.* London: Longmans, Green and Co., 1956.

Leenhardt, Franz J. *Le baptême chrętien, son origine, sa signification.* Neuchâtel: Delachaux et Niestlé, 1946.

Lestringant, Pierre. *Le ministère catéchétique de l'église; esquisse théorique et pratique.* Paris: Éditions "Je Sers," 1945.

Liber Sacramentorum Romanae Aeclesiae Ordinis anni circuli. Ed. Leo Cunibert Mohlberg. Roma: Herder, 1968.

Locher, Gottfried Wilhelm. *Die Zwinglische Reformation im Rahmen der europäischen Kirchengeschichte.* Göttingen: Vandenhoeck und Ruprecht, 1979.

Lohmeyer, Ernst. *Das Evangelium des Matthäus.* 3. Aufl. Ed. Werner Schmauch. Göttingen: Vandenhoeck & Ruprecht, 1962.

Lowenberg, Bruno. "Das Rituale des Kardinals Julius Antonius Sanctorius." Part of a dissertation at the Papal Gregorian University, Munich, 1937.

Lundberg, Per. *La typologie baptismale.* Leipzig: A. Lorenta; Uppsala: Lundquista bokhandeln, 1942.

Luther, Martin. *Theologia Germanica.* Ed. Hoffman. New York: Paulist Press, 1980.

Macdonald, Alexander B. *Christian Worship in the Primitive Church.* Edinburgh: T. & T. Clark, 1934.

Magne, J. "Le bénédictione romaine de l'eau baptismale: prehistoire du texte," *Revue de l'histoire des religions* 68 (1959): 25-63.

Manuale Curatorium secundum usum ecclesiae Roskaldensis. Ed. Joseph Freisen. Paderborn: s.n., 1898.

Marsh, H. G. *The Origin and Significance of the New Testament Baptism.* Manchester: University of Manchester Press, 1941.

Martimort, A. G. *L'église à priére.* Tournai: Desclée, 1961.

Maurer, Wilhelm. "Geschichte von Firmung und Konfirmation bis zum Ausgang der Lutherischen Orthodoxie," *Confirmatio, Forschungen zur Geschichte und Praxis der Konfirmation.* Munich: Evangelischer Presseverband für Bayern, 1959.

Maxwell, William D. *John Knox's Genevan service book, 1556: the liturgical portions of the Genevan service book . . .* Westminster: Faith Press, 1965.

Meister, Willi. *Volksbildung und Volkserziehung in der Reformation Huldrych Zwinglis.* Zurich: Zwingli-Verlag, 1939.

Michaud-Quantin, Pierre. "Guy de Montrocher," *Dictionnaire de spiritualité ascetique et mystique, doctrine et histoire.* Paris: G. Beauchesne, 1932: vol. 6, pp. 1303-04.

Michaelis, W. "Zum jüdischen Hintergrund der Johannestaufe," *Judaica* 8 (1951): 81-120.

Michel, A. and E. Amman. "Penitance," *Dictionnaire de théologie catholique.* Paris: Librairie Letouzey et Ané, 1933: t. 12, cols. 722-1138.

Michel, O. "Die Umkehr nach der Verkundigung Jesu," *Evangelische Theologie* 5 (1938): 403-13.

Moeller, Bernd. "Die deutschen Humanisten und die Anfänge der Reformation," *Zeitschrift für Kirchengeschichte* 70 (1959): 46-61.

Moeller, Bernd. *Johannes Zwick und die Reformation in Konstanz.* Heidelberg: G. Mohn, 1961. (*Quellen und Forschungen zur Reformationsgeschichte,* 28).

Molin, J. B. "A Bibliography of Rituals," *Ephemerides Liturgicae* 73 (1959): 218-24.

Moody, Dale. *Baptism: Foundation for Christian Unity.* Philadelphia: Westminster Press, 1967.

Mortimer, R. C. *The Origins of Private Penance in the Western Church.* Oxford: Clarendon Press, 1939.

Müller, Alfons. *Die Lehre von der Taufe bei Albert dem Grossen.* Munich: Schöningh, 1967. (*Veröffentlichungen des Grabmann-Instituts zur Erforschung der Mittelalterlichen Theologie und Philosophie,* n.f. 2).

Müller, Joseph. *Die deutschen Katechismen der Böhmischen Brüder.* Berlin: A. Hofmann & Co., 1887. (*Monumenta Germaniae Paedagogica,* 4).

Muralt, Leonhard von. *Glaube und Lehre der Schweizerischen Wiedertäufer in der Reformationszeit.* Zurich: Kommissionsverlag Beer, 1938.

Muralt, Leonhard von. "Zum Problem: Reformation und Täufertum," *Zwingliana* 6/2 (1934): 65-85.

Murphy, F. X. "Penitential Controversy," *New Catholic Encyclopedia* 9: pp. 84-85.

Neunheuser, Burkhard. *Baptism and Confirmation.* Trans. John Hay Hughes. New York: Herder and Herder, 1964.

Neunheuser, Burkhard. "De benedictione acquae baptismalis," *Ephemerides Liturgicae* 44 (1930): 194-207, 258-81, 360-412, 455-92.

Neuser, Wilhelm H. *Die reformatorische Wende bei Zwingli.* Neukirchen-Vluyn: Neukirchener Verlag, 1977.

Nümann, F. K. "Zur Entstehung des lutherischen Taufbüchleins von Jahre 1523," *Monatschrift für Gottesdienst und kirchliche Kunst* 33 (1928): 214-19.

Oberman, Heiko Augustinus. *The Harvest of Medieval Theology.* Cambridge, Mass.: Harvard University Press, 1963.

Oberman, Heiko Augustinus. "Some Notes on the Theology of Nominalism, with Attention to its Relation to the Renaissance," *Harvard Theological Review* 53 (1960): 74-76.

Oecolampadius, John. *Antwort auff Balthasar Huobmaiers büchlein wider der Predicanten gesprach zu Basel, vom dem Kindertauff.* Basel: A. Cratander, 1527.

Oecolampadius, John. *Ein gesprech etlicher predicanten zuo Basel, gehalten mitt etlichen bekennern des widertouffs.* Basel: V. Curione, 1525.

Oecolampadius, John. *Vnderrichtung von dem Widertauff, von der Oberkeit vnd von dem Eyd, auff Carlins N. widertauffers artickel.* Basel: A. Cratander, 1527.

Oepke, Albrecht. "βάπτω," *Theologisches Wörterbuch zum Neuen Testament* 1: pp. 527-44.

Old, Hughes Oliphant. "Bullinger and the Scholastic Works on Baptism," *Henry Bullinger, 1504-1575, Gesämmelte Aufsätze zum 400. Todestag.* Zurich: Theologische Verlag, 1975: pp. 191-207. (*Zürcher Beiträge zur Reformationsgeschichte,* 7-8).

Old, Hughes Oliphant. "John Oecolampadius and the Patristic Argument in the Defense of Infant Baptism." Paper read to the American Church History Society, Washington, D.C., 1979.

Old, Hughes Oliphant. *Patristic Roots of Reformed Worship.* Zurich: Theologischer Verlag, 1975.

Ozment, Steven. "Humanism, Scholasticism, and the Intellectual Origins of the Reformation," *Continuity and Discontinuity in Church History: Essays Presented to George Huntston Williams on the Occasion of his 65th Birthday.* Leiden: Brill, 1979. (*Studies in the History of Christian Thought,* 19).

Ozment, Steven. *Mysticism and Dissent: Religious Ideology and Social Protest in the Sixteenth Century.* New Haven, Conn.: Yale University Press, 1973.

Packull, Werner O. "Denck's Alleged Baptism by Hübmaier: Its Significance for the Origin of South German-Austrian Anabaptism," *The Mennonite Quarterly Review* 47 (1973): 327-38.

Packull, Werner O. *Mysticism and the Early South German-Austrian Anabaptist Movement, 1525-1531.* Scottsdale, Pa.: Herald Press, 1977. (*Studies in Anabaptist and Mennonite History,* 19).

Padberg, Rudolf. *Erasmus als Katechet.* Freiburg: Herder, 1956.

Pascoe, Louis B. *Jean Gerson: Principles of Church Reform.* Leiden: E. J. Brill, 1973. (*Studies in Medieval and Reformation Thought,* 7).

Patzelt, Erna. *Die Karolingische Renaissance.* Graz, Austria: Akademische Druck, 1965.

Payne, John B. *Erasmus: His Theology of the Sacraments.* Richmond, Va.: John Knox Press, 1970.

Pfister, Rudolf. "Kirche und Glaube auf der Ersten Zürcher Disputation vom 29. Januar 1523," *Zwingliana* 13 (1973).

Pfister, Rudolf. *Das Problem der Erbsunde bei Zwingli.* Leipzig: Verlag von M. Heinsius Nachfolger, 1939.

Plummer, Alfred. *An Exegetical Commentary on the Gospel According to St. Matthew.* Grand Rapids: Eerdmans, 1953.

Pohlman, H. *Die Metanoia als Zentralbegriff der Christlichen Frömmigkeit.* Leipzig: J. C. Hinrichs, 1938.

Porter, H. B. "Maxentius of Aquileia and the North Italian Baptismal Rites," *Ephemerides Liturgicae* 69 (1955): 3-9.

Poschmann, B. *Paenitentia secunda: die kirchliche Busse im ältesten Christentum bis Cyprian und Origines.* Bonn: P. Hanstein, 1940.

Post, R. R. *The Modern Devotion: Confrontation with Reformation and Humanism.* Leiden: Brill, 1968.

Potter, G. R. *Zwingli.* Cambridge: University Press, 1976.

Puniet, Pierre de. "Baptême," *Dictionnaire d'archéologie chrétienne et de liturgie* 2/1: cols. 251-346.

Puniet, Pierre de. "Bénédictions de l'eau," *Dictionnaire d'archéologie chrétienne et de liturgie* 2: cols. 685-713.

Puniet, Pierre de. "Catéchuménat." *Dictionnaire d'archéologie chrétienne et de liturgie* 2/2: cols. 2579-2621.

Puniet, Pierre de. "La liturgie baptismale en Gaule avant Charlemagne," *Revue des questions historiques* 72 (1902): 382-423.

Quellen zur Geschichte der Täufer in der Schweiz. Eds. L. von Muralt and W. Schmid. Zurich: Theologischer Verlag, 1952.

Ratschow, C. H., W. Michaelis and W. Nagel. "Exorzismus," *Die Religion in Geschichte und Gegenwart.* 3rd ed. Vol. 2, pp. 832-34.

Reitzenstein, Richard. *Die Vorgeschichte der christlichen Taufe.* Leipzig: B. G. Teubner, 1929.

Repp, Arthur C. *Confirmation in the Lutheran Church.* St. Louis, Mo.: Concordia, 1964.

Reu, M. *Dr. Martin Luther's Small Catechism: A History of its Origin, its Distribution and its Use.* Chicago: Wartburg Publishing House, 1929.

Das Rheinauer Rituale. Hrsg. von Gebhard Hurlimann. Freiburg: Universitätsverlag, 1939.

Das Rituale des Bischofs Heinrich I. von Breslau. Hrsg. von Adolph Franz. Freiburg: Herder, 1912.

Das Rituale von St. Florian aus dem zwölften Jahrhundert. Ed. Adolf Franz. Freiburg: Herder, 1904.

Rohrich, G. E. *Essai sur la vie des escrits, et la doctrine de l'anabaptiste Jean Denk.* Strasbourg: s.n., 1853.

Rondt, H. "La croix sur le Front," *Revue des Sciences Religieuses* 42 (1954): 388-94.

Rordorf, Willy. *Liturgie, foi, et vie des premiers chrétiens, études patristiques.* Paris: Beauchesne, 1986.

Roth, Friedrich. "Zur Lebensgeschichte des Meisters Michael Keller, Prädikanten in Augsburg," *Beiträge zur bayrischen kirchengeschichte* 5 (1889): 149-63.

Sachsse, Karl. D. *Balthasar Hübmaier als Theologe.* Berlin, 1914. (*Neue Studien zur Geschichte der Theologie und der Kirche,* 20).

Das Sacramentarium Gregorianum nach dem Aachener Urexemplar. Hrsg. von Hans Lietzmann. Münster: Aschendorff, 1921. (*Liturgiegeschichtliche Quellen,* 3).

Scheidt, Hubert. *Die Taufwasserweihegebete im Sinne vergleichender Liturgieforschung untersucht.* Münster: Aschendorff, 1935. (*Liturgiegeschichtliche Quellen und Forschungen,* 29).

Schillebeeckx, Edward. *Christ, the Sacrament of the Encounter with God.* Trans. Paul Barrett. New York: Sheed and Ward, 1963.

Schmidt-Clausing, Fritz. "Die liturgietheologische Arbeit Zwingli's am Sintflutgebet des Taufformulars: ein weiterer Blick in Zwingli's liturgische Werkstatt," *Zwingliana* 13 (1972): 516-43, 591-615.

Schmidt-Clausing, Fritz. "Die Neudatierung der liturgischen Schriften Zwinglis," *Theologische Zeitschrift* 25 (1969): 252-65.

Schmidt-Clausing, Fritz. *Zwingli als Liturgiker.* Göttingen: Vandenhoeck und Ruprecht, 1952.

Schmidt-Clausing, Fritz. *Zwinglis liturgische Formulare.* Frankfurt am Main: O. Lembeck, 1970.

Schnackenburg, Rudolf. *Baptism in the Thought of St. Paul.* Trans. G. R. Beasley-Murray. Oxford: Blackwell, 1964.

Schneider, Johannes. *Die Taufe im Neuen Testament.* Stuttgart: W. Kohlhammer, 1952.

Schulz, Karl. "Thomas Müntzers liturgische Bestrebungen," *Zeitschrift für Kirchengeschichte* 74 (1928): 369-401.

Schwarz, Reinhard. *Die apokalyptische Theologie Thomas Müntzers und der Taboriten.* Tübingen: J. C. B. Mohr, 1977.

Sider, Ronald J. *Andreas Bodenstein von Karlstadt: The Development of His Thought, 1517-1525.* Leiden: E. J. Brill, 1974. (*Studies in Medieval and Reformation Thought,* 11).

Sider, Ronald J. "Karlstadt's Orlamünde Theology: A Theology of Regeneration," *The Mennonite Quarterly Review* 45 (1971): 191-218, 352-76.

Smend, Julius. *Die evangelischen deutschen Messen bis zu Luthers Deutscher Messe.* Göttingen: Vandenhoeck und Ruprecht, 1896.

Smirin, M. M. *Die Volksreformation des Thomas Münzer und der grosse Bauernkrieg.* Berlin: Dietz, 1952.

Spital, Hermann Josef. *Der Taufritus in den deutschen Ritualien.* Münster: Aschendorff, 1968. (*Liturgiewissenschaftliche Quellen und Forschungen,* 47).

Spitz, Lewis W. *The Religious Renaissance of the German Humanists.* Cambridge, Mass.: Harvard University Press, 1963.

Staehelin, Ernst. *Das theologische Lebenswerk Johannes Oekolampads.* Leipzig: M. Heinsius Nachfolger, 1939. (*Quellen und Forschungen zur Reformationsgeschichte,* 21).

Stahelin, Rudolf. *Huldreich Zwingli.* Basel: B. Schwabe, 1895-97. 2 vols.

Stayer, James M., Werner O. Packull, and Klaus Deppermann. "From Monogenesis to Polygenesis: The Historical Discussion of Anabaptist Origins," *The Mennonite Quarterly Review* 49 (1975): 83-121.

Steinmetz, David C. "The Baptism of John and the Baptism of Jesus in Huldrych Zwingli, Balthasar Hübmaier and Late Medieval Theology," *Continuity and Discontinuity in Church History: Essays Presented to George Huntston Williams on the Occasion of His 65th Birthday.* Leiden: Brill, 1979. (*Studies in the History of Christian Thought,* 19).

Steinmetz, David C. "Scholasticism and Radical Reform: Nominalist Motifs in the Theology of Balthasar Hübmaier," *The Mennonite Quarterly Review* 45 (1971): 123-44.

Stenzel, Alois. *Die Taufe, eine genetische Erklarung der Taufliturgie.* Innsbruck: F. Rauch, 1958. (*Forschungen zur Geschichte der Theologie und des innerkirchlichen Lebens,* 7/8).

Stephens, W. P. *The Holy Spirit in the Theology of Martin Bucer.* London: Cambridge University Press, 1970.

Stommel, Eduard. "Die Benedictio Fontis in der Osternacht," *Liturgisches Jahrbuch* 7 (1957): 8-24.

Stommel, Eduard. *Studien zur Epiklese der römischen Taufwasserweihe.* Bonn: P. Hanstein, 1950. (*Theophaneia,* 5).

Strathmann, Hermann. "Die Entstehung der Lehre Calvins von der Busse," *Calvin Studien* (1909): 185-234,

Surgant, Johann Ulrich. *Manuale Curatorum.* Basel: M. Furter, 1503.

Tertullian. *Traité du Baptême.* Texte, introd. et notes de R. F. Refoulé. Paris: Editions du Cerf, 1952.

Theobald, L. "Balthasar Hübmaier," *Zeitschrift für bayerische Kirchengeschichte* 16 (1941): 3-38.

Thomas, Joseph. *Le mouvement baptiste en Palestine et Syrie.* Gembloux: J. Duculot, 1935.

Tractatus de Sacramentis, Strassburg 1512. In Gustave Kawerau, "Liturgische Studien zu Luthers Taufbüchlein von 1523," *Zeitschrift für kirchliche Wissenschaft und kirchliches Leben* 10 (1898): 416-17.

Traede, K. "Exorcismus," *Reallexikon für Antike und Christentum* 7: cols. 44-117.

Tschakert, Paul. "Urbanus Rhegius," *New Schaff-Herzog Encyclopedia,* vol. 10. New York: Funk and Wagnalls, 1911.

Turck, André. *Evangelisation et catéchése aux deux premiers siècles.* Paris: Editions du Cerf, 1962.

Usteri, Johann Martin. "Darstellung der Tauflehre Zwinglis, mit besonderer Berücksichtigung der widertäufischen Streitigkeit," *Theologische Studien und Kritiken* 55 (1882): 205-84.

Usteri, Johann Martin. "Oekolampads Stellung zur Kindertaufe," *Theologische Studien und Kritiken* (1883): 155-74.

Usteri, Johann Martin. "Die Stellung der Strassburger Reformatoren Bucer und Capito zur Tauffrage," *Theologische Studien und Kritiken* 57 (1884): 456-525.

van der Meer, Frederik, and Christine Mohrmann. *Atlas of the Early Christian World.* Trans. and eds. Mary F. Hedlund and H. H. Rowley. London: Nelson, 1958.

Vedder, H. C. *Balthasar Hübmaier: The Leader of the Anabaptists.* New York: G. P. Putnam's Sons, 1905.

Vischer, Eberhard. "Utenheim, Christoph von," *Realencyklopädie für protestantische Theologie und Kirche,* vol. 20. 3rd ed. Leipzig: s.n., 1908.

Vittali, Otto Eric. *Die Theologie des wiedertaufers Hans Denck.* Offenberg: s.n., 1932.

Vogel, Cyrille. *La réforme culturelle sous Pepin le Bref et sous Charlemagne.* Graz, Austria: Akademische Druck, 1965.

Vogel, Cyrille. "La réforme liturgique sous Charlemagne," *Karl der Gross,* vol. 2. Ed. Bernhard Bischoff. Düsseldorf: L. Schwann, 1965: 217-32.

Wackernagel, Rudolf. *Humanismus und Reformation in Basel.* Basel: K. Helbing & Lichtenhahn, 1924.

Wagner, Günter. *Das religionsgeschichtliche Problem von Römer 6,11.* Zurich: Zwingli-Verlag, 1962.

Wallace, Ronald A. *Calvin's Doctrine of the Christian Life.* Grand Rapids, Mich.: William B. Eerdmans, 1959.

Wallace, Ronald A. *Calvin's Doctrine of Word and Sacrament.* Edinburgh: Oliver and Boyd, 1963.

Walton, Robert C. "The Institutionalization of the Reformation at Zurich," *Zwingliana* 13 (1972).

Weigand, Friedrich. *Erzbischof Odilbert von Mailand über die Taufe.* Leipzig: Dieterich, 1899. (*Studien zur Geschichte der Theologie und der Kirche,* 4/1).

Weis, Frederick Lewis. *The Life, Teachings and Works of Johannes Denck, 1495-1527.* Strasbourg: s.n., 1924.

Weisz, Leo, "Heinrich Bullingers Agenda," *Zwingliana* 10 (1954): 1-23.

Weisz, Leo. *Leo Jud, Ulrich Zwinglis Kampfgenosse, 1482-1542.* Zurich: Zwingli-Verlag, 1942.

Wendel, Francois. *L'Église de Strasbourg, sa constitution et son organisation, 1532-1535.* Paris: Presses universitaires de France, 1942.

West, Andrew Fleming. *Alcuin and the Rise of the Christian Schools.* New York: Charles Scribner's Sons, 1892.

Williams, George H. *The Radical Reformation.* Philadelphia: Westminster Press, 1962.

Wilmart, A. "Un florilège carolingien sur le symbolisme des cérémonies du baptême," *Analecta Reginensia.* Città del Vaticano: Biblioteca apostolica Vaticana, 1933: 153-79. (*Studi e Testi,* 59).

Wilson, H. A. *The Gregorian Sacramentary under Charles the Great.* London: Henry Bradshaw Society, 1915.

Wimpfeling, Jakob. *Jakob Wimpfelings Adolescentia.* Ed. Otto Herding, with Franz Josef Worstbrock. Munich: Fink Verlag, 1965.

Windhorst, Christof. *Täuferisches Taufverstandnis: Balthasar Hübmaiers Lehre zwischen traditioneller und reformatorischer Theologie.* Leiden: Brill, 1976. (*Studies in Medieval and Reformation Thought,* 16).

Wisswedel, Wilhelm. "The Inner and Outer Word: A Study in the Anabaptist Doctrine of Scripture," *The Mennonite Quarterly Review* 62 (1952): 171-91.

Wymann, Eduard. "Liturgische Taufsitten in der Diözese Konstanz," *Der Geschichtsfreund, Mitteilungen der fünf Orte Luzern, Uri, Schwyz, Unterwalden und Zug* 60 (1905): 1-151.

Yoder, John Howard. "Balthasar Hübmaier and the Beginnings of Swiss Anabaptism," *The Mennonite Quarterly Review* 33 (1959).

Yoder, John Howard. *Täufertum und Reformation in der Schweiz I, die Gespräche zwischen Täufern und Reformatoren, 1523-1538.* Karlsruhe: H. Schneider, 1962.

Yoder, John Howard. *Täufertum und Reformation in der Schwiz,* Part 2, *Dogmengeschichtliche Untersuchung der frühen Gespräche zwischen Schweizerischen Täufern und Reformatoren.* Zurich: EVZ-Verlag, 1968.

Index of Liturgical Terms, Documents, and Subjects